Zlatka Guentchéva (Ed.)

Epistemic Modalities and Evidentiality in Cross-Linguistic Perspective

Empirical Approaches to Language Typology

Volume 59

Epistemic Modalities and Evidentiality in Cross-Linguistic Perspective

Edited by
Zlatka Guentchéva

DE GRUYTER
MOUTON

ISBN 978-3-11-108618-7
e-ISBN (PDF) 978-3-11-057226-1
e-ISBN (EPUB) 978-3-11-056988-9
ISSN 0933-761X

Library of Congress Control Number: 2018934804

Bibliographic information published by the Deutsche Nationalbibliothek
The Deutsche Nationalbibliothek lists this publication in the Deutsche Nationalbibliografie; detailed bibliographic data are available on the Internet at http://dnb.dnb.de.

This volume is text- and page-identical with the hardback published in 2018.
Typesetting: Integra Software Services, Pvt. Ltd.
Printing and binding: CPI books GmbH, Leck
∞ Printed on acid-free paper
Printed in Germany

www.degruyter.com

Contents

Part III: Baltic and Slavonic languages

Part IV: Non Indo-European languages

Part V: Theoretical perspectives

Editorial Preface

The papers gathered in this volume stem from a research project, initiated jointly with Jon Landaburu, in collaboration with leading European scholars, and the support of the *Fédération de Typologie et Universaux Linguistiques* of the CNRS (French National Center for Scientific Research). This volume explores the complex issues pertaining to the expression of epistemic modality and evidentiality in relation to other linguistic categories and notions in the languages of Europe and the world from different angles and perspectives (semantic, functional, pragmatic). It reflects the diversity of theoretical currents and the heterogeneity of the phenomena grouped together under the heading of evidentiality or (epistemic) modality in linguistic research. It follows on an earlier publication (*L'énonciation médiatisée II. Le traitement épistémologique de l'information: illustrations amérindiennes et caucasiennes*, ed. by Zlatka Guentchéva & Jon Landaburu. 2007. Louvain: Éditions Peeters), but differs in that its coverage is not restricted to specific linguistic areas or language families, and that it integrates recent advances in the domains covered.

This collective volume focuses on semantic-functional oriented analyses but also on discourse-pragmatic studies related to socio-cultural interactional practices. It reflects the diversity of theoretical currents relating to semantic, functional, typological and pragmatic perspectives. It offers re-examination of known phenomena, and raises new questions in the areas of epistemic modality and evidentiality.

In spite of the authors' diverse frameworks, one of the most common and prominent features is the semantic-pragmatic analysis of these phenomena, based on large corpora of spoken and written texts. Grounded in solid empirical knowledge, each article contributes in its own way to the following central issues in languages: (i) how notions associated with evidentiality (information source, evidence, justification, access to knowledge) and epistemic modality (possibility, probability, reliability, belief) are expressed in relation to their co-text and how these various notions interact; (ii) how to disentangle notions such as evidence, judgement, speaker's attitude, stance, (inter)subjectivity, etc.; (iii) how to define the boundaries between evidentialty and epistemic modality in the semantic areas where they overlap functionally.

This book is not meant to be a comprehensive survey of current descriptive, theoretical and typological approaches to epistemic modality and evidentiality. It presents both the diversity of current research and linguistic traditions, and aims to provide new insights in a domain which has given rise to a considerable number of publications in the past two decades. The studies concentrate on the manifestations of epistemic and evidential distinctions as conveyed by linguistic expressions, mostly in Indo-European languages (Germanic: Danish, English; Romance: French as well as a regional variety of French, Italian, Portuguese, Spanish; Balto-Slavonic:

https://doi.org/10.1515/9783110572261-201

Russian and Lithuanian) but also beyond (Hungarian, Tibetan, Yucatec and Lakandon Maya, and Ika and Kogi, two Arwako-Chibchan languages). Many of them offer cross-linguistic comparisons and new data analyzed in the light of current debates.

The book is divided into five parts. In the three first parts, the authors discuss the semantics and expression of different subtypes of epistemic modality and/or evidentiality in Germanic (Part 1), Romance (Part 2) and Baltic and Slavonic (Part 3) languages. Taking the discussion beyond Indo-European languages, Part 4 investigates these issues in typologically different language groups, some of which have received little attention in previous works. Finally, Part 5 proposes a more theoretical approach for these issues.

The contributions align with different theoretical orientations; from broad surveys to in-depth studies, they address a number of foundational issues, bear on various aspects of epistemic modality and evidentiality, enlarge the scope of previously available research and invite further research.

I am grateful to all the participants in the research project who responded to the call for papers as well as to Henrik Bergqvist, Jean Léo Léonard and Zuzana Vokurková who were subsequently invited to join in. My thanks also go to all the scholars who came to present and discuss their approaches and theoretical frameworks with the members of the research project: Kasper Boye, Marc Duval, Peter Kosta, Djamel Kouloughli†, Samia Naïm, Paola Pietrandrea, Alain Peyraube, Bernard Pottier, Nicole Rivière, Claude Rivière, Martine Vanhove, Aude Vinzerich, Björn Wiemer, and especially Patrick Dendale and Johan Van der Auwera for their stimulating scientific debates. Special thanks go to the many reviewers for their comments, observations, and suggestions which greatly contributed to improving quality. I also wish to express my gratitude to this volume's authors for their extreme patience during the drawn out preparation process.

I gratefully acknowledge financial assistance from the *Fédération de Typologie et Universaux Linguistiques* of the CNRS and support from Lacito (*Langues et Civilisations à Tradition Orale*), a research unit of the French CNRS. I would also like to thank Raphaëlle Chossenot for her technical assistance in bringing this volume to press, and Birgit Sievert, Julie Miess, and Stefan Diezmann for their support and assistance during the production process.

I am particularly thankful to Professor Bernard Comrie for his interest in the topic of the present volume, for his constructive comments and invaluable advice which greatly helped to improve this volume.

Zlatka Guentchéva
Emerita Senior Researcher of the CNRS
LACITO – CNRS, 7, rue Guy Môquet
94800 Villejuif (France)
e-mail: guentche@vjf.cnrs.fr

List of Contributors

Henrik Bergqvist
Stockholm University
Department of Linguistics
Universitetsvägen 10 C
106 91 Stockholm, Sweden
E-mail: henrik.bergqvist@ling.su.se

Anna Bonola
Catholic University of the Sacred Heart
Department of Foreign Languages and literature
Largo Gemelli, 1
20123 Milan, Italy
E-mail: anna.bonola@unicatt.it

Agnès Celle
University Paris Diderot – Paris 7
UFR Etudes Anglophones
Bât. Olympe de Gouges, Case 7046
5 rue Thomas Mann
75205 Paris Cedex 13, France
E-mail: agnes.celle@univ-paris-diderot.fr

Adrián Cabedo Nebot
University of Valencia
Departamento de Filología Española
Avda.Blasco Ibáñez, 32
46025 – Valencia, Spain
E-mail: adrian.cabedo@uv.es

Bert Cornillie
University of Leuven
Department of Linguistics
Blijde-Inkomststraat 21, Box 3308
B-3000 Leuven, Belgium
E-mail: bert.cornillie@kuleuven.be

Jean-Pierre Desclés
University Paris-Sorbonne & STIH
Maison de la Recherche
28, rue Serpente
75006 Paris, France
E-mail: Jean-Pierre.Descles@paris-sorbonne.fr

Lionel Dufaye
University Paris Est – Marne La Vallée
Equipe d'accueil LISAA (4120)
5 Bd Descartes,
77420 Champs Sur Marne, France
E-mail: dufaye@sfr.fr

Laurent Gosselin
University of Rouen-Normandie
Département des Sciences du Langage et de la Communication
1, Rue Lavoisier
76821 Mont Saint Aignan Cedex, France
E-mail: laurent.gosselin@univ-rouen.fr

Michael Herslund
Department of Management, Society and Communication
Copenhagen Business School
Dalgas Have 15
DK-2000 Frederiksberg, Denmark
E-mail: mh.ibc@cbs.dk

Axel Holvoet
Vilnius University
Institute for the Languages and Cultures of the Baltic
Universiteto g. 5
LT-01513 Vilnius, Lithuania
E-mail: axel.holvoet@flf.vu.lt

https://doi.org/10.1515/9783110572261-202

Ferenc Kiefer
Hungarian Academy of Sciences
Research Institute for Linguistics
Teréz krt. 13
H-1067 Budapest, Hungary
E-mail: kiefer@nytud.hu

Hans Kronning
Uppsala University
Department of Modern Languages
Romance Languages
Box 636, 751 26 Uppsala, Sweden
E-mail: hans.kronning@moderna.uu.se

Brenda Laca
University Paris 8
UMR Structures Formelles du Langage
2 rue de la Liberté
93526 St Denis, France
E-mail: brendalaca@gmail.com

Jean Léo Léonard
Université Paris-Sorbonne
UFR de langue française
1, rue Victor Cousin
75005 Paris, France
E-mail: leonardjeanleo@gmail.com

Daniel Petit
Ecole Normale Supérieure,
Centre d'études anciennes
45, rue d'Ulm
F-75005 Paris, France
E-mail: petit.daniel.dpt@gmail.com

Mario Squartini
University of Turin
Dipartimento di Studi umanistici
via s. Ottavio 20
I-10124 Turin, Italy
E-mail: mario.squartini@unito.it

Valentina Vapnarsky
National Centre for Scientific Research
LESC / EREA – CNRS &
University Paris-Ouest
Maison Archéologie & Ethnologie René-Ginouvès
21, allee de l'Université
92023 Nanterre cedex, France
E-mail: vapnarsk@cnrs.fr

Zuzana Vokurkova
Charles University in Prague
Department of South and Central Asia
nám. Jana Palacha 2
116 38 Prague 1, Czech Republic
E-mail: vokurkova@hotmail.com

Part I: **Germanic languages**

Michael Herslund

Epistemic modality, Danish modal verbs and the tripartition of utterances

Abstract: The Danish modal verbs are basically polysemous in the sense that they convey different kinds of modality. The verb *kunne* 'can' e.g. both expresses dynamic modality (capacity, viz. *He can/is able to swim*), deontic modality (permission, viz. *He can/is allowed to swim*), or epistemic modality (supposition, viz. *He can/is assumed to swim*).

The article attempts to explain this distribution of the three kinds of modality by linking it to the tripartition of the sentence proposed by R. M. Hare (1971). According to this philosopher every sentence can be broken down into a *neustic* ('I say'), a *tropic* ('it is the case') and a *phrastic* ('the lexical content') component. The idea is then simply to relate the different readings of a modal to the different components, so that the dynamic and deontic are both related to the phrastic component, the deontic furthermore to the tropic, but the epistemic reading exclusively to the tropic component, cf. e.g. Herslund (2003). The three readings are thus the results of three different positions of the modal verb. The use of the terms 'component' or 'position' does not imply any concrete localisation in the sentence with the exception of certain cases of iconicity. A number of semantic and syntactic arguments are adduced in favour of the proposed analysis.

Keywords: modal verb, modal value, modal intensity; neustic, tropic, phrastic component; dynamic, deontic, epistemic modality

1 Introduction

Modality is a difficult and controversial concept – for a number of reasons. First, there seems to be no consensus on its ontological status: is it a linguistic category or is it a semantic field ("a content domain")? Insofar as linguistic categories usually are conceived as (numerically limited) sets of linguistic forms with a rather

---

Note: The present article is a revised and updated version of the article in French, Herslund (2003). I thank two anonymous reviewers for their constructive and helpful criticism of an earlier version.

Michael Herslund, Copenhagen Business School

https://doi.org/10.1515/9783110572261-001

precise meaning within the overall linguistic system, there seems to be no reason to assume it is a category on line with tense, aspect and mood for instance. As is well known, modality can be expressed in a number of ways (special verbs or verb forms, adverbs, whole phrases, etc.), so we are left with the conception of modality as a semantic field. Second, what is the content of the field? A common definition is that modality characterises sentences conveying the speaker's attitude towards the propositional content of his utterance, i.e. his evaluation of the possibility or necessity for the description of a given state of affairs to be true; hence the field's affinity with related areas such as subjectivity and evidentiality. Third, how can this field be described and subdivided? A widespread subdivision partitions the field into root (or dynamic) modality, epistemic and deontic modality (Boye 2001, 2005, Nuyts 2005),[1] but other types are also found in the literature, such as alethic and boulomaic modalities. This proliferation of modality types leads to the final question: do we need this ill-defined semantic area at all as a linguistically relevant concept? The answer of Nuyts (2005) is that we do not. He prefers to treat the different types of modality as levels within a larger "category" of qualifications. He may have a point here, but the very fact that epistemic and deontic modalities constitute separate identifiable levels casts doubt upon his conclusion. I shall therefore take the more traditional view that it makes sense to speak of modality, and that it can be fruitful to distinguish between dynamic (or root), epistemic and deontic modality.

One reason for this is that the retention of the three kinds of modality, dynamic, epistemic and deontic is justified by their close resemblance and affinity to the three fundamental functions of the utterance that are identified by Benveniste (1974: 84): *assertion* (dynamic), *interrogation* (epistemic) and *intimation* (deontic).

However one defines the field, the Germanic languages possess a special class of verbs, the modal verbs, whose only, or at least primary, function is to convey the speaker's evaluation of the possibility or necessity of a certain state of affairs to obtain, in contradistinction to so-called categorical sentences, which are simply asserted as true. So modality can be seen as, if not grammaticalised, to a certain extent lexicalised in these languages – which does not preclude that modal values can be expressed in numerous other ways.

The modal verbs constitute in Danish a class with special morphological and syntactic features. Historically, they are so-called preterite-present verbs characterised by the Ablaut of their present tense forms and the absence of the present tense ending *-r*, but contrary to the English modals their inflection is not

1 Some authors doubt that root or dynamic modality belongs to the field at all, e.g. Palmer (1986: 12). In his treatment of modality, Lyons (1977) doesn't mention it at all.

Table 1.1: Modal Morphology

a.	*kunne* can-INF	*skulle* shall-INF	*måtte* may/must-INF
	han kan he can-PRES	*han skal* he shall-PRES	*han må* he may/must-PRES
b.	*han kan gøre det* he can-PRES do it	*han skal gøre det* he shall-PRES do it	*han må gøre det* he may/must-PRES do it
	vs.		
	han prøver at gøre det he tries to do it		

defective insofar as they have their own infinitive form (cf. Table 1.1a); syntactically, they are directly followed by an infinitive, i.e. without the complementiser *at* 'to' (cf. Table 1.1b), together with which they constitute a *modal expression*. The present article will concentrate on the three central Danish modal verbs *kunne* 'can', *skulle* 'shall' and *måtte* 'may/must', which all have clear epistemic uses.[2]

2 Modal value and intensity

As in other (Germanic) languages the modal verbs in Danish are polysemous and convey the three different *modal values*: dynamic (or root modality),[3] deontic and epistemic (Section 2.1); there is not a single modal verb that carries only one of these values, and they all seem to be able to express them all. These three

---

2 The full list of the Danish modal verbs is somewhat disputed. Davidsen-Nielsen (1990: 38) gives the following list of "modal auxiliaries": *kunne* 'can', *måtte* 'may/must', *behøve* 'need', *burde* 'ought' and *skulle* 'shall'; the most extensive list is probably found in Brandt (1999: 25): *behøve* 'need', *burde* 'ought', *gide* 'bother', *kunne* 'can', *måtte* 'may/must', *skulle* 'shall', *turde* 'dare' and *ville* 'will'; the most "authoritative" list is to be found in Hansen and Heltoft (2011: 765): *kunne* 'can', *måtte* 'may/must', *behøve* 'need', *skulle* 'shall' and *burde* 'ought', and they add as a particular case *ville* 'will', which they consider to be a "broken" modal verb because of its use as a future auxiliary too (Hansen and Heltoft 2011: 795ff). Whereas both *behøve* 'need' and *turde* 'ought' also carry epistemic modal values I shall disregard them in the present context because they predominantly have non-modal values. In contradistinction the three *kunne*, *skulle* and *måtte* have only modal values and no "independent" uses.

3 This type has different labels attached to it. I shall however follow Nuyts (2005) and retain the label 'dynamic'.

values can be graduated into *modal intensities* ranging from the possible to the necessary (Section 2.2).

2.1 Modal values

To take a first example, the verb *kunne* 'can' has as its semantic core the notion of 'possibility'. The sentence *Han kan svømme* of Table 1.2 has consequently three interpretations:

(1) *Han* *kan* *svømme.*
he can-PRES swim-INF

Table 1.2: Modal Values

1. 'He has the capability to swim'	(physical possibility: dynamic modality)
2. 'He has the permission to swim'	(social possibility: deontic modality)
3. 'He has the possibility to swim'	(mental possibility: epistemic modality)

Such (multiple) ambiguity is inherent in any modal verb, but in actual use one is seldom in doubt.

2.2 Modal intensity

The three modal values, dynamic, deontic and epistemic, can be further described in terms of degrees on a scale of *modal intensity* ranging from 'possible' to 'necessary' (Lyons 1977: 787ff, Herslund 1989: 13). The degrees of intensity are mutually defined within modal logic by the negation (Lyons 1977: 787), as in Table 1.3.

The field of 'possibility' can in natural languages be subdivided into 'possible' and 'probable', although e.g. Nuyts (2005: 16) contests the scalar nature of the dynamic, which yields the following interpretations in terms of modal intensity for the three readings, as in Table 1.4.

Table 1.3: Modal Intensity

	Dynamic	**Deontic**	**Epistemic**
POSSIBLE (= not necessary)	Capability	Permission	Possibility
NECESSARY (= not possible not)	Need	Duty	Necessity

Table 1.4: Modal Value and Intensity

	Dynamic	Deontic	Epistemic
POSSIBLE	Capability	Permission	Conjecture
PROBABLE	Disposition	Obligation	Conclusion
NECESSARY	Need	Duty	Conviction

The three values are illustrated for our three modal verbs *kunne* 'can', *måtte* 'may/must' and *skulle* 'shall':

(2) **Dynamic**:
  a. *Ællinger kan svømme.* (capability)
   'Ducklings can swim'
  b. *Ællinger må svømme* (disposition)
   'Ducklings have to swim'
  c. *Ællinger skal svømme.* (natural need)[4]
   'Ducklings must swim'

(3) **Deontic:**
  a. *Han kan/må komme.* (permission)
   'He can/may come'
  b. *Han må komme.* (obligation)
   'He must come'
  c. *Han skal komme.* (duty)
   'He shall come'

(4) **Epistemic:**
  a. *Han kan være syg.* (conjecture)
   'He can be ill'
  b. *Han skal være syg.* (conclusion, external source)[5]
   'He will be ill'
  c. *Han må være syg.* (conviction)
   'He must be ill'

4 One might in fact wonder whether such expressions should not rather be seen as instances of objective deontic modality, cf. Herslund (2005).
5 This use of *skulle* 'shall' is of course akin to the related field of *evidentiality*.

3 Modal values and the tripartition of utterances

How then can we explain such multiple meanings for the same verb, and how can we account for the special status of the epistemic value? According to the British philosopher Richard M. Hare (1971) the logical structure of an utterance (cf. Lyons 1977: 750) contains three components: the Neustic component (a sort of sender signature: 'I say so'); the Tropic component (the truth value: 'it is the case'); and the *Phrastic* component (the propositional content). These three components are part and parcel of any utterance, but they are not necessarily located topologically in the sentence, i.e. their position cannot normally be specified; it might however, as suggested below, sometimes be possible to identify such positions.

3.1 Modal verbs and the three components

The hypothesis I want to examine – and defend – in what follows, is simply that the three modal values, dynamic, epistemic and deontic follow from the location of a modal verb in one of the above mentioned components, so that the same modal receives three different interpretations according to which component it is located in: the degree 'possible', for instance, will be interpreted as dynamic, deontic or epistemic according to which component the modal is associated with.

What I propose is the distribution of the three modal values over Hare's three components depicted in Table 1.5.

Table 1.5: Three Components

Neustic	Tropic	Phrastic
'I say so'	Epistemic	Dynamic
	Deontic	

The proposal is simply that dynamic modality consists in a modification of, or is located in, the phrastic component, deontic modality in both the phrastic and the tropic, and epistemic modality in the tropic component. The neustic component may play an important part in the distinction between subjective and objective modality, cf. Herslund (2005), but this issue will not be discussed in the present context.

Most authors seem to agree that dynamic modality must belong to the phrastic – or whatever similar analytical category is chosen. So, Le Querler (1996: 67ff) speaks of an "*intra-predicative*" modality, i.e. a modification of the link between the subject and the predicate (Subject – Mod – Predicate) expressing the possibility, probability or necessity of the realisation of the state of affairs described by the propositional content, i.e. the phrastic component. And this possibility, probability or necessity is, so to speak, located, has its root in the subject (or, mostly, the agent).

There seems also to be a widespread consensus as to the location of the epistemic modality in the tropic component. For Le Querler (1996: 67ff) it is an *"extra-predicative"* modality (Mod → [Subject – Predicate]), and for Boye (2001: 41f.) we have to do with a raising construction of the subject of a subordinate predication, cf. also the analyses of Brandt (1999: 41f.). In fact, an epistemic expression is not about the possible, probable or necessary realisation of the state of affairs described in the phrastic component, but about the truth of these degrees, i.e. the evaluation inherent in the tropic component.

But what about deontic modality? How can we make sense of the proposal that it affects both the tropic and the phrastic components? Let us note first of all that some authors in fact group it together with the dynamic modality (and other types) in a super-category of 'agent-oriented modality' as opposed to epistemic modality (Bybee and Fleischman 1995, Heine 1995). This means that the deontic reading affects the phrastic component because that is where the agent is located. But if the deontic value expresses the social or moral possibility, probability or necessity of the realisation of the state of affairs described in the phrastic, there is obviously more to it than the mere modification of this component. I shall therefore suggest that the deontic value is distributed over, or shared by the tropic and the phrastic, because the meaning of a sentence such as *He must come* is not just the necessity of the realisation of a certain state of affairs, but also the *will* to see this change come about. It is thus a complex modality, and this is acknowledged in the analysis of Kronning (1994: 96ff) of the deontic modality as a complex predicate (FAIRE-ETRE), or, following the suggestions by Le Querler (1996) that one can distinguish extra- and intrapredicative modalities, we can say that it is an "extra-intra-predicative" modification. Furthermore, Le Querler (1996: 65) characterises the deontic value as an "intersubjective" modality insofar as the speaker expresses his relation with another subject by ordering, advising, allowing, etc.

The deontic value is, in other words, related to the epistemic, insofar as it constitutes a modification of the tropic component, which can be paraphrased by 'it be so' (instead of "it is so"). But on the other hand it is also related to the dynamic value because it carries a special link to the subject (agent or 'first participant')[6] of the sentence, hence the phrastic component (Nuyts 2005: 13): the participant

---

6 Compare the notion above of 'agent oriented modality' covering both the dynamic and the deontic reading.

who is obliged, allowed or forbidden to realise a certain state of affairs. Notice that no such link exists in the case of the epistemic reading.

We thus have the following analysis of the three modal values (Table 1.6):

Table 1.6: Simple and Complex Modality 1

	Neustic	Tropic	Phrastic
Dynamic	I say so	it is the case	he **Mod** + comes
Deontic	I say so	it is + **Mod** the case	he **Mod** + comes
Epistemic	I say so	it is + **Mod** the case	he comes

This analysis then yields the following picture of the modality (Table 1.7):

(5) *Han kan komme.*
'He can come'

Table 1.7: Simple and Complex Modality 2

Dynamic (phrastic, "intra-predicative"):
'I say so – it is the case – he has the capability to come'
Deontic (tropic + phrastic, "extra-intra-predicative"):
'I say so – it be the case – he exploits his capability to come'
Epistemic (tropic, "extra-predicative"):
'I say – it is possibly the case – he comes'

The special status of the epistemic modality stands out as the only exclusively tropic modification.

3.2 Ambiguity and disambiguation

As seen above, the same modal verb can often be interpreted in two or even three different ways, as dynamic, deontic or epistemic. There are however certain morphological or syntactic features which distinguish between, on the one hand, the epistemic and, on the other, the two other readings. Such features thus isolate the epistemic reading.

A first criterion is linked to the existence of two passives in Danish: a synthetic passive with the ending -s, and a periphrastic passive, which is a regular predicative construction with the verb *blive* 'become' (Sørensen 1986), and thus not, as traditionally assumed, an auxiliary construction. A modal verb followed by a synthetic passive infinitive has dynamic or deontic meaning, whereas the same verb followed by a periphrastic passive infinitive is only interpreted as epistemic (Heltoft and Jakobsen 1996: 209ff, Hansen and Heltoft 2011: 787ff):

(6) a. *Hønen kan spises.*
hen-DEF can eat-INF-PASS
Dynamic: 'The hen is edible'
Deontic: 'It is allowed to eat the hen'
b. *Hønen kan blive spist.*
hen-DEF can become-INF eat-PAST-PART
Epistemic: 'There is a risk that the hen will be eaten (e.g. by the fox)'

This fact can be linked to and explained in terms of the proposed differences in the location of modality: if we assume that the periphrastic passive is a regular predicative construction (Sørensen 1986), one can see that the epistemic modal in the tropic governs a subordinate predication in the phrastic, cf. that Boye (2001) as noted above, assumes a kind of raising-construction (6b'):

(6) b'. poss hønen [blive + spist]

whereas the two modalities located, at least partially, in the phrastic are part of a "normal" modal + infinitive construction:

(6) a'. [hønen poss spises]

The second criterion is the tense/aspect of the infinitive following the modal. As a deontic expression necessarily concerns the future the opposition between the simple and the perfect infinitive (infinitive + past participle) conveys a difference between a deontic or epistemic reading, or an exclusively epistemic reading with the perfect infinitive (similar facts from French, German, Greek and Arabic are cited by Palmer (1986: 37, 61):

(7) a. *Jane kan / må / skal anmelde bogen.*
Jane can / may / must / shall review-INF book-DEF
Deontic (permission, obligation, duty) or epistemic (possibility)

b. *Jane kan / må / skal have anmeldt bogen.*
Jane can / may / must / shall have-INF review-PAST-PART book-DEF
Only epistemic (possibility)

As a further observation along this line one may add that only the deontic interpretation is compatible with a following telic phrase or particle, but no infinitive. As in the case of the synthetic passive the modal combines with a "pseudo-predicate" and therefore must be located in the same component as this. So a modal followed by a synthetic passive infinitive or a telic particle will inevitably have a deontic or, in the case of the passive infinitive, a dynamic reading (Hansen and Heltoft 2011: 808ff):

(8) a. *Brevene* *må* ***sendes*** *i* *tide.*
letter-PL-DEF must-PRES send-INF-PASS in time
'The letters must be sent in time'

b. *Brevene* *må* *frem* *i* *tide.*
letter-PL-DEF must-PRES PARTC in time
'The letters must (arrive) at their destination in time'

The epistemic interpretation is excluded as soon as there is no complete subordinate predication in the phrastic component to modify: the tropic must obviously have a predication to operate on. It is noticeable that the epistemic interpretation becomes possible as soon as an infinitive is inserted, i.e. when a full predication is (re)established:

(8) c. *Brevene* *må* *komme* *frem* *i* *tide.*
letter-PL-DEF must-PRES come PARTC in time
'The letters must arrive at destination in time'

This fact supports the interpretation of the location in the tropic of the modal in the epistemic reading: the modal has no room in the full predication of the phrastic component.

Here too, then, it appears that the epistemic reading is singled out, whereas the borderline between the other two readings is more blurred. This and other features contributing to the particular status of the epistemic value are discussed below.

3.3 Further syntactic and semantic arguments

Several features of the syntax and semantics of the Danish modals seem to lend support to the hypothesis that different modal values are the consequences of the modal verb being associated with different components.

3.3.1 Iconicity

Whereas the three components of the utterance cannot in general be identified with fixed positions in the sentence (or clause), there is, though, an ordering relation between them: logically, the neustic ('I say so') precedes the tropic ('It is the case'), which precedes the phrastic (propositional content). Therefore it seems justified to look for some sort of iconic relation between the three components and their associated modal values, and the actual sequencing of the modal verbs, especially in a language like Danish, whose sentence structure is extraordinarily tight-knit, topologically speaking.[7] So the first argument comes from the order of constituents.

Danish modals can combine mutually and such combinations seem to iconically reflect the three proposed locations even if, as noted, the three components are not in general identifiable by actual fixed positions in the clause. Insofar as the combination of three modals is possible (cf. Brandt 1999: 125ff), their order will definitely be Epistemic > Deontic > Dynamic:

(9) *Han må skulle kunne lose dette problem.*
     må = Epistemic, skulle = Deontic, kunne = Dynamic
     he must shall-inf can-inf solve this problem
     'He must be obliged to be able to solve this problem'

Combinations of two modal verbs are, on the other hand, quite common and their order is invariably the same: the first modal will always, depending on the second, have an epistemic or deontic interpretation, the second a deontic or dynamic interpretation. The possible combinations are accordingly as depicted in Table 1.8.

Table 1.8: Modal Combination

Epistemic > Dynamic (ex. 10a)
Epistemic > Deontic (ex. 10b)
Deontic > Dynamic (ex. 10c)

7 One might even argue that the very tripartition of the Danish clause in the classical "sentence schema" (Diderichsen 1946) is a reflection of the three logical components (Herslund 2002: 95ff): (1). the fundament field (where the illocutionary force is expressed (= neustic), (2). the nexus field, where the predication is established (= tropic), and (3). the content field (= phrastic).

The epistemic (in the tropic) always precedes everything else, the dynamic (the phrastic) comes always last:

(10) a. *Han må kunne løse problemet.*
   må | Epistemic; kunne | Dynamic
   'He must be able to solve the problem'

b. *Han kan skulle løse problemet.*
   kan | Epistemic; skulle | Deontic
   'He can be obliged to solve the problem'

c. *Han skal kunne løse problemet.*
   skal | Deontic; kunne | Dynamic
   'He shall be able to solve the problem'

The deontic reading of (10c) is readily understood in a context where someone is looking for a man to solve a certain problem ("We need a man for this job").

These sequences are also in conformity with the general observation that an epistemic modal never occurs in the scope of another modal, cf. Brandt (1999: 128), as predicted by the proposed analysis.

3.3.2 Cleft Sentences

In cleft sentences, modals can, instead of remaining in the subordinate clause (11b), be "raised" together with the focalised constituent into the presentative clause, and attach syntactically to the verb *være* 'be' (11c). Such raised modals are invariably interpreted with an epistemic or deontic value, i.e. the two modalities associated with the tropic component:

(11) a. *Peter kan bære fanen.*
   'Peter can bear the standard' (Epistemic, Deontic or Dynamic)

b. *Det er Peter der kan/skal bære fanen.*
   'It is Peter that can/shall bear the standard' (Deontic or Dynamic, never Epistemic)

c. *Det kan/skal være Peter der bærer fanen.* (Epistemic or Deontic, never Dynamic)
'It can/shall be Peter that bears the standard'

This phenomenon is easily explained by assuming that the cleft construction is a kind of "grammaticalisation" or materialisation of the tropic component: only modal values associated with this component can occur in the presentative clause 'It is x that ...', hence only deontic or epistemic readings are possible.

3.3.3 Data from other languages

That the epistemic modality is associated with the tropic component is further corroborated by certain syntactic data from other languages. Palmer (1986: 19f.), for instance, cites the Modern Greek *boró* (μπορώ) 'can', which in its epistemic use occurs in the impersonal 3. sing. (*borí*) without regard for the person of the grammatical subject, which, obviously belongs to the phrastic:

(12) a. *Ta peđjá borí na fíyun ávrio.*
the children can-3-SG that leave-3-PL tomorrow
'The children can leave tomorrow' (Epistemic)

b. *Ta peđjá borún na fíyun ávrio.*
the children can/may-3-PL that leave-3-PL tomorrow
'The children can/may leave tomorrow' (Deontic)

Van der Auwera et al. (2005: 253f.) cite similar data from Maltese and Irish. Such data are paralleled by the existence in French of the impersonal expression *il se peut* 'it can be', which has only an epistemic value, whereas the verb *pouvoir* 'can' in general has both dynamic, deontic and epistemic values.

Also in Danish an impersonal expression with the verb *kunne*, *det kan være* 'it can be' expresses the epistemic conjecture:

(13) a. *Børnene kan tage afsted i morgen.*
'The children can leave tomorrow' (Dynamic, Deontic or Epistemic)

b. *Det kan være (at) børnene tager afsted i morgen.*
it can be (that) the children go away tomorrow'
'Maybe the children leave tomorrow' (Epistemic)

The existence of epistemic impersonal expressions, and the absence of such expressions with a dynamic value, corroborates the hypothesis of the different locations of these two modal values, in the tropic and phrastic respectively: the impersonal expression is but the "materialisation" of the tropic component.

3.3.4 Diachronic excursus

The three modal values seem to constitute a hierarchy reflecting the development of the modal verbs from a primary dynamic sense via an intermediate deontic sense to the derived epistemic reading, cf. Traugott (1989) on the evolution of English *can*, Kronning (1990, 1994) on the evolution of the French verb *devoir* 'may/must', Bybee and Fleischman (1995: 5), Heine (1995: 17), Auwera et al. (2005), and Nuyts (2005: 14).

A verb like *kunne* 'can' has a historically primary dynamic meaning. And from this primary meaning 'have the capability to' it can easily be seen how it evolves into the more general meaning of 'possibility', hence the modal values deontic permission and epistemic possibility:

(14)	*Han*	*kan*	*svømme.*	'He can swim'	
		↓			
	Han	*kan*	*svømme.*	'He has the permission to/can swim'	(Deontic)
				'It is possible he can swim'	(Epistemic)

To account for this evolution one only has to assume that the meaning component 'possible' moves into the tropic. Such a development, where a word "migrates" from the phrastic into the tropic component, is also found in the evolution of the French adverb *or*, which from a clear temporal meaning, 'now', i.e. belonging to the phrastic, nowadays only has a logical meaning as introducing a weak opposition (as the minor in a syllogism), cf. Herslund (2008).

3.4 The modal *måtte*

The modal verb *måtte* 'may, must', which corresponds to the two German verbs *dürfen* and *müssen*, and Englsh *may* and *must*, exhibits at a first glance a bewildering distribution.[8] It participates in two pairs of oppositions.

8 In closely related Norwegian the cognate verb *måtte* only expresses the necessary.

In the epistemic use it is opposed to *kunne* 'can' and expresses the necessary:

(15) POSSIBLE: *kunne* / NECESSARY: *måtte*

In the deontic use it is opposed to *skulle* 'shall, must' and expresses, this time, the possible, but also the necessary:

(16) POSSIBLE: *måtte*, (*kunne*) / NECESSARY: *skulle*, (*måtte*)

The same verb has thus two diametrically opposed intensity values. What is necessarily the case, conviction or certainty, in the epistemic reading:

(15') *Han må være rejst.*
'He must have left'

but the possible in the deontic reading, i.e. a permission:

(16') *Han må rejse.*
'He may leave'

The meaning of deontic possibility, permission, can be underlined by adverbs such as *gerne* or *godt* 'gladly, it's ok':

(17) *Du må gerne komme nu.*
'It's ok for you to come now'

To confuse matters further, this modal can also, in particular when stressed, have the meaning of deontic necessity, i.e. express a duty:

(18) *Du må tage dig sammen.*
'You must pull yourself together'

If *måtte* is opposed to *kunne* in the epistemic system, i.e. in the tropic, cf. (15) above, it shares with this verb the domain of the possible in the deontic system, cf. (16) above. The two verbs express an active permission (*måtte*) and a passive permission, indifference (*kunne*), respectively:

(19) a. *Han må komme når jeg siger til.*
'He may come when I say so'

b. *Han kan komme når han vil.*
'He can come whenever he likes to'

And if *måtte* is opposed to *skulle* in the deontic system it also shares, as seen in (16), the domain of the necessary, in particular with the negation, *måtte ikke* 'must not' being the negative counterpart to positive *skulle* 'shall, must':

(20) a. *Du skal komme nu.*
'You must come now'
b. Du må ikke komme endnu.
'You mustn't come yet'

This apparently bizarre distribution of a single lexeme has led several authors such as Sørensen (2001) and Boye (2001) to assume the existence of two homonymous verbs, *måtte*-p (cf. German *dürfen* 'may', permission) and *måtte*-n (cf. German *müssen* 'must', duty or certainty). It is however possible, and perhaps even desirable, to maintain the unity of the lexeme and try to explain the distribution as an effect of the different locations of the epistemic value in the tropic, and the deontic both in the tropic and the phrastic.

In the epistemic reading, when the verb is located in the tropic, it remains unambiguous and expresses only the necessary intensity. Now, it is precisely in the deontic system, the complex modality, that the verb has two different intensity values, both 'possible' and, in particular when negated, 'necessary'. And it is perhaps the relation with the negation that is the key to the riddle. If we look at the distribution in the shape of the schema in Table 1.9:

Table 1.9: Modality and Negation

Epistemic		Deontic	
POSS	NEC	POSS	NEC
kunne	*måtte*		*skulle*

It appears that the deontic poss intensity (permission) is minoritarian and that most of the uses of *måtte* have the value nec, which is also the only meaning of the cognate verb in Norwegian, i.e. you cannot ask permission by using *måtte* in this language.

The negative version, Neg + *måtte*, is in a sense a neutralisation of the intensities poss and nec: what is not possible is, a fortiori, not necessary either. So whereas:

(21) *Han må ikke komme.*
'He must not come'

is the negative version of both:

(22) a. *Han må komme.*
'He may come' (permission)
b. *Han skal komme.*
'He must come' (duty)

it is a difference in the location of the negation that accounts for the inherent ambiguity of the negative sentence. If (21) *Han må ikke komme* is understood as cancelling a duty, (22b) *Han skal komme*, we have the logical transcription:

(23) a. nec (Neg he come)
'It is necessary that he doesn't come'

with propositional negation, i.e. the negation of the phrastic. But if the same sentence is understood as the negation of a permission, (22a) *Han må komme*, the negation is modal, i.e. located in the tropic component:

(23) b. Neg poss (he come)
'It is not possible that he comes'

and one can speak of a neutralisation of the two negative versions because of the logical equivalence:

(24) Neg poss ≡ nec Neg
'What is not possible is necessarily not'

It is the two possibilities for the location of the negation as tropic or phrastic, which is made possible by the double or complex nature of the deontic modality, that account for the at first glance bewildering distribution of the Danish modal *måtte*. On the other hand, this distribution corroborates the hypothesis defended, i.e. that the deontic value is complex, both tropic and phrastic, whereas the epistemic value is simple, only tropic. That is why it is precisely in the deontic, and not in the epistemic system that one finds this puzzling ambiguity of the modal verb *måtte* 'may, must'.

4 Conclusions

The original proposal by Hare (1971) was not constructed specifically in order to handle the analysis of modal verbs, but to assess the overall organisation of the semantic content of utterances, their logical structure as it were (Lyons 1977: 749f.), in the analysis of speech acts. The capability of the proposed hypothesis to account for the general distribution of modal values over the three examined modal verbs, to single out the special status of the epistemic modality, and in particular its contribution to solving the riddle of the distribution of the modal *måtte* constitutes a test of its explanatory power in a field it was not especially designed for.

Abbreviations: DEF – definite; INF – infinitive; PART – participle; PARTC – particle; PASS – passive; PAST – past (tense); PL – plural; SG – singular

References

Benveniste, Emile. 1974. L'appareil formel de l'énonciation (1970). In *Problèmes de linguistique générale, 2*, 79–88. Paris: Gallimard.
Boye, Kasper. 2001. The Force-Dynamic Core Meaning of Danish Modal Verbs. *Acta Linguistica Hafniensia* 33. 19–66.
Boye, Kasper. 2005. Modality and the Concept of Force-Dynamic Potential. In Alex Klinge & Henrik H. Müller (eds.), *Modality. Studies in Form and Function*, 49–80. London: Equinox.
Brandt, Søren. 1999. *Modal Verbs in Danish* (Travaux du Cercle Linguistique de Copenhague XXX). Copenhagen: Reitzel.
Bybee, Joan & Suzanne Fleischman. 1995. Modality in Grammar and Discourse. An Introductory Essay. In Joan Bybee and Suzanne Fleischman (eds.), *Modality in Grammar and Discourse*, 1–14. Amsterdam/Philadelphia: John Benjamins.
Davidsen-Nielsen, Niels. 1990. *Tense and Mood in English. A Comparison with Danish.* Berlin/New York: Mouton de Gruyter.
Diderichsen, Paul. 1946. *Elementær Dansk Grammatik* [Elementary Danish Grammar]. Copenhagen: Gyldendal.
Hansen, Erik & Lars Heltoft. 2011. *Grammatik over det Danske Sprog, I-III* [Grammar of the Danish language]. Copenhagen: Det Danske Sprog- og Litteraturselskab.
Hare, Richard M. 1971. *Practical Inferences*. London: Macmillan.
Heine, Bernd. 1995. Agent-Oriented vs. Epistemic Modality. Some Observations on German Modals. In Joan Bybee & Suzanne Fleischman (eds.), *Modality in Grammar and Discourse*, 17–53. Amsterdam/Philadelphia: John Benjamins.
Heltoft, Lars & Lisbeth Falster Jakobsen. 1996. Danish passives and subject positions as a mood system. A content analysis. In Elisabeth Engberg-Pedersen, Michael Fortescue, Peter Harder, Lars Heltoft & Lisbeth Falster Jakobsen (eds.), *Content, Expression and Structure. Studies in Danish functional grammar* (Studies in Language Companion Series 29), 199–234. Amsterdam/Philadelphia: John Benjamins.

Herslund, Michael. 1989. Modality. A Presentation. In Michael Herslund (ed.), *Modality* (Travaux du Cercle Linguistique de Copenhague XXIII), 7–15. Copenhagen: Reitzel.
Herslund, Michael. 2002. *Danish* (Languages of the World. Materials 382). Munich: Lincom Europa.
Herslund, Michael. 2003. Sur la modalité en danois et la tripartition de la phrase. In André Rousseau (ed.), *La modalité dans tous ses états. Revue Belge de Philologie et d'Histoire*, 81 (3). 867–882.
Herslund, Michael. 2005. Subjective and Objective Modality. In Alex Klinge & Henrik H. Müller (eds.), *Modality. Studies in Form and Function*, 39–48. London: Equinox.
Herslund, Michael. 2008. Temporalité et connexion: le cas de *or*. In Merete Birkelund, Maj-Britt Mosegaard Hansen & Coco Norén (eds.), *L'énonciation dans tous ses états. Mélanges offerts à Henning Nølke à l'occasion de ses soixante ans*, 391–402. Bern: Peter Lang.
Kronning, Hans. 1990. Modalité et diachronie: du déontique à l'épistémique. L'évolution sémantique de *debere/devoir*. In Odile Halmøy, Arne Halvorsen & Lise Lorentzen (eds.), *Actes du onzième congrès des romanistes scandinaves. Trondheim 13–17 août 1990*, 301–312. Trondheim: Institut d'Etudes Romanes.
Kronning, Hans. 1994. *Modalité, cognition et polysémie: sémantique du verbe modal* devoir. Uppsala: University of Uppsala.
Le Querler, Nicole. 1996. *Typologie des modalités.* Caen: Presses Universitaires de Caen.
Lyons, John. 1977. *Semantics.* Cambridge: Cambridge University Press.
Nuyts, Jan. 2005. The modal confusion: on terminology and the concepts behind it. In Alex Klinge & Henrik H. Müller (eds.), *Modality. Studies in Form and Function*, 5–38. London: Equinox.
Palmer, Frank. 1986. *Mood and Modality*. Cambridge: Cambridge University Press.
Sørensen, Finn. 1986. Passivkonstruktioner er prædikatskonstruktioner [Passive constructions are predicative constructions]. In Niels Davidsen-Nielsen and Finn Sørensen (eds.), *Festskrift til Jens Rasmussen* (CEBAL 8), 230–249. Copenhagen: Nyt Nordisk Forlag Arnold Busck.
Sørensen, Finn. 2001. Modals and Modality. Some Issues and some Proposals. In Henrik H. Müller (ed.), *Reflections on Modality* (Copenhagen Studies in Language 26), 11–37. Frederiksberg: Samfundslitteratur.
Traugott, Elizabeth. 1989. On the rise of epistemic meanings in English: an example of subjectification in semantic change. *Language* 65. 31–55.
Van der Auwera, Johan, Andreas Ammann & Saskia Kindt. 2005. Modal polyfunctionality and Standard Average European. In Alex Klinge and Henrik H. Müller (eds.), *Modality. Studies in Form and Function*, 247–272. London: Equinox.

Agnès Celle

Epistemic evaluation in factual contexts in English

Abstract: This article accounts for the use of *should* and *would* in factual contexts where there is no doubt as to the actualisation of the modalised proposition. The focus is on two types of construction – *why*-questions in which *should* or *would* is used, and content clauses introduced by predicative lexemes expressing surprise or evaluation as in *It's surprising that he should have been so late*. It is argued that modals used in these positions combine layers of modality. In *why*-questions, epistemic modality is part of an evaluative judgement that requests either the cause of a surprising state of affairs (with *would*) or the justification of an event or a speech act (with *should*). In content clauses, epistemic evaluation comes under the scope of an evaluative superordinate expression. Whether the content clause is evaluated as concordant with the speaker's expectations or not, the use of *should* and *would* signals that the speaker does not commit himself / herself to the truth of that proposition. This may be for pragmatic reasons in cases where hearer-new information prompts the speaker to anticipate the hearer's surprise.

Keywords: epistemic evaluation, factual context, expectation, meditative polemic, concordance, discordance, surprise, questions, content clauses, past tense modals, modal remoteness

1 Introduction

The aim of this paper is to account for the use of *should* and *would* in factual contexts where there is no doubt as to the actualisation of the modalised proposition. We concentrate on two types of utterances: *why*-questions, in which a question is asked about the cause of a state of affairs, and content clauses introduced by predicative lexemes indicating surprise or evaluation as in *It's surprising that he should have been so late*. This use of *should* is called "emotive" by Huddleston and Pullum (2002), "meditative-polemic" by Behre (1950, 1955), "theoretical" by Leech

Note: I would like to express my thanks to the anonymous reviewers and to Bernard Comrie for their valuable comments and suggestions. Any remaining errors are my sole responsibility.

Agnès Celle, University Paris Diderot

https://doi.org/10.1515/9783110572261-002

(1971: 112). These various labels reflect the relation between modality and speaker's stance. In contrast to *should*, *would* in content clauses embedded in a superordinate clause expressing emotion or evaluation has scarcely been described in studies of modality in English – with the notable exceptions of Jacobsson (1988), Larreya (2015) and Furmaniak & Larreya (2015). The use of *would* and *should* in these contexts raises several questions. Firstly, what is the nature and function of epistemic modality when it is put into service to evaluate a proposition not in terms of likelihood, but in terms of appropriateness? Secondly, what is the connection between affect, and more specifically surprise, and epistemic modality? While acknowledging the emotive function of *should* in content clauses, Huddleston and Pullum (2002: 187) classify this use under the heading "low degree modality", which they further define as "with little discernible modal meaning of its own". We argue that the modal forms under study combine layers of modality, possibly including dynamic modality, which makes their modal meaning not weaker or lower, but more elusive. Finally, we aim to explain why *would* is used in such contexts, especially – but not only – in American English, a fact that goes unaccounted for in English grammars. Although a few linguists (Jacobsson 1988, Larreya 2015) have examined this use of *would*, they did not attempt to account for the distribution of *should* and *would* in subordinate position.

2 *Would* and *should*: layers of modality

Before examining the factual uses this paper is about, let us outline the meaning(s) of *should* and *would*.

Would and *should* are preterite forms of the modal auxiliaries *will* and *shall* respectively. *Will* expresses a relation of inference that depends on some inherent conformity between the subject and the predicate based on the volition, the willingness, or the propensity of the subject to carry out the eventuality expressed by the verb base.[1] *Shall* expresses necessity. Contrary to the preterite forms of lexical verbs, the meaning of preterite modals cannot be derived from the combination of past meaning with the meaning of the present tense modals, as pointed out by Bybee (1995: 503). Past tense modals are unlikely to have past meaning. If they

1 There is general agreement that *will* expresses the speaker's confidence based on knowledgeability (Palmer 1979: 47; Joos 1964: 156–157). This "adequate assurance of eventual occurrence", to use Joos's terminology, is assured by the properties of the predication. In contrast, *shall* expresses "contingent casual assurance", i.e. the eventual occurrence is not congruent with the properties of the predication.

do, there are restrictions on their use. The preterite forms of modal auxiliaries are commonly subdivided into three categories (see Coates 1983: 111, 211, Bybee 1995: 503–504):

- Hypothetical uses, which are the most frequent uses:

(1) *If I knew a lady of birth such as her in person and mind, I* ***would*** *marry her tomorrow.* (BNC)

(2) *Well, Mistress Pamela, I can't say I like you so well as this lady does for I* ***should*** *never care, if you were my servant, to have you and your master in the same house together.* (BNC)

In (1) and (2), the relation of inference between the protasis and the apodosis is framed in a remote conditional by the *if*-clause in the preterite tense. The modal in the apodosis is therefore to be interpreted as a modal preterite.

- Present context uses, where the past form introduces modal remoteness (Huddleston & Pullum 2002: 148–151, 196–201), possibly, but not necessarily, with tentative meaning:

(3) *I* ***would*** *suggest a counter-proposition: that we are living in a society that is sick and tired of information.* (BNC)

(4) *Er that's our reduced one. That* ***would*** *be sixty nine pounds.* (BNC)

(5) *A valid passport is essential when you travel abroad. You* ***should*** *allow at least 12 weeks to obtain a British passport.* (BNC)

(6) *With departure from Vanov scheduled for 9.30am, you* ***should*** *be in Decin for 1.00pm.* (BNC)

Modal remoteness as defined by Huddleston and Pullum covers a great variety of uses. They point out that the modal meaning of the preterite is highly frequent with modal auxiliaries (2002: 196). In (3) and (4), the meaning of *would* can be derived from *will* + past inflection. In (3), the volitional sense of *will* is weakened by the past form and the act of suggesting is performed at the time of utterance in a tentative way. In (4) however, the past form does not introduce tentative meaning, as the speaker's certainty about the price is not weakened. There is no doubt at all as to the truth of the proposition. However, the speaker does not commit herself to the truth of the proposition, as shown by Celle (2012). The past form introduces affective hedging rather than epistemic hedging (Dixon & Foster 1997: 3) by anticipating potential disagreement or discordance. In (5) and (6), it is questionable whether the meaning of *should* can be derived from *shall* + past inflection, as *shall* cannot be used in such contexts. Compared with *must*, the past form *should* conveys a weakened sense of obligation in (5), and the meaning is one of advice given to anyone preparing to travel abroad. In (6), the past form expresses logical necessity qualified by a sense of doubt. Noteworthy is the fact that *should* cannot express just any kind of logical relation. As shown by Rivière (1981), *should* cannot be used to express an inferential judgement about the cause of a state of affairs (**There is light in his room. He should be back home*) while it may express a deductive judgement about the consequence of a state of affairs (*He is back home. He should be able to help you*).

- Past time uses, further subdivided into two categories:
- Backshift:

(7) *Bradford North Labour MP Terry Rooney said he* ***would*** *send Simon some cash personally.* (BNC)

In this backshifted report, the preterite indicates that the past situation referred to by the main verb *said* functions as the time of utterance.

- Past time reference:

Past time uses are the least common with modal auxiliaries. They always involve dynamic modality (see Huddleston & Pullum 2002: 197):

(8) *It was the start of a genuine friendship. I told Frankie about my deafness and my Dad being away. And we* ***would*** *go for walks together or just sit in the garden, talking. I told him how I had to go for special lessons and how other kids* ***would*** *sometimes laugh or pick on me. And he* ***would*** *listen and try to talk up my confidence.* (BNC)

(9) *After her mother died she went on many trips abroad with him. She was always impressed by his fame and* ***would*** *have liked a theatrical career. She did appear in amateur shows just as he had, but he* ***would*** *not allow any of his children to become professional performers. So Jessie became a secretary to a Manchester solicitor and eventually fell in love with and married an officer during the First World War.* (BNC)

In (8), *would* expresses a propensity of the subject. This typical behaviour is actualised in a series of situations iterated in the past. In (9), volitional *would* is negated, so that the preterite form of *would* expresses the subject's refusal in the past.

As noted by Bybee (1995: 504) and Huddleston & Pullum (2002: 197), *should* has no past time uses at all, unlike *would*.

The addition of the preterite to *shall* and *will* may thus be said to create layers of modality, one of them being modal remoteness in present context uses. An important feature of modal remoteness is that it is perfectly compatible with the speaker's absolute certainty in factual contexts. This is the case in (4), where the proposition holds despite the use of the past morpheme. Interestingly, epistemic *would* in factual contexts cannot be accounted for in terms of tentativeness, as pointed out by Birner et al. (2007), Ward et al. (2003), Ward et al. (2007) and Ward (2011). Birner et al. (2007: 326–327) and Ward et al. (2003: 71) claim that epistemic *would* conveys commitment to the truth of the modalised proposition because it expresses a higher level of confidence than any other epistemic modal. They also contend that this epistemic use requires an open proposition, i.e. "a proposition with one or more underspecified elements" (2003: 72). However, Ward et al. limit their study of *would* to equative constructions such as "That would be X" where an open proposition is necessarily implied.

It is argued in Celle (2012) that this use is possible independently of an open proposition and with verbs other than the copula. Celle (2012) also stresses that the modal contribution of *would* in factual contexts should not be underestimated. Even if the speaker's confidence in the truth of the proposition is not at stake, it does not mean that this use conveys commitment to the truth of the proposition. Celle (2012) argues that epistemic *would* expresses modal remoteness because it is not for lack of knowledge or confidence that the speaker does not ascribe actuality to some fact, but for pragmatic reasons. Celle upholds the view that *would* in itself is truth-neutral, and that information about the actualisation of the verb can only be provided by its contextual environment. The following example yields two readings which are made explicit with more context in (a) and (b):

(10) *'How old is Benjamin?'*
'Benjamin was *born in 2006. He* **would** *be ten.'*
a. *Benjamin was born in 2006. He* **would** *be ten if he were still alive.*
b. *Benjamin* was born in 2006. So he **would** be ten.'

In (a), the protasis sets an unreal condition. Consequently the apodosis is interpreted as counterfactual, the implicature being that Benjamin is dead. In (b), the existence of Benjamin is presupposed by the *how*-question. On the basis of objective evidence, that is, his year of birth, it is possible to infer Benjamin's age.

To our knowledge, the only full account of all modals used in factual contexts as opposed to non-factual contexts is the one offered by Larreya (2015). Larreya (2015) makes a systematic distinction between a priori and a posteriori modalisation that cuts across the distinction between epistemic and root modality. Larreya defines modalisation as "the way modality is used": (a) "depending on the speaker's state of knowledge of the modalised fact" and (b) "depending on the addressee's state of knowledge of the modalised fact as assumed by the speaker".[2] When the speaker does not present himself / herself as knowing the truth value of the modalised proposition, modality is used a priori (as in (1), (2), (3), (5), (6) and (7)). In contrast, when the speaker presents himself / herself as aware of the truth value of the proposition, modality is used a posteriori under Larreya's account (as in (8) and (9), where the modal expresses dynamic modality, and as in (4), where the epistemic use of the modal is not motivated by the speaker's uncertainty). Larreya further distinguishes between two cases of a posteriori modalisation: constative uses, and evaluative uses. Constative modalisation is concerned with hearer-new facts that the speaker modalises when reporting them, as in (4), (8) and (9). Evaluative modalisation presupposes the existence or the non-existence of a modalised fact and is typically conveyed in predicative expressions that have scope over a content clause. Section 3 is devoted to a special case of constative modalisation (the one illustrated in (4)), and section 4 deals with evaluative uses.

3 *Would* and *should* in *why*-questions

3.1 Epistemic *would* in answer to a question

As mentioned above, the use of epistemic *would* in factual contexts is documented in several studies by Birner et al., Ward et al., Celle (2012), Furmaniak & Larreya (2015) and Larreya (2015). These studies are concerned with declarative sentences, in which epistemic *would* – as opposed to *should* – may convey evidence-based modalised assertions, as in the following example:

(11) *'Ew, what smells?'*
*'That **would** be me, or more specifically, my patient's insides all over me.'*
(cited in Celle 2012: 153)

In (11), the speaker does not express the slightest doubt about himself being the source of a bad smell. In answer to a question asked by the addressee, the speaker supplies a piece of information that will predictably sound surprising to the addressee. Epistemic *would* signals that the proposition was expected to be unlikely. The speaker anticipates that reality contradicts the addressee's expectations and distances himself from the situation of utterance for purely pragmatic

2 Our translation.

reasons. As pointed out by Bybee (1998: 267) in her definition of the irrealis, modal categories may perform an illocutionary "discourse-oriented function", rather than express the speaker's stance on objective reality. The choice of the past tense modal exhibits the fact that the speaker is not asserting the truth of the proposition, even if he does not have the slightest doubt about it: "epistemic moods mollify the strength of a statement so that it is not a bald assertion" (Bybee 1998: 268).

There is no similar pragmatic use for *should.*[3] In (11), the modalised proposition expresses the speaker's knowledge that he is the source of the foul smell. The assertion is qualified by the past tense modal form in order to anticipate and defuse the addressee's surprise, not to weaken the speaker's level of certainty. The context implies too high a level of certainty on the part of the speaker to license *should.* In (12), however, *should* may substitute for *would*, but with a different implicature:

(12) A. *'How old is Benjamin?'*
B. *'Benjamin was born in 2006. He* ***should*** *be ten.'*

The second proposition in B's utterance is presented as the result of an inference. Unlike *would*, *should* weakens the level of certainty associated with the modalised proposition. This explains why only epistemic *would* is attested in factual contexts where the speaker's judgement is based on available evidence.

3.2 *Why-would* questions

Why-questions are about the cause of a proposition. In combination with *would*, the actual validity of that cause is challenged by modal remoteness. As mentioned above, *would* is truth-neutral per se. It is the context that allows either a factual reading or a hypothetical one. *Why-would* questions may cast doubt on a prior proposition. They may also do the exact opposite in factual contexts and convey the speaker's surprise at some event without calling that event into question. Any kind of variable question may be found in factual contexts. Our focus will be on

---

3 However, Larreya & Rivière (2010: 119–120) note that under certain circumstances, *should* implies actualisation: *'He's in good shape.'*

'So he should be, after three weeks' holiday!' (Larreya & Rivière 2010: 120).

They analyse this utterance as a case of understatement. Although *should* is used in an independent clause, we argue that this use is evaluative and comparable to the use of *should* in content clauses, as the following paraphrase suggests: "It is normal that he should be in good shape after three weeks' holiday."

why-questions that bear on the cause of a state of affairs. In the following pair of examples, *would* is hypothetical:

(13) A. *'Are you sure you don't mind?'*
B. *'Why* **would** *I mind?'* (BNC)

(14) A. *'Louis probably started that rumour himself.'*
B. *She rubbed her temples. 'I don't understand. Why* **would** *he do that?'* (BNC)

In the first utterance of (13), the speaker seeks confirmation of non-*p*: "you don't mind". The rhetorical *why-would* question indirectly confirms non-*p* by undermining the belief that the causal grounds for *p* are justified. As a result, non-*p* sounds self-evident, and "I don't mind" is implied. As pointed out by Furmaniak (2014), in such cases, the preceding proposition modalised by *would* conforms to the speaker's expectations, and non-*p* is viewed as not surprising. This implicitly suggests that *p* would run counter to B's norm.

In (14), the cause for *p* (*Louis started that rumour himself*) is called into question in a context where speakers do not understand each other and disagree. The epistemic status of *p* is an issue for both speakers: A's utterance is modalised by the adverb *probably*, and B's question indicates that this proposition does not make sense to her. *Would* conveys the meaning that no actual existence can be assigned to that cause, which amounts to denying *p*. The question implies *Louis did not start that rumour himself* and signals that speaker B does not believe in the truth of *p*. It is the discordant status of *p* that triggers B's epistemic judgement.

In factual contexts, *p* corresponds to an actualised proposition. The past tense morpheme is not counterfactual. Note that *would* is time-neutral and compatible with past reference as well as present reference. In the following examples, *why-would* questions refer to a past event:

(15) *'He's a politician: Northern Ireland Office.' 'House-sweeps on a regular basis, mirrors under the car each morning, a discreet bodyguard and,' Pascoe added, 'a gun.' 'He's on their list; not high, but he's there.' 'How did you get it?' 'I went to see him one evening and asked to borrow it.' 'He handed it over?' 'Yes.' 'Why* **would** *he do that?' 'We're divorcing. I'm being nice about it. Apart from other things, I'm not bringing into court the fact that he liked to beat me. One time, he cut me.'* (BNC)

(16) *'Why were you offended? Even if you think me the most immoral bastard ever to walk the face of the earth, why* **would** *you react so personally? And why* **would** *you have set out to humiliate me?'* (BNC)

It is the context that tells us how to interpret the temporal reference of these questions. In (15), *do that* refers to the past situation framed by the event *He handed it over*. The context is less clear in (16), where the first *why-would* question can be interpreted either as referring back to the past situation set up by the question *why were you offended?*, or as referring to a generic present. This ambiguity can only be lifted with the addition of the perfect aspect as in the second *why-would* question, which unambiguously refers to the past.

In the following examples, *why-would* questions refer to the present:

(17) *'Then who's the woman in the photographs?' Robbie was still sceptical. 'My sister – Fenella. She's a photographic model. Those were copies of two of her recent portfolio photographs.' 'Why* **would** *you keep photos of your sister in your cabin?'* (BNC)

(18) *'If there is one thing I definitely need at this moment, it is a commentary on Italian traffic from a girl from the American midwest.' Caroline's brows lifted in puzzlement. 'Why* **would** *you think that?' 'Only one born to the insanity of Italian traffic should make observations about it,' he answered tersely. 'I meant, why* **would** *you think I'm from that part of America?'* (BNC)

In (17) and (18), the *why-would* question is formed in reaction to the addressee's discourse content, which violates the speaker's expectations. In (18), the discourse content referred to by *that* is viewed as the reflection of the addressee's erroneous thinking. Verbs of saying are frequently used this way:

(19) [...] *she interrupted eventually, 'why* **would** *you be telling me these things when I know them already?'* (BNC)

(20) *'Where were you last night, McKenzie?'*
'Are you asking if I have an alibi, Mr. Donatucci? Why **would** *you ask?'* (COCA)

In (19) and (20), the *why-would* questions seek information about the cause of the addressee's speech act.

In these factual contexts, the speaker's judgement is based on evidence provided by some surprising discourse content. Emotionally, these *why-would* questions convey the speaker's surprise. This emotional experience activates a cognitive process whereby the speaker adapts to the unexpected situation, as stated by Miceli and Castelfranchi (2015: 52):

> [S]urprise is likely to induce epistemic causal search and consequent belief revision, thus favoring a more coherent (and hopefully reliable) predictive belief system, and in so doing a long-term adaptation to unexpected events through future adaptive action.

This adaptation process involves an abductive inference. Epistemic modality is here characterised by the speaker's attempt to account for unexpectedness in an abductive evidence-based judgement that goes from a discordant state of affairs to its cause.[4] Although the starting point of abductive reasoning is some surprising observation made at the time of utterance, the past form of the modal is used. This mirative stance is adopted in reaction to some surprising information that the speaker has not fully assimilated yet.[5]

However, not all *why-would* questions in factual contexts are induced by a reaction of surprise. If these questions are anaphoric to propositions that convey discourse-old information, they seek the cause of some tendency, propensity or behaviour that is evaluated. In that case, *would* refers to the past:

(21) A. *... Once something like that has happened there's always another disaster coming behind that actually takes over the headlines, so, about six months, a year, two years afterwards they were still finding that in parts of Europe the general level of nuclear activity was higher than it had been before Chernobyl, why* ***would*** *that happen?*
B. *Erm ...*
A. *Welsh Wales, in Wales and in the Lake District they found that the er level of nuclear activity on the surface of, of the field as it were and therefore reached the animals is higher than it has been, how* ***would*** *they manage to do that?* (BNC)

(22) Kendall: *You just found out that your real dad is not the guy who abused you, but someone who would take a bullet for you.*
Ryan: *Exactly! He took a bullet for me. I know that. That's the point. That's the point. Why* ***would*** *he do that?*

4 Based on Peirce (1966), Desclés and Guentchéva (forthcoming) distinguish abduction from two other inferential processes, i.e. deduction and induction. They define abduction as follows: "Abduction (or retroduction) is based on facts (observed or known) and the law of inference (relation of implication) across propositions, states the plausibility of a hypothesis." They also stress that abduction is characterised by "a certain disengagement on the speaker's part" and that the hypothesis suggested may be contradicted: "stating that a hypothesis is plausible leaves the field open for competing explanations (often unknown as yet)."

5 On the mirative stance, see Celle and Lansari (2014), Celle and Lansari (2015) and Celle et al. (2017).

Kendall: *Well, maybe because he cares whether you live or die?*
Ryan: *Or maybe because it's just in his training.* (CASO)

In (21) and (22), the underlined sequences correspond to actualised past events which are in focus in discourse. This information being shared by speaker and addressee, the questions cannot be motivated by a feeling of surprise on the part of the speaker at the time of utterance. In (21), the *why*-question seeks the cause of a physical phenomenon, namely the high level of nuclear activity in parts of Europe long after the Chernobyl accident. The *how*-question asks about the manner in which the investigation was carried out. What is questioned in both cases is how and why these events conform to some congruent property – be it a physical principle in the first case or the propensity of the subject in the second. The question is thus about the predictability of these propositions. The epistemic meaning of predictability associated with these propositions is grounded in the properties of the subject, which shows that epistemic modality and root modality are closely intertwined.

Similarly in (22), the speaker wonders why it was predictable that the referent of the subject would take a bullet for him. In this example, predictability is based on the subject's willingness to adopt that attitude. In all these questions, the speaker attempts to account for past events with hindsight. He wonders why such events were predictable on the basis of the properties of the subject. This epistemic judgement intersects with root modality. The following example can be accounted for along the same lines:

(23) Lee: *Why* ***would*** *you let her watch something called "Bloody stranger two"?*
Gaby: *I know, I know. I'm an idiot. Now she's having nightmares and crawling into our bed every night.* (*Desperate Housewives*)

Although there is no prior discourse the question can be anaphoric to, the proposition challenged by the question is discourse-old information. Lee is reacting not to something that unexpectedly arises in the situation of utterance, but to a past event he already knows about and disapproves of. The question is rhetorical and not informative. More specifically, the question is not about the cause of a past event – as would be the case with *why did you let her watch something called "Bloody stranger two"?*. The rhetorical question implies rather that there is no justification for the addressee's foolish behaviour and invites the addressee to commit herself to that point of view. This reading is confirmed by Gaby's answer, *I know, I know, I'm an idiot*, which does not supply a cause, but "a shared sense of absurdity", to use Rohde's expression (2006: 140).

Significantly, Rohde (2006: 152) correlates the lack of surprise in rhetorical questions with their uninformativity. We further suggest that the lack of surprise in *why-would* questions about discourse-old information hinders abductive reasoning.[6] The state of affairs may well be discordant, which explains why a modalised question is asked. And yet, if the question is about discourse-old information, however discordant the state of affairs, the root foundation of the proposition will be challenged, rather than its epistemic character. Furthermore, this discordant state of affairs is in a past situation. The behaviour of the subject in a past situation may be evaluated and indirectly criticised, as in (23). Crucially, the evaluation of some past event is made possible by the ability of root *would* to refer to the past. By contrast, the starting point of abductive reasoning is some surprising observation made at the time of utterance.

3.3 *Why-should* questions

Why-questions have the form of open interrogatives. However, *why-should* questions are not ordinary information questions about a cause. They may question modality in three different ways.

Why-should questions may seemingly ask about the cause of a weak obligation while they actually aim to persuade the addressee to accept that obligation:

(24) *ARRANGING YOUR AFFAIRS AND MAKING A WILL # A GUIDE FOR PEOPLE WITH AIDS OR HIV INFECTION # The Terrence Higgins Trust # Why* ***should*** *you make a will? # If you die without making a will (sometimes called 'dying intestate'), strict rules govern who will inherit your property, including money and personal possessions.* (BNC)

(25) *Your investment will buy units in that fund and you will therefore have access to a far wider-ranging portfolio of investments than most individuals could realistically set up and manage on their own. # WHY* ***SHOULD*** *I INVEST IN A PEP NOW? # History has shown that investing in the stock market during times of economic recovery has proved rewarding for investors who are looking for a good return over the longer term. Most commentators agree that, with interest rates and inflation at a low level, the UK economy is now well placed to emerge out of recession.* (BNC)

6 As such, rhetorical questions are not an obstacle to the expression of surprise. It is argued in Celle (forthc.) that rhetorical questions may indeed serve a mirative function in English, which is not predicted by Rohde's (2006) theory.

These questions are not genuine directives because they do not attempt to get the addressee to do something. They may, however, be considered directive in the sense that they aim to get the addressee to accept the presupposed deontic modality. Schematically, they may be represented by "Why (obligation) *p*?" and imply "(obligation) *p*". They are not ordinary questions as they do not request an informative answer from the addressee. In (24) and (25), *why* could be followed by *for what reasons*: *why and for what reasons should you make a will?*; *why and for what reasons should I invest in a PEP now?*. In answer to these questions, the reasons for investing straight away in (25), for making a will in (24) are listed. It is worth noting that the answers are provided by the speaker, not by the addressee, the latter being not expected to know the answers. *Why-should* questions are used as directives in guidelines that formulate advice for patients or customers. These spurious questions imply "you should make a will", "you should invest in a PEP now." This reveals both the deontic meaning of *should* and the directive nature of the question, which prompts the addressee to accept the following: "I should invest in a PEP now because..." and "I should make a will because...", hence to fulfill an obligation and to commit to the causal link suggested by the speaker.

However, in their overwhelming majority, *why-should* questions have an evaluative function in an anaphoric context. They serve to characterise a state of affairs as absurd. In first-person questions, *should* tends to cancel the question-answer presupposition. The necessity applied to the proposition is rejected by the speaker.

First, it should be stressed that *should*, like *would*, is truth-neutral:

(26) *He said Vera could have her job back if she apologised. Angry Vera replied: 'Why* ***should*** *I apologise for helping charity? I am not going back.'* (BNC)

(27) PAMELA: *Sir, sir, as you please, I can't... I can't... be displeased...*
BELVILLE: *Displeased? Why that word? And why that hesitation?*
PAMELA: *Why* ***should*** *I hesitate? What occasion is there for it?* (BNC)

As in the previous examples, these questions may be schematically represented by "Why (obligation) *p*?". However, they imply "there is no obligation for *p*, hence *p* does not hold". In (26), the question refers back to a condition expressed by the addressee. The condition requires that Vera apologise. Vera's question cancels that prerequisite. The *why-should* question amounts to cancelling that obligation and implies "I will not apologise". In first-person *why-should* questions with an agentive verb, deontic modality is prone to appear. It is precisely that sense of obligation that is called into question. The question is used rhetorically and implies that there is no logical reason for Vera to apologise. In (27), deontic modality is also called into question. However, no obligation such as "you should hesitate" can be recovered from the context. On the contrary, Belville assumes that Pamela should not be hesitating. It is the addressee's choice of words, and more specifically his choice of the word *hesitate* that is challenged by the *why-should* question. The speaker argues that this word is wrongly applied to her behaviour. It is not, then, the actual de re event that is called into question by the speaker, but the addressee's de dicto statement. This use of *should* is compared by Arigne (2007) and Larreya & Rivière (2010: 121) with the use of *vouloir* in second person questions in French.[7] *Why should I hesitate*, like *pourquoi voudrais-tu que j'hésite*, is a metalinguistic question. It does not presuppose the obligation for the subject to hesitate. It does, however, presuppose the existence of some necessity wrongly applied by the addressee to characterise the subject's attitude. It is the addressee's speech act itself that is being modalised. This can be paraphrased as follows: "why is it necessary for you to *say* that I am hesitating?".

To sum up, the presupposition of a de re proposition is cancelled by the *should* question in (26), while the presupposition of a de dicto proposition is cancelled in (27). But *should* does not always cancel the presupposition derived from the addressee's prior statement. In second person questions, the actuality of the modalised proposition is not necessarily challenged:

(28) *He made no attempt at any civility, and left Elizabeth to do the talking. She said, 'I cannot imagine why you have returned here, Mr Bodenland. Do you have any more messages to bring me from Victor Frankenstein?' 'Am I so unwelcome, ma'am? I did you a small service once by delivering a letter. Perhaps it is fortunate for my own sake that I have no further letter now.' 'It is unfortunate for you that you brazenly appear at all.' 'Why* ***should*** *you say that? I had not intended to trouble you on this occasion. Indeed, I may say it was not my wish to see you at all.'* (BNC)

(29) *'He tells me he is going straight on to Australia to see Greg,' Hugo said. 'Let's hope the whole thing ends there. Though somehow I doubt it.' 'Why? Why* ***should*** *you doubt it?' Sally demanded. Harriet noticed her hands were shaking. 'Because the son of a bitch won't let up while he thinks there is the slightest chance of getting back his quarter of a million,' Hugo said.* (BNC)

7 Milner and Milner (1975) analyse the syntax and function of quotative second person *pourquoi*-questions with *vouloir*. They show that in such questions, *vouloir* does not convey the subject's volition. It is to be understood metalinguistically. They also stress that the proposition anaphorically referred to is taken up as a *dictum*.

(30) *'You've heard the news, of course.' 'Yes.' Even without the simple affirmation his face would have given her the answer; he looked pale and drawn, as if he had slept even less than she had. 'I tried to call you but there was no reply from your flat.' 'I was in Paris on a job. I saw a newspaper there. I rushed back to London, packed a few fresh things and came straight here.' 'Harriet... I'm so sorry.' 'Why* ***should*** *you be sorry?' 'It must have been a terrible shock for you...' 'And for you!' she said hotly. 'After all this time – it's almost unbelievable. Do you suppose there's any truth in it?' He spread his hands helplessly. 'I wish I knew. But I can't see why anyone should invent a story like that.'* (BNC)

Strikingly, the existence of *p* is not affected by the question on modality. *Why should you say that, why should you doubt it* and *why should you be sorry* presuppose *you said that, you doubt it* and *you are sorry* respectively. These questions imply "*p* holds, although there is no obligation for *p*". In these second-person questions, *should* is based on logical necessity and conveys a sense of evaluation. These questions typically appear in dialogue and are anaphoric to a prior statement made by the addressee. They clearly have a quotative function, referring back either to some discourse content or to the addressee's speech act. The speaker challenges either the discourse content or the speech act itself. *Why-should* questions request a justification for the logical necessity of the proposition. They are triggered by a sense of surprise on the part of the speaker, because the addressee's statement violates their expectations. These examples are very close in meaning to the *why-would* questions examined above. However, it should be stressed that this quasi-equivalence in meaning results from different modal judgements. The logical necessity expressed by *should* is evaluated according to the speaker's moral standards, hence the evaluative judgement. With *would*, on the other hand, the inherent conformity between subject and predicate is checked against evidence in an unexpected situation, hence the abductive inferential judgement. In an evidence-based *why-would* question, the speaker attempts to account for a surprising state of affairs that they fail to understand by seeking its cause. In dialogue, such abductive questions are not quotative (see (17)). The quotative function, however, is typically served by *should*-questions. Such questions do not ask about the cause of a proposition. They cancel the addressee's commitment to the truth of a prior proposition and invite them to justify themselves. This is particularly clear in (30), where the validity of the proposition *I am sorry* is disclaimed by the modalised question, which forces the addressee to justify his statement. Note that a *because*-answer introduces the justification requested in (29) as in the following example. As the proposition to be justified refers to a past event in (31), the perfect aspect is required:

(31) *'I'm pleased with it,' Maria responded warily, reminding herself that she worked for the man. 'And you feel the people here are pleased with you?' Luke probed. 'I believe they are.' She was cautiously confident. 'Although it's not so much I who has to please them as my ideas, since a lack of support would hamper or even prevent their implementation – but those I've already mooted have met with even less resistance than I anticipated.' 'Why* ***should*** *you have anticipated any, if they're good ideas?' Briefly, his interest was in her as a person with opinions and particular professional attitudes of her own, rather than as a female body he wanted to possess, and Maria responded with relief. 'Because any changes, however positive, require adjustment, and most people feel more comfortable with the familiar.'* (BNC)

Should having no past time reference, past time reference can only be marked by the perfect aspect. As we have seen in (16), past time reference is not as clear-cut with *would*, which may, or may not, combine with the perfect aspect to refer to the past. However, past time reference need not be marked with *should*:

(32) *'She looked an interesting girl. I had a sort of fellow feeling for her.' 'Really?' Hargazy looked at her sharply. 'Why* ***should*** *you have a fellow-feeling for her?'* (BNC)

The statement quoted is in the preterite. Without the perfect aspect, the quotative question does not refer to that past situation. This signals that *should*-questions may abstract away from a spatio-temporal situation. What is being referred to here is the fact of having a fellow-feeling rather than the corresponding actual event anchored to a past situation. The metalinguistic use illustrated in (27) points in the same direction.

A further argument to support this claim is provided by rhetorical *should*-questions. In the following example, *should* is followed by the verb base *suffer*, not by the perfect infinitive *have suffered*. It indicates that the *should*-question does not refer to the past situation defined by *yesterday*, but rather to some idea or conception that runs counter to the speaker's norm. This rhetorical question can be construed as a present comment on some misconception, rather than as a judgement on a past event:

(33) *HOSPITAL patients were given a COLD lunch yesterday – because the cooks were too busy preparing a HOT one for a royal visit. The Duchess of Kent and 60 guests sat down to a delicious fish meal while patients had to make do*

with quiche or ham salad. Last night NUPE official Alex Rennie slammed the bosses of Milton Keynes Hospital, Bucks. 'I think it is outrageous,' he stormed. 'If anyone had to have the cold meal, it should have been the bigwigs. Why ***should*** *the patients suffer because one of the royal family is invited to a junket? The hospital is for patients, not just for a load of hangers-on.' The Duchess visited the 358-bed hospital, which got NHS Trust status in April, to open an 18 million extension.* (BNC)

This question does not request a causal answer. Interestingly, the cause for the patients' suffering is supplied in the question in the form of a *because*-clause. The rhetorical question implies that this cause is no good reason. The logical necessity that seems to have prevailed is in contradiction with the speaker's ethics and is presented as outrageous. In other words, there is no justification at all for the causal relationship expressed in the rhetorical question. This purely evaluative function is exploited in the following example drawn from a speech:

(34) *That's quite ridiculous. He says seventy to seventy five percent are being directed towards the private sector (pause) so why. I thought our social services people did that (pause) if they run that why* ***should*** *they direct people away from their own livelihoods. That's quite ludicrous, why* ***should*** *they shoot themselves in the foot (pause) and is Mr (-----) seriously suggesting the same thing? I mean apart from a monstrous attack on our own officers who can't answer for themselves in this place. Why* ***should*** *they be prejudicing the the jobs of the their colleagues, I, it doesn't make any sense whatsoever.* (BNC)

In (34), *why-should* rhetorical questions repeatedly suggest that there is no logical explanation to be found. These questions collocate with assertive statements that also evaluate an idea as absurd. No accurate temporal reference, whether past, present or future, can be assigned to the modalised propositions because what matters is some idea rather than some precise event. The figurative expression *shoot oneself in the foot* also indicates that it is an attitude that is being criticised, not a specific event, even if some event may be the source of this generalisation.

Why-should questions and *why-would* questions both have an evaluative dimension. However, only *why-would* questions may go from an observation to its cause in abductive reasoning. By contrast, *should*-questions may abstract away from a specific event and evaluate an idea.

4 *Would* and *should* in content clauses

Would and *should* may both be used in content clauses introduced by evaluative impersonal superordinate expressions such as *it is strange that, it is surprising that, it is odd that, it is natural that, it is inevitable that*, or *I find it strange that*. Such content clauses are extraposed subject clauses or complement clauses respectively.

It should be stressed that the use of these modals is not compulsory in this syntactic position.[8] The distribution of the modals in the fiction subcorpora of the British National Corpus (BNC) and the Corpus of American Contemporary English (COCA) is represented in Table 1.

These figures confirm Johannsson's observation that *would* is more frequently used in American English than in British English. After *it's surprising*, it

Table 1: Distribution of the modals in content clauses

BNC CORPUS	*Surprising*	*Odd*	*Strange*	*Natural*	*Inevitable*
Would	0	1; 2%	2; 3%	2; 7%	7; 29%
Should	6; 17%	13; 22%	21; 36%	21; 75%	13; 54%
Bare infinitive	0	0	0	0	0
Other*	29; 83%	44; 76%	36; 61%	5; 18%	4; 17%

COCA CORPUS	*Surprising*	*Odd*	*Strange*	*Natural*	*Inevitable*
Would	6; 7%	16; 9%	20; 9%	16; 18%	36; 53%
Should	8; 9%	8; 4%	28; 12%	23; 26%	10; 15%
Bare infinitive	0	0	0	4; 5%	1; 1%
Other	72; 84%	156; 87%	179; 79%	45; 51%	21; 31%

Note: *This category includes factual uses (present tense, preterite, past perfect) as well as non factual uses (*can, could, may, might, will*) which are not dealt with in this study.

8 For lack of space, we leave aside the use of *should* after directive superordinate expressions.

may be hypothesised that the uses conveyed by *should* in British English are split between *should* and *would* in American English. The figures also show that the bare infinitive is used in American English after *it's natural* and marginally after *it's inevitable*, a fact that is not attested at all in British English.

Overall, there is a tendency to use the modal forms, and specifically *should*, much more frequently in British English than in American English. By contrast, the use of full verbs in the preterite, the past perfect and the present tense is statistically significantly higher in American English. In both varieties, the use of *should* and *would* is strikingly higher after *it's natural* and *it's inevitable*, a tendency that is even more pronounced in British English. *Would* and *should* are the majority only after these expressions in British English, and only after *it's inevitable* in American English. Interestingly, these figures suggest a similar correlation in American English and in British English between the semantic contribution of the superordinate expression and the use of modality in the content clause. If the superordinate expression evaluates the propositional content of the subordinate clause as contrary to expectations, the verb form in the subordinate clause appears less likely to be a modal. In contrast, if the superordinate expression evaluates the propositional content as being in accordance with the speaker's expectations, the subordinate clause is more likely to contain *should* or *would*. However, we will see that this counterintuitive observation will need to be qualified when the context is examined in more detail.

For lack of space, the full description of the corpus data cannot be carried out in the present article. We limit ourselves to stressing some salient facts.

This construction combines two levels of modality, whose linear order does not reflect chronological order. Firstly, the content clause – which appears in extraposed position – contains discourse-old information. The modal that appears in this subordinate clause combines epistemic modality and evaluative modality exactly in the same way as in the *why-would* and *why-should* clauses examined in section 3. Secondly, the superordinate expression appears in focus and conveys an evaluative judgement about the content clause. Even at the superordinate level, evaluative and epistemic modality can hardly be disentangled. On the one hand, the adjectives *surprising, strange, odd, natural* and *inevitable* evaluate the content clause. On the other, this evaluation has to do with the expected or unexpected character of the propositional content, which allows for assessing its likelihood in retrospect. This use of past tense modals in content clauses is discourse-oriented. As Bybee (1998: 268) writes:

> [I]t is not perceived reality or unreality that is at issue, but rather how the speaker is positioning the proposition in the discourse.

4.1 Discordance between the superordinate expression and the content clause

We first examine the relationship between the superordinate clause and the content clause when they stand in contradiction to each other.

4.1.1 *Surprising that*

The use of *should* in content clauses introduced by the adjective *surprising* amounts to 17% in the BNC subcorpus. In the COCA subcorpus, modalised content clauses with either *should* or *would* amount to 16%.

However, this raw figure should be qualified in view of the fact that in the BNC as well as in the COCA corpus, this adjective is systematically negated or questioned. In the BNC, 67% of the *surprising* type superordinate expressions contain the negated adjective *not surprising*, which we analyse as an instance of concordance between the two clauses. In the other examples, the discordant character of the content clause is questioned (*is it surprising that…*). Likewise, *would* and *should* are found after the negative adjectival phrase *not surprising* in the COCA corpus.

If the propositional content is said to have been felt surprising in a past situation, past tenses of full verbs are used in both varieties of English:

(35) *It was surprising that she* ***did*** *not feel embarrassed at being caught in floods of tears.* (BNC)
(36) *All the same, it was surprising that Nick* ***dealt*** *with him, Kelly thought to herself as she drove her car.* (BNC)
(37) *He'd told me that Danforth did not give interviews, so it was quite surprising that* ***I'd been singled out*** *for this audience.* (COCA)

The preterite is systematically found in the superordinate clause, indicating that the evaluative judgement was formed in the past. The content clauses in the preterite or past perfect are purely factual. Although each content clause is embedded in a superordinate clause, the evaluative phrase exerts no modal influence on the subordinate clause. The two clauses can be coordinated without any significant change in meaning, but for the information structure:

(35') *She did not feel embarrassed at being caught in flood of tears, and it was surprising.*
(36') *Nick dealt with him, and it was surprising.*

(37') *I'd been singled out for this audience, and it was quite surprising.*

This suggests that each proposition is an assertion the speaker commits himself to at the time of utterance.

4.1.2 *Strange that*

Non-modalised content clauses are the majority after a superordinate expression containing the adjective *strange*. They are comparable to the ones examined in 4.1.1:

(38) *I greet the mothers, but they look past us. It's strange that they* ***don't think*** *us strange.* (COCA)
(39) *It seemed strange that John* ***didn't want*** *to transform George, y'know.* (COCA)

The two clauses may be viewed as two separate assertions:

(38') *They don't think us strange. That's strange.*
(39') *John didn't want to transform George. It seemed strange, y'know.*

However, the use of modalised forms is higher than it is with the adjective *surprising*. In the BNC, *should* is found in 36% of the content clauses. In the COCA subcorpus, 9% of the content clauses contain *would* and 12% *should.*

In the BNC, 40% of these superordinate clauses are verbless, possibly exclamative. In the COCA, this figure drops to 21%. Another 17.5% of these superordinate clauses are modalised with the copular verb *seem* in the BNC, against 25% in the COCA corpus. All in all, 57.5% of the superordinate clauses are not assertions in the BNC, against 46% in the COCA corpus. In the COCA corpus, *would* and *should* are evenly distributed after the modalised superordinate clause. After a verbless superordinate expression, however, *should* is systematically preferred to *would* – the corpus yields only one instance of *would* after *strange that.* Let us start with *would.* The salient feature of *would* is that epistemic modality in the content clause is assigned in retrospect to the content clause in relation to the evaluative judgement expressed in the superordinate expression:

(40) *It might seem strange that a person so young* ***would*** *deny herself those things that most of the rest of the world took for granted: a husband, a child, a family of her own. But Old World customs were strange, and stranger still were the traditions that had been formed in the small villages that nestled in the rolling hills of Avellino.* (COCA)

(41) *Neither of them had much information that I could use. My interview with the Media Lab Director also didn't help. He knew about Gerber's research, of course, and was extremely cooperative, but he had nothing to add to what he had already told the Cambridge police. He found it strange that Gerber* ***would*** *commit suicide, but he did hazard a guess as to what might have caused it. 'Perhaps he was worried about what might happen to his research,' he said.* (COCA)

It is still possible to derive the following paraphrases, which reveal the modal meaning of *would*:

(40') *Predictably, she denied herself those things that most of the rest of the world took for granted: a husband, a child, a family of her own. It might seem strange.*
(41') *Predictably, Gerber committed suicide. He found that strange.*

These content clauses are very close in meaning to the *why-would* questions analysed in the previous section:

(40'') *Why would she deny herself those things?*
(41'') *Why would he commit suicide?*

In these examples, *would* refers to the past and its epistemic meaning is not affected by the superordinate predicate. The construction highlights discordance between an unlikely state of affairs and reality by stressing that the predictability of the modalised proposition runs counter to expectations. As pointed out by Larreya (2015), epistemic modality appears as part of an a posteriori modalisation in a judgement that goes "from effect to cause". Epistemic modality is reconstructed in an evaluative judgement that aims to account for a discordant state of affairs. We further suggest that epistemic modality is fictitiously and provisionally assigned to the content clause for the sake of evaluation. Indeed, in (41), the cause of Gerber's death is unclear, and suicide is far from predictable prima facie.

The relation between the superordinate expression and the content clause is different in the case of *should*:

(42) *He is just sitting there, in deep meditation, staring into the glowing yellow and red coals, examining each burning log looking for an answer, or looking for some personal satisfaction. It seems strange that he* ***should*** *find this answer, or satisfaction, written in a fire. As he keeps staring into the fire, the crackling becomes louder and the burning more intense.* (COCA)

(43) *'Can I get you some coffee?' inquired the visitor.*
'Strange that you ***should*** *ask,' said Perera. 'Got my thermos here.'* (COCA)

(44) *How strange that such an excellent king* ***should*** *not take the chance I was offering him!* (BNC)

Modality in the content clause cannot be understood separately from modality in the superordinate clause. The following paraphrases would not be correct:

(42') *# He should find this answer, or satisfaction, written in a fire. It seems strange.*

(43') *# You should ask. Strange.*

(44') *# The king should not take the chance I was offering him. How strange!*

In these examples, the superordinate expression indicates that the state of affairs expressed in the content clause violates the speaker's expectations. In addition, as pointed out by Behre (1950) and Arigne (2007), the subordinate clause is presented as an instance of "fatal necessity": "the thing or event referred to by the proposition was originally felt as being imposed or imposing itself upon the subject" (Arigne 2007). Arigne argues that this inverted relation produces a sense of conflict that is reflected in the superordinate clause.

A parallel may here again be drawn with the corresponding *why*-questions:

(42'') *Why should he find this answer, or satisfaction, written in a fire?*

(43'') *Why should you ask?*

(44'') *Why should the king not take the chance I was offering him?*

Both constructions are motivated by a sense of puzzlement and an attempt to account for some discordant state of affairs. However, content clauses contain discourse-old information, unlike questions. The specific contribution of superordinate expressions is that they verbalise the speaker's evaluative judgement and put it in focus, content clauses being presupposed. This is particularly clear in exclamative constructions, which imply that the degree of strangeness applied to the presupposed proposition exceeds the speaker's expectations. Exclamative as well as verbless superordinate clauses are not assertions. They express a purely evaluative judgement about a propositional content abstracted away from a referential situation. In (42), what matters is not whether the subject actually found an answer or some personal satisfaction written in a fire. It is the fact that the subject may find an answer or some personal satisfaction that is being evaluated. As stressed by Arigne (2007), a fact should not be confused with an event, as it is the representation of an event.

4.2 Concordance between the superordinate expression and the content clause

4.2.1 *Not surprising that*

At first sight, it might seem a bit of a paradox that modal verbs are used so frequently with superordinate clauses containing the adjectives *natural* and *inevitable*, which do not convey a sense of discordance per se. And yet, these adjectives indicate that the state of affairs expressed in the content clause is being reconsidered and positively evaluated after being first negatively evaluated. These stages in the reasoning process are explicit with *not surprising*. In addition, the adjective *surprising* is modified by degree words (*so*, comparative *less*):

(45) *There are some very pertinent reasons why this memory has remained with me, as I wish to explain. Moreover, now that I come to think of it, it is perhaps not so surprising that it **should** also have made a deep impression on Miss Kenton given certain aspects of her relationship with my father during her early days at Darlington Hall.* (BNC)

(46) *Once over the first fright of finding out that this was an unconventional arrangement, Alexandra found it less surprising that her mother **should** have married her father, than vice versa.* (BNC)

The state of affairs expressed in the content clause is not self-evident. It only comes to be partly accepted after being initially rejected. The underlined segments signal a change in the speaker's emotional state or in her cognitive ability to account for some state of affairs.

4.2.2 *Natural that*

Likewise, *natural* is typically found in collocation with *only* and *perfectly*, i.e. adverbs which indicate that a conclusion is reached after considering the opposite proposition:

(47) *I thought I saw a face in one of the windows – a queer, white face ... It scared me – I don't know why. But it's only natural that one **should** see things after eating mousetrap cheese!* (BNC)

(48) *The rules of the local game didn't apply to us. I didn't appreciate this freedom until I lost it. I took it for granted that I could associate with people from all walks of life, from every background. It seemed perfectly natural that I **should***

spend one evening being waited on by uniformed retainers at the home of an important industrialist whose son I taught, and the next in a seedy bar drinking beer with a group of workers from the factory where I gave private courses in technical English. (COCA)

In (47), the proposition *see a face in one of the windows* is first presented as scary. It is only once the connection with a potential cause, *eating mousetrap cheese*, has been established that this idea can be deemed natural. What was assumed to be discordant is deemed minimally natural on second thought. Minimal concordance is attained as a result of reasoning.

A similar reasoning process is at stake in (48), but it is reversed. The proposition *spend one evening being waited on by uniformed retainers...* is first assumed to be perfectly natural, "taken for granted". Once some change has occurred – i.e. the loss of freedom – the speaker is led to reevaluate that proposition, which can no longer be deemed natural. "Perfectly natural" is then evaluated as applying to the past, not to the present. What seemed to be perfectly in accordance with the speaker's norm is eventually considered discordant.

The use of *should* in such contexts gives credence to Behre's claim (1950) that *should* expresses "mental resistance". Even when the orientation of the superordinate clause seems to be in accordance with that of the content clause, *should* conveys "mental resistance" and indicates that the modalised proposition cannot be straightforwardly asserted.

As opposed to the utterances examined in 4.1, these utterances cannot be paraphrased using a *why*-question. A *why*-question would imply a feeling of surprise on the part of the speaker that is not present when the superordinate clause expresses a seemingly positive evaluation. This suggests that epistemic modality is not only triggered by a sense of surprise. It can also be motivated by the persistence of some mental resistance, which prevents the subordinate clause from being asserted.

4.2.3 *Inevitable that*

When the superordinate clause is in the present (*it is / seems inevitable that*), the verb forms that appear in the content clause are in the present:

(49) *It becomes inevitable that my mother **packs** food in more than one lunch box for me.* (COCA)

(50) *Whenever a man swears not to love, it becomes almost inevitable that he **will**.* (COCA)

In contrast, *would* and *should* are systematically found after superordinate clauses in the preterite. The preterite indicates that the evaluative judgement is formed in retrospect. On the one hand, the propositional content is said to be predictable, but only in hindsight. In other words, the propositional content is not assumed to have been taken for granted. On the other hand, it is evaluated negatively.

It is with this superordinate expression in the past that the modals *should* and *would* are most frequently found both in American English and in British English. This superordinate expression also exhibits the contrast between the two varieties of English: *would* accounts for 29% of the modalised content clauses in British English, and for 53% in American English. *Should* accounts for 54% of the modalised content clauses in British English, and for 15% in American English.

The retrospective comment conveyed by the preterite in the superordinate clause explains the systematic use of modality in the content clause. *Would* tends to be used when the retrospective evaluative judgement is emphasised:

(51) *Looking back, it seemed inevitable that Evelyn* ***would*** *go down with some sort of psychological trouble.* (BNC)

(52) *I guess it was inevitable that Clavius* ***would*** *charm her. He had won me over the same way.* (COCA)

It is the predictable character of the propositional content that is stressed. By contrast, *should* is preferred when the proposition is contrary to what might have been predicted:

(53) *It might have been predictable, and yet few saw the answer coming. In a later day of harder times, of short resources and mandatory recycling, it was inevitable that those landfills* ***should*** *draw the eyes of innovators, looking for ways to get rich.* (COCA)

(54) *But then she had never met a man like Damian Flint before; a man who was as masculine as she was feminine. Perhaps it was inevitable that an attraction* ***should*** *have blazed between them from the first.* (BNC)

The context here implies that the propositional content cannot be taken for granted. In hindsight it can be assessed as predictable. But this retrospective evaluation stands in contrast to a prior assessment.

However, when it is not possible to recover such a clear contrast from the context, the default form is *would* in American English, *should* in British English:

(55) *In the air, they introduced an element of beauty and grace. It was inevitable that new religions* ***should*** *develop round them.* (BNC)

(56) *It was inevitable that there* ***would*** *be serious problems.* (COCA)

This suggests that the evaluative judgement is formed along different lines of epistemic reasoning in American English and in British English. The more the content clause is claimed to be in accordance with the speaker's expectations, the more problematic its assertion. In British English, *should* signals the speaker's "meditative" attitude adopted in reaction to a proposition that may give rise to controversy. Although the content clause is seemingly in accordance with the evaluative judgement expressed in the superordinate clause, it is not vouched for by the speaker. The speaker only asserts the evaluative judgement expressed at the superordinate level. In this complex argumentative process, the speaker "may be anticipating some sort of reluctance in the mind of the hearer to accept a proposition" (Behre 1955: 149). The use of *should* is thus motivated by pragmatic considerations. In American English, *would* stresses the predictability of the content proposition and the content proposition has the same orientation as the superordinate expression, the predictability of the latter being evaluated as inevitable in the former. *Would* is used as a result of backshift. The evaluative judgement expressed in the superordinate clause prevails and is not assumed to enter into conflict with potentially different points of view.

5 Conclusion

We hope to have shown that *would* and *should* used in *why*-questions and in content clauses combine different layers of modality. In *why*-questions, epistemic modality is part of an evaluative judgement that requests either the cause of a surprising state of affairs (with *would*) or the justification of an event or a speech act (with *should*). In content clauses, epistemic evaluation comes under the scope of an evaluative superordinate expression. The use of *would* and *should* is far from obligatory. It depends on the nature of the evaluative judgment expressed at the superordinate level and on its temporal location. If a content clause is evaluated as concordant with the speaker's expectations, the fact that it is said to be normal, natural or not surprising is indicative that the speaker cannot commit himself or herself to the truth of that proposition, hence the use of *would* or *should* in the subordinate clause. In that position, *should* marks what Arigne (2007) calls "fatal necessity" and is not in line with the evaluative judgement expressed at the superordinate level. *Would* marks predictability and has the same orientation as the superordinate proposition.

We have also shed light on two pragmatic uses of *should* and *would*. These uses serve a similar illocutionary function by anticipating and defusing potential disagreement between speaker and hearer. Assertion is prevented by the modal remoteness marked by the past tense morpheme. However, the two modals are not found under the same conditions. Pragmatic *should* is encountered in content clauses that convey hearer-old information. This use is 'meditative-polemic' and not generated by a sense of surprise. Pragmatic *would*, on the other hand, is found when hearer-new information is supplied by the speaker. For example, *would* is found in equative utterances that identify a variable on the basis of objective evidence. The modal does not assess the likelihood of a proposition, but signals that the speaker anticipates the hearer's surprise. This epistemic use, called "brave new *would*" by Ward (2011), is supposedly recent. Although more investigations would be needed to substantiate this claim, we argue that this use is more frequently found in American English.

Finally, only *would* can mark abductive inference in questions about the cause of some surprising state of affairs. We contend that this type of modal inference is made possible by the ability of *would* to refer to the past. *Should* having no past time reference, its epistemic uses are much more limited.

Corpus data

British National Corpus
http://corpus.byu.edu/bnc/
Corpus of Contemporary American English
http://corpus.byu.edu/coca/
Corpus of American Soap Operas
http://corpus.byu.edu/soap/

References

Arigne, Viviane. 2007. "Grammaticalization, Polysemy and Iterated Modality: The Case of *Should*." *Corela* [online], 5–1. http://corela.revues.org/343 (accessed 29 October 2015).

Behre, Frank. 1950. "The Origin and Early History of Meditative-Polemic *should* in *that*-clauses." *Symbolae Philologicae Gotoburgenses, Göteborg Högsolas Arsskrift* 56. 275–309.

Behre, Frank. 1955. *Meditative-Polemic* should *in Modern English* that*-clauses* (Studies in English 4). Stockholm: Gothenburg.

Birner, Betty, Jeffrey Kaplan & Gregory Ward. 2007. "Functional Compositionality and the Interaction of Discourse Constraints." *Language* 83/2. 317–343.

Bybee, Joan. 1995. "The Semantic Development of Past Tense Modals in English." In J. Bybee & S. Fleischman (eds.), *Modality in Grammar and Discourse*, 503–517. Amsterdam: John Benjamins.

Bybee, Joan. 1998. "'Irrealis' as a Grammatical Category." *Anthropological Linguistics* 40. 257–271.

Celle, Agnès. 2012. "Epistemic *would* – A Marker of Modal Remoteness." *Faits de Langue* n°40, *Ultériorité dans le passé, valeurs modales, conditionnel*. 149–156.
Celle, Agnès (forthcoming) "Questions as Indirect Speech Acts in Surprise Contexts." In D. Ayoun, A. Celle & L. Lansari (eds.), Tense, aspect, modality, evidentiality: crosslinguistic perspectives. Amsterdam, Philadelphia: John Benjamins.
Celle, Agnès & Laure Lansari. 2014. "Uncertainty as a Result of Unexpectedness." *Language and Dialogue* 4/1: 7–23.
Celle, Agnès & Laure Lansari. 2015. "On the Mirative Meaning of *aller* + Infinitive Compared with Its Equivalents in English." *Cahiers Chronos* n°27, *Taming the TAME systems*. 289–305.
Celle, Agnès, Anne Jugnet, Laure Lansari & Emilie L'Hôte. 2017. "Expressing and Describing Surprise." In Agnès Celle & Laure Lansari (eds.), *Expressing and Describing Surprise*, 215–244. Amsterdam: John Benjamins Current Topics.
Coates, Jennifer. 1983. *The Semantics of the Modal Auxiliaries*. London: Croom Helm.
Desclés, Jean-Pierre & Zlatka Guentchéva (forthcoming) "Inference Processes Expressed by Languages: Deduction of a Probable Consequent vs. Abduction." In Viviane Arigne and Christiane Migette, *Theorization and Representations in Linguistics*. Cambridge: Cambridge Scholars Publishing.
Dixon, John & Don Foster. 1997. "Gender and Hedging: From Sex Differences to Situated Practice." *Journal of Psycholinguistic Research* 26(1). 89–107.
Furmaniak, Grégory. 2014. "Entre logique et réalité: le cas des interrogatives en *Why would*... ?. " In Catherine Moreau, Jean Albrespit and Frédéric Lambert (eds.), *Du réel à l'irréel. Travaux Linguistiques du CerLiCO*, Vol. 25 – 1. 341–360. Presses Universitaires de Rennes.
Furmaniak, Grégory & Paul Larreya. 2015. "On the Uses of *Would* in Epistemic Contexts." In Juan Rafael Zamorano-Mansilla, Carmen Maíz, Elena Domínguez & Mª Victoria Martín, de la Rosa (eds.) *Thinking Modally : English and Contrastive Studies on Modality*, 105–124. Newcastle upon Tyne: Cambridge Scholars Publishing.
Huddleston, Rodney & Geoffrey Pullum. 2002. *The Cambridge Grammar of the English Language*. Cambridge: Cambridge University Press.
Jacobsson, Bengt. 1988. "*Should* and *Would* in Factual That-Clauses." *English Studies* 69/1. 72–84.
Joos, Martin. 1964. *The English Verb, Form and Meanings*. Madison and Milwaukee: The University of Wisconsin Press.
Larreya, Paul & Claude Rivière. 2010. *Grammaire explicative de l'anglais*. Paris: Longman Pearson.
Larreya, Paul. 2015. "Modalisations *a priori* et *a posteriori:* le cas de *would*." *Anglophonia* 19. http://anglophonia.revues.org/457; DOI: 10.4000/anglophonia.457 (accessed 05 November 2015).
Leech, Geoffrey. 1971. *Meaning and the English Verb*. London: Longman.
Miceli, Maria & Cristiano Castelfranchi. 2015. *Expectancy and Emotion*. Oxford: Oxford University Press.
Milner, Jean-Claude & Judith Milner. 1975. "Interrogations, reprises et dialogue. " In Julia Kristeva, Jean-Claude Milner & Nicolas Ruwet (eds.), *Langue, discours, société: Pour Emile Benveniste*, 122–148. Paris: Editions du Seuil.
Palmer, Frank. 1979. *Modality and the English Modals*. London: Longman.
Peirce, Charles S. 1966. *The collected papers of Charles Sanders Peirce* [1839–1914] (8 vols). Cambridge, MA: Harvard University Press.
Rivière, Claude. 1981. "Is *Should* a Weaker *Must*?." *Journal of Linguistics* 17. 179–195.

Rohde, Hannah. 2006. "Rhetorical Questions as Redundant Interrogatives." *San Diego Linguistic Papers*, Issue 2. http://escholarship.org/uc/item/4xd7t5ww (accessed 25 November 2013).

Ward, Gregory, Jeffrey Kaplan & Betty Birner. 2003. "A Pragmatic Analysis of the Epistemic Would Construction." In Roberta Facchinetti, Manfred Krug & Frank Palmer (eds.), *Modality in Contemporary English*, 71–79. Berlin, New York: Mouton de Gruyter.

Ward, Gregory, Jeffrey Kaplan & Betty Birner. 2007. "Epistemic *Would*, Open Propositions, and Truncated Clefts." In Nancy Hedberg and Ron Zacharski (eds.), *Topics on the grammar-pragmatics interface: Papers in honor of Jeanette K. Gundel*, 77–90. Amsterdam & Philadelphia: John Benjamins.

Ward, Gregory. 2011. Brave new *would*: Demonstrative Equatives and Information Structure. In Christina Galeano, Emrah Görgülü and Irina Presnayakova (eds.), *Proceedings of the Fortieth Western Conference on Linguistics, volume 21, WECOL 2011*, 139–160. Fresno: Department of Linguistics, California State University.

Lionel Dufaye

SHOULD in Conditional Clauses: When Epistemicity Meets Appreciative Modality

Abstract: Depending on the context, epistemic uses of SHOULD can take on two contradictory values. In main clauses, it expresses high probability (*The plane should be on time*), but in conditional clauses, SHOULD can only express improbability: *If the plane should be delayed, please call.* To account for this semantic shift, it will be hypothesized that SHOULD and IF (or any other conditional markers) refer to two distinct enunciative viewpoints. On the one hand, conditional clauses imply an enunciative disendorsement of the speaker, who does not validate the event denoted by the conditional; on the other hand SHOULD is always the expression of the speaker's judgement. For instance *Your husband should pull through* is fine whereas ? *Your husband should succumb to his injuries* is problematic in the sense that with SHOULD the speaker qualifies the event as normal or expected according to her line of reasoning or her set of values. The two markers thus express conflicted forms of endorsement: the speaker's appreciative modality with SHOULD, the speaker's refusal to validate the event with IF.

Keywords: should, endorsement. endorsement, disenunciation, clause, conditional epistemicity, epistemic, modality, if

1 Introduction

SHOULD can have two opposite epistemic values, depending on whether it occurs in a conditional clause or in a main clause:

(1) *Labour should win the election.*
(2) *If Labour should win the election, what would you do?*

In the first example, SHOULD expresses both likelihood and the positive expectation of a Labour victory; conversely, in the second example SHOULD carries both a sense of unlikelihood and the negative apprehension of a Labour victory. This semantic alternation will be construed as a two-pronged approach: on the one hand, SHOULD will be analyzed as a marker that expresses the speaker's point

Lionel Dufaye, University Paris Est – Marne La Vallée

https://doi.org/10.1515/9783110572261-003

of view by qualifying the event as epistemically (un)expected and/or subjectively (un)desirable. On the other hand, IF-conditional clauses will be analyzed as suspending the speaker's endorsement. The combination of the two results in the primary value of SHOULD being reversed.

2 An overview of the problem

SHOULD can occur in conditional clauses, be they IF-clauses or inverted forms:

(3) *The clayish soil there absorbs too much when water is run down the furrows, he said;* ***if it should rain****, plants could drown.*

(4) *As he worked, Ernie explained that the thick cushion of needles he was piling up would level the slope, make a soft mattress, provide insulation from the chilly ground and,* ***should it rain****, allow water to flow beneath, keeping his bed high and dry.*

The difference between these two types of conditionals will not be discussed in this article; only IF-clauses will serve to illustrate the purpose of the current demonstration.[1] In both examples, the event is presented as unlikely and/or undesirable. One may wonder why SHOULD does not express high probability. Indeed, since epistemic uses of SHOULD express confident assumption (*He should be safe now*), and since it occurs within a clause expressing condition, why is it that these co-occurring operations do not combine to express some "highly probable condition"? It is this specific question that will be addressed in this article.

The central idea is that SHOULD and IF (or any other conditional marker for that matter) imply different sources of endorsement, so that the co-occurrence of the two markers induces polyphonic interference. SHOULD, as it will be described later on, always expresses the speaker's evaluation, whereas conditionals can be characterized as a disendorsement on the part of the speaker, who does not assert the truth of the proposition: IF (or inversion) sets up a scenario which is not validated by the "actual speaker" but by what we shall call a "fictitious speaker".[2]

1 For a discussion on this topic from an enunciative perspective, see: Chuquet 1994, Celle 2004, Bourdier 2009.

2 The concepts of "actual speaker" and "fictitious speaker", as they are used in this article, are not unlike the concepts of "locuteur" and "énonciateur" in Ducrot's theory (see Ducrot 2001 for instance). In other words, the "fictitious speaker" is to be understood, not as a physical entity, but as a discursive point of view, which differs from the actual speaker's stance.

The co-occurrence of these contradictory subjective sources can be represented as follows[3]:

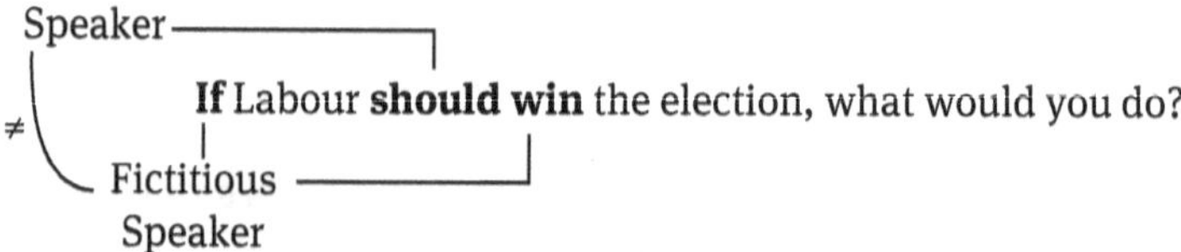

If one accepts the idea that the reversal in the value of SHOULD derives from a divergence in subjective endorsement, the nature of the operations in play still needs to be explained. To do so we will first consider SHOULD itself in order to highlight the fact that, contrary to SHALL, SHOULD is essentially judgmental, in the sense that it qualifies the propositional content as appropriate or normal for the speaker without ever carrying a factive meaning. Conversely, IF will be analyzed as an operator that validates the propositional content relative to a secondary (fictitious) speaker. In other words, it will be argued that SHOULD and IF cohabit within the same propositional content to express semantically contradictory – yet enunciatively complementary – polyphonic modalities: SHOULD is the marker of a "Qualitative" operation expressing the speaker's "judgment"; IF, on the other hand, is the marker of a "Quantitative" operation which validates an "event" (which is not validated by the actual speaker but by a fictitious speaker or "secondary enunciator").

---

3 For the sake of simplicity, we use fabricated examples, but actual occurrences are not hard to come by:

According to the natural political cycle and to the awesome size of the Labour Party victory in 2013, a careful Labour should win the next general election quite handsomely.

(http://www.timesofmalta.com/articles/view/20130512/opinion/Simon-depends-on-Joseph.469384); March 2017.

If Labour should win the next election, the 164 grammar schools will be lucky to survive. But if the Tories were to emerge victorious, and David Cameron were at last to show some guts and conviction, there is a chance that the greatest single engine of social mobility could be restored. (http://www.dailymail.co.uk/debate/article-2869395/STEPHEN-GLOVER-does-fact-half-schools-fail-send-pupils-study-doctors-say-Britain.html); March 2017.

3 *SHOULD* as an expression of conformity

The qualitative (i.e. non-occurrential[4]) core value of SHOULD can be characterized as an expression of conformity, whereby the speaker states that validation fits with the way they expect things to happen, which could be paraphrased by expressions such as "barring accidents" or "in the normal course of events" (Salkie 2009: 95).

(5) *The Tories **should win** the next election if everything continues along its current path.*

(6) *Flynn says barring another hurricane or other catastrophe, oil and gas prices **shouldn't spike** again like they did last week.*

Conformity may actually take on two different, yet compatible, qualitative values: it can express "subjective valuation" (the speaker's emotive stance) and/or "objective evaluation" (congruence with material facts). With SHOULD, it is not unusual for these two values to dovetail (as is the case in the previous examples for instance).

When SHOULD expresses objective evaluation, there is no emotive value at stake (i.e. good/bad; right/wrong; desirable/undesirable...). The speaker simply assesses the likelihood of the event according to their inductive knowledge base.

(7) *Today will be sunny in southwestern* Connecticut, *the National Weather Service says, but **rain should start falling overnight**.*

(8) *The return fare for a family of four, occupying a sleeper section on the Ocean is $694 plus taxes. Dinner for each person on board the train **should** cost between $7.50 and $11.95, with two choices.*

In this case, the information *Dinner for each person on board the train **should** cost between $7.50 and $11.95* is supposed to be in accordance with the speaker's mode of reference, provided that the actual situation is still in keeping with their knowledge base. The example could easily be completed as follows:

(9) *Dinner for each person on board the train **should** cost between $7.50 and $11.95* [... that is, if the prices haven't gone up *in the meantime*].

---

4 Contrary to other modals such as CAN (*When he was young, he **could** swim across the river*) or WILL (*Every morning, she **would** go for a stroll in the park*), SHOULD can no longer express (occurrential) past values, which is why we hypothesize that, unlike Deschamps & Dufaye's model (2001), SHOULD has no corresponding Quantitative dimension, and is thus represented by a single Qualitative operation.

Accordingly, it will be hypothesized that SHOULD expresses a complex modality which takes into account a dual scenario, and which can be schematized by an asymmetrical bifurcation (based notably on Culioli 1990, Deschamps 1999, Dufaye 2001, Gilbert 1987):

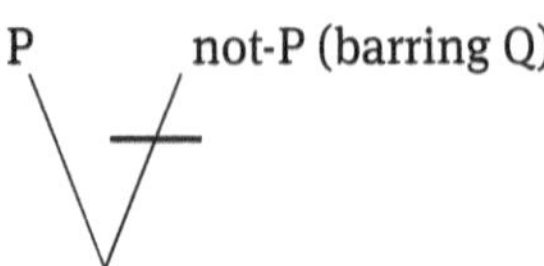

This implies that SHOULD favors one polarity over the other by rejecting one of the two scenarios as improbable and/or undesirable.

4 *SHOULD* as an appreciative modality

As a consequence, it can be argued that SHOULD always expresses some form of subjective (hence "Qualitative") modality, which may be backgrounded – as is the case in the preceding examples – or predominant. Contrary to other modals, it may seem difficult to isolate the two values. SHOULD is ambivalent where MUST, for instance, is at best ambiguous:

(11) *She must be cured*: is either strictly appreciative or strictly epistemic.
(12) *She should be cured*: can be either appreciative, epistemic or both depending on pragmatic interpretation.

As a consequence, only MUST can express non-judgmental epistemic evaluations whereas SHOULD usually carries an appreciative modality. Compare:

(13) *She must be cured by now.*
(14) **She must be cured by now, but she's not.*
(15) *She should be cured by now.*
(16) *She should be cured by now, but she's not.*[5]

5 Again, for the sake of argumentation we use fabricated sentences that may seem artificial, but it is easy enough to collect actual examples such as: *Why Labour should win the next election but won't* (www.wessexscene.co.uk/politics/2015/05/04/why-labour-should-win-the-election-but-wont/).

Interestingly enough, SHOULD is particularly compatible with positive (desirable) scenarios. Conversely, it would seem unlikely for the covert condition to refer to a positive context (which is why the right path is crossed out in the diagram above):

(17) *Dinner for each person on board the train* ***should*** *cost between $7.50 and $11.95 (?that is, unless prices have gone down in the meantime).*

The fact that SHOULD expresses the scenario generally favored by the speaker is further evidenced by searches on Mark Davies's Contemporary Corpus of American English (COCA-BYU[6]) such as *tomorrow should be*, which yields the following contexts: *tomorrow should be: a good day/ great / a very quiet and a very private time / a great day / a pretty easy day.* Along the same line, the following search clearly confirms that SHOULD tends to select mostly positive contexts (where [j*] = "any *Adjective*", [r*] = "any *Adverb*" and the Sheffer stroke | = "*or*" (but not both)):

<table>
<tr><td colspan="4">COCA: should be a [j*] day|week|evening
should be a [r*] [j*] day|week|evening</td></tr>
<tr><td>should be a</td><td>good</td><td>day</td><td>4 occ.</td></tr>
<tr><td>should be a</td><td>paid</td><td>day</td><td>1 occ.</td></tr>
<tr><td>should be a</td><td>great</td><td>day</td><td>1 occ.</td></tr>
<tr><td>should be a</td><td>cold</td><td>day</td><td>1 occ.</td></tr>
<tr><td>should be a</td><td>beautiful</td><td>Day</td><td>1 occ.</td></tr>
<tr><td>should be a pretty</td><td>easy</td><td>Day</td><td>1 occ.</td></tr>
<tr><td>should be a</td><td rowspan="3">big</td><td>day</td><td>1 occ.</td></tr>
<tr><td>should be a very</td><td>day</td><td>1 occ.</td></tr>
<tr><td>should be a</td><td>week</td><td>1 occ.</td></tr>
<tr><td>should be a</td><td rowspan="2">fun</td><td>week</td><td>1 occ.</td></tr>
<tr><td>should be a</td><td>evening</td><td>1 occ.</td></tr>
<tr><td>should be a</td><td>lovely</td><td>evening</td><td>1 occ.</td></tr>
</table>

The presence of an adjective like COLD shows that SHOULD does not filter out all negative contexts (a few other similar cases occurred in further searches: e.g. *should be a long year*); in such cases, the context was clear enough to leave no doubt about the fact that the speaker was expressing an objective epistemic evaluation rather than conveying their own judgment:

(18) ***Most likely****, the Panthers will win the NFC South en route to a date with destiny. The Colts will win Super Bowl XL in what* ***should be a cold day*** *in Detroit.*

6 http://corpus.byu.edu/coca/

Similarly, the following search string returned consistent results:

COCA: prices should		
And in true Silicon Valley fashion, as LED-makers expand their volumes, manufacturing	**prices should**	***drop**, pushing this energy saving technology into wider use, he argued.*
"Unless that recovers, you know, (copper)		***stay pretty much** where they are now," Argus research analyst Bill Selesky said.*
Better lending and cheaper		*eventually **restore balance** to the market, economists say.*
Accumulatively,		***fall** somewhere between 5 and 10 percent nationwide.*
driving season won't be any more painful than last years. The Energy Department says		***be roughly the same**, averaging around $2.81 a gallon, nationwide.*
Flynn says barring another hurricane or other catastrophe, oil and gas		***n't spike** again like they did last week.*

Among the 82 contexts there were two occurrences of *prices should increase*, which may be felt to be negative. However both contexts depicted negative backgrounds (drugs and stolen goods), which modifies the pragmatic conditions and turns the *increase* into a desirable consequence:

(19) *If law enforcement approaches are successful in reducing supply and deterring demand through stiffer penalties and greater risk of arrest, then the outcome should be reduced drug use, with an uncertain effect on drug prices. If law enforcement approaches, as commonly believed, have greater effects on the supply side, then* **prices should increase**. *With successful deterrence and interdiction along with higher prices, outcomes such as the use, abuse, and addiction associated with illegal drugs should be lower.*

(20) *Arrest a thief, and at the margin fewer goods will be stolen; the scarcity of stolen goods will increase, which means that* **prices should increase** *[...].*

In IF subordinates, SHOULD still conveys a judgmental value, however the polarity is consistently reversed: the event no longer refers to a normal or desirable scenario according to the speaker; quite the contrary, it refers to an unexpected or unsatisfactory state of affairs:

(21) *Now* ***if Labour should win*** *the next election (dafter things have happened) they've really got to sort the country out, which they were never capable of doing.* (Our emphasis)

(22) *So in a way this is a – this is a luxury – it's the luxury of having a big enough majority that even if you* ***should lose one or two seats on this issue****, it's not going to make a difference to who controls Congress, you think.*

(23) *Corry watched him in the flickering light, wondering how he had managed to survive such a wound, and what might happen to her* ***if he should succumb to his injuries****.*

Consider the following pairs:

(24) *?Your brother should succumb to his injuries.*

(25) *Your brother should succumb to his injuries without suffering.*

(26) *If your brother should succumb to his injuries,...*

(27) *If your brother should succumb to his injuries without suffering,...*

Clearly, *Your brother should succumb to his injuries* sounds odd due to the fact that it could hardly be interpreted as referring to a positive event under normal circumstances; on the contrary, *If your brother should succumb to his injuries...* is perfectly normal. To account for this polarity reversal, we need a closer understanding of the type of operation at stake with IF conditionals (as mentioned above, the difference between IF and inverted conditionals is not dealt with in this article: see among others Chuquet 1994, Iatridou and Embick 1994, Bourdier 2009).

5 *IF* as a polyphonic marker

Our analysis advocates that IF conditionals ascribe the validation of the propositional content to a secondary speaker, who may or may not be fictitious. Let us start by considering the fact that, in itself, IF is unable to express counterfactual premises; other markers such as the preterit and the past perfect are generally[7] required to prompt an explicit counterfactual interpretation:

7 Counterfactual value can also be derived from an explicit modus tollens (if *p then q*, but *not q*, therefore *not p*) such as:

If she's a size 6, then I'm the Queen of England.

If you're the pope, I'm the Empress of China. (Akatsuka 1986: 335)

In such cases, the counterfactual value of the protasis can only be logically (and pragmatically) inferred from the explicit counterfactual value of the apodosis.

(28) *Jesus died too soon.* ***If*** *he* ***had lived*** *to my age he would have repudiated his doctrine*

(29) ***If*** *I* ***was*** *a giraffe, and someone said I* ***was*** *a snake, I'd think, no, actually I'm a giraffe.*

Conversely, when the verb does not combine with any specific aspectual or temporal marker, IF can refer to non-counterfactual situations:

(30) *If he's working, let him work.*

Or even to factual states of affairs (for a detailed analysis of such cases: Kitis 2004), as it is the case with so-called "given conditionals":

(31) *Well if (as you say) he had lasagna for lunch, he won't want spaghetti for dinner.* (Sweetser 1990: 126)

And "concessive conditionals":

(32) *If I was a bad carpenter, I was a worse sailor.* (Sweetser 1990: 129)

(33) *If you're so smart (as you seem to think), what was the date of Charlemagne's coronation?* (ibid.)

According to these observations, it would seem that the core property of IF clauses consists in setting a secondary speaker[8] to endorse a propositional content that the primary (or actual) speaker does not validate. In other words, IF clauses are a type of assertive modality endorsed by what Chuquet 1984 calls a "fictitious" speaker, created by the real speaker:

> "[...] to state Q, the speaker needs to posit himself or herself, not as an "actual" speaker [...] but as a fictitious one." (Chuquet 1984: 48)[9]

And it is perhaps noteworthy that, be it in French or in English, the conditional mood occurs within the apodosis, never within the protasis; the subordinate clause expressing the condition indeed takes an indicative verb form which sets an anchoring situation:

---

8 As mentioned above, the secondary speaker does not correspond to an actual speaker but to a discursive (or "enunciative") point-of-view.

9 "[...] l'énonciateur a besoin, pour énoncer Q, de se poser non plus tant comme énonciateur "actuel" [...] mais en tant qu'énonciateur FICTIF [...]." (Our translation)

(34) ***If I was** sick, I **would** still go to work.*
(35) ***Si** j' **étais** malade, j' **irais** quand même travailler.*

It can thus be considered that IF introduces statements, which may be modulated by modal, aspectual or temporal markers. What differentiates an IF statement from a standard statement is that it is endorsed, not by the actual speaker, but by a secondary speaker, who may be "fictitious" or real (reported speech). Hence the existence of the concessive values conveyed by *given conditionals* or *modus tollens*; in any case, we are led to posit an alternative speaker whose statement is granted and/or quoted:

(36) *Well if (**as you say**) he had lasagna for lunch, he won't want spaghetti for dinner.*
(37) *If you're so smart (**as you seem to think**), what was the date of Charlemagne's coronation?* (Sweetser 1990: 126)

In short, the potentially hypothetic value of IF clauses is first and foremost derived from a polyphonic discordance whereby the main speaker explicitly defers the validation of the propositional content to a secondary speaker. It is this polyphonic discordance which causes the subjective judgment expressed by SHOULD to be interpreted negatively.

6 *IF* and *SHOULD*: The co-occurrence of two different kinds of endorsement

We can now return to our initial question, which was: since epistemic SHOULD expresses confident probability and since it occurs within a clause expressing condition, why is it that these co-occurring operations do not combine to express a "highly probable condition"? To put it differently, why does the overall meaning not reflect the addition of the expected values of the two markers? Actually, part of the answer lies in the fact that the question is ill-stated. In order to understand the versatility of SHOULD, the markers should not be apprehended in terms of values, but in terms of primitive semantic operations. In other words, SHOULD does not in itself express high probability, or even weak necessity. As suggested above, its fundamental operation consists in projecting the speaker's positive judgment onto a propositional content. To better understand the complexity of the operation, let us consider the case of expletive NE in French:

(38) *Je crains qu'il (**ne**) vienne.*[10]

The predicate *craindre que p* (*to fear that p*) implies a dual scenario. On the one hand, an event is envisaged as likely to take place, on the other hand the speaker expresses his or her concern about that possibility. What is particularly noteworthy is that, in this particular context, the negation marker NE does not reverse the polarity of the predicate (hence an *expletive* use). In a discussion on the topic, Ducard 2013 refers directly to Culioli, who considers that NE is the explicit trace of the speaker's attitude regarding the possible occurrence of the event:

> *Once again, we establish a relation between the event which we fear will take place (i.e. what might be the case) and the event we wish would take place, but which we fear will not (i.e. what might not be the case). NE is the trace of the subjective orientation (the desire) from <he-come> to <he-not come>.*[11] (Culioli 1999: 73)

In our diagram, the subjective negation, which bears on the actualization of the event, can be represented by a crossed out path towards the positive scenario:

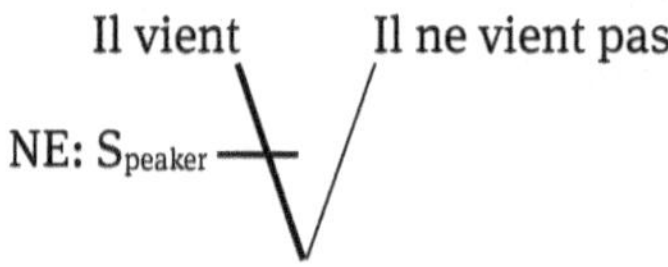

We will hypothesize that SHOULD acts in a similar fashion. For one thing, even though SHOULD (in conditional clauses) cannot exactly be classified as a true "expletive" (its semantic value is far from being as colorless as is NE in French), its presence is never compulsory either. What is more, if we consider the phrase *for fear that X should*, which is almost a word for word translation of *par crainte que X ne*, it is interesting to note that SHOULD and NE have a similar distribution. Consequently, SHOULD may be analyzed as the trace of the speaker's attitude vis-à-vis a dual scenario where an event may (or may not) take place (hence the two-prong diagram). Again the speaker's negative inclination is represented by a dash crossing out the path towards the positive scenario:

10 *I'm afraid that he might come here.*

11 "Ici encore, on construit une relation entre l'événement dont on craint qu'il ait lieu (ce qui risque d'être le cas) et l'événement que l'on souhaiterait voir se produire, mais dont on pense qu'il n'aura pas lieu (ce qui risque de ne pas être le cas). Ne marque l'orientation subjective (le souhait) de <lui-venir> à <lui-ne pas venir>" (Our translation).

(39) [. . .] *we dread to sleep again for fear the whole vision should come back.*

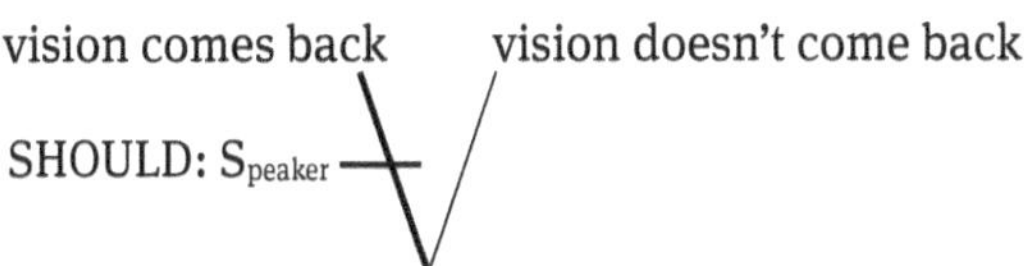

The difference between IF and *for fear that* is that IF does not convey any negative dimension in itself. Yet, it can be assumed that SHOULD acts alike in both contexts, in the sense that it projects the speaker's negative valuation onto the scenario which is depicted by the subordinate clause in both cases. Let's consider the initial examples once more:

(40) *Labour should win the election.*
(41) *If Labour should win the election, what would you do?*

In the first sentence, SHOULD expresses objective and subjective conformity. At the moment of speech, Labour may or may not win the election, but the speaker evaluates the positive scenario as probable (objective epistemicity) and desirable (subjective modality). The imbalance can here again be noted by a dash that crosses out the scenario rejected by the speaker:

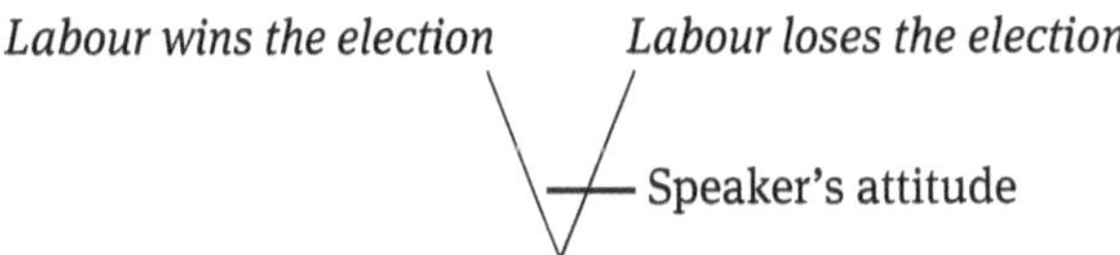

In the second sentence, the situation is different since IF signals that the propositional content <*Labour – win the next election*> is validated by a secondary speaker; it can thus no longer be endorsed by the primary speaker. Because of the polyphonic conflict between the two speakers, the modality expressed by SHOULD favors the opposite scenario, and hence rejects the scenario favored by the secondary speaker:

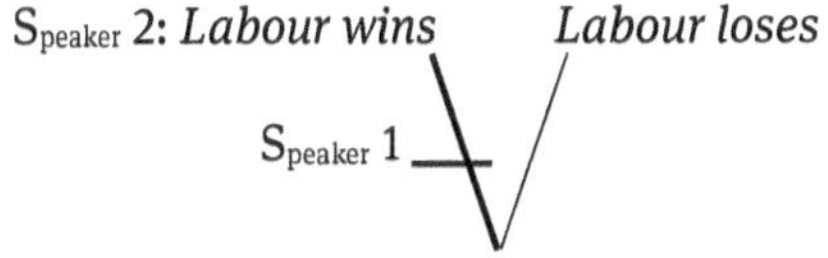

In other words, it is the polarity validated by the IF clause that determines the scenario affected by the negative facet of SHOULD:

- when IF validates *P*, the negative valuation bears on *P*,
- when IF validates not-P, the negative valuation bears on *not-P*:

In all cases, SHOULD works by rejecting the scenario (positive or negative) validated by the IF-clause. Hence the following paraphrases:

(42) *If Labour SHOULD Ø win the election...: If Labour wins the election (which I hope they won't)...*
(43) *If Labour SHOULD not win the election...: If Labour does not win the election (which I hope they will)...*

It is noteworthy that, even when the sentence has a negative polarity, SHOULD itself can never fall under the scope of negation, as is evidenced by the fact that enclitic negation, and even more so double negation, sound ill-formed:

(44) *If Labour should not win the election, what would you do?*
(45) *???If Labour shouldn't win the election, what would you do?*
(46) ** If Labour shouldn't not win the election, what would you do?*

This constraint comes as yet another argument in favor of the two-fold analysis proposed here. As a first step, which could be called "quantitative" in Antoine Culioli's theoretical framework, a secondary speaker validates a propositional content, which refers to either a positive or a negative state-of-affairs. In a second step, which could be called "qualitative", SHOULD somehow superimposes a modal operation upon the preconstructed statement conveyed by the conditional. Thus, negation, when there is one, is part of the initial phase and can only bear on the predicate. In sum, it is the negation that falls under the scope of modality in these contexts, not the other way round.

7 Conclusion

Beyond the specificity of the subject addressed in this article, what this analysis has sought to demonstrate is that the metalinguistic discourse on modal operators – probably on any operators – requires a formal semantics that transcends the values induced by contextual variations. The versatility of SHOULD in conditional clauses can only be accounted for if it is apprehended as an interaction of the semantic components of the markers involved. Moreover, the study also highlighted that the porosity between traditional modal values such as "epistemic" and "appreciative" modalities can be resolved by hypothesizing the existence of two cognitive levels of operations – namely quantitative and qualitative operations – which can interact to create complex modal interpretations.

References

Akatsuka, Noriko. 1986. Conditionals are Discourse-bound. In Elisabeth C. Traugott, Alice ter Meulen, Judith S. Reilly & Charles A. Ferguson (eds.), *On Conditionals*, 333–351. Cambridge: Cambridge University Press.

Bourdier, Valérie. 2009. SHOULD antéposé dans les propositions hypothétiques, *Anglophonia / Sigma 26*, 23–43. Toulouse: Presses Universitaires du Mirail.

Chuquet, Jean. 1984. *If..., Cahiers de recherche T2*, 45–87. Paris: Ophrys.

Chuquet, Jean. 1994. *Forme interrogative et hypothèse en anglais contemporain*. In Paul Boucher & Jean-Marie Fournier, L'interrogation (I), *Travaux linguistiques du CERLICO*, 7, 213–236. Rennes: Presses Universitaires de Rennes II.

Culioli, Antoine. 1985. *Notes du séminaire de D.E.A. 1983–1984*, (notes de séminaire recueillies par J.-C. Souesme). Université Poitiers et Université Paris 7, Département de Recherches Linguistiques: www.dufaye.com/documents/culioli-83-84.pdf

Culioli, Antoine. 1999. Existe-t-il une unité de la négation ? *Pour une linguistique de l'énonciation. Opérations et représentations*, Tome 3 (Collection L'Homme Dans la Langue), 67–98. Paris: Ophrys.

Deschamps, Alain. 1999. Essai de formalisation du système modal de l'anglais. In Jeanine Bouscaren (ed.), *Les opérations de détermination: quantification/qualification* (Collection L'Homme Dans la Langue), 269–285. Paris: Ophrys.

Deschamps, Alain & Lionel Dufaye. 2006. For A Topological Representation of the Modal System, Proceedings of the 2d International Conference. University of Pau. Reprinted in Raphael Salkie, Pierre Busittil & Johan van der Auwera, *Modality in English: Theory and Description*, 123–144. Berlin, New York: Mouton de Gruyter.

Ducard, Dominique. 2013. Que ne se sont-ils compris ! Benveniste, Lacan, Culioli, *Les théories de l'énonciation: Benveniste après un demi-siècle*, 25–40. Paris: Ophrys.

Ducrot, Oswald. 2001. Quelques raisons de distinguer 'locuteurs' et 'énonciateurs', *Polyphonie – linguistique et littéraire*, III. 19–41.

Dufaye, Lionel. 2001. *Les Modaux et la négation en anglais contemporain*. In Jeanine Bouscaren (ed.), n° spécial des *Cahiers de Recherche*. Paris: Ophrys.

Dufaye, Lionel. 2002. La Représentation de l'irréel : de l'intuition aux opérations. In Wilfrid Rotgé (ed.), *Anglophonia n° 12*, 29–61. Toulouse: Presses Universitaires du Mirail.

Gilbert, Eric. 1987. *May, Must, Can* et les opérations énonciatives. In Jeanine Bouscaren (ed.), *Cahiers de recherche*, T. 3. Paris: Ophrys.

Iatridou, Sabine & David Embick. 1994. Conditional Inversion. *Proceedings of North East Linguistic Society 24th*, 189–203. UMass, Amherst: GLSA.

Kitis, Eliza. 2004. Conditional Constructions As Rethorical Structures, *Working Papers in Linguistics*, Department of Theoritical and Applied Linguistics, Aristotle University, 30–51. Thessaloniki: Altintzis.

Rivière, Claude. 1980. Is *should* a weaker *must*? *Journal of Linguistics* 17. 179–191.
Salkie, Raphael. 2009. Degrees of Modality. In Raphael Salkie, Pierre Busuttil and Johan van der Auwera (eds.), *Modality in English: Theory and Description*, 79–104. Berlin, New York: Mouton de Gruyter.
Sweetser, Eve. 1990. *From Etymology to Pragmatics. Metaphorical and Cultural Aspects of Semantic Structure* (Cambridge Studies in Linguistics 54). Cambridge: Cambridge University Press.

Part II: **Romance languages**

Hans Kronning

Epistemic modality and evidentiality in Romance: the Reportive Conditional

Semantics and variation

Abstract: In this article we study the Reportive Conditional (RC) in Romance, in French (1), Italian (2) and Spanish (3), using both unidirectional translation corpora and comparative corpora: (1) *Kadhafi serait*$_{RC}$ *malade* 'Gaddafi is reportedly ill', (2) *Gheddafi sarebbe*$_{RC}$ *malato*, (3) *Kadafi estaría*$_{RC}$ *enfermo*. The Reportive Conditional (RC) is analysed as a *bicategorial epistemic marker* denoting *reportive evidentiality* and *zero modalization* (the refusal to epistemically endorse the mediated content of the utterance).

The arguments for this analysis are in large measure derived from the RC's discourse properties and functions as shown outside its *mediation domain* (the sequence conveying the mediated cognitive content), as well as outside and inside *discourse frames* opened by prepositional phrases of the type *Selon* X ('According to X'). It is shown that the speaker's epistemic attitude is variable (dubitative and non-dubitative), whereas the modal orientation inherent in the epistemic RC is invariably positive (towards 'true'). It is further shown that this verb form is exploited rhetorically to establish ascending gradations: the epistemic distancing intensifies from a first discourse frame, in the Indicative, to a second one, in the RC.

From a comparative point of view and even though the sets of epistemic uses of the Conditional are not identical in the different Romance languages, the Reportive Conditional seems to be semantically fairly equivalent in these languages, whereas the normative attitude towards the Reportive Conditional varies considerably from one language to the other, which entails differences in frequency among the Romance languages and among discourse genres within these languages. More specifically, it is shown that *diaphasic* ("situational"), *diatopic* ("geographic") and *diachronic* aspects of variation are interdependent in the case of the Spanish RC.

Keywords: evidentiality, hearsay, epistemic modality, reported speech, linguistic variation, Romance languages

Hans Kronning, Uppsala University

https://doi.org/10.1515/9783110572261-004

1 Introduction: epistemic modality and evidentiality

The principal function of *epistemic markers* (EM) is to regulate the *epistemic utterance responsibility* of the speaker[1] in order to allow him or her to conform to the social norm that s/he be truthful. The epistemic auxiliary *devoir*$_{\mathrm{EM}}$ (1), the epistemic adverb *apparemment* (2) and the Reportive Conditional (often described as "journalistic") (3) are some examples of such markers in French:

(1) *Marie* ***doit***$_{\mathrm{EM}}$ *être malade. Elle est si pâle.* 'Marie must be ill. She is so pale.'
(2) *Marie est* ***apparemment***$_{\mathrm{EM}}$ *malade.* 'Marie is apparently ill.'
[a] *Elle est si pâle.* 'She is so pale.'
[b] *Pierre l'a dit.* 'Pierre said so.'
(3) *Marie se**rait***$_{\mathrm{EM}}$ *malade.* 'Marie is reportedly ill.'
(4) *Marie est malade.* 'Marie is ill.'

By using a *simple assertion* (4) (with no epistemic marker), the speaker, should s/he be contradicted or contradict him- or herself, risks violating this norm, and as a consequence, "losing face" (Brown & Levinson 1987).[2] If on the other hand s/he reduces the enunciative responsibility by inserting an epistemic marker in the utterance (1–3),[3] s/he will be presenting the truth of the utterance as more readily "negotiable", thus mitigating the danger of "losing face".[4]

---

1 We will follow "the widespread practice in linguistics of extending the ordinary sense of 'speaker' so as to subsume 'writer' [...]. We likewise take 'utterance' to be neutral between the mediums" (Huddleston & Pullum 2002: 11).

2 Epistemic markers – such as *je crois*, verb forms expressing epistemic stance in *si*-conditionals (Kronning 2009a, 2009b, 2014b) – are also used when truth is not primarily at stake to prevent the hearer from "losing face": *Écoutez, monsieur le commissaire,* ***je crois que*** *cela* ***irait*** *plus vite si vous me laissiez parler* 'Listen, Superintendent, I believe this would go faster if you would let me speak'.

3 There are also epistemic markers (*Je t'assure*) that augment the enunciative responsibility of the speaker, used, for example, when the hearer seems to be especially incredulous.

4 Desclés (2009), in his theoretical framework, sets "declaration" (corresponding to "simple assertion" [4]), which, according to him, is negotiable, in opposition to "assertion" (*Je t'assure que P* 'I assure you that P'), called *assertion forte* ('strong assertion') (cf. Kronning 2003: 140) by others. So defined, the "assertion" is "non-negotiable by the speaker" (Desclés 2009: 36). For our part, we consider "negotiability" as a gradable property. If "strong assertion" is presented as non-negotiable, "simple assertion" (4), surely more negotiable than strong assertion, is presented as clearly less negotiable, and more likely to result in "loss of face", than assertions including

However, epistemic markers differ in terms of the semantic categories – in the first place *epistemic modalization* and *evidentiality* – to which they have recourse in order to realize this regulatory function. Thus, *epistemic modalization* carries out an "epistemic quantification" (Kronning 2003: 137–138) of the utterance, assigning it a quantificational value, such as "true" (2), "probably true" (1) or "zero" (equivalent to a refusal to attribute a truth value to the utterance) (3), whereas *evidentiality* (or *epistemic mediation*)[5] defines the "mode of access to knowledge" (Guentchéva 2004: 21), such as "perception", "inference" (1), "borrowing information from others" (3), "indirect unspecified mediation" (2). This latter type of mediation is just as compatible with contexts from which it emerges that the mediation is of inferential nature (2a) as with contexts from which it emerges that this process involves borrowing (2b). These evidential categories, in the same way as modal categories such as "probably true" or "zero", all imply, in varying degrees, the "dissociation" of the speaker towards the fact s/he is presenting.

Many epistemic markers are bicategorial markers (1–3) that fall under the category of epistemic modalization as well as under the category of evidentiality. Thus the epistemic adverb *apparemment* ('apparently') (2), denotes, according to our hypothesis, simple modalization ("true") and unspecified indirect mediation, and thus performs a "dissociation", which, solely as a result of the indirect nature of the epistemic mediation, is relatively weak. This explains why dictionaries sometimes give as synonyms of *apparemment* markers such as *probablement* ('probably') and *sans doute* ('probably'), which also realize a relatively weak "dissociation", due, in part, to inferential evidentiality, but essentially to modal quantification.

---

epistemic markers (1–3). Negotiability could moreover vary within the category of the simple assertion. Thus, an assertion like *Il fait plus beau aujourd'hui* 'The weather is nicer today', which contains the axiological predicate *beau* ('beautiful, nice'), is certainly more negotiable than (4). Desclés and Guentchéva (2013: 92–93) discuss our position on "assertion" and "negotiability".

5 In French, *évidentialité* is an Anglicism that Guentchéva (1994: 9) criticizes, because *evidence* in English means 'proof,' 'indication', while *évidence* in French means 'something that enters your mind with such force that there is no need for proof'. Italian and Spanish generally use *evidenzialità* and *evidencialidad*, although Guentchéva's criticism could also apply to these terms (cf. Kronning 2013b: 126). In our works in French, we use *médiation épistémique* ('epistemic mediation'), while Anscombre prefers *médiativité* (Anscombre et al. 2014). Desclés & Guentchéva (2013) and Guentchéva (2014) have long used *médiatif*, a term that has a more restrictive sense, related to abduction, than those mentioned above.

2 Semantic aspects

2.1 Introduction

The principal hypothesis we will defend is that the Reportive Conditional (RC) in French (5, 8), Italian (6, 9) and Spanish (7, 10), whether simple (5–7) or compound (8–10), is a *bicategorial grammatical marker* that expresses *zero modalization* – the refusal of the speaker to epistemically endorse the cognitive content of his utterance – and a particular type of *evidentiality*: the borrowing of this content from others (reportive evidentiality).[6] Zero modalization is brought about by "showing" *hic et nunc* the zero *modus* ('neither true nor false') in and through the utterance act[7]:

(5) *Kadhafi* ***serait*** *malade avec besoin urgent de soins hors Libye. Manière de sortir en sauvant la face ? Rumeur ?* (Twitter, 17.08.2011)
'Gaddafi *is reportedly* ill and in urgent need of care outside Libya. A way of leaving while saving face? Rumour?'

(6) *Il leader libico Muammar Gheddafi* ***sarebbe*** *malato* (agenzianova.com, 17.08.2011)
'The Libyan leader Muammar Gaddafi *is reportedly* ill'

(7) *Kadafi* ***estaría*** *enfermo y busca cobijo de Zuma / Estambul. El líder libio Muamar Kadafi está muy enfermo y pretende viajar a Sudáfrica para tratarse, según informó ayer el diario árabe "Al Sharq Al Awsat"* (territoriodigital.com, 18.08.2011)
'Gaddafi *is reportedly* ill and seeking shelter with Zuma. Istanbul. The Libyan leader Muammar Gaddafi is very ill and is trying to go to South Africa in order to get medical treatment, according to what the Arabic daily *Al Sharq Al Awsat* reported yesterday.'

---

6 By way of example we can cite among semantic analyses of the RC in terms of modality and/or evidentiality, for French: Abouda 2001, Bres 2010, Coltier & Dendale 2004, Gosselin 2005, Haillet 2002, Korzen & Nølke 2001, Kronning 2002, 2005, 2012, Rossari 2009, Provôt-Olivier & Desclés 2012; for Italian: Kronning 2013ab, Petitta 2006; for Spanish: Bermúdez 2016, Böhm & Henneman 2014, Sarrazin 2010, Vatrican 2010; in a Romance perspective: Kronning 2009, 2014a, 2015, Squartini 2001, 2004; for Germanic languages: Kronning 2007; and for other European languages: Wiemer 2010.

7 The fact that the *modus* denoting the RC is "shown" (Ducrot 1984: 151; Kronning 2013c, 2013d) implies that one cannot retort *That's false; you haven't presented the dictum 'She is ill' as borrowed from others, while refusing to endorse it epistemically* to someone who said *Elle serait malade* ('She *be*-RC.3sg ill'), whereas one can respond to that person *That's false: she's not ill.*

(8) *Berlusconi* ***aurait songé*** *à éliminer Kadhafi* (20minutes.com, 13.06.2013)
'Berlusconi *is said to have considered* eliminating Gaddafi.'

(9) *Silvio Berlusconi, nel 2011,* ***avrebbe chiesto*** *al capo dei servizi segreti Gianni De Gennaro di uccidere il Raìs Gheddafi.* (today.it, 13.06. 2013)
'Silvio Berlusconi *had reportedly asked* the head of the secret services Gianni De Gennaro in 2011 to kill the leader Gaddafi.'

(10) *Silvio Berlusconi, de 76 años,* ***habría iniciado*** *el año con una nueva conquista, una guapa actriz colombiana* (LaVanguardia.com, 06.02.2012)
'Silvio Berlusconi, 76 years old, *have*-RC.3sg *begun* the year with a new conquest, a beautiful Colombian actress'

These two semantic categories constituting the signification of the RC concur to maximally reduce the utterance responsibility of the speaker.

Among the more than sixty denominations of the RC found in French linguistic literature, some allude to zero modalization (the conditional of "non-commitment", of "non-assertion", of "dissociation"); others to mediation by borrowing from others (the conditional of "quotation", of "enunciative otherness", of "hearsay", the dialogic conditional); still others (the conditional of "uncertainty", of "doubtful fact") suggest a hypothesis according to which the RC is a modal marker that expresses a dubitative epistemic attitude (Lazard 2000: 214), a hypothesis that we reject. We can also add that it has been suggested by some that the RC is an *evidential marker* that does not express "non-commitment" "by its own semantics" (Coltier & Dendale 2004: 592).

2.2 The Reportive Conditional and the Inferential Conditional

It appears that in principle the RC has the same semantic and syntactic properties in the Romance languages treated here,[8] in contrast to the *Inferential Conditional* (IC), whose conditions of use diverge radically in these three languages (Kronning 2007, Squartini 2001, 2004).[9]

---

8 Similarly in Catalan (*Gaddafi estaria*$_{RC}$ *malalt* 'Kadafi is reportedly ill') (Solà et al. 2002) and in Portuguese (*Kadafi estaria*$_{RC}$ *doente* 'Kadafi is reportedly ill') (Kronning 2009c; Squartini 2004). This use of the conditional also exists in Romanian (Popescu 2011).

9 In Romanian, the markers corresponding to the IC (the *Prezumtivul* 'presumptive') and to the RC (the *Condiţional* 'conditional') are morphologically distinct (Pană Dindelegan, 2013: 53–54, Popescu 2011).

Thus, lodged in French in utterances accompanied by a "mirative" (DeLancey 2012) intonation expressing surprise (11a), in present-day Italian the IC is archaic, hence the translation *sei affezionata* in (11b), whereas in Spanish, the IC, by no means limited to mirative utterances, is used only if the reference time is in the past (t'_0) (12), the IC being replaced by the *Inferential Future* (IF) (often called "conjectural") if the reference time is simultaneous with the utterance time (t_0) (11c):

(11) a. – *Alors ... c'est seulement pour l'argent que tu le vois. – Non ...* [...] *Pas seulement. La mère étonnée,* [...], *dit tout bas: – Tu te* ***serais attachée*** *à lui ...?* (Duras, Marguerite. 1991. *L'amant de la Chine du Nord*. Folio, p. 207)
'– So ... you're only seeing him for the money. – No ... Not only. The mother astonished, [...] says to herself: – *Be*-IC.2sg you attached to him ...?'

b. «*Ti* ***sei affezionata*** *a lui ...?*» (It. trans.)
'Are you becoming attached to him?'

c. *¿Te* ***habrás encariñado*** *con él ...?* (Sp. trans.)
'*Have*-IF.2sg attached to him?'

(12) ***Serían*** *las diez de la mañana. Yo estaba recostado en un banco, frente al río Charles.* (Borges, Jorge Luis. 1975. *El libro de arena*. Folio bilingue, p. 16)
'It *must have been* ten in the morning. I was stretched out on a bench facing the Charles River.'

Put differently, the Inferential Conditional in Spanish could be regarded as the transposition of the Inferential Future (*Serán las diez de la mañana*) to the past.

2.3 The Reportive Conditional – a grammatical marker

We qualify the RC as a *grammatical marker* because, first of all, the RC of French and other Romance languages constitutes a paradigm of flexional suffixes, while the corresponding markers of Germanic languages are typically less grammaticalized expressions, like the auxiliary *sollen* in German (Provôt-Olivier 2011: 401), or lexical expressions, like the adverbs *reportedly* and *reputedly* in English (Ramat 1996: 290):

(13) a. *This Mass* [Missa Papae Marcelli] ***reputedly*** *reconciled the Church to contrapuntal music.* (A. Short *in* Pfitzner, Hans. *Palestrina*. DVD, EuroArts 2009, p. 6)

b. *Diese Messe* **soll** *die Kirche mit der kontrapunktischen Musik versöhnt haben.* (Germ. trans. by S. Wollny, p. 10)
c. *Cette Messe* ***aurait****, dit-on,* ***réconcilié*** *l'Église avec la musique contrapuntique.* (Fr. trans. by G. Bégou, p. 14)

Secondly, the RC is systematically opposed to evidentially neutral forms of the indicative (cf. Gougenheim 1938: 188), such as the present (*est*), the compound past (*a été*) (14) or the future (*partira*) (15):

(14) *Marie* ***serait***$_{RC}$ (+ ***aurait***$_{RC}$ ***été***) *malade* vs. *Marie* **est** (+ ***a été***) *malade.*
'Marie is *reportedly* (+ *is said to have been*) ill' vs. 'Marie is (+ has been) ill'.

(15) *Marie* ***partirait***$_{RC}$ *pour Paris demain* vs. *Marie* ***partira*** *pour Paris demain.*
'Marie *will reportedly leave* for Paris tomorrow' vs. 'Marie *will leave* for Paris tomorrow'.

In contrast, the inferential interpretation of the compound past (16) is not a grammatical marker of evidentiality in French, but only a contextual interpretation that is not opposed to a non-evidential verbal form (17):

(16) *Marie voyant Pierre rentrer tout mouillé dit: Tiens ! Il a plu !*
'Seeing Pierre come in all wet, Marie said: Ah! It's been raining!'

(17) *En rentrant tout mouillé, Pierre dit, à titre explicatif: Il a plu.*
'Coming in all wet, Pierre said, by way of explanation: It's been raining.'

Thirdly, as a grammatical marker, the RC does not specify the original speaker, as does a discourse frame of the type *Selon X* ('According to X'). Thus, the original speaker in (5–10) could equally well be a specific third person or a collective with more or less well-defined contours. It is indeed a primordial function of this grammatical form to allow the speaker not to specify the identity of the original source.

In our opinion, there is no reason to reduce the RC to a simple "contextual interpretation" or to a "pragmatic inference" (Anderson 1986: 274) or an "evidential strategy" (Aikhenvald 2004: 105–107), although evidentiality is not an obligatory grammatical category in French, as it is in an Amerindian language like Tuyuca.

2.4 Mediation domain, epistemic modalization and modal orientation

The RC establishes a *mediation domain* ({...}), according to rules that have been only partially described (Kronning 2004: 101–106). This domain is constituted by the continuous (18) or discontinuous (19) discursive sequence that transmits the cognitive content (the *dictum*) borrowed from others and subject to zero modalization:

(18) {*Ben Laden ne* ***serait*** *pas à Tora Bora*} *où les combats se poursuivent* [headline] (*Le Monde* 08.12.2001)
'Bin Laden *is reportedly* not in Tora Bora where the fighting continues'

(19) {*Kandahar*}$_{i}$, *le dernier grand bastion taliban*, {***aurait capitulé***}$_{i}$ [headline] (*Le Monde* 06.12.2001)
'Kandahar, the last great Taliban bastion, *is said to have capitulated*'

If we reject the hypothesis that the RC expresses a *dubitative epistemic attitude*, it is because the speaker is able to show, outside the mediation domain of the RC, a more or less dubitative attitude, by evaluating the credibility of the sources (20–21), as well as a non-dubitative attitude ("certainty" regarding the truth or falseness of the borrowed *dictum*) (22–23):

(20) ***Secondo fonti non certe***, *proprio nel corso di uno dei raid aerei su Tripoli*, {***sarebbe stato ucciso*** *un figlio di Gheddafi, Khamis*}. (www.topnotizie.it, 21.03.2011)
'According to uncertain sources, Gaddafi's son Khamis *have*-RC.3sg *been killed* precisely during one of the air raids over Tripoli.'

(21) ***Selon des sources bien informées***, {*Washington* ***serait*** *« activement engagé » dans la création d'une coalition militaire* [...] *pour assurer la sécurité de l'Afghanistan à la suite de la chute de Kaboul*}. (*Le Monde* 14.11.2001)
'According to well-informed sources, Washington *be*-RC.3sg "actively engaged" in the creation of a military coalition [...] to guarantee the security of Afghanistan following the fall of Kabul.'

(22) *Beaucoup d'idioties ont été écrites sur le film* [Tony Palmer's film "Wagner" from 1983] *depuis son achèvement*. {*Il* ***durerait*** *9 heures ; 2 heures ; 5 heures*}$_{A–C}$. ***Tout cela est faux. Le film fait exactement 7 heures 46 minutes***. {*Il* ***aurait*** *complètement* explosé *le budget*}$_{D}$ *et* {***aurait été considéré*** *comme une « perte fiscale »*}$_{E}$. {*La chaîne britannique ITV* ***aurait refusé*** *de le diffuser*}$_{F}$. {*Les producteurs* ***auraient demandé*** *à ce que le film soit brûlé*}$_{G}$. ***Seule cette dernière affirmation*** [= G] ***est vraie***. (Wagner. TP-DVD157. 2011)
'Much rubbish has been written about the film since its completion. It *is said to be* 9 hours long; 2 hours long; 5 hours long. It is none of those. It is 7 hours and 46 minutes in length precisely. It *has reputedly gone* hugely over budget; it *is said to be made* as a 'tax loss'. ITV *is said to have refused* to show it; the producers *have reportedly ordered* the negative to be burned. Only the last is true.'

(23) *El oso común que,* ***según Zimmermann, estaría*** *difundido por todo el globo, no existe en América* (Francisco Jorge Torres Villegas. 1857^2. *Cartografía hispano-científica; ó sea, Los mapas españoles ...*, I. Madrid: Ramón Ballone, p. 250)
'The common bear, which, according to Zimmermann, *is said to be* disseminated all over the globe, does not exist in America.'

When the epistemic attitude is not dubitative (22–23), the RC does not have the function to regulate utterance responsibility, but rather a text-organizational function that allows the speaker to refer to a point of view of others without endorsing it, in order to be able to disconfirm (22A–C, 23)[10] or confirm it (22G) in his or her subsequent discourse. This supports the notion that zero modalization is inscribed in the RC's "specific semantic content", contrary to the hypothesis put forward by Coltier and Dendale (2004: 592).

Moreover, the disconfirmation or confirmation of the *content* transmitted in its *mediation domain* shows that the RC, like reported speech (RS), has an invariably positive *modal orientation* in accordance with a general pragmatic principle. The transmitted content is oriented towards "true", not towards "false", as is shown by the possibility to annul (24) or to corroborate (25) this positive orientation, but not the opposite orientation:

(24) */Selon Pierre,/ {Marie* serait *malade}, mais, en fait, elle ne l'est pas* (+ **elle l'est*).
'According to Pierre, Marie *be*-RC.3sg ill, but, in fact, she is not (+ *she is.)'
(25) */Selon Pierre,/ {Marie* ***serait*** *malade}, et, en effet, elle l'est* (+ **elle ne l'est pas*).
'According to Pierre, Marie *be*-RC.3sg ill, and, indeed, she is (+ *she is not)'

The general pragmatic principle that explains this modal orientation is a *topos* (cf. Anscombre 1995) deriving from Grice's maxim of quality, according to which the speaker must try to see to it that his or her discourse is truthful. According to this *topos* (Kronning 2005: 304, 2010: 26; cf. Ducrot 1984: 157), if someone says something, the fact that s/he is saying it is an argument for its being true. This *topos* is explicitly invoked in (26):

10 In this case, the RC is sometimes described as *conditionnel polémique* ('polemical conditional').

(26) *Elle m'a dit qu'elle viendrait te voir bientôt mais pourquoi ? – Alors là ! Si elle a dit qu'elle viendrait me voir, c'est qu'elle va venir !*
'She told me she would come to see you soon, but why? – Well then, if she said she would come to see me, then she's coming.'

On the one hand, this *topos*, being positively oriented, only provides an argument for the truth of the borrowed cognitive content and thus in principle leaves this truth in doubt. This has presumably led certain linguists to unduly regard the RC as a modal marker invariably expressing a dubitative epistemic attitude. On the other hand, this *topos* enables the speaker to abusively communicate information lacking any foundation and, without endorsing it, to shirk all responsibility, as it leaves the modal semantic value of the RC (zero modalization) unaffected. Furthermore, the positive *pragmatic* modal orientation of the content in the mediation domain implied by this *topos* explains that it is worth transmitting this content even if the mediation domain is in the scope of an explicitly negative *semantic* modal evaluation (*Secondo fonti non certe*) outside the mediation domain, as in (20). There is no contradiction in expressing a dubitative epistemic attitude (outside this domain) concerning a borrowed, and thus presented as positively oriented, cognitive content that the speaker refuses to epistemically endorse. Rather, there would be no point in referring to such an actively non-endorsed content if it were not pragmatically and argumentatively oriented towards "true".

2.5 Discourse frames, reportive evidentiality and reported speech

It is important to distinguish the *reportive evidentiality* (or "reportive epistemic mediation") expressed by the RC from *reported speech*[11] (or "enunciative mediation"), and notably from *indirect speech* (IS).

Indirect speech is a discourse configuration representing a mediated utterance act (*Il a dit que* ... 'He said that') and its cognitive content (or *dictum*) (... *Marie est malade* 'Marie is ill'), all the while giving an image of the original discourse which is "homogeneous" from a semiotic and enunciative point of view "with the discourse where it is produced" (Authier-Revuz 2004: 41). This image proceeds from a reformulation of the original utterance, a reformulation that subsumes paraphrase, inference and/or translation.

11 "What, following the grammatical tradition, we call *reported speech* covers the reporting of spoken and written text but also that of unspoken thoughts" (Huddleston & Pullum 2002: 1023).

Unlike indirect speech, the RC is not a discourse configuration, but a *grammatical marker* (see Section 2.3) that does not represent the original utterance act, but, if s/he hints at it, the speaker merely borrows the cognitive content from it, normally reformulated and invariably subjected to zero modalization.

As it is not represented by the RC, the original utterance act cannot, although it is conceptually anterior to the borrowed *dictum*, serve the function of reference time in relation to which this *dictum* could be temporally located. The result of this is that the temporal localization of this eventuality is essentially dependent on its *actionality*, as well as on the *simple* or *compound form* of the conditional. Thus, if it is atelic (27), the mediated eventuality is localized simultaneously with the utterance time, t_0[12]:

(27) {*Le président* **serait** *malade*}.
'The president *is said to be* ill.'

If this eventuality is telic, it is localized after t_0 (28–29a), unless this telic eventuality is an "accomplishment" (29), in which case the eventuality can also be localized simultaneously with t_0 (Gosselin 2001: 47) (29b):

(28) {*Le président* **partirait** *pour Londres /lundi/*}
'The president *is said to leave* for London /Monday/'

(29) {*La coalition* **déploierait** *une « force de sécurité » dans les villes afghanes*} [headline] (*Le Monde* 14.11.2001)
a. 'The coalition *will reportedly deploy* a security force in Afghan towns'
b. 'The coalition *is reportedly deploying* a security force in Afghan towns'

If, finally, the RC is in the compound form, the eventuality is localized before t_0 (30):

(30) {*Le président* **aurait** été *malade* (+ **serait parti** *pour Londres*)}.
'The president *is said to have been* ill (+ *has reportedly left* for London)'

It commonly happens that the RC is inscribed in a *discourse frame* (Charolles & Péry-Woodley 2005) ([...]) opened by a prepositional phrase such as *Selon Pierre*

12 The mediated eventuality may also be localized in relation to a reference time in the past (Kronning 2005: 306–307).

('According to Pierre'). We will consider constructions of the type *Selon X*[13] as falling by default under a subcategory of indirect speech (IS) where the mediated utterance is embedded in a discourse frame. We will call this type of indirect speech *discourse frame embedded indirect speech* (DFIS).

Unlike the RC (31), the DFIS (32) indicates the identity of the author (*According to Pierre*) of the original utterance act – like prototypical IS (33) (*Pierre says that*) –, but DFIS does not allow the categorization of this act with the help of a reporting verb:

(31) {*Marie **serait** malade*}
(32) *Selon Pierre,* [< *Marie **est** malade* >].
'According to Pierre, Marie is ill.'
(33) *Pierre dit que* < *Marie **est** malade* >.
'Pierre says that Marie is ill.'

The *embedded utterance* (<...>) of IS (33) and of DFIS (32), like the mediated *dictum* of the RC (31), results from a *reformulation* of the original utterance, to which the hearer normally has no access.

When the RC is inscribed in a discourse frame ([...]), the reported speech interpretation (in the present case the DFIS) assigned by default to the discourse frame construction may, however, be annulled and replaced by a reportive evidentiality interpretation ({...}):

(34) *Selon Pierre,* [{*Marie **serait***$_{RC}$ *malade*}]
'According to Pierre, Marie *be*-RC.3sg ill.'

In this case, the discourse frame (*Selon Pierre*) specifies the source to whom the borrowed *dictum* ('Marie est malade', 'Marie is ill') is attributed.

Now, the framing construction conserves its reported speech interpretation if the reportive epistemic mediation ({*Marie serait*$_{RC}$ *malade*}) is interpreted as *reported* (< {...} >), in which case the discourse frame indicates the speaker (*Pierre*) of the original utterance, which is in the RC, and not the unspecified source of the borrowed *dictum* ({...}):

(35) *Selon Pierre,* [< {*Marie **serait***$_{RC}$ *malade*} >]
'According to Pierre, Marie *is reportedly* ill.'

13 These constructions are often characterized as *médiatives* ('mediative') or *évidentielles* ('evidential') (Coltier & Dendale 2004: 596, Charolles & Péry-Woodley 2005: 6).

Contexts in which one of these interpretations – *reportive evidentiality* (34) and *reported reportive evidentiality* (35) – of the RC inscribed in a discourse frame introduced by *selon X* are absolutely mandatory are relatively rare. Now, there is no doubt that utterance (36) falls within the reportive evidentiality interpretation, the speaker having extracted the *dictum* of his utterance from an original utterance such as *Je ne me suis pas échappé en même temps que les cinq autres fuyards* ('I did not escape at the same time as the other five fugitives'):

(36) ***Selon ses propres aveux,*** [{*Bavone ne se* ***serait*** *pas* ***échappé*** *en même temps que les cinq autres fuyards /.../*}]. (*Tribune de Genève* 29.02.1988)
'According to his own account, Bavone *have*-RC.3sg not *escaped* at the same time as the other five fugitives.'

It is natural on the other hand to interpret the RC of (37) as falling under the category of "reported reportive evidentiality", which would explain the at first disconcerting juxtaposition of the indicative present and the RC in one and the same discourse frame:

(37) ***Selon certaines sources,*** [< *la fuite du mollah Omar n'****est*** *pas totalement inattendue* > *et* < {***aurait été facilitée*** *par des complicités dans le camp adverse*} >]. (*Le Monde* 08.12.2001)
'According to certain sources, the flight of Mullah Omar is not totally unexpected and *is said to have been facilitated* by some collusive activity in the enemy camp.'

2.6 Discourse frames, absence of epistemic endorsement and zero modalization

From the point of view of modality, it is advisable to distinguish two types of discourse frame constructions: those which enclose verbal forms other than the RC (38) and those which enclose the RC (39):

(38) *Selon Pierre, Marie* ***est*** *(****était, fut****, etc.) malade.*
'According to Pierre, Marie is (was, etc.) ill.'

(39) *Selon Pierre, Marie* ***serait*** *malade.*
'According to Pierre, Marie *be*-RC.3sg ill.'

By contrasting the use of verbal forms in the indicative other than the RC with the RC in these constructions, we are hypothesizing that these two types of verbal forms denote two degrees of intensity of non-commitment towards the mediated eventuality: the indicative (apart from the RC) expresses the *absence of epistemic commitment* towards the mediated eventuality (38), whereas the RC denotes *zero modalization* which – since it signifies an absolute refusal to epistemically endorse the eventuality (39) – performs a more emphatic epistemic distancing on the part of the speaker.

This hypothesis is corroborated by the rhetorical exploitation that is made of this opposition of the two degrees of intensity of non-commitment – absence vs. refusal of commitment – in order to form *ascending binary gradations*. Thus, in (40a–40b), the epistemic distancing intensifies from the first discourse frame (absence of commitment) (A) to the second (refusal of commitment) (B):

(40) a. [< *Judas* >]$_{A}$, ***selon l'unanime tradition des premiers temps,*** [< ***accompagnait*** *lui-même l'escouade* >]$_{A}$, *et même,* ***selon quelques-uns,*** [{*il* ***aurait poussé*** *l'odieux jusqu'à prendre pour signe de sa trahison un baiser*}]$_{B}$. (Renan, Ernest. 1867[13]. *Vie de Jésus*. Paris: Folio 1974, p. 381, Chap. XXIV)

b. *Giuda,* ***secondo l'unanime tradizione dei primi tempi, accompagnava*** *personalmente il drappello e* ***secondo alcuni avrebbe spinto*** *la scelleratezza al punto di dare un bacio come segno del tradimento.* (It. trans. by A. Pasquali)
'Judas, according to the unanimous tradition of the earliest times, *accompanied* the detachment himself, and according to some, he *have*-RC.3sg *carried* his hateful conduct even to betraying him with a kiss.'

This binary gradation is supported by the differences in the credibility assessment of the sources invoked for the eventualities mediated in the two discourse frames. The positive assessment of sources in the first frame (A), which is quantitative (*selon l'unanime tradition* ... 'according to the unanimous tradition') as well as qualitative (... *des premiers temps* 'of the earliest times'), contrasts with the exclusively quantitative (*selon quelques-uns* 'according to some') negative assessment of the second frame (B).[14]

14 Added to this ascending gradation of the intensity of epistemic distancing expressed by the verbal forms is another ascending gradation that reinforces the rhetorical structure of the Renanian discourse. This other gradation, marked linguistically by the operator *même* ('even'), is axiological and thus fundamentally different in nature: the behaviour of Judas described in

3 Variational aspects

If the semantic and syntactic properties of the RC in French, Italian and Spanish appear to be the same in principle, we will attempt to show in the following (a) that Spanish stands out in a *diaphasic* and *diachronic* sense from French and Italian, (b) that the diaphasic properties of Spanish ensue from *normative discourses* based on, among other things, the supposed diachronic properties of the RC in this language and (c) that there is a *diatopic* variation in Spanish between its *peninsular* and *Latin-American* varieties, and (d) that this diatopic variation is dependent on *diaphasic* variation.

3.1 Diaphasic variation

From a theoretical point of view, we regard *diaphasic variation*, usually seen as being of "situational or functional-contextual" nature (Berruto 1993: 8), as defined in relation to discourse genres, which are "types of socio-discursive practices" (Adam 1999: 83), governed by "norms" (Coseriu 1969), situated between *langue* and *parole*.[15] In other words, discourse genres largely determine both diaphasic variation and diaphasic properties of linguistic units.

Given that the RC is a relatively infrequent phenomenon in our three Romance languages, we will limit ourselves here to *hypergenres of discourse* – whether it be *journalistic discourse* (see Section 3.1.1),[16] *historical* and *scientific discourse* (see Section 3.1.2), or novelistic *literary discourse* (see Section 3.1.3) – before investigating the *normative discourses* (see Section 3.2) to which the RC is subjected.

3.1.1 Journalistic discourse

According to a particularly tenacious received notion, the RC is said to be, in French as well as in Italian and Spanish, restricted to a specific genre: journalistic discourse.

the second discourse frame (B) is presented as more reprehensible from a moral point of view (... *poussé l'odieux jusqu'à* ... 'carried his hateful conduct even to') than that in the first frame (A).

15 Cf. Glessgen (2007: 105) and above all Rastier (2011).

16 Our quantitative data (see Section 3.4.2) for this hypergenre fall under a "paratextual" journalistic subgenre, the headline, which is particularly conducive to the study of the RC (Kronning 2004: 69–71, 2013b: 221–222, Sullet-Nylander 2005).

Thus, “almost exclusively reserved for journalistic discourse” in French, “whence the recurrent use of the term *conditionnel journalistique* in grammars”,[17] the RC, described as the *condizionale giornalistico* in Italian (Rocci 2005: 121), is said to be used “nella lingua dell’informazione giornalistica” (‘in the language of journalistic information’) (Patota 2006: 116). Similarly, in Spanish, called the *condicional periodístico*,[18] the RC is said to be “propio del lenguaje periodístico” (‘characteristic of journalistic language’) (*Nueva Gramática* 2010, § 23.8.1f). In fact, the RC is even seen as being intrinsically bound to journalistic discourse, as, according to Petitta (2006: 259), “è indubbia l’incidenza diafasica: mettere in discussione la propria fonte è un atteggiamento tipicamente giornalistico” (‘the diaphasic incidence is clear: questioning one’s own sources is a typically journalistic attitude’), which would also explain the supposedly late emergence of this type of conditional: “Le attestazioni [of the RC] sono dunque” (‘Attestations of the RC are thus’), she continues, “inevitablemente legate al fenomeno di diffusione della stampa periodica” (‘inevitably tied to the phenomenon of the spread of the periodical press’).

To be sure, the RC is characteristic of the journalistic genre (see Section 3.3.2), but, as we shall see, this use of the conditional is by no means limited to this discourse genre.

3.1.2 Historical and scientific discourse

The RC is also typical of historical and scientific discourse in the three languages, as Serianni (1989: 516) underlines, affirming that “il ‘condizionale di dissociazione’ si adopera spesso” (‘the RC is often used’) in Italian “anche in àmbiti lontani dal giornalismo, per esempio nella trattatistica scientifica” (‘also in contexts far removed from journalism, such as scientific treatises’). It is in fact easy to attest the RC in these discourse genres, including history (41a–41c), chemistry (42) and ethnology (43) – and that, in French (41a), in Italian (41b, 42) and in peninsular (41c) and Latin-American Spanish (43):

(41) a. *L’opinion d’après laquelle Jean, fils de Zébédée,* ***aurait écrit*** *l’ouvrage* [...] *est ici écartée comme improbable.* (Renan, Ernest. 1867[13]. *Vie de Jésus.* Préface. Paris: Folio 1974, p. 41)
‘The opinion that John, the son of Zebedee, *have*-RC.3sg *written* the work [...] is dismissed here as improbable.’

17 Anonymous reviewer of an abstract of a conference paper by the present author.
18 Cf. Vatrican (2010: 83).

b. *L'opinione secondo la quale Giovanni, figlio di Zebedeo,* ***avrebbe scritto*** *l'opera* [...], *è qui scartata come improbabile.* (It. trans. by A. Pasquali)
c. *La opinión según la cual Juan, hijo de Zebedeo,* ***habría escrito*** *la obra* [...] *queda aquí descartada como improbable.* (Sp. trans. by A. G. Tirado)

(42) *L'orina de' bambini* ***sarebbe, secondo SCHEELE,*** *molto somigliante a quella del cavallo* (Luigi Valentino Brugnatelli. 1797. *Annali di chimica e storia naturale.* Tomo quattordicesimo. Pavia: Bolzani, p. 211)
'The urine of infants *be*-RC.3sg, according to Scheele, very similar to that of the horse.'

(43) *Esta escritura de naturaleza muy primitiva* ***estaría, según nuestro autor, emparentada*** *con las pictografías de los Pieles Rojas* (*Anales de arqueología y etnología* 11–13. 1950. Universidad Nacional de Cuyo, p. 136)
'This writing, which is very primitive in nature, *be*-RC.3sg, according to our author, *related* to the pictographs of the Red Indians.'

3.1.3 Literary discourse

Linguists and grammarians have often excluded the RC from literary language, as stated by Petitta (2006: 262). Actually, literary discourse by no means eschews the RC, as is shown by the following famous passage (44) from Proust, which contains three occurrences (a.–c.) of the RC:

(44) *M. le marquis de Norpois* [a.] ***aurait eu*** *plusieurs entretiens avec le ministre de Prusse, afin d'examiner* [...] *les différents motifs de friction existants* [...] *Dernière heure : on a appris avec satisfaction dans les cercles bien informés, qu'une légère détente semble s'être produite dans les rapports franco-prussiens. On* [b.] ***attacherait*** *une importance toute particulière au fait que M. de Norpois* [c.] ***aurait rencontré*** unter den Linden *le ministre d'Angleterre* (Proust, Marcel. 1925. *Albertine disparue.* Pléiade 1989, IV, p. 216)[19]
'M. de Norpois [a.] *have*-RC.3sg *held* several discussions with the Minister of Prussia, in order to examine [...] the various causes of tension [...] Latest news: it has been learned with satisfaction in well-informed circles that Franco-Prussian relations have apparently experienced a

19 An example that we have analysed in depth elsewhere (Kronning 2012: 93–94, 2013a: 219–221, 2013b: 131–132).

slight improvement. Very special importance [b.] *is said to be attached* to the fact that M. de Norpois [c.] *is reported to have met* the British Minister "unter den Linden".'

These occurrences of the RC are systematically rendered with the conditional by four Italian translators of Proust's novel:

(44) a. *avrebbe avuto*[20] / *avrebbe avuto*[21] / *avrebbe avuto*[22] / *avrebbe avuto*[23]
b. *si attribuirebbe* / *si attribuirebbe* / *si attribuirebbe* / *si attribuirebbe*
c. *avrebbe incontrato* / *avrebbe incontrato* / *avrebbe incontrato* / *avrebbe incontrato*

On the other hand, two translators into Spanish systematically avoid the conditional, whereas one Spanish-speaking translator resorts systematically to this verbal form:

(44) a'. *parece haber mantenido*[24] / *Al parecer, el señor marqués ha celebrado*[25] / *habría mantenido*[26]
b'. *parece concederse* / *parece atribuirse* / *se le atribuiría*
c'. *se entrevistó al parecer* / *se haya reunido* / *se habría encontrado*

3.2 Normative discourses

The RC is the subject of normative discourses in Spanish, as is evidenced, among other places, in the notes regarding the RC that two of the Spanish-speaking translators – Javier Albiñana and Carlos Manzano – append to the Proust passage (44).

According to Albiñana, the RC is a "construcción imposible en castellano".[27] Manifestly erroneous from a descriptive point of view, this statement must be interpreted as a normative judgement.

20 It. trans. by F. Fortini.
21 It. trans. by M. T. Nessi Somaini.
22 It. trans. by R. Stajano.
23 It. trans. by G. Raboni.
24 Sp. trans. by J. Albiñana.
25 Sp. trans. by C. Manzano.
26 Sp. trans. by E. Canto.
27 Note from the translator in Proust, Marcel, 1988, *Albertine desaparecida*, translated by Javier Albiñana, Barcelona: Anagrama, p. 188.

To Manzano, the RC gives rise to a *purist* normative discourse: this use of the conditional is a *Gallicism* to be avoided, although it is frequent in journalistic discourse:

> En la traducción [...] se ha substituido ese condicional (llamado 'de rumor') por la expresión 'al parecer, + indicativo' para no cometer un gravísimo calco sintáctico del francés, pese a que en la actualidad esté tan generalizado en el lenguaje de la prensa –a diferencía del de los hablantes comunes y corrientes y del de los escritores [...]–, que ha acabado denominándoselo también 'condicional periodístico'.[28]

Now, others, like Seco (1998: 350), maintain that the RC is only used "esporádicamente" ('sporadically') in the journalistic discourse of peninsular Spanish, a quantitative appreciation that squares well with the *purist* and allegedly *deontological normative discourse* found in the *Libro de estilo* of *El País*, according to which the use of the RC is proscribed in this daily because it is supposed to be grammatically incorrect and to compromise the credibility of the information:

> Este uso del condicional de indicativo [the RC] es francés. [...] Los giros adecuados para sustituir el condicional francés pueden ser éstos u otros parecidos [...]: 'el ministro parece estar dispuesto ...'; 'según indicios, el obispo ha establecido ...' [...] El uso del condicional en ese tipo de frases queda terminantemente prohibido en el periódico. Además de incorrecto gramaticalmente, resta credibilidad a la información.[29]

If we consider this discourse to be deontological only in appearance, it is because the substitute expressions (*parece* 'seems', *según indicios* 'according to evidence') recommended by the *Libro de estilo* do not provide the exact sources of the information conveyed either. Curiously, the *Nueva Gramática de la lengua española* (2009, § 23.15m) denies explicitly, and obviously incorrectly, the very existence of this type of purist normative discourse:

> Algunos diarios hispanohablantes han optado por excluir este uso particular del condicional de conjetura [the RC] en sus libros de estilo. No lo hacen, sin embargo, porque exista incorrección gramatical en dicha construcción, sino porque el rumor no debe ser presentado como noticia.

In French, there is also a deontological normative discourse regarding the RC. Thus, the authors of *Le Style du Monde* (Paris 2002: 55, *apud* Sullet-Nylander

---

28 Note from the translator in Proust, Marcel, 2007, *Albertine desaparecida*, translated by Carlos Manzano, Barcelona: Lumen, p. 243.
29 http://estudiantes.elpais.com/libroestilo/apartado12_037.htm

2005) decree that "l'usage du conditionnel doit être exceptionnel et se justifier par la citation de nos sources" ('the use of the conditional should be exceptional and be justified by quoting our sources'). Now, this discourse, which is hardly respected (see Section 3.4.2), is deontological not only in appearance, given that the RC is admissible according to *Le Style du Monde* if it is justified by quoting the exact sources of the information.

3.3 Diaptopic variation

It is probable that the RC is subject to diaptopic variation in Spanish. Thus, some linguists (Butt & Benjamin 2000: 217) deem that the RC is used above all in Latin-American Spanish. The third Spanish-speaking translator of the Proust passage above (44), in contrast with the first two, systematically rendered the RC in French with the conditional in Spanish (44a'–44c': *habría mantenido, se le atribuiría, se habría encontrado*). It turns out that the translator, Estela Canto, is, as it happens, Argentinian and writes, according to the literary critic Herbert E. Craig, "un español totalmente normativo, pero de América".[30]

3.4 Evidence from the corpora

It is time to bring to bear the *quantitative evidence* provided by a *translation corpus* (see Section 3.4.1) and by *comparative corpora* (see Section 3.4.2).

3.4.1 Translation corpus: literary discourse

Our corpus of Italian and Spanish translations of instances in French of the simple and compound RC is based on novelistic literary discourse from Balzac to Ndiaye (Table 4.1).

The corpus shows that *in French* the RC, though not used frequently, is certainly not markedly unusual in this discourse genre and that *in Italian* the RC is regularly translated with the conditional. While it is true that one cannot exclude that it may be "overused" (Johansson 2007: 32) under the influence of the French original text, nothing indicates that the RC is exceptional in Italian literary discourse.

30 lanacion.com, 6.11.2005.

Table 4.1: Translation of French source RC into Italian and into Spanish in literary discourse

Author and Title of work	French Source RC	Italian Target RC	Spanish Target RC
Balzac, *Le père Goriot*, 1835	4	4	1
Zola, *Nana*, 1880	1	–	–
Proust, *Sodome et Gomorrhe II*, 1922	4	4	2* Arg.
Proust, *Albertine disparue*, 1925	12	12	3* Arg.
Cohen, *Belle du Seigneur*, 1968	1	1	–
Perec, *La vie mode d'emploi*, 1978	7	4	–
Duras, *L'amant de la Chine du Nord*, 1991	2	–	–
Houellebecq, *La possibilité d'une île*, 2005	1	1	1
Littell, *Les bienveillantes*, 2006	17	12	–
Ndiaye, *Trois femmes puissantes*, 2009	3	3	1
TOTAL	52	41	8
%RC	100%	79%	15%

On the other hand, the corpus shows that *in peninsular Spanish*, the RC is exceptional in literary discourse. Our corpus provides only five instances of the RC translated into *Latin-American Spanish*, but they are all rendered with a conditional.

Novelistic fiction is peculiar in that it can contain within its fictive mode numerous other genres (journalistic, historical and scientific, conversational, etc.). The RC occurs in this discourse genre both from the pen of the narrator (45a–45c) and in the mouth (46a–46c) and from the pen (44) of characters:

(45) a. *« Bien entendu », **aurait dit** M. Bergson à M. Boutroux, à en croire le philosophe norvégien, « les hypnotiques pris de temps en temps à doses modérées n'ont pas d'influence sur cette solide mémoire de notre vie de tous les jours* [...] » (Proust, Marcel. 1922. *Sodome et Gomorrhe II.* Chap. III. Pléiade 1988, III, p. 373)

b. *avrebbe detto* '*have*-RC.3sg *said*' (It. trans. by G. Raboni)

c. *habría dicho* '*have*-RC.3sg *said*' (Sp. trans. by E. Canto, Argentina)

d. *dijo, al parecer*, '*said apparently*' (Sp. trans. by C. Manzano, Spain)

'"Of course," M. Bergson *is to have said* to M. Boutroux, if the Norwegian philosopher is to be believed, "moderate doses of hypnotics from time to time have no influence on this solid memory of our everyday life [...]"'

(46) a. – [...] *Eugène, reprit-elle à voix basse, elle y va pour dissiper d'affreux soupçons. Vous ne savez pas les bruits qui courent sur elle ?* [...] ***Selon certaines personnes** monsieur de Trailles **aurait souscrit** des lettres*

de change montant à cent mille francs, presque toutes échues, et pour lesquelles il allait être poursuivi. Dans cette extrémité, ma sœur ***aurait vendu*** *ses diamants à un juif* (Balzac, H. de. 1835. *Le Père Goriot*. Édition de P.-G. Castex. Paris: Garnier 1963, p. 247)

b. *avrebbe firmato – avrebbe venduto* '*have*-RC.3sg signed – *have*-RC.3sg sold' (It. trans. by C. De Marchi)

c. *ha suscrito – habría vendido* 'has signed – *have*-RC.3sg sold' (Sp. trans. by M. Gutiérrez)

'– Eugene, she went on, lowering her voice, she will go to dispel ugly suspicions. You do not know the things that people are saying about her. [...] According to some people, M. de Trailles *have*-RC.3sg *put* his name to bills for a hundred thousand francs, nearly all of them are overdue, and proceedings are threatened. In this predicament, my sister *have*-RC.3sg *sold* her diamonds to a Jew'

Thus, the Proust passage quoted above (44) falls in the fictional universe under the genre of journalistic discourse: it is an "editorial" written by a character in the Proust novel, the Marquis de Norpois. It is all the more remarkable that one of the Spanish translators, Carlos Manzano, affirms – in the note just quoted (see Section 3.2) where he explains his refusal to resort to the conditional in translating Proust's RC – that the RC is "generalizado en el lenguaje de la prensa" ('generally used in press language') in Spanish.

In the light of our quantitative evidence, it seems permissible to conclude that the diaphasic effects of the purist normative discourse are particularly powerful and significant in literary discourse in peninsular Spanish and that in this case the diaphasic marking of the RC is diatopically determined.

3.4.2 Comparative corpora: journalistic discourse

By searching comparative corpora based on journalistic discourse for all instances of the (simple and compound) conditional forms *serait*, *aurait*, *sarebbe*, *avrebbe* and *estaría*, *habría* in press headlines (print and/or electronic) published by *Google Actualités*, *Google News Italia* and *Google Noticias* during the month of May 2012, we can compare the frequency of the RC interpretation (+RC) of these forms with the frequency of these forms not having this interpretation (–RC) (Table 4.2).

This evidence makes it clear that, on the one hand, *diaptopic variation* between *peninsular Spanish* and *Latin-American Spanish* is particularly important in the "paratextual" journalistic genre of headlines and, on the other hand, that

Table 4.2: The forms *serait, aurait, sarebbe, avrebbe* and *estaría/habría* representing the RC (*+RC*) in relation to these forms not representing the RC (*–RC*) in these comparative journalistic corpora

Serait, aurait; sarebbe, avrebbe; estaría, habría /+PP/	***–RC***	***+RC***	**% +RC (%)**
French Le Figaro, Le Monde, Libération, Le Parisien, La Croix, Ouest-France, Le Progrès de Lyon, Le Républicain lorrain	22	43	**66**
Italian Corriere della Sera, La Repubblica, La Stampa, Il Tempo, Il Mondo, L'Osservatore Romano, Il Gazzettino, Liberazione	19	10	**34**
Peninsular Spanish ABC, El Mundo, El País, La Vanguardia, Diario Vasco, El Comercio, El Economista, La Voz de Galicia, La Verdad	34	20	**37**
Latin-American Spanish Clarín (Arg.), Cronista (Arg.), Diario Época (Arg.), El Mercurio (Chi.), Diario de Yucatán (Mex.), La Crónica de hoy (Mex.), El Universal (Col.), Noticias en linea (Ecu.), La República (Per.), ABC Color (Par.)	6	42	**87**

the frequency of the RC in peninsular Spanish (37%) is little different from that of Italian (34%). Consequently, it cannot be affirmed, as Seco does (see Section 3.2), that the RC is used only "sporadically" in journalistic discourse in Spain.

Now, peninsular journalistic discourse is governed by conflicting diaphasic norms. Thus, in a newspaper like *El País*, which subscribes to a purist prescriptive (and supposedly deontological) norm, instances of the RC are rare, but not non-existent (1 inst.), while in other newspapers, such as *ABC* (8 insts.), which do not subscribe to – or do not observe, which comes to the same thing – this norm, the frequencies of the RC are clearly higher.

On the other hand, despite the negative deontological discourse of *Le Monde* towards the RC (see Section 3.1.4), use of the RC (8 insts.) is frequent in this French newspaper.

3.5 Diachronic perspectives

Is the purist normative discourse regarding the RC in Spain supported by diachronic differences among the three languages?

Traditionally, the RC is considered a phenomenon of the 20th century in French as well as in Italian and Spanish. Thus, in French, "exemples avec le conditionnel de reprise donnés par la littérature ne sont jamais antérieurs au XXe siècle" ('examples of the reportive conditional quoted in the literature are never prior to the 20th century') (Dendale 2010: 307).[31] In Italian, "no indisputable example of reportive usage is documented in the 19th century" (Squartini 2001: 325).[32] In Spanish, one finds "nulle trace [of the RC] avant la première moitié du XXe siècle" ('no trace [of the RC]' before the first half of the 20th century) (Sarrazin 2010: 101).

Now, recently, Dendale (2010: 308) has been able to push back the dating of this usage in French to 1574, and below is an attestation of the RC that is some twenty years prior to Dendale's (47)[33]:

(47) *Luther* [...] *s'adressant à eux, monstre ce sien souhait par lequel il desiroit vn tel decret estre fait par le Concile, n'estre digne de reprehensiõ, non plus que s'il se disoit souhaiter que par l'ordonnance du Concile il fust permis aux prestres de se marier. Ce qu'autrefois le pape Pie second* ***auroit dit & desiré****. Parquoy on ne doit le blasmer s'il souhaite le pareil.* (Iean Sleidan, HISTOIRE ENTIERE *Deduite depuis le Deluge iusques au temps present*, Second liure, Chez Jean Crespin, 1561)
'Luther, who turned to them, made it known that he wanted such a regulation to be issued by the Council and that this would be no more blameworthy than if he had wished it were permitted, by decree of the Council, for priests to marry. Pope Pius II *have*-RC.3sg *said* and *wished* so. Therefore, he should not be blamed for wishing the same.'

It will be noticed that the occurrences of the RC are not accompanied in this example by a lexical marker of mediation (*According to X*) and that the epistemic attitude adopted by the speaker towards the borrowed cognitive content is not dubitative. Thus, in concluding *Parquoy on ne doit le blasmer s'il souhaite le pareil*, the Luxembourgian diplomat and historian Johannes Sleidanus (1506–1556) connects on to the eventuality mediated by the RC – that Pope Pius II was reported to have said that he wished that "il fust permis aux prestres de se marier" – and

31 A somewhat overly categorical affirmation, as Dendale and Coltier (2012) moreover show themselves. We had already cited (Kronning 2004, 2005) several examples from the 19th century, taken from Renan, Zola and *Le Figaro*.

32 Masini (1977) nevertheless attested the RC in Italian as early as the middle of the 19th century. Cf. Petitta (2006: 258): "Il condizionale di dissociazione come espressione di dato riportato non sembra diffuso prima del XIX secolo" ('The RC as the expression of reported information does not seem to have spread before the 19th century').

33 Damourette and Pichon (1911–1940, § 1846) quote some "legal" examples from 1541 that are similar to an example we cited in Kronning (2014a: 81). Baeyen (2012) brings to bear even earlier attestations of the same type from the 14th century, but the texts are 16th-century copies.

hence makes known his own non-dubitative attitude towards the mediated eventuality. Perhaps the speaker's taking recourse to the RC in this case simply serves, by the epistemic dissociation that it implies, to underscore his objectivity.

What about Italian and Spanish? In order to provide parts of an answer to this question, we ran systematic searches in *Google Livres* (1500–1900), retrieving the forms *sarebbe/saria, avrebbe/avria* and *estaría, habría* in combination with *secondo/según X*.[34]

For Italian, we were able, it seems, to push back this dating to 1550 (Kronning 2013ab). The instances of the RC prior to the 19th century that we have been able to find primarily come from scientific or historical discourse. Thus, our first attestation of the RC in Italian is found from the pen of the famous geographer Ramusio (1485–1557) (48):

(48) *Conciosia cosa che il paese intermedio fra il Nilo & il detto porto sia largo da cento venti miglia, che* ***saria secondo l'opiniõ di Strabone*** *vna distanza di sei in sette giornate.* (Giovanni Battista Ramusio, 1550, *Primo volume delle navigationi e viaggi nel qval si contiene la descrittione dell'Africa*, Venetia: Gli Heredi di Lvcantonio Civnti, p. 400)
'Because the territory between the Nile and the aforementioned port is a hundred and twenty miles, which *be*-RC.3sg, in Strabo's opinion, a distance of six to seven days' journey.'

Searching for instances of the conditional combined with discourse frames such as *selon X*, *secondo X*, and *según X* is not an infallible way to single out RCs, for, in this context, the conditional can also receive a hypothetical interpretation (Kronning 2013a: 225–226, 2013b: 135–136; Rossari 2009). It seems, moreover, that the conditional in combination with a discourse frame like *secondo X* could also – as still is the case in Spanish[35] – be interpreted as a transposition, in a past context, of the non-mirative Inferential Future, called "conjectural" (*Adesso saranno le quattro* 'Now *be*-IF.3pl four o'clock'). Such a transposition is attested in indirect speech in the past up to Manzoni (Squartini 2002). Now, in (48), the conditional is found in a present context (*sia*), and the reference time of the epistemic mediation – the borrowing of cognitive content from Strabo – seems to be simultaneous

34 Of course, an in-depth diachronic study of the RC would require that all instances of the conditional (of all verbs) be taken into account, including those that are not accompanied by a lexical marker of "borrowing" (*secondo/según X*).
35 Cf. (12) above.

to the utterance time, since the opinion of Strabo is pertinent in the *hic et nunc* of the speaker-writer (Ramusio).

For Spanish, we were only able, by searching *Google Livres*, to push back the dating to the middle of the 19th century (23).

However, using CORDE (*Corpus diacrónico del español*), we could retrieve some probable instances of the RC from the early 16th century (cf. Kronning 2014a: 82–84), including (49a):

(49) a. [...] *un solo fraile* [Luther] [...] *nos quiera pervertir y hacer conocer según su opinión que toda la dicha cristiandad* ***sería y habría estado*** *todas horas en error.* [...] *Hecho en Bormes a 19 de abril en 1521. De mi mano. Yo el Rey.* (Fray Prudencio de Sandoval. 1604–1618. *Historia de la vida y hechos del Emperador Carlos V.* Alicante: Universidad de Alicante, 2003. CORDE)

b. *toute ladite crestienité* ***seroit*** *et* ***auroit*** *tousjours* ***esté*** *en erreur* (Fr. orig.)[36]

c. *tutta laditta christianità* ***staria*** *e* ***saria*** *sempre* ***stata*** *in errore* (It. transl.)[37]
'a sole brother wants to corrupt us and makes known in accordance with his understanding that all of the aforementioned Christendom *be*-RC.3sg and always *have*-RC.3sg (it. *be*-RC.3sg) *been* deluded. [...] Signed in Worms 19 April 1521. In own hand. I, the king.'

In this example (49a), where Charles V (1500–1558), as emperor of the Holy Roman Empire and king of Spain, defends Catholic doctrine and rebels against the ideas of Luther, the epistemic conditional, being in a present context, probably denotes reportive – and not inferential – evidentiality, given that the Inferential Conditional (IC) is only used in Spanish, as we have pointed out (see Section 2.2), in a past context.[38]

---

36 Quoted by Escamilla, Michèle. 2007. Charles Quint: un Quichotte historique ? In Estrella Ruiz-Galvez Priego & Gilles Groult (eds.), *Don Quijote de la Mancha dans la Manche*, 18. Paris: L'Harmattan.

37 Quoted in *Martin Luther und die Reformationsbewegung in Deutschland vom Jahre 1520–1532 in Auszügen aus Marino Sanuto's Diarien.* Ansbach: C. Brügel, 1883, p. 18.

38 The context also excludes a temporal interpretation ("the future in the past") of the conditional forms. Likewise, a hypothetical (counterfactual) interpretation of these verb forms seems less probable, because the prepositional phrase *según su opinión* is less readily conceived as the protasis ('if we were to subscribe to his opinion') of a hypothetical (predictive) relation than prepositional phrases such as *according to this theory* and *according to this doctrine* ('if one adopted this theory'), and because the phrase *según su opinión* is syntactically related to the reporting verb *hacer conocer* of the matrix phrase and not to the subordinated clause it embeds.

Now, Charles V "wrote [this] declaration against Luther in the French language, on 19 April 1521" and "its publication was planned not only in French but also in Latin, in Italian, in German, in Spanish, and in Dutch" (Braun 2010: 237). Consequently, this example allows us in principle to push back the dating of the RC in French (49b) and in Italian (49c) as well as in Spanish (49a) to the early 16th century – in Spanish, however, on the condition that the historian Prudencio de Sandoval (1552–1620) did not translate the declaration of Charles V himself.

The diachronic evidence thus seems to indicate that the emergence of the RC goes back to (at least) the 16th century, in French and Italian as well as in Spanish. Without more precise and exhaustive data collection, it is not possible to settle the question whether the RC is, as might be suggested by (49a–49c), a Gallicism in Italian and in Spanish – an idea that, as we have seen, underpins the purist normative discourse in Spain – or whether this usage of the conditional is the result of Romance polygenesis.

4 Conclusion

In describing the syntactic, semantic and discursive properties of the Reportive Conditional, as well as its rhetorical functions, which seem to be the same in French, Italian and Spanish, we have sought to find arguments in favour of our analysis of this epistemic marker, whereby it is a *bicategorial grammatical marker* expressing *reportive evidentiality* and *zero modalization* (the refusal to epistemically endorse the cognitive content of the utterance).

We have put forward arguments against the notion that the RC is a simple "pragmatic inference" or "evidential strategy". In our view, there is good reason to treat the RC as a *grammatical marker*, although "evidentiality" is not an obligatory grammatical category in Romance, which is generally considered, in linguistic typology, a necessary condition for a marker of evidential interpretation to be regarded as belonging, in this use, to the grammar of a language.

By drawing attention to the possibility of expressing a variable epistemic attitude – dubitative or non-dubitative – outside the *mediation domain* established by the RC, we have provided a powerful argument against the hypothesis according to which the RC is a *modal marker* expressing an invariably dubitative epistemic attitude.

Besides its function of reducing the speaker's utterance responsibility the RC can fulfil – owing to the zero modalization it denotes – a text-organizational function, allowing the speaker to evoke someone else's point of view without epistemically endorsing it in order to refute or confirm it in the subsequent discourse. By signalling this possibility we have provided a strong argument against the hypothesis that the RC is a *purely evidential marker* that does not include 'non-commitment' in its distinctive semantic content (its *sémantisme propre*).

If it is important to distinguish epistemic modalization from evidentiality (or epistemic mediation) conceptually, although they are often conveyed simultaneously by one and the same bicategorial marker, it is equally vital to distinguish *reportive evidentiality* from *reported speech* (or *enunciative mediation*). We have attempted to show that discourse frame constructions (*Selon X, [p]*), often regarded as "evidential", falls by default under the reported speech category "discourse frame embedded indirect speech". Under certain conditions, this interpretation can be cancelled in favour of the reportive evidentiality interpretation, uniquely by the RC.

By contrasting the use of verbal forms in the indicative other than the RC with the RC in these constructions, we have hypothesized that these two types of verbal forms denote two degrees of intensity of non-commitment towards the mediated eventuality: the indicative (apart from the RC) expresses the *absence of epistemic commitment* towards the mediated eventuality, whereas the RC denotes *zero modalization*, which, signifying an actual refusal to epistemically endorse the eventuality, performs a more emphatic epistemic distancing on the part of the speaker.

This hypothesis is corroborated by one of the *discourse functions* of the RC that we have identified.[39] The use of verbal morphology in the discourse frame constructions studied here can be exploited rhetorically to form a *binary ascending gradation* (indicative vs. RC) in accordance with the intensity of the epistemic distancing.

From the point of view of *variation*, we have attempted to show that the widely held notion that the use of the RC is restricted to journalistic discourse is erroneous, although the RC is indeed common in that discourse genre. In fact, though it is primarily characteristic of journalistic, historical and scientific discourse genres, there is nothing exceptional about the RC in literary discourse in French, in Italian and in Latin-American Spanish; it is even attestable, though rare, in informal conversational discourse, at least as this is recreated by authors and translators (50–51), no doubt owing to the diaphasic flexibility (Gadet 2003), the diaphasic properties of a marker being renegotiable by the interactants in the discourse:

39 For some other discourse functions of the RC, see Kronning (2012: 91–94).

(50) a. *– enfin* [...] *d'après ce qu'elle nen* [sic] *dit dans son cahier intime il* ***serait*** *beau comme je sais pas quoi, son cahier que j'ai un peu lu dedans c'est pas indiscrétion* (Cohen, Albert. 1968. *Belle du Seigneur.* Paris: Gallimard, Folio, p. 643.)
'– anyway [...] from what she says about him in her private diary he *be*-RC.3sg as handsome as I don't know what, her diary that I read little bits of that ain't no indiscretion'

b. *«comunque* [...] *secondo quelle che dice lei nel suo quaderno intimo* ***sarebbe*** *bello come chissacché, il quaderno che ho letto un tantino che non è mica indiscrezione* [...]*»* (It. trans.)

(51) a. *Elle a beaucoup d'amants, c'est de ça que vous vous souvenez ... – Je crois ...* [...] *– Il y en a eu un, très jeune, il se* ***serait tué*** *pour elle ... je ne sais pas bien.* (Duras, Marguerite. 1991. *L'amant de la Chine du Nord.* Paris: Gallimard, Folio, p. 40)
'She has many lovers, is that what you remember... – I think so ... [...] there was one, very young, he's *said to have killed* himself for her...I don't really know.'

b. *–Hubo uno, muy joven, se* ***habría matado*** *por ella ... no sé muy bien.* (Sp. trans.)

Primarily associated, in the Romance varieties treated here, with "serious" genres – journalism, history and science – the RC is diaphasically oriented towards the elevated, that is towards lofty or formal registers.

On the other hand, there are conflicting diaphasic norms in peninsular Spanish inasmuch as the RC can be "perceived"[40] as being oriented towards the elevated as well as towards the quotidian. Thus, in one part of the peninsular press, the RC is perceived as oriented towards the formal, whereas in another part of the peninsular press, and, in a particularly strong and significant manner, in peninsular literary discourse, the RC is subject to a purist normative discourse that considers the RC to be a Gallicism to be avoided and thus, when used (51b), as diaphasically oriented towards the quotidian. This discourse is not univocally supported by diachronic facts, as the RC seems to have emerged in the 16th century in French as well as in Italian and Spanish.

Abbreviations: DFIS – Discourse Frame embedded Indirect Speech;
EM – Epistemic Marker; Fr. – French; IC – Inferential Conditional;

40 Cf. Moreno Fernández 2012.

IF – Inferential Future; IS – Indirect Speech; It. – Italian; orig. – original; RC – Reportive Conditional; RC.3sg – Reportive Conditional third person singular; RS – Reported Speech; Sp. – Spanish; t_0 – utterance time; t'_0 – reference time in the past; trans. – translation; + – or; {...} – mediation domain; [...] – (after *Selon X*, 'According to X') discourse frame; <...> – embedded utterance.

References

Abouda, Lotfi. 2001. Les emplois journalistique, polémique et atténuatif du conditionnel. In Patrick Dendale & Liliane Tasmowski (eds.), *Le conditionnel en français*, 277–294. Paris: Klincksieck.

Adam, Jean-Michel. 1999. *Linguistique textuelle. Des genres de discours aux textes*. Paris: Nathan.

Aikhenvald, Alexandra Y. 2004. *Evidentiality*. Oxford: OUP.

Anderson, Loyd B. 1986. Evidentials, Paths of Change, and Mental Maps. In Wallace Chafe & Johanna Nichols (eds.), *Evidentiality: the Linguistic Coding of Epistemology*, 261–272. Norwood, NJ: Ablex.

Anscombre, Jean-Claude (ed.). 1995. *Théorie des topoï*. Paris: Kimé.

Anscombre, Jean-Claude, Evelyne Oppermann-Marsaux & Amalia Rodríguez Somolinos (eds.). 2014. *Médiativité, polyphonie et modalité en français. Études synchroniques et diachroniques*. Paris: Presses Sorbonne Nouvelle.

Authier-Revuz, Jacqueline. 2004. La représentation du discours autre: un champ multiplement hétérogène. In Juan Manuel Lopez Muños, Sophie Marnette & Laurence Rosier (eds.), *Le discours rapporté dans tous ses états*, 35–53. Paris: L'Harmattan.

Baeyen, Lien. 2012. *Le conditionnel épistémique dans les textes juridiques du XVIe siècle*. Antwerp: Universiteit Antwerpen MA thesis.

Bermúdez, Fernando. 2016. Rumores y otros malos hábitos. El condicional de evidencia en español. *Cuadernos de Lingüística de El Colegio de México* 3 (2). 35–69.

Berruto, Gaetano. 1993. La varietà del reportorio. In Alberto A. Sobrero (ed.) 2004[2], *Introduzione all'italiano contemporaneo. La variazione e gli usi*, 3–36. Roma-Bari: Laterza.

Böhm, Verónica & Anja Henneman. 2014. The Evidential Use of the Spanish Imperfect and Conditional in Journalistic Contexts, *Studia Neophilologica* LXXXVI:2. 183–200.

Braun, Guido. 2010. *La connaissance du Saint-Empire en France du baroque aux Lumières 1643–1756*. Munich: Oldenbourg.

Bres, Jacques. 2010. *Robert aurait pris sa retraite et passerait du bon temps* ... Du conditionnel *dit* journalistique. In Claire Maury-Rouan (ed.), *Regards sur le discours*, 15–33. Aix-en-Provence: Presses de l'Université de Provence.

Brown, Penelope & Stephen Levinson. 1978. *Politeness*. Cambridge: CUP.

Butt, John & Carmen Benjamin. 20003. *A new reference grammar of modern Spanish*. London: Arnold.

Charolles, Michel & Marie-Paule Péry-Woodley (eds.). 2005. *Les adverbiaux cadratifs. Langue française* 148.

Coltier, Danielle & Patrick Dendale. 2004. Discours rapporté et évidentialité: comparaison du conditionnel et des constructions en *selon N*. In Juan Manuel Lopez Muños, Sophie

Marnette & Laurence Rosier (eds.), *Le discours rapporté dans tous ses états*, 587–597. Paris: L'Harmattan.

Coseriu, Eugenio. 1969 [1952]. Sistema, norma e 'parola'. In *Studi in onore di Vittore Pisani*, I, 235–233. Brecia: Paideia.

Damourette, Jacques & Édouard Pichon. 1911–1940. *Des mots à la pensée. Essai de grammaire de la langue française*. I–VII. Paris: D'Artrey.

Dendale, Patrick. 2010. *Il serait à Paris en ce moment. Serait-il à Paris ?* A propos de deux emplois épistémiques du conditionnel. Grammaire, syntaxe, sémantique. In Camino Álvarez Castro, Flor Mª Bango de la Campa & Maria Luisa Donaire (eds.), *Liens linguistiques. Études sur la combinatoire et la hiérarchie des composants*, 291–317. Bern: Peter Lang.

Dendale, Patrick & Danielle Coltier. 2012. La lente reconnaissance du 'conditionnel de reprise' par les grammaires du français. In Bernard Colombat, Jean-Marie Fournier & Valérie Raby (eds.), *Vers une histoire générale de la grammaire française*, 631–652. Paris: Champion.

DeLancey, Scott. 2012. Still mirative after all these years. *Linguistic Typology* 16. 529–564.

Desclés, Jean-Pierre. 2009. Prise en charge, engagement et désengagement. *Langue française* 162. 29–53.

Desclés, Jean-Pierre & Zlatka Guentchéva. 2013. L'abduction dans l'analyse sémantique. In Coco Norén, Kerstin Jonasson, Henning Nølke & Maria Svensson (eds.), *Modalité, évidentialité et autres friandises langagières. Mélanges offerts à Hans Kronning à l'occasion de ses soixante ans*, 81–102. Bern: Peter Lang.

Ducrot, Oswald. 1984. *Le dire et le dit*. Paris: Minuit.

Gadet, Françoise. 2003. *La variation sociale en français*. Paris: Ophrys.

Glessgen, Martin-Dietrich. 2007. *Linguistique romane*. Paris: Armand Colin.

Gosselin, Laurent. 2001. Relations temporelles et modales dans le « conditionnel journalistique ». In Patrick Dendale & Liliane Tasmowski (eds.), *Le conditionnel en français*, 45–66. Paris: Klincksieck.

Gosselin, Laurent. 2005. *Temporalité et modalité*. Brussels: Duculot.

Gosselin, Laurent. 2010. *Les modalités en français*. Amsterdam & New York: Rodopi.

Gougenheim, Georges. 1938. *Système grammatical de la langue française*. Paris: D'Artrey.

Guentchéva, Zlatka. 1994. Manifestations de la catégorie du médiatif dans les temps du français. *Langue française* 102. 8–23.

Guentchéva, Zlatka. 2004. La notion de médiation dans la diversité des langues. In Régine Delamotte-Legrand (ed.), *La Médiation*, I, 10–33. Rouen: Publications de l'Université de Rouen.

Guentchéva, Zlatka. 2014. Peut-on identifier, et comment, les marqueurs dits 'médiatifs' ? In Jean-Claude Anscombre, Evelyne Oppermann-Marsaux & Amalia Rodríguez Somolinos (eds.), *Médiativité, polyphonie et modalité en français. Études synchroniques et diachroniques*, 35–50. Paris: Presses Sorbonne Nouvelle.

Haillet, Pierre Patrick. 2002. *Le conditionnel en français*. Paris: Ophrys.

Huddleston, Rodney & Geoffrey K. Pullum. 2002. *The Cambridge Grammar of the English Language*. Cambridge: CUP.

Johansson, Stig. 2007. *Seeing trough Multilingual Corpora. On the use of corpora in contrastive studies*. Amsterdam / Philadelphia: Benjamins.

Korzen, Hanne & Henning Nølke. 2001. Le conditionnel: niveaux de modalisation. In Patrick Dendale & Liliane Tasmowski (eds.), *Le conditionnel en français*, 125–146. Paris: Klincksieck.

Kronning, Hans. 2002. Le conditionnel 'journalistique': médiation et modalisation épistémiques. *Romansk forum* 16, 2. 561–575.

Kronning, Hans. 2003. Modalité et évidentialité. In Merete Birkelund, Gerhard Boysen & Poul Søren Kjærsgaard (eds.), *Aspects de la Modalité*, 131–151. Tübingen: Max Niemeyer.

Kronning, Hans. 2004. Kunskapens källa och kunskapens styrka. Epistemisk konditionalis i franskan som evidentiellt och modalt grammatiskt uttryck [The source of knowledge and the strength of knowledge. The epistemic conditional in French as an evidential and modal grammatical expression]. In *Annales Societatis Litterarum Humaniorum Regiae Upsaliensis 2002*, 43–123. Uppsala: Swedish Science Press.

Kronning, Hans. 2005. Polyphonie, médiation et modalisation: le cas du conditionnel épistémique. In Jacques Bres, Pierre Patrick Haillet, Sylvie Mellet, Henning Nølke & Laurence Rosier (eds.), *Dialogisme et polyphonie*, 297–312. Brussels: De Boeck Duculot.

Kronning, Hans. 2007. Les auxiliaires médiatifs en suédois à la lumière du conditionnel épistémique et du futur aléthique en français. In Louis Begioni & Claude Muller (eds.), *Problèmes de sémantique et de syntaxe. Hommage à André Rousseau*, 287–309. Lille: Éditions du Conseil Scientifique de l'Université Charles-de-Gaule – Lille 3.

Kronning, Hans. 2009a. Polyphonie, constructions conditionnelles et discours rapporté. *Langue française* 164. 97–112.

Kronning, Hans. 2009b. Constructions conditionnelles et attitude épistémique en français, en italien et en espagnol. *Syntaxe & Sémantique* 10. 13–32.

Kronning, Hans. 2009c. Talarens ansvar för sitt yttrande. Om epistemiska uttryck i de romanska språken [The Speaker's responsibility for his utterance. On epistemic expressions in the Romance languages]. *Kungl. Vitterhetsakademien / Académie Royale Suédoise des Belles-Lettres, de l'Histoire et des Antiquités. Årsbok 2009*. 177–199.

Kronning, Hans. 2010. Prise en charge épistémique et non-concordance des temps dans le discours indirect (libre) en français, en italien et en espagnol. *Sens Public, Les Cahiers* 13–14. 19–33.

Kronning, Hans. 2012. Le conditionnel épistémique: propriétés et fonctions discursives. *Langue française* 173. 83–97.

Kronning, Hans. 2013a. Le conditionnel épistémique *riportivo* en italien. *Arena Romanistica* 13. 210–235.

Kronning, Hans. 2013b. Il condizionale epistemico di attribuzione in italiano. *La lingua italiana. Storia, strutture, testi* IX. 125–142.

Kronning, Hans. 2013c. Ducrot et Wittgenstein: le 'dit', le 'montré' et le *logos apophantikos*. In Françoise Sullet-Nylander, Hugues Engel & Gunnel Engwall (eds.), *La linguistique dans tous les sens*, 165–177. Stockholm: Académie Royale Suédoise des Belles-Lettres, de l'Histoire et des Antiquités.

Kronning, Hans. 2013d. Monstration, véridiction et polyphonie. Pour une théorie modale de la polyphonie. In Hugues de Chanay, Marion Colas-Blaise & Odile Le Guern (eds.), *Dire / Montrer. Au cœur du sens*, 93–115. Chambéry: Université de Savoie, Coll. Langages.

Kronning, Hans. 2014a. Pour une linguistique contrastive variationnelle: le conditionnel épistémique d''emprunt' en français, en italien et en espagnol. In Hans Petter Helland & Christine Mecklenborg Salvesen (eds.), *Affaire(s) de grammaire. Mélanges offerts à Marianne Hobæk Haff à l'occasion de ses soixante-cinq ans*, 67–90. Oslo: Novus.

Kronning, Hans. 2014b. La théorie modale de la polyphonie et les conditionnelles prédictives en *si*. *Langages* 193. 17–31.

Kronning, Hans. 2015. El condicional epistémico de «attribución» en francés, italiano y español: aspectos diafásicos, diatópicos y diacrónicos. In Jan Lindschouw & Kirsten Jeppesen Kragh (eds.), *Les variations diasystématiques dans les langues romanes et leurs interdépendances* (TraLiRo), 507–518. Strasbourg: Éditions de linguistique et de philologie.
Lazard, Gilbert. 2000. Le médiatif: considérations théoriques et application à l'iranien. In Lars Johanson & Bo Utas (eds.), *Evidentials: Turkish, Iranian and Neighbouring Languages*, 209–228. Berlin & New York: Mouton de Gruyter.
Masini, Andrea. 1977. *La lingua di alcuni giornali milanesi dal 1859 al 1865*. Florence: La Nuova Italia.
Moreno Fernández, Francisco. 2012. *Sociolingüística cognitiva*. Madrid & Frankfurt: Iberoamericana & Vervuert.
Nueva gramática de la lengua española, I–II. 2009. Real Academia Española & Asociación de Academias de la lengua española. Madrid: Espasa.
Nueva gramática de la lengua española. Manual. 2010. Real Academia Española & Asociación de Academias de la lengua española. Madrid: Espasa.
Pană Dindelegan, Gabriela (ed.). 2013. *The Grammar of Romanian*. Oxford: OUP.
Patota, Giuseppe. 2006. *Grammatica di riferimento dell'italiano contemporaneo*. Novara: Garzanti.
Petitta, Giulia. 2006. Sull'origine del condizionale di dissociazione. *Studi linguistici italiani* XXXII.2. 246–276.
Popescu, Mihaela. 2011. Le 'conditionnel journalistique' dans le discours médiatique roumain. *Analele Universităţii din Craiova, Seria Ştiinţe Filologice, Lingvistică* 1–2. 226–238.
Provôt-Olivier, Agnès. 2011. *Le conditionnel en français et ses équivalents en allemand*. Université Paris IV Sorbonne dissertation.
Provôt-Olivier, Agnès & Jean-Pierre Desclés. 2012. Existe-t-il un 'conditionnel médiatif' en français ?, *Faits de langues* XL. 45–52.
Ramat, Paolo. 1996. *Allegedly, John is ill again*: stratégies pour le médiatif. In Zlatka Guentchéva (ed.), *L'énonciation médiatisée*, 287–298. Louvain-Paris: Peeters.
Rastier, François. 2011. *La mesure et le grain. Sémantique de corpus*. Paris: Champion.
Rocci, Andrea. 2005. *La modalità epistemica tra semantica e argomentazione*. Milan: I.S.U. Università Cattolica.
Rossari, Corinne. 2009. Le conditionnel dit épistémique signale-t-il un emprunt ? , *Tranel* 51. 75–96.
Sarrazin, Sophie. 2010. Le conditionnel journalistique espagnol: du modèle français aux nouveaux usages. *Cahiers de l'Association for French Language Studies*, 16.1. 99–128.
Seco, Manuel. 1998[10]. *Diccionario de dudas y dificultades de la lengua española*. Madrid: Espasa Calpe.
Serianni, Luca. 1989. *Grammatica italiana. Italiano comune e lingua letteraria*. Torino: UTET.
Solà, Joan, Maria Rosa Lloret, Joan Mascaró & Manuel Pérez Saldanya (eds.). 2002. *Gramàtica del català contemporani I–III*. Barcelona: Empúries.
Squartini, Mario. 2001. The internal structure of evidentiality in Romance. *Studies in language* 25. 297–334.
Squartini, Mario. 2002. Futuro e Condizionale nel discorso riportato. In Gian Luigi Beccaria & Carla Marello (eds.), *La parola al testo. Scritte per Bice Mortara Garavelli*, 451–462. Alessandria: Edizioni dell'Orso.
Squartini, Mario. 2004. La relazione semantica tra Futuro e Condizionale nelle lingue romanze. *Revue Romane* 39. 68–96.

Sullet-Nylander, Françoise. 2005. De l'emploi du conditionnel journalistique: du titre à l'article et de l'article au titre. *Le Monde* 2005. http://www.rucsdigitaleprojektbibliotek.dk

Sullet-Nylander, Françoise. 2013. De l'emploi du conditionnel journalistique et du discours rapporté dans quatre journaux – français et suédois – au cours de "l'affaire DSK" (mai-août 2011). In Coco Norén, Kerstin Jonasson, Henning Nølke & Maria Svensson (eds.), *Modalité, évidentialité et autres friandises langagières. Mélanges offerts à Hans Kronning à l'occasion de ses soixante ans*, 291–309. Bern: Peter Lang.

Vatrican, Axelle. 2010. La modalité et le 'conditionnel de rumeur' en français et en espagnol. *Modèles linguistiques* XXXI (62). 83–94.

Wiemer, Björn. 2010. Hearsay in European languages: toward an integrative account of grammatical and lexical marking. In Gabriele Diewald & Elena Smirnova (eds.), *Linguistic Realization of Evidentiality in European Languages*, 59–130. Berlin & New York: De Gruyter Mouton.

Brenda Laca

Epistemic modality and perfect morphology in Spanish and French

Abstract: In current approaches to the interaction between modality and temporality, there has been widespread consensus as to the fact that, in epistemic readings, modal verbs outscope tense and aspect (Condoravdi 2001, Hacquard 2006, Demirdache & Uribe-Etxeberria 2006, 2008 among many others). This generalization, which is semantic in nature, conflicts with the actual realization of tense-aspect morphology on epistemically interpreted modal verbs, a regular phenomenon in languages in which modal verbs are transparently and fully inflected for TMA categories. Among these, the Romance languages figure prominently, and they have provided a number of researchers with evidence against the hypothesis according to which epistemic modals outscope tense and aspect (Boogart 2007, Mari 2015, Homer 2010, Martin 2011). In this contribution, I will concentrate on the interaction between modals and perfect morphology in French and Spanish, which can be shown to vary in an intriguing way.

The article is organized as follows: section 1 provides an introduction to temporal configurations in modal environments and to the characterization of epistemic readings; section 2 gives an overview of the interpretation of epistemic modals bearing past morphology; section 3 is devoted to the contrast between higher perfects and perfect infinitives in French and Spanish; section 4 concludes.

Keywords: modal verbs, tense, aspect, epistemic readings, perfect

1 Introduction: Temporal configurations and epistemic readings

Interactions between modal verbs and tense-aspect morphology are extremely complex, and give rise to interpretive patterns that constitute a challenge to compositional approaches to interpretation; in fact, they look at first sight like instances of morphology gone awry. Such patterns, which are illustrated for Spanish below, comprise (i) multiple ambiguities, (ii) apparently redundant morphology, (iii) apparently equivalent different linearizations, and (iv) unexpected morphological equivalences.

Brenda Laca, University Paris 8

https://doi.org/10.1515/9783110572261-005

(i) Multiple ambiguities

As shown by the English paraphrases, a sentence like (1), with a modal in the simple (perfective) past, has at least three distinct readings, which are arguably associated with different temporal configurations

(1) *El ladrón pudo entrar por la ventana.*
the thief CAN.SP enter by the window
(i) The thief was able/managed to come in through the window. (IMPLICATIVE READING)
(ii) The thief had the opportunity/possibility to come in through the window (but he didn't). (COUNTERFACTUAL READING)
(iii) As far as I know, it might have been the case that the thief came in through the window. (EPISTEMIC READING)

(ii) Redundant morphology

When a modal in the simple (perfective) past embeds a perfect infinitive, the sentences thus obtained (cf. (2)) preserve the counterfactual and epistemic readings of the sentences lacking a perfect infinitive, only the implicative reading disappears. For the admissible readings, perfect morphology on the infinitive seems to be redundant (see Bosque 1999).

(2) El ladrón pudo haber entrado por la ventana.
the thief CAN.sp have entered by the window
(i) The thief had the opportunity/possibility to come in through the window (but he didn't). (COUNTERFACTUAL READING)
(ii) As far as I know, it might have been the case that the thief came in through the window. (EPISTEMIC READING)

(iii) Equivalent linearizations

In the presence of conditional morphology, the site of realization of perfect morphology (on the modal in (3a) or on the infinitive in (3b)) does not seem to affect interpretation. For all practical purposes, (3a) and (3b) are synonymous.

(3) a. *María habría podido quedarse en México.*
M. have.COND CAN.PP stay-REFL in Mexico
b. *María podría haberse quedado en México.*
M. CAN.cond have-REFL stayed in Mexico
'María could have stayed in Mexico'

(iv) Unexpected morphological equivalences

As all Romance languages, Spanish exhibits a very clear semantic contrast between the simple (perfective) past and the imperfect. However, in the counterfactual reading, which is the only one admitted by the context for sentences (4a) and (4b), both containing a perfect infinitive, this contrast seems to be neutralized.

(4) *Ella no te encerró con mil cerrojos. La casa estaba abierta.*
'She didn't lock you under a thousand locks. The door was open'
a. *Tú pudiste haber escapado.*
you CAN.SP have escaped
b. *Tú podías haber escapado.*
you CAN.IMPF have escaped
'You could have escaped'

These patterns indicate that modal verbs interact with tense and aspect in a peculiar way, which is not paralleled by any other lexical items. As we will see, in the case of epistemic readings, which are the focus of this paper, it has been argued that this interaction is constrained by the impossibility of obtaining epistemic readings in certain temporal configurations, and by the near-obligatoriness of epistemic readings in certain other temporal configurations.

Temporal configurations in modal environments are more complex than they are in non-modal environments, because the former must determine not only the temporal location of the event or situation described in the sentence, but also the temporal location of the time of modal evaluation.[1] Modalized sentences are interpreted against a background of possibilities (a set of worlds constituting the domain of quantification for the modal operator, henceforth modal base, see Kratzer 1981, Kaufmann, Condoravdi and Harizanov 2006; Portner 2009 among many others), and possibilities change (actually diminish) with the flow of events in time. Just as the occurrence of any new event eliminates from a circumstantial/metaphysical modal base all the worlds in which the event does not occur, the acquisition of a piece of propositional knowledge eliminates from an epistemic modal base all the worlds in which the proposition is not verified. Thus, modal bases change inexorably with time, and the point in time from which a modal base is accessed (the time of modal evaluation) is never indifferent.

1 As stated in Laca (2014), the complexity arises from the fact that this double temporal location has to be determined in monoclausal structures which, as such, have only one Tense projection.

Condoravdi (2001) has considerably contributed to clarifying the issue of temporal configurations in modal environments by distinguishing what she calls the temporal perspective (**Tpersp**) of the clause from its temporal orientation (**Torient**). **Tpersp** is a relationship between the time of modal evaluation (Tmod) and the highest anchor for tense, which is generally speech time (S) in main clauses and the time of the matrix (Tmatrix) in the object clauses of attitude verbs. **Torient** is the relationship between the time of the described situation/ of the prejacent proposition (Tprej) and Tmod.[2] Thus, sentences (5a) and (5b) both illustrate a past temporal orientation and a simultaneous temporal perspective, the difference between them being that in (5b) Tmod is simultaneous with Tmatrix, which is itself past.

(5) a. *He must have left early.*

TPersp: Tmod SIMUL S
TOrien: Tprej BEFORE Tmod

b. *She thought that he must have left early.*

Tmatrix BEFORE S
TPersp: Tmod SIMUL Tmatrix
TOrien: Tprej BEFORE Tmod

Such temporal configurations almost invariably give rise to epistemic readings. The explanation that may be invoked for this constraint has to do with the fact that past and present issues are objectively decided at the time of evaluation, whereas only the future contains open possibilities. Whenever the issue whether the prejacent is true or false is already objectively decided at Tmod, only the subjective uncertainty that goes hand in hand with epistemic readings is apt to ensure that the modal base is p-diverse, i.e. that it contains both worlds which verify the prejacent and worlds which don't. P-diversity is a pragmatic constraint on modal bases (and as such it may be circumvented in some cases), arguably motivated by a number of semantic anomalies that arise with non-p-diverse domains (cf. Condoravdi 2001, Werner 2003).

On the other hand, certain temporal configurations exclude epistemic readings. This is clearly the case in sentence (6a), which has a future temporal per-

2 Following a suggestion by von Fintel (2005), we call 'prejacent' the proposition which is the argument of the modal verb, i.e. the modalized proposition minus the modal expression. Some authors have suggested that a third relationship might be necessary in order to account for certain interpretations (Laca 2012; Martin 2011).

spective and a future temporal orientation, and in (6b), which has a past temporal perspective and a future temporal orientation. Both sentences can only receive a root interpretation (obligation, requirement and the like):

(6) a. *He'll have to leave early.* **TPersp**: Tmod AFTER S
TOrien: Tprej AFTER Tmod

b. *He had to leave early.* **TPersp**: Tmod BEFORE S
TOrien: Tprej AFTER Tmod

In fact, syntactic approaches have claimed for the best part of three decades that the difference between epistemic and root modals is a difference in scope, with epistemic modals outscoping other operators, most notably tense and/or aspect (Picallo 1990, Cinque 1999, Butler 2004, Hacquard 2006). Semantic approaches, by contrast, claim that the unavailability of epistemic readings for (6a–b) is due to the fact that epistemic readings have to be anchored to the *now* of the relevant epistemic agent, which normally coincides with the speaker in main sentences (Papafragou 2006, Boogaart 2007). Only a simultaneous temporal perspective could guarantee this anchoring.

The generalizations that emerge are thus:

1. Epistemic readings are the only available option when the temporal orientation is past or simultaneous (i.e. when the truth value of the prejacent is decided at the time of modal evaluation). The modals in examples (5a–b) can only have an epistemic reading because, their temporal orientation being past, the truth value of the prejacent is objectively decided at Tmod, and the requirement of p-diversity can only be fulfilled by the uncertainty of an epistemic agent as to this truth value.
2. Epistemic readings are impossible when the temporal perspective is not simultaneous. The modals in examples (6a–b) cannot have an epistemic reading because their temporal perspective is future, resp. past.

These generalizations can only be tested without circularity if we have a precise understanding of what epistemic readings are.

First and foremost, epistemic readings rely on the epistemic uncertainty of the relevant epistemic agent(s), and they are excluded whenever there is direct evidence for the truth of the prejacent (von Fintel & Gillies 2007). Thus, (7) is acceptable in context (A), but it is not adequate in context (B):

(7) *It must be raining outside.*

A. Speaker sees people entering the buiding with umbrellas and wet shoes.

#B. Speaker looks out of the window and sees the rain.

In epistemic readings, universal (necessity) modals mean that the prejacent is inferrable from the available evidence/from what is known and what is believed by the relevant epistemic agent. In fact, most assertions containing universal epistemic modals express abductive inferences (Desclés & Guentcheva 2001), though deductive and inductive (probabilistic) inferences are not impossible. Existential (possibility) modals mean that the prejacent is not incompatible with the available evidence/with what is known or believed by the relevant epistemic agent.

(8) a. *It must be raining outside.*
'From the available evidence, Speaker concludes that it is raining outside'.
b. *It may be raining outside.*
'From the available evidence, Speaker cannot conclude that it isn't raining outside'

One of the most reliable tests for epistemic readings is the naturalness of continuations with tags like *for all I know*, or *let's check*, which target the issue of the truth value of the prejacent (and not of the whole modalized proposition).

2 Epistemic readings and tense-aspect morphology

Generalization (2) above has received a syntactic explanation in line with the general tendency for epistemic modals to have wider scope than other operators. For some authors, epistemic modals obligatorily outscope tense and/or aspect either because they are base generated at a higher position (Picallo 1990; Butler 2004; Cinque 1999; Hacquard 2006) or as the result of movement (Demirdache and Uribe-Etxeberria 2006, 2008). This syntactic explanation is challenged by overtly realized and interpretable tense-aspect morphology on the modal verb.

So, for instance, cases in which the temporal perspective is simultaneous, but there are nonetheless interpretable morphological contrasts in tense-aspect morphology, show that a semantic-pragmatic account fares better than the syntactic explanation. The contrast between modals in the present tense and modals in the imperfect in embedded contexts in Romance languages is one of these cases. In fact, this contrast replicates an identical contrast in non-modalized sentences. In languages exhibiting sequence of tense, a present tense embedded under the past form of an attitude or speech-act verb gives rise to a so called "double-access" reading, in which the time of the complement clause is simultaneous to both the time of the attitude and to speech time. By contrast, an imperfect only requires simultaneity to the (past) time of the attitude. This is the reason why (9a) is strange, since it requires a duration of pregnancy which largely exceeds what world knowledge dictates, whereas (9b) is perfectly fine:

(9) a. # *Juan me dijo hace un año que María está embarazada.*
J. me tell.SP make a year that M. be.PRES pregnant
'Juan told me a year ago that Maria is pregnant'

b. *Juan me dijo hace un año que María estaba embarazada.*
J. me tell.SP make a year that M. be IMPF pregnant
'Juan told be a year ago that María was pregnant'

In languages exhibiting sequence of tense, present tense is deictic in nature, whereas there is a dedicated anaphoric tense, corresponding in Romance to the imperfect, which can express simultaneity to a past attitude. Now, this contrast is preserved when the complement clause contains an epistemic modal:

(10) a. #*Juan me dijo hace un año que María debe estar embarazada.*
J. me tell.SP make a year that M. MUST.PRES be pregnant
'Juan told me a year ago that María must be pregnant'

b. *Juan me dijo hace un año que María debía estar embarazada.*
J. me tell.SP make a year that M. MUST.IMPF be pregnant
'Juan told me a year ago that María must be pregnant'

From this we conclude – against the syntactic hypothesis – that modal verbs in epistemic readings may be dominated by a projection which at the very least distinguishes between a deictic and an anaphoric tense. This projection cannot but be the tense projection.[3]

3 See also Homer (2010), who argues in favor of the presence of tense above epistemic modals on the grounds of scopal interaction with other operators, such as negation. Homer's reasoning is the following: the epistemic existential modal *pouvoir* 'can' always scopes under negation, tense is known to scope above negation, so it follows by scope transitivity that the epistemic existential modal must scope under tense.

The anaphoric interpretation of imperfect morphology on an epistemic modal is also available in main clauses, i.e. in the absence of overt embedding under a past attitude verb. Thus, in (11a), it is the (past) thoughts of Marie when she checks the time that are being reported, and (11b) reports the (past) thoughts of the parents when learning about the facts:

(11) a. *Marie regarda sa montre. Il était très tard.* [FRENCH]

Pierre devait s'inquiéter de son absence.
Pierre MUST.IMPF REFL-worry of her absence
'Marie looked at her watch. It was very late. Pierre must be worrying that she was not there'

b. *Cuando los padres se enteraron, montaron en furia, la golpearon sin piedad y no le permitieron explicar los reales hechos.* [SPAN.]
Decididamente, la cosa tenía que haber sucedido tal como
decidedly the thing HAVE.IMPF that have happened such as

la gente decía. La culpa de todo debía tenerla ella.
the people say.IMPF the guilt of all MUST.IMPF have+it she.

[Dimas Aranda, S. *Tiempo de agonía*
<http://www.biblioteca.org.ar/libros/88623.pdf>]

'When the parents learned about it, they became furious, they beat her remorselessly and didn't let her explain the real facts. Definitely, the whole thing had to have happened as people were saying. Everything must have been her fault'

Boogaart (2007) has assimilated these cases to free indirect speech sentences, which reproduce the thoughts or the words of an epistemic agent at a past time.[4] Although Boogaart does not adopt the anaphoric or zero tense interpretation for the imperfect, he accurately observes that such interpretations involve a temporal perspective which is simultaneous to the *now* of the epistemic agent whose thoughts or words are being reproduced.

However, it can be shown that modals in the imperfect may also have epistemic readings in contexts in which the imperfect cannot possibly function

4 But see Homer (2010) for a different opinion, based on the fact that such examples do not comply with all the requirements for free indirect speech.

as an anaphoric or zero tense, most notably when embedded under a present tense form of an attitude verb:

(12) a.

Jean	*pense*	*que*	*à*	*ce*	*moment-là,*	*Marie*	*devait*
J.	think.PRES	that	to	that	moment-there	M.	MUST.IMPF

être	*enceinte.*	[FR]
be	pregnant.	

'Jean believes that Maria must have been pregnant at that time'

b.

Creo	*que,*	*en*	*aquella*	*época,*	*el*	*río*	*debía*
believe.PRES 1SG	that	in	that	time	the	river	MUST.IMPF

estar	*menos*	*contaminado*	que	hoy	en	día	[SPAN.]
be	less	contaminated	than	today	in	day	

'I think that at the time, the river must have been less polluted than it is nowadays.'

In (12a) and (12b), the relevant epistemic agent is the subject of the attitude (Jean in (12a), the Speaker in (12b)), and the relevant time is the time of the attitude, a time which coincides with speech time. These sentences are not reporting past, but present thoughts of the epistemic agent with regard to a past situation. The imperfect is functioning as a *bona fide* past tense, but it is not locating Tmod in the past, it is locating the described situation in the past. The temporal configuration of (12a) and (12b) combines a simultaneous temporal perspective with a past temporal orientation:

(13) Tmatrix SIMUL S

TPersp: Tmod SIMULTmatrix
TOrien: Tprej BEFORE Tmod

Now, the temporal configuration (13) attributed to (12a–b) is in accordance with generalizations (1) and (2) above: we obtain an epistemic reading with a simultaneous temporal perspective and a past temporal orientation. This temporal configuration, however, poses an evident compositionality problem: imperfect morphology is realized on the modal, but its past component affects temporal orientation, i.e. it locates the time of the prejacent. Attempts at solving this compositionality problem mostly involve scope inversion mechanisms (Tasmowski 1980; Stowell 2004; Borgonovo and Cummins 2007; Demirdache and Uribe-Etxeberria 2008 among others). We will not delve into the various mechanisms that have been proposed. It suffices to say that they all strive at aligning the overt structure represented in (14a) with the structure (14b), which best captures the temporal configuration of the epistemic interpretation:

(14) a. [TP [T impf [Modal [vP... OVERT SYNTACTIC STRUCTURE
b. Modal [T impf [vP... INTERPRETATION

The plausibility of analyses postulating that the particular past tense appearing on the modal originates or is interpreted in the prejacent, and not above the modal, is increased by an observation originally due to Tasmowski (1980)[5]: for an epistemic reading to emerge, the choice of the past tense form must coincide with the one that would be mandatory for the prejacent without the modal. Thus, a simple (perfective) past is the only acceptable choice in sentence (15a), and correspondingly, only the modalized sentence (15b), which replicates this choice on the modal, may have an epistemic interpretation.

(15) a. *Marie escribió/ *escribía esta novela en menos de un año.*
M. write.SP/ write.IMPF this novel in less of a year
'Marie wrote this novel in less than a year.'

b. *Marie debió escribir esta novela en menos de un año.* [√EPIST]
M. MUST.SP write this novel in less of a year
'Marie must have written this novel in less than a year.'

c. *Marie debía escribir esta novela en menos de un año.* [*EPIST]
M. MUST.IMPF write this novel in less of a year
'Marie had to write this novel in less than a year.'

The accuracy of Tasmowski's generalization has been recently questioned by Martin (2011) and Mari (2015), who argue:

(i) that there are clear counterexamples to it, in which the choice of past tense on the modal does not replicate the mandatory choice for the corresponding non-modalized sentences. This is the case with individual level states, which require an imperfect (16a) and do not allow the *passé composé* (16b), but can give rise to an epistemic reading when the modal verb is in the *passé composé* (16c):

5 See Borgonovo and Cummins (2007) for further evidence on the matching between tense-aspect morphology on the epistemic modal and in the corresponding unmodalized sentences.

(16) a. *Hélène avait les yeux bleus.*
H. have.IMPF the eyes blue
'Helène was blue-eyed'

b. **Hélène a eu les yeux bleus.*
H. have.PRES had the eyes blue
*'Hélène has been blue-eyed'

c. *Hélène a dû avoir les yeux bleus.*
H. have.PRES MUST.PP have the eyes blue
'Hélène must have been blue-eyed'

(ii) that sentences with an epistemic modal in the *passé composé* are not equivalent to sentences in which perfect morphology is realized on the infinitive, thus contradicting an apparent prediction of scope inversion mechanisms:

(17) a. *Il a pu être recompensé de la médaille Fields quand*
he have.PRES CAN.PP be awarded of the medal Fields when

il est rentré au CNRS
he be.PRES entered to+the CNRS

b. *Il peut avoir été recompensé de la médaille Fields quand il*
he CAN.PRES have been awarded of the medal Fields when he

est rentré au CNRS
be.PRES. entered to+the CNRS
'He may have been awarded the Fields medal when he joined the CNRS'

Both sentences allow for an interpretation in which the temporal clause gives the time at which he was (possibly) awarded the Fields medal, but only (17b) has a second reading in which the (possible) award precedes the time of the temporal clause.

Notice that both arguments involve perfect morphology on the modal verb, to which we turn now.

3 Epistemic modals and higher perfects

3.1 Variation in the epistemic readings of higher perfects

By contrast with tense morphology, which in Romance is morphologically linked to person agreement morphology and thus cannot be realized on infinitives, perfect morphology can be realized on infinitives. Past temporal orientation can thus be expressed by a perfect infinitive, as in (17b) above, or by perfect morphology on the modal verb, which we will call a higher perfect, as in (17a) above. Before discussing the semantics of the two possible realization sites of perfect morphology and evaluating Mari and Martin's objections to Tasmowski's generalization, it is important to realize that there is considerable macro- and micro-variation as to the possibility of higher perfects with epistemic modals. We will successively discuss pluperfects, perfect conditionals, and present perfects in French and Spanish, in order to show (i) that there is a general tendency for French to allow or prefer higher perfects, and (ii) that there is a correlation between the acceptability of higher present perfects and the aoristic drift of the perfect.

3.1.1 Pluperfects

As illustrated in (18a–b), French admits quite freely epistemic readings with a pluperfect on the modal verb:

(18) a.

Quelqu'un	*avait*	*dû*	*le*	*jeter*	*dehors,*	*mais*	*qui ?*	*Qui ?*
somebody	have.IMPF	MUST.PP	him	throw	outside,	but	who	who

Qui	*avait*	*pu ?*
who	have.IMPF	CAN.PP

Il ne se souvenait pas.

'Somebody must have thrown him outside, but who? Who? Who could have? He didn't remember'

b.

Ces	*pièces,*	*il*	*avait*	*dû*	*les*	*garder*
these	coins	he	have.IMPF	MUST.PP	them	keep

en se disant qu'elles prendraient de la valeur un jour. Il ne s'était pas trompé.

'Those coins, he must have saved them, assuming that their value would eventually increase. He had not been proven wrong'

The most natural Spanish translations of such examples exhibit perfect infinitives, and not higher perfects:

(19) a.

Alguien	*debía*	*haberlo*	*arrojado*	*fuera,*	*pero*	*¿quién?*
somebody	MUST.IMPF	have+him	thrown	outside	but	who

¿Quién	*podía*	*haberlo*	*hecho?*	*No*	*se*	*acordaba.*
who	CAN.IMPF	have+it	done.	not	REFL	remember.IMPF

b. *Esas monedas, las debía haber conservado*
these coins THEM MUST.IMPF have keep.PP
diciéndose que algún día tendrían más valor. No se había equivocado.

While epistemic readings for the sequences pluperfect+modal are frequent in French, they are extremely rare in Spanish. A search of the Davies corpus (<corpusdelespanol.org>) gives only four clear examples – two of them from the same novel[6] illustrated in (20a–b) –, a range of frequency contrasting with the dozens of examples patterning like (19a–b), and in fact as low as that of epistemic readings for sequences in which the modal bears progressive aspectual morphology, which are exceptional (21).

(20) a. *De un gran sobre de papel estraza comenzó a sacar papeles, dinero, cartas, fotografías..., varios objetos que Pedro llevaba encima*
y otros que habían debido coger en su domicilio.
and other.PL that have.IMPF.3PL MUST.PP take in his lodging
'From a big brown envelope he started taking out papers, money, cards, pictures...., several objects that Pedro carried on him and others that they must have picked up at his lodgings ...'

b. *quedaba perplejo al comprobar el extraño género de relaciones que frecuentaba este mozo, aparentemente algo descarriado del que*
alguno quizá había podido oír comentarios referentes a tales
somebody may be have.IMPF CAN.PP hear comments referring to such
y cuales aficiones literarias y tales y cuales fracasos académicos
and which tastes literary and such and which failures academic
'he remained astonished at the strange sort of people this young man consorted with, an apparently dissolute young man about whom some people might have heard comments referring to these or those literary preferences and these or those academic failures' ...

(21) *ya había puesto en conocimiento del Ministerio Fiscal las situaciones*
que se ***estaban pudiendo producir a tenor*** *de las*
that REFL be.IMPF CAN.GER produce to tenor of the
denuncias que había hecho la OCU [Cortes CL-M54]
complaints that had made the OCU
'I had already informed the Attorney General of the situations that might have been happening according to the complaints filed by the OCU'

6 *Tiempo de silencio*, by L. Martín-Santos, Barcelona, Seix Barral, 1961.

Informal consultation of 5 native speakers of European and American varieties confirms the preference for perfect infinitives above the pluperfect+modal sequences when the context imposes an epistemic reading. Thus, in a set of contrasting sentence pairs of the type illustrated in (22a–b) and (23a–b), the (a) sequences are unanimously accepted whereas the (b) sentences are judged doubtful or less acceptable by all the consultants:

(22) a. *Ofrecía en un vaso un poco de agua en la que debía haber*
offered in a glass a little of water in the which MUST.IMPF have
exprimido un limón a juzgar por una pepita que flotaba en él
press.PP a lemon to judge by a seed that float.IMPF in it

b. *Ofrecía en un vaso un poco de agua en la que había debido*
offered in a glass a little of water in the which have.IMPF MUST.PP
exprimir un limón a juzgar por una pepita que flotaba en él
press a lemon to judge by a seed that float.IMPF in it
'He offered in a glass a little water in which he might have pressed a lemon, to judge by the seed floating therein'

(23) a. *Pedro admitió que al terminar la lectura el sueño lo había vencido,*
y que bien podía haber dejado caer el manuscrito
and that well CAN.IMPF have let fall the manuscript
sobre la alfombra.
on the rug

b. *Pedro admitió que al terminar la lectura el sueño lo había vencido,*
y que bien había podido dejar caer el manuscrito
and that well have.IMPF CAN.PP let fall the manuscript
sobre la alfombra.
on the rug
'Pedro admitted that, when finishing reading, sleep had overcome him, and that he might have just as well let the manuscript fall on the rug.'

In sum, in pluperfect contexts there is a clear difference between French, which freely admits higher perfects and Spanish, which prefers perfect infinitives.

3.1.2 Perfect conditionals

The argument involving perfects and conditional morphology is slightly more complex. Combinations of conditional morphology and the perfect can give rise either to construals of epistemic uncertainty or to counterfactual readings. Thus, sentence (24) below shows an ambiguity concerning the epistemic state of the speaker, which is resolved by the two possible continuations (i) and (ii). In the epistemic reading, the speaker does not know whether Mary won or not, in the counterfactual reading, the speaker assumes that she did not win.[7]

(24) *Marie aurait pu gagner la course.* [FR]
M. have.COND CAN.PP win the race
'Marie might have won the race'

(i) C'est une possibilité à ne pas exclure. [EPISTEMIC][8]
'We shouldn't ignore this possibility'

(ii) Mais elle a perdu. [COUNTERFACTUAL]
'But she lost'

This ambiguity also exists in the case of the necessity modal:

(25) *Pierre aurait dû arriver chez lui il y a une heure.*
P. have.COND MUST.PP arrive home him there has an hour
'Pierre should have arrived home an hour ago'

(i) *Appelle pour vérifier qu'il est bien là.* [EPISTEMIC]
'Call up to check whether he's there all right'

---

7 The very existence of this ambiguity casts doubt on the explanation offered in Condoravdi (2001) for the parallel ambiguity of the English sentence *Mary might have won the race*, which relies on covert perfect raising for generating the counterfactual reading, see Laca (2012). In fact, Condoravdi's approach predicts, contrary to fact, that higher perfects will uniformly give rise to counterfactual readings in these contexts, whereas perfect infinitives will uniformly give rise to epistemic readings.

8 A reviewer expresses doubts as to the possibility of an epistemic reading for example (24). However, there are a host of attested examples in which the sequence *aurait pu Vinf* clearly conveys epistemic uncertainty, and not counterfactuality. Cf. for instance:

(i) *Au vu du terrain, un hélicoptère aurait bien pu venir de derrière la colline proche sans être entendu*
'Due to the characteristics of the terrain, a helicopter might well have arrived from behind the nearby hill without being heard'

(ii) *Il y a eu plusieurs décès en détention, que la torture et d'autres mauvais traitements auraient pu causer ou auxquels ils auraient pu contribuer.*
'There have been several deaths in custody which might have been caused by torture and mistreatment or to which the latter might have contributed'.

(ii) *Mais il n'y est pas encore arrivé.* [COUNTERFACTUAL]
'But he hasn't arrived yet'.

The counterfactual/epistemic ambiguity is also attested in Spanish, but in this case, it is the sequence with the perfect infinitive that exhibits the ambiguity:

(26) *María ya debería haber llegado a su casa.*
M. already MUST.COND have arrived at her house
'María should have arrived home by now'
(i) *¿Porqué no llamas para confirmar?* [EPISTEMIC]
'Why don't you call up to check?'
(ii) *Pero no ha llegado.* [COUNTERFACTUAL]
'But she hasn't arrived'.

As discussed in Laca (2012), the epistemic-counterfactual ambiguity exhibits different patterns in French and Spanish, which are summarized in Table 5.1.

The linearizations freely allowing for the ambiguity in each language involve higher perfects in French, and perfect infinitives in Spanish. Leaving aside the complexities arising from lexical differentiation among modals, the patterns represented in the last row of Table 1 show, once again, that higher perfects in French are perfectly compatible with epistemic readings, whereas they only restrictedly receive epistemic readings (namely for the existential modal *poder*) in Spanish.

3.1.3 Present perfects

As illustrated in (27a–c), French freely admits epistemic readings for modals in the *passé composé*:

Table 5.1: Possible construals with conditional modals and perfect mophology

	French		Spanish	
MOD_{COND} + PERF.INF	√EPIST	CF *pouvoir (√)devoir	√EPIST	√CF
$PERF_{COND}$ + MOD	√EPIST	√CF	EPIST(√)poder *deber *tener que	√CF

Source: From Laca (2012).

(27) a. *J'ai pu me tromper.*
I have CAN.PP me err
'I might have been mistaken'

b. *Le voleur a dû se cacher dans l'entrée.*
the thief has MUST.PP REFL hide in the entrance
'The must have hidden in the entrance'

c. *Hélène a dû avoir les yeux bleus.*
H. hwas MUST.PP have the eyes blue
'Hélène must have been blue-eyed'

Spanish shows considerable variation as to the possibility of epistemic readings for modals in the *perfecto compuesto*. A corpus study by Vázquez Laslop (2004) demonstrates that such sequences exhibit epistemic readings in European Spanish in 264 ocurrences out of a total of 422 (62.6%), whereas in Mexican Spanish they only exhibit epistemic readings in 1 occurrence out of a total of 31 (3.2%). These results indicate (i) that modals in the *perfecto compuesto* show an overall much lower frequency in Mexican Spanish (n=31) than in European Spanish (n=422) and (ii) that epistemic readings for such sequences are much less frequent in Mexican Spanish (3.2%) than in European Spanish (62.6%).

A search of the Davies corpus confirms these results. Epistemic readings for modals in the *perfecto compuesto* are attested mainly in examples from European Spanish (28a–b) and from Andean Spanish (29a–b), and are practically non-existent in other varieties.

(28) a. *podemos afirmar que, como hemos obrado así, ése ha debido*
we can assert that, since we have acted thus this has MUST.PP
ser el motivo
be the reason
'We are in a position to assert that, since we have thus acted, this must have been the reason'

b. *Si incluimos a aquellos que han sido desplazados dentro de sus propios países, la cifra se aproxima a los 50 millones de personas*
que han podido ser obligadas a dejar sus hogares en todo el mundo
that have CAN.PP be forced to leave their homes in all the world
'If we also count those that have been displaced inside their home countries, the numbers approach the 50 million people worldwide who may have been forced to quit their homes'.

(29) a. *Somoza ha podido ser un criminal sangriento*
S. has CAN.PP be a criminal bloody
o lo que usted quiera, pero no es un hombre inculto [Habla Culta, La Paz]

'Somoza may have been a bloody criminal or what you'd like to call him, but he is not an uncultivated man'

b. *entonces el gasto de taxi ha debido ser grande* [Habla Culta, La Paz]
then the expense of taxi has MUST.PP be big
'Then taxi expenses must have been considerable'

This internal variation in Spanish is clearly correlated with variation in the distribution and interpretation of the *perfecto compuesto* accross Spanish varieties. It is an established fact (see, among others, Real Academia Española 2009, Laca 2009, Howe 2013) that the *perfecto compuesto* in American varieties only exhibits specific aspectual values, whereas it is well advanced on the grammaticalization path known under the label of 'aoristic drift of the perfect' (Squartini and Bertinetto 2000) in most European Spanish varieties. As shown in example (30), the *perfecto compuesto* can appear in typical aoristic (perfective past) contexts in such varieties:

(30) *Esta mañana cuando he salido al jardín Gladys me ha llamado, como anoche. Ya estaba fuera, esperándome. He ido a su instalación, me he asomado a la ventana de su dormitorio y, ¿adivinas lo que he visto entre sus patas?* (Real Academia Española: Banco de datos (CREA) [online]. Corpus de referencia del español actual. <http://www.rae.es> [IX-2008])

'This morning, when I went into the garden Gladys called me, as last night. She was already outside, waiting for me. I went to her cabin, peeked through her bedroom window and guess what I saw between her paws?'

The *perfectos compuestos* in this fragment are combined with temporal adverbials not containing the time of utterance ('this morning'), they appear in temporal clauses ('when I went out'), they are modified by temporal clauses ('she called me when I went out'), and they constitute a narrative sequence. These are precisely the contexts that are incompatible with (aspectual) perfect semantics, and indicate the existence of (temporal) simple past values. Uses of the *perfecto compuesto* of this type are only possible in (most) European Spanish varieties.

It is thus possible to establish a correlation between the possibility of epistemic readings for a modal in combination with a higher perfect and the aoristic drift of the perfect. This correlation is reinforced by the comparison with French, which, as we saw, freely admits epistemic readings for modals in the *passé composé*: the French *passé composé* has for all practical purposes completed the aoristic drift, and can function as a simple past tense.

The explanation for the existence of epistemic readings for modals in the *perfecto compuesto* in Andean varieties is different, and has to do with the rise of evidential values for perfect forms in such varieties (see Howe 2013). It is the match between these evidential values and the inferences conveyed by modals in epistemic readings that could account for the existence of such combinations.[9]

We would like to add that microvariation as to the possibility of epistemic readings for modals with higher perfects is also attested for Italian. In fact, Mari (2015: 178 & passim) observes that Italian shows variation as to the possibility of epistemic readings with the possibility modal *potere* 'can' in the *passato prossimo* and explicitly invokes an ongoing linguistic change. According to her hypothesis, this change involves a lexico-syntactic property of the modal, which would gradually evolve from a control to a raising verb. For reasons of space, we cannot go into the details of her hypothesis, but it is important to bear in mind that, next to the hypothetical change of status of the modal verb, Italian exhibits a well documented evolution in the use and interpretation of the *passato prossimo*, which places it somewhere between Spanish and French on the process of aoristic drift (cf. Squartini and Bertinetto 2000).

Epistemic readings for higher perfects are also sporadically attested in Dutch (Boogaart 2007) and in some Norwegian dialects (Eide 2001), both of which are languages exhibiting a past-tense-like present perfect. Curiously, the Norwegian dialects are characterized by a form of 'perfect doubling', combining the higher perfect on the modal with a perfect participle on the embedded verb:

(31) *Han har måtta arbeidd med det i heile natt.* [Norwegian]
he has must.PERF work. PERF on it in all night
'He must have worked on it all night through.' (Eide 2001: 233–234)

'Perfect doubling' appears sporadically in contemporary French, as shown in (32a–b), but a google search shows that the vast majority of such examples date from the 18th and 19th century (33a–b):

(32) a. *Le premier suspect a pu avoir été en contact avec Coulibaly,*
the first suspect has CAN.PP have be.PP in contact with C.
selon une source policière. [Le Monde 18/06/2015]
'The first suspect might have been in contact with Coulibaly, according to police sources'

9 In fact, we predict that in varieties that make frequent use of evidential values for the *perfecto compuesto*, it will be possible to obtain epistemic readings for modals in the perfecto compuesto. This prediction stands to be tested, taking into account that evidential values for the perfecto compuesto do exist in varieties other than the Andean varieties.

b. *Elle a dû avoir été piquée partout,*
she has MUST.PP have be.PP sting.PP every where
car son corps était tout boursouflé. [Europe 1 21/08/2013]
'She must have gotten stung all over, since her body was all swollen'O

(33) a. *l'on est parfaitement convaincu que le marquis de Castries*
n 'a pu avoir parlé ainsi [1782]
not has CAN.PP have talk.PP thus
'Every body is fully convinced that the Marchess of Castries cannot have talked in this way.'

b. *Hégésippe vivoit dans ce tems-là,* &
n'a dû avoir écrit ces discours que six ans après [1737]
not has MUST.PP have write.PP these speeches that six years after
'Hegesippe lived in that time, and he must have written these speeches six years later at the earliest'

A question that certainly deserves further research concerns the likelihood of 'perfect doubling' as a stage in the development of higher perfects in epistemic readings. If this is indeed the case, the process by which such higher perfects come into existence shows a tantalizing analogy to the better known process of externalization of inflection, by which inflectional morphology that becomes trapped between a stem and other morphological material migrates towards the edge of the word (Haspelmath 1993). Revealingly, in intermediate stages this process involves doubling of the inflectional material, which appears both at its original site and at the edge of the word. Mutatis mutandis, in the case of perfect morphology, we would have perfect morphology which has acquired past-tense-like properties and is trapped in the infinitival complement of the modal migrating towards the standard site of realization of tense morphology, the inflection on the modal.[10] At the present moment, this is only a speculative suggestion, but it may give rise to a line of research which we think is worth pursuing.

---

10 Notice that Italian seems to resort to "perfect doubling" quite freely. Thus, Mari (2015) cites a number of examples like:

(i) *Jean a potuto avere spostato la macchina*
Jean has CAN.PP have move.pp the car
'Jean might have moved the car'.

3.2 Higher perfects and Tasmowski's generalization

Recall that Tasmowski's generalization states that the choice of past tense on a modal in an epistemic reading replicates the choice that would be mandatory for the prejacent in the absence of a modal verb, and suggests that the past tense in some way originates in the prejacent. Two types of counterexamples have been put forward by Mari (2015) and Martin (2011). The first type of counterexample involves realization of the *passé composé* on a modal in cases in which the prejacent would require an imperfect. We will call these cases *non-conform* higher perfects. The second type of counterexample involves cases where there is a semantic difference between the higher perfect and the corresponding sequence with a perfect infinitive. We will call these cases *non-equivalent* higher perfects.

3.2.1 Non-conform higher perfects

As stated above (see section 2), individual level states require an imperfect (34a) and do not allow the *passé composé* (34b), but can give rise to an epistemic reading when the modal verb is in the *passé composé* (34c):

(34) a. *Hélène avait les yeux bleus.*
H have.IMPF the eyes blue
'Helène was blue-eyed'

b. **Hélène a eu les yeux bleus.*
H have.PRES had the eyes blue
'Hélène has been blue-eyed'

c. *Hélène a dû avoir les yeux bleus.*
H. have.PRES MUST.PP have the eyes blue
'Hélène must have been blue eyed'

This phenomenon also arises with other state verbs. Homer (2010) observes that the *passé composé* with some states gives rise to a coerced interpretation, so that (35) only has a reading in which the house cost 100,000 euros and was bought for that price, the buying event supervening on the property of having such a price[11]:

(35) *Cette maison a couté 100.000 euros.*
This house has cost 100,000 euros

11 As pointed out by one of the reviewers, the coerced eventive reading is clearly preferred, but a stative reading is not categorically excluded, as assumed by Homer.

However, *pace* Homer, with an epistemic modal in the *passé composé*, the coerced eventive reading easily disappears. Thus, (36) does not imply that the house was bought at all:

(36) *A l'époque, cette maison a dû coûter environ un million d'euros.*
at the time, this house has MUST.PP cost around one million of euro
Pas étonnant qu'ils n'aient pas trouvé d'acheteur.
'At the time, this house must have cost around 1 million euros. No wonder they did not find a buyer'

Non-conform higher perfects pose a serious problem for Tasmowski's generalization in its original formulation, which requires a match between the tenses that appear in the the modalized and in the unmodalized sentence. But it is less of a problem for a refinement of this generalization, according to which this match reflects the fact that morphology that originates in the infinitival complement of the modal verb raises to be expressed on the modal. In this case, this would mean that a structure containing a perfect infinitive is transformed into one containing a higher perfect:

(37) a. MODAL + PERFECT INFINITIVE
b. PERFECT MODAL + INFINITIVE

Now, as correctly pointed out by Martin (2011), the aspectual makeup of perfect infinitives is underspecified by comparison with the aspectual makeup of perfect tenses: perfect infinitives can have perfect(ive) or imperfective readings. As shown by the choice of tenses in the (a) and the (b) sentences in each pair, imperfective readings arise not only with infinitives as complements of modals (38a–b), but also in other contexts (39a–b, 40a–b):

(38) a. *#Pierre a été albinos.*
P. has been albino
b. *Pierre peut très bien avoir été albinos.*
P. may very well have been albino

(39) a. *Le Colosse de Rhode pesait/ # a pesé trois tonnes.*
the Colossus of Rhodes weigh.IMPF / # has weighed three tons
'The Colossus of Rhodes weighed three tons'
b. *Le Colosse de Rhode est censé avoir pesé trois tonnes.*
'The Colossus of Rhodes is thought to have weighed three tons'

(40) a. *Il dit qu'il ignorait /# a ignoré l'existence de cet enfant.*
He says that he ignore.IMPF/ # has ignore.PP the.existence of this child

'He says that he was not aware of this child's existence'

b. *Il dit avoir ignoré l'existence de cet enfant.*
he says to+have ignore.PP the.existence of this child
'He pretends not to have been aware of this child's existence'

If higher perfects have their origin in a perfect which is generated on the infinitive, and are attracted by the modal verb by a sort of overt perfect raising mechanism, examples like (34c) and (36) do not pose more of a problem than examples like (38b): the higher perfects inherit the aspectual makeup of the perfect infinitives, which, as we have just shown, may have imperfective readings. Recall that in the last section we have surmised that the existence of "perfect doubling" may indicate that such a mechanism is or has been at work in French.

3.2.2 Non-equivalent higher perfects

However, the hypothesis of a perfect raising mechanism is now confronted with the second objection raised by Mari (2015), namely that one can devise contexts in which higher perfects are not equivalent to the corresponding sequences with perfect infinitives. Counterexamples of this kind always follow the same pattern: the sequence with the perfect infinitive has an extra reading corresponding to a temporal configuration which is impossible with the higher perfect.

Thus, for instance, (41b) has a reading in which he might have already been awarded the Fields medal when he joined the CNRS, whose temporal configuration is represented as (42). This temporal configuration cannot be associated with (41a), which, according to Mari (2015), only admits the interpretation in which the time of the award coincides with the time at which he joined the CNRS.

(41) a. *Il a pu être recompensé de la médaille Fields quand*
he have.PRES CAN.PP be awarded of the medal Fields when
il est rentré au CNRS.
he be.PRES entered to+the CNRS

b. *Il peut avoir été recompensé de la médaille Fields quand*
he CAN.PRES have been awarded of the medal Fields when
il est rentré au CNRS. [ex. from Mari 2015: 210]
he be.PRES entered to+the CNRS
'He may have been awarded the Fields medal when he joined the CNRS'

(42) he-be-awarded-the-Fields-medal____ he join the CNRS ________**S**________
Tmod

Analogously, (43a) is acceptable because it allows for a temporal configuration (44) in which the (possible) event of getting a promotion precedes 'tomorrow', but not Speech Time, whereas the event can only precede Speech Time in the case of the anomalous (43b):

(43) a. *Il peut avoir reçu sa promotion demain et*
He CAN.PRES have gotten his promotion tomorrow and
quand même changer d'entreprise tout de suite après
nonetheless change of_enterprise all of sequence after
b. **Il a pu recevoir sa promotion demain et*
he has CAN.PP get his promotion tomorrow and
quand même changer d'entreprise tout de suite après
nonetheless change of_enterprise all of sequence after
'He may have gotten his promotion by tomorrow and nonetheless change companies right after that' [ex. from Mari 2015: 210]

(44) **S** ____he get a promotion____tomorrow____he change company_____
Tmod

Note first that the temporal configuration (44) is actually a future perfect configuration. Whereas both (41b) and (43a) share a simultaneous temporal perspective, (41b) has a past temporal orientation, but (43a) has a future temporal orientation. Now, as stated in section 1 above, there is consensus as to the existence of epistemic readings for decided issues (propositions whose truth value depends on facts which are past or simultaneous wrt. Tmod), but there is an ongoing debate as to the wisdom of attributing the label 'epistemic' to readings in which, due to the indeterminacy of the future, the subjective uncertainty characterising epistemic readings goes hand in hand with the objective uncertainty pertaining to contingent futures (cf. Condoravdi 2001, Portner 2009: 222–236).

Leaving aside the issue of the debatable epistemic status of (43a), what Mari's counterexamples actually show is that the anteriority relation conveyed by the perfect can only be computed with regard to Speech Time in the case of a higher present perfect, but it can also be computed with regard to a temporal adverbial clause or a temporal adverb in the case of a perfect infinitive. Anchoring the anteriority relation to the temporal adverbial clause in (41b) produces the pluperfect-like configuration in (42), anchoring it to the temporal adverb in (43a) produces the future-perfect-like configuration in (44). Crucially, what Mari's counterexamples do not show is that there is a difference in temporal perspective between (41a) and (41b) or between (43a) and (43b). And Tasmowski's generalization and its refinement target precisely the possibility of maintaining a simultaneous temporal perspective for epistemic readings when the modal verb bears past or perfect morphology.

To sum up, Martin's and Mari's counterexamples, while undoubtedly contributing to refine Tasmowski's generalization, do not offer conclusive evidence for the existence of a past temporal perspective in epistemic readings of modals bearing past or perfect morphology. They show, however, that -at least in the case of perfects- Tasmowski's generalization should be better formulated as "perfect raising", correlating perfect infinitives with higher perfects, and not as as a sort of "copying" on the modal of a tense which has its origin in the unmodalized version of the sentence. They also show that higher perfects, which are necessarily tensed, do not have the same privileges of occurrence and interpretation as perfect infinitives, which are necessarily non-tensed.[12]

4 Concluding remarks

In this paper, we have examined the hypothesis that modal verbs in epistemic readings require a simultaneous temporal perspective in the light of the morphological evidence from Romance languages, in which modal verbs are fully inflected for TMA categories, paying particular attention to the interaction of modal verbs with perfect morphology.

We have first shown that the semantic formulation of the hypothesis, based on the type of temporal perspective required, fares much better than the syntactic formulation, which requires epistemic modals to outscope tense. In fact, the semantic contrast between a deictic tense (the present) and an anaphoric tense (the imperfect) evidenced by epistemic modals demonstrates that tense morphology on modals is interpretable. Secondly, starting from Tasmowski's observation as to the matching tense-aspect categories of modals in epistemic readings and of the corresponding unmodalized sentences, we have compared the linearizations of perfect morphology in French and Spanish by contrasting perfect infinitives with higher perfects. We have been able to show that Spanish exhibits a clear preference for the former, whereas French shows a clear preference for the latter, thus indicating the existence of variation. This variation is probably due to a diachronic process of perfect raising which correlates with the 'aoristic drift' of the

12 Martin (2011) discusses a number of revealing contrasts between higher perfects and perfect infinitives which – we believe – can all be explained by (i) the fact that higher perfects, being tensed, are always anchored to Speech Time in matrix contexts, and (ii) the fact that perfect infinitives have a less specified aspectual contour than tensed perfects.

perfect. Finally, we have discussed the counterexamples to Tasmowski's generalization put forward by Mari (2015) and Martin (2011), showing that, although they contribute to refine Tasmowski's generalization, which should be interpreted in terms of perfect raising, they do not provide decisive arguments against the hypothesis that epistemic readings require a simultaneous temporal perspective.

If the idea of perfect raising suggested by our materials is on the right track, much further work on larger databases is required in order to adequately describe this process. It should be stressed that the picture that emerges from our materials, particularly from the comparison of different varieties, is not necessarily one of a (synchronic) syntactic derivation, by means of which higher perfects are derived from perfect infinitives, but rather that of a diachronic process of syntactic change, producing alternative linearisations with nearly equivalent temporal interpretations.

Abbreviations: COND – conditional tense; GER – gerund; IMPF – imperfect tense; PERF – perfect; PP – past participle; PRES – present tense; REFL – reflexive; SP – simple past tense

References

Boogaart, Ronnie. 2007. The Past and Perfect of Epistemic Modals. In Louis de Saussure, Jacques Moeschler & Genoveva Puskas (eds.), *Recent advances in the syntax and semantics of tense, aspect, and modality?*, 47–71. Berlin: Mouton de Gruyter.

Borgonovo, Claudia & Sarah Cummins. 2007. Tensed Modals. In Juis Eguren & Olga Fernández-Soriano (eds.), *Coreference, Modality, and Focus*, 1–18. Amsterdam: John Benjamins.

Bosque, Ignacio. 1999. ¿Qué sabe el que sabe hacer algo? Saber entre los predicados modales. In Kepa Korta & Fernando García Murga (eds.), *Palabras. Victor Sánchez de Zavala in memoriam* (Filosofía 3), 303–323. Bilbao: Universidad del País Vasco.

Butler, Jonny. 2004. *Phase Structure, Phrase Structure, and Quantification*. University of York: PhD Dissertation.

Cinque, Guglielmo. 1999. *Adverbs and Functional Heads. A Cross Linguistic Perspective*. Oxford: Oxford University Press.

Condoravdi, Cleo. 2001. Temporal interpretations of modals. Modals for the present and for the past. In David Beaver, Luis D. Casillas Martinez, Brady Z. Clark & Stefan Kaufmann (eds.), *The Construction of Meaning*, 59–88. Stanford: CSLI Publications.

Demirdache, Hamida & Miriam Uribe-Etxeberria. 2006. Scope and Anaphora with Time Arguments: The Case of "Perfect Modals". In Heidi Harley & Raffaella Folli (eds.), *Lingua* 118. 1798–1815.

Demirdache, Hamida & Miriam Uribe-Etxeberria. 2008. Morfosintaxis e interpretación de los verbos modales. In A. Carrasco Gutiérrez (ed.), *Tiempos compuestos y formas verbales complejas*, 443–497. Madrid-Frankfurt: Iberoamericana.

Desclés, Jean-Pierre & Zlatka Guentcheva. 2001. La notion d'abduction et le verbe *devoir* "épistémique". In Patrick Dendale & Johan van der Auwera (eds.), *Les verbes modaux* (Cahiers Chronos 8), 103–122. Amsterdam: Rodopi.
Eide, Kristen M. 2001. *Norwegian modals*. Berlin: Mouton de Gruyter.
Fintel, Kai von. 2nd edn. 2005. Modality and Language, *Encyclopaedia of Philosophy*.
Fintel, Kai von & Antony Gillies. 2007. An Opinionated Guide to Epistemic Modality. In Tamar Szabó Gendler & John Hawthorne (eds.), *Oxford Studies in Epistemology*, 36–62. Oxford: Oxford University Press.
Hacquard, Valentine. 2006. *Aspects of Modality*. Cambridge, Mass.: MIT dissertations in linguistitcs.
Haspelmath, Martin. 1993. The Diachronic Externalization of Inflection, *Linguistics* 31: 2, 279–309.
Homer, Vincent. 2010. Epistemic Modals: High ma non troppo, *Proceedings of NELS* 40. 273–286.
Howe, Chad L. 2013. *The Spanish perfects: pathways of emergent meaning*. London: Palsgrave-Macmillan.
Kaufmann, Stephen, Cleo Condoravdi & Valentine Harizanov. 2006. Formal Approaches to Modality. In William Frawley (ed.), *The expression of modality*, 71–106. Berlin: Mouton De Gruyter.
Kratzer, Angelika. 1981. The Notional Category of Modality. In Hans-Jürgen Eikmeyer & Hans Rieser (eds.), *Words, Worlds, and Contexts: New Approaches in Word Semantics*, 38–74. Berlin: De Gruyter.
Laca, Brenda. 2009. Perfect semantics. How universal are Ibero-American Present Perfects? In Claudia Borgonovo, Manuel Español-Echevarría & Philippe Prévost (eds.), *Selected Proceedings of the 12th Hispanic Symposium*, 1–16. Laval: Cascadilla Press.
Laca, Brenda. 2012. On Modal Tenses and Tensed Modals. In Chiyo Nishida & Cinzia *Russi* (eds.), *Building a Bridge between Linguistic Communities of the Old and the New World* (Cahiers Chronos 25), 163–198. Amsterdam: Rodopi.
Laca, Brenda. 2014. Epistemic Modals and Temporal Anchoring, *Modality. [Special Issue]. ReVEL* 8. 76–104. http://www.revel.inf.br/files/4357ef41070a1ebd45f071737a5d3c51.pdf (accessed 10 May 2016).
Mari, Alda. 2015. *Modalités et temps. Modèles et données*. Bern: Peter Lang.
Martin, Fabienne. 2011. Epistemic Modals in the Past. In Janine Berns, Haike Jacobs & Tobias Scheer (eds.), *Romance Languages and Linguistic Theory 2009. Selected Papers from "Going Romance", Nice [3–5 december] 2009* (Romance Languages and Linguistic Theory 3), 185–202. Amsterdam: Benjamins.
Papafragou, Anna. 2006. Epistemic Modality and Truth Conditions. *Lingua* 116, 1688–1702.
Picallo, Carme. 1990. Modal verbs in Catalan. *Natural Language and Linguistic Theory* 8 (2), 285–312.
Portner, Paul. 2009. *Modality*. Oxford: Oxford University Press.
Real Academia Española. 2009. *Nueva gramática de la lengua española*. Madrid: Espasa Calpe.
Squartini, Mario & Pier Marco Bertinetto. 2000. The Simple and Compound Past in Romance Languages. In Osten Dahl (ed.), *Tense and aspect in the languages of Europe*, 405–475. Berlin: Mouton de Gruyter.

Stowell, Tim. 2004. Tense and Modals. In Jacqueline Guéron & Jacqueline Lecarme (eds.), *The Syntax of Time*, 621–636. Cambridge, Mass.: MIT Press.
Tasmowski, Lilianne. 1980. Un devoir épistémique. *Travaux de linguistique* 7. 43–58.
Vázquez Laslop, Maria E. 2004. Modalidad de *deber* (de) + Infinitivo en antepresente: México frente a España. ms. México: El Colegio de México.
Werner, Thomas. 2003. *Deducing the Future and Distinguishing the Past: Temporal Interpretation in Modal Sentences in English*. Rutgers University: PhD Dissertation.

Jean Léo Léonard

Anchoring evidential, epistemic and beyond in discourse: *alào*, *vantér* and *vér* in Noirmoutier island (Poitevin-Saintongeais)

Abstract: This chapter uncovers a complex system of evidential and epistemic adverbs in Poitevin-Saintongeais – an Oïl dialect spoken in western-central France. Pragmatic orientation (egocentric vs. dialogic) and assertive/negative polarity in discourse provide the basic framework to explore intricate subsystems of adverbial modality embedded in diglossic code-switching patterns. First-hand data recorded in the island of Noirmoutier in the 1980s highlight similarities and differences with standard or regional French, from the standpoint of language documentation techniques (i.e. through oral texts rather than elicited data).

Keywords: Modality, Evidentiality, Epistemic, Dialect, Discourse, Orality, Poitevin-Saintongeais, French

> *E tu para queres um barco, pode-se saber, foi o que o rei de facto perguntou (...). Para ir à procura da ilha desconhecida, respondeu o homem, Que ilha desconhecida, perguntou o rei (...), A ilha desconhecida, repetiu o homem, Disparate, já não há ilhas desconhecidas, Quem foi que te disse, rei, que já não há ilhas desconhecidas, Estão todas nos mapas, Nos mapas só estão as ilhas conhecidas, E que ilha desconhecida é essa de que queres ir à procura, Se eu to pudesse dizer, então não seria desconhecida.* José Saramago, 1997: O conto da ilha desconhecida.[1]

1 Introduction

In the above quotation from José Saramago, a simple man comes up to the King's house to stubbornly demand a boat, in order to search for an undiscovered island.

1 "Why do you want me to give you a boat? May I ask you?' the king indulged in asking (...). 'In order to look for the undiscovered island', the man answered. 'What undiscovered island?' asked the king (...). 'The undiscovered island', the man repeated. 'Nonsense! There are no undiscovered islands whatsoever: if any existed, all of them have already shown up in maps'. 'In maps one finds but islands which have already been discovered'. 'And what sort of undiscovered island do you pretend to find?' 'If I could tell you, it wouldn't be an undiscovered island in the first place".

Jean Léo Léonard, Université Paris-Sorbonne

https://doi.org/10.1515/9783110572261-006

The man insists that such an island exists, even though the King claims his clerks have already mapped out all existing islands to be found, that none are left to be discovered on earth. The man wittily answers that the only way to prove the existence of uncharted islands would be to go look, if one is sufficiently stubborn to take on such an endeavour – as he proves himself to be. Moreover, when the King asks him who he thinks he is to presume demanding such a favour, the man returns the question, asking him in turn who he is not to indulge in providing him with a boat to make his discovery. Indeed, he says, the King belongs more to his navy than the boats of his navy belong to him, because without a navy, the King would be powerless. The King ends up providing the man with a boat from his navy, and whether the man eventually discovers an unknown island or not will not be told here, we leave the reader to find out the answer on his/her own.

1.1 A subset of evidential and epistemic adverbial patterns in Noirmoutier

This tale by José Saramago has much to do with the present study. When any outsider first asks about the local Poitevin-Saintongeais dialect (henceforth, PS), called 'Patois' /*patoj*/, (s)he is told, among other examples, that islanders say *alào* /alaw/ for 'yes', *vér* /*vaer*/ for 'indeed' and *vantér* /*vãter*/ for 'perhaps'. However, it can take a lifespan for an outsider – but also for a native speaker not devoted to formally analysing his/her linguistic knowledge – to understand that *alào*, *vér* and *vantér*, as I will now spell these items, make up a subset of an unexpected evidential and epistemic system. One needs modelling and analytical grids, but also a closer look at transcribed material to fathom this system. The tendency to boast about these items as if they were mere curiosities and dully matched their alleged Standard French equivalents 'oui' [yes], 'certes' [certainly], 'peut-être' [maybe] in *ad hoc* dictionaries (*glossaires, dictionnaires de régionalismes*, etc.) obstructs us from seeing that they make up an unexpected – and thus undiscovered – island within the grammar-lexicon subset of adverbial categories available in the dialect.

Table 6.1 shows the system under survey from Noirmoutier island, with tentative translations in Standard French (henceforth, SF) and English. See Tables 6.1–6.2 below for details of the Poitevin-Saintongeais orthography.

In order to explore the evidential/epistemic dimension of these items in Noirmoutier Poitevin,[2] I have had to rely on transcriptions of oral texts carried out

2 While discourse and pragmatic particles in Oïl dialects have not yet been surveyed, the reader will find many references on this issue in SF in Auchlin (1981), Beeching (2002), Bouchard

Table 6.1: Evidential/Epistemic Adverbs vs. Assertive/Assumptive Adverb subsets in Noirmoutier PS and SF

	Poitevin-Saintongeais	Standard French	Gloss
Evidential	*alào*	'en effet, effectivement'	indeed, in effect
Confirmative	*vér*	'certes'	certainly
Assertive	*oalle*	'oui'	yes
Corroborative	*sia !*	'si !'	yes!
Epistemic	*vantér, censémint*	'peut-être'	maybe, perhaps
Admirative	*dame !*	'bah!' 'pour sûr!' 'pardi!'	well, surely, gosh!

in the 1980s, when I was gathering material for my Ph. D. in the form of oral narratives in various insular subdialects. Rather than eliciting data from questionnaires, I engaged elderly speakers aged 50–90 for hours in free conversations, entirely held in the local dialect. Having lived in the island in the years 1968–72, and having been at school with their grandchildren, not only could I monitor these narrative sessions in the dialect during all these years, but no one doubted the interviewer's ability to speak it and understand it, which provided reliable conditions for observing genuine speech without too much interference from SF. This detail is important, as we will see that the subset of Evidential/Epistemic Adverbs (henceforth, EEA) is prone to undergoing alternation with the SF Assertive/Assumptive Adverb subset (henceforth, AAA).

As a set of adverbial lexemes, the EEA system belongs to the periphery of Evidential/Epistemic systems proper, as defined by Aikhenvald (Aikhenvald 2004, Narrog 2005): Noirmoutier PS adverbs are not grammaticalised; they are not integrated in inflection, nor in morphosyntax, nor can they be considered as clitics proper. Nevertheless, they do make up a consistent adverbial system based on the *source of information* as core meaning (firsthand vs. non-firsthand information) or the speaker's commitment embedded in the assertive-negative polarity. As such, they are not scattered among various morphosyntactic or lexical classes. They also extend their function and meaning towards *mirativity*, being the category of a "speaker's 'unprepared mind', unexpected new information, and concomitant surprise" (Aikhenvald 2004: 195). Moreover, not only does

(2002), Hwang (1992), Ducrot (1980) and Hansen Mosegaard (1998). See Pusch (2007) for an account of evidentiality in Gascony Occitan – another Gallo-Romance variety, somewhat akin to PS, though from the Oc domain.

the Noirmoutier EEA system shed more light on evidentiality in discourse and in the lexicon, it also provides insights on how evidentiality, especially adverbial, goes far beyond modality, as a pragmatic and rhetoric asset for speakers, and how it can be embedded in diglossic constraints sociolinguistically.

1.2 Transcription conventions and grammar in the Noirmoutier dialect

All original transcriptions were carried out in the IPA (International Phonetic Alphabet), but here I prefer to use a revisited version of the unified orthography, made available by Gautier et al. 1993, and summarised in Table 6.2.1 and 6.2.2 below[3].

Last, but not least, in order to make Noirmoutier PS data easier to read, I must point out that geolinguistic patterns in the island are fairly complex and intricate, due to consecutive waves of settlement in the history of this territory beginning in the Middle Ages. For instance, two pronominal systems have coexisted since the foundation of the island at the turn of the first millennium A.D.: a typically PS system in the centre and the south of the island (i.e. Barbâtre, La Guérinière, L'Epine) versus a classic Oïl system in the north (L'Herbaudière, Le Vieil, Noirmoutier-en-l'Île), as presented in Table 6.3. Both subdialects have symmetrical 1 Sg & Pl AGRS pronouns, as in most Oïl dialects (South & Centre *i dis* 'I

Table 6.2.1: Consonants in PS, Noirmoutier: Graphemic conventions

	Labial	Coronal	Palatal-alveolar	Mediopalatal	Dorsal
Stops	*p* = /p/	*t* = /t/	*ty* = /tʲ/	*çh* = /ç/	*c, qu*[i, e] /k/
	b =/b/	*d* = /d/			*g, gu*[i, e] /g/
Fricatives	*f* = /f/	*s(s), ç* = /s/	*ch* = /ʃ/		
	v = /v/	*z, s* = /z/	*jh* = /h/		
Nasals	*m* = /m/	*n*= /n/	*gn* = /ɲ/		
Approximants		*r, l* = /r, l/	*ll* = /ʎ/		
				i, y =/j/	

3 See Léonard (2004) for allophonic details and Léonard (2005) and Léonard & Jagueneau (2013) for a contextualisation of sociolinguistic trends in the Poitevin-Saintongeais area. On the spelling tradition, see Gautier & Jagueneau (2002), Devineau (2015) for Noirmoutier specifically; on the standardised orthography, see http://www.arantele.org/ortho/grammaire.pdf.

Table 6.2.2: Vowels in PS, Noirmoutier: Graphemic conventions

	Front	Labial	Back
+High	*i* = /i/	*u* = /y/	*ou*= /u/
–High	*e* = /e/	*eu* = /ø/	*o, au* = /o/
Rising Back Long Complex Nucleus			*oé* = /oj/
Long Complex Nuclei	*àe; èr, èa* = /ae; ɛa/		*ào* = /aw/
Short Complex Nuclei	*ai* = /éi/		
Schwa		*e* = /ə/	
+Low	*a* = /a/		*â* = /ɑ/

Note: *Vn* for nasal vowels (*in, en, an*, etc.).

say', *i disuns* 'we say', North *jhe dis* 'I say', *jhe disuns* 'we say'; SF 'je dis', 'nous disons'), as they do for *le* and *il(s)* e.g. in msc. AGRS 3 *le dit* 'he says', *le disant* 'they say' versus *il dit, ils disant* in the northern part of the island. Strikingly enough, the former system is closer to Poitevin proper, whereas the latter is reminiscent of Saintongeais (in the south of the domain), although the configuration is inverted (the Saintongeais-like system being used in the north of the island, whereas the Poitevin-like system occurs in the centre and in the south). Actually, this geolinguistic distribution could be explained by the fact that the Saintongeais-like system is more akin to the central Oïl and SF model, so that *jhe* and *il(s)* for AGRS 1 and AGRS 3 could have been imported from the so called Gallo contact area, from Pays de Retz, rather than having radiated from the South (see Léonard 1991). Nevertheless, pronominal systems are far more intricate than suggested in Table 6.3, as far as AGRS 3 Pl is concerned in particular, as *a(l)s* tends to generalise as an AGRS 3 Pl portmanteau form – not only in the north, but also in the centre and the south, especially in the speech of younger speakers.

The neutral pronoun *o(l)* (gloss abbreviated as Neuter, e.g. *o moll* 'it rains'; SF 'il pleut', *ol ét venu daus mundes* 'Some people have come'; SF 'il est venu du monde / des gens sont venus') is common to all localities, and unlike in common PS, it strongly competes with *çhe* SF 'ce' [this], or *çha* SF 'ça' [that] in the north of the island, in contexts such as the presentative (i.e. cleft sentences) and other constructions of the same kind (*ol/çh'ét facile d'o dire/de dire çheu* 'It is easy to say'; SF 'il/c'est facile de (le) dire ça'), as described in Léonard 1995.

In order to make the data easier to read and interpret for the reader, translations in standard French are given below every example given in the dialect, followed by a translation in English. As the reader will notice, in many cases, the

Table 6.3: *Subject agreement pronouns* in Noirmoutier PS and SF

	Noirmoutier PS, Centre & South	Noirmoutier PS, North	SF
1 Sg	*i*	*jhe*	*je*
2 Sg	*te*		*tu*
3 Sg	*le, a(l)*	*il,* (msc) *a(l)* (fem)	*il, elle*
3 Ntr	*o(l)*		–
1 Pl	*i*	*jhe*	*nous*
2 Pl	*vous, ve*	*vous*	*vous*
3 Pl	*le, a(l)s*	*ils* (msc), *a(l)s*	*ils, elles*

univocity of the items from the Eea System in the Noirmoutier dialect strongly contrasts with the translation in Standard French. Many times, the PS system has to be translated with idioms (as "pour sûr", "tu penses bien!" [for sure, you'd better believe it!], etc. for an item as *alào*).

2 Modelling the local eea system

In short, from the empirical standpoint of the discourse analysis implemented here, we will postulate (1) – according to Rooryck (2001) revisited:

(1) *Evidentiality* points at the source of information, and pragmatically relies on, or is mainly grounded on first-hand information, whereas *epistemicity* evaluates available information, according to personal assumption, reported information or any kind of second-hand information.

The former conceptual realm strongly depends on knowledge of the source of information, while the latter has to do with the speaker's commitment to what (s)he is saying (Palmer 1986: 51), or whether it equates to reality – a subdivision which is reminiscent of Bally's opposition between the *Modus* and the *Dictum* (Bally 1932). Nevertheless, these notions make up a continuum, rather than a clear-cut dichotomy, and they tend to be distributed across Ego (the speaker) and his/her interlocutors (dialogic),[4] as suggested in Table 6.4, where

4 See Alrahabi & Desclés (2009) on the pragmatic and enunciative framework of evidentiality and epistemicity.

Table 6.4: Polarity of the Evidential/Epistemic system of adverbial particles in Noirmoutier PS

Categories	Orientation	Assertion	Negation
Evidential	Ego	*alào*	*nào, poét*
+/−Confirmative	Dialogic	*vér*	*poét*
+/−Assertive	Ego	*oalle, oelle*	*nun*
+/−Corroborative	Dialogic	*sia !*	*nan-ni !*
Epistemic	Ego	*vantér, censément*	*jha*
Admirative	Dialogic	*dame (sia)!*	*dame (nào)!*

adverbial resources in Noirmoutier PS are listed along the assertive/negative polarity system of adverbial particles, echoing comparative data already presented in Table 6.1 and accounting for correspondences between local PS and SF. As for categories linked with evidentiality proper, I claim that *alào* is strictly evidential, oriented towards Ego, i.e. it is a definite assertion based on uncontroversial evidence, and is morphologically symmetrical to its corresponding negative particle *nào* or to the proclitic *poét* /pojt/ lit. 'point' [not], SF 'pas' [not], whereas *vér* can be defined as +/-Confirmative, and therefore dialogic, with *poét* as a potential negative counterpart. Ego-centred and dialogic items alternate in the table: the +/-Assertive set is the more neutral, while the *sia !* /sja/ SF 'si !' [but yes!] versus *nan-ni !* /nãni/ 'no way', 'not at all!' SF 'non pas', 'pas du tout !' couple can be defined as +/-Corroborative and strongly dialogic.[5] I claim that *vantér* matches *alào* in its own category, as an epistemic adverb *par excellence*, competing with a less frequent dialectal item *censément* 'supposedly', and with interferential resources from SF such as 'peut-être' [maybe], 'sans doute' [undoubtedly] or calques, such as *soé-disant* 'soi-disant' [allegedly] or the metaplasm *probabllement* SF 'probablement' [probably]. The negative particle *jha* has a very restricted distribution, akin to phraseology – it often occurs alongside AGR 1 Sg with cognitive verbs, as in *i o sé jha* /j o se ha/ 'je ne (le) sais pas' [I don't know]. However, it is nonetheless worth mentioning as it expresses a strongly negative commitment of Ego as regards access to the source of knowledge. The last item *dame!* is an interjection widely used in

5 All these categories participate in 'an implicational ranking of evidential meaning' (Nichols 1986: 239); they illustrate within the assertive-negative polarity the 'linguistic coding of epistemology' (Chafe & Nichols 1986).

Western France, often associated with local PS items, such as evidential *alào, nào, sia!*

Interestingly enough, the exclamation tag *dame!* is translated in the French-Gallo dictionary as SF 'assurément, bah, bien sûr, eh!, évidemment, certes' [assuredly, but of course, obviously, certainly] and as an exclamation, equivalent to 'naturellement', 'soit !' [naturally, so be it!] (Auffray 2007: 191). The author gives examples such as '– *a caoze don ? – Dame, je velaes pas perdre !*' ('– Why then?' '– Well, you know, I didn't want to lose the game!' SF '– Pourquoi cela ? – Eh bien, je ne voulais pas perdre!'). Poitevin-Saintongeais bilingual dictionaries provide few or no examples of *dame!*[6] In our opinion this gap is due to underestimation of the tag's use as an interjection, at least in the Poitevin-Saintongeais tradition. Indeed, elsewhere in Vendée, Pierre Rézeau duly mentions *dame !* < lat. *domina* in his monograph on a Bocage variety, Vouvant, as an interjection: 'signalons à part la très haute fréquence de *(bé) dàm* qui ponctue chaque phrase, marquant tour à tour la surprise, l'hésitation, la certitude ...'[7] (Rézeau 1976: 92). All these clues point to what could be considered an *admirative*, as labelled in Table 6.4, i.e. a polyvalent exclamation tag, conveying, as Rézeau puts it, 'in turn surprise, hesitation or certainty', with a strong phatic load in face to face interaction. This brief survey of this tag's occurrences in regional monographs confirms how much the evidential-epistemic value of this kind of lexeme may be underestimated in descriptive works, both academic and from grass-root linguists. They always show up as curiosities, instead of being viewed as part of a genuine EEA modal and adverbial system embedded in the positive-negative polarity of these dialects.

In the following subsections, we will observe examples of discourse providing evidence for these categorisations, but as an EEA system, rather than a collection of separate AAA items. In other words, a yet undiscovered EEA "island" (or *subsystem*) looms upon the lexical and pragmatic inventory. Most of our examples will be anchored in narrative contexts, in order to enhance the properties of this relevant subset.

6 The Poitevin-Saintongeais reference dictionary by Vianney Pivetea, though outstanding on many points, gives but marginal hints: '*Dame !* interjection: certes ! *(bé dame !)* évidemment; *(dame aran!)* alors ! à ce compte !' (Pivetea 2006: 473) ('*Dame !* interjection: indeed ! *(bé dame !)* of course; *(dame aran!)* now then! in that case!). This looks more like an understatement than a proper definition of this strategic conversational tag.

7 'Let us mention incidentally the very high frequency of *(bé) dàm*, which punctuates every sentence, conveying in turn surprise, hesitation or certainty ...'. The same remark for Pivetea's definition holds here: more an understatement than a positive categorisation of this item.

3 The undiscovered eea island on Noirmoutier Island: alào, vantér, vér and beyond

3.1 Evidential *Alào*

The following sample comes from an extensive narrative about how fishermen in L'Herbaudière – the island's main harbour – have to cope with bureaucracy to control the supplying of facilities for their work. The fishermen's cooperative had initially been funded out of contributions made by individual fishermen themselves, despite their very low incomes. Although it was supposed to provide them with fuel, clothing and tools at better prices than in shops for tourists, the administration of this institution is now in the hands of white-collar professionals and clerks. Assemblies and meetings are held regularly, but AB, a retired fisherman aged 62 in 1987, when the recording was carried out at his home, had many complaints about the way things were handled by the local cooperative: he wondered why some conciliatory fishermen would be invited out of the blue to be co-opted to the board when important decisions were to be made, as in (2) below, and why some chairmen behaved as if the institution were not a democratic organisation, but rather a business of their own, as in (3).

(2) – *jhe vas en faere partie [dau cunsell d'administrasiun], pasque le directeur m'a demandai*
– Ah bun? *!* Ah, bé',[8] *jhe li dis, 'jhe savoés que çh'étét comme çheu que çhe se passét. Més là, jh'é dit, te me fournis vrémint la preuve'; bé* ***alào*** !

SF: '– Je vais en faire partie [du conseil d'administration], parce que le directeur m'a demandé [d'y entrer]'. ' – Ah bon? ! Eh bien', je lui dis, 'je savais que c'était comme ça que ça se passait. Mais là', j'ai dit, 'tu m'en fournis vraiment la preuve ; ah ça, *pour sûr* !'

ENG '– I'm going to join [the board of directors], because the chairman asked me to'
– Really?! Gosh!' I say, 'I knew that that was how things were handled [co-opting people to the board]. But now you've really given me proof of it; *Yes indeed!* [AB_L'Herbaudière, born in 1925].

8 Complementary tags or sequences linked with main EEA strategies highlighted in the examples are underlined. They can be considered as associated *shifters*.

(3) *Pasque çh'ét noutre coopérative. Çh'ét pas sa coopérative à li [le directeur]. Çh'ét la coopérative daus marins-pàecheurs. Eh oui ! [çh'ét noutre coopérative] qu'at étai fundai avec les parts [daus marins].* ***Alào*** *! Daus parts de qui ? Mun père à moé, à l'époque, çh'étét mun père [qu'at apportai daus funds, comme les àotres]'*

SF: 'Parce que c'est vraiment notre coopérative. C'est pas sa coopérative à lui [le directeur]. C'est la coopérative des marins-pêcheurs. Eh oui ! [C'est notre coopérative] qu'a été fondée avec les parts [des marins]. *Pour sûr !* Des parts de qui ? Mon père à moi, à l'époque, c'était mon père [qui a apporté des fonds, comme les autres]'.

'Because it really is our cooperative. It doesn't belong to him [the chairman]. It is the fishermen's cooperative Yes indeed! [it is our cooperative] which was funded through shares [belonging to the fishermen]. *Truly!* Who bought the shares? My own father, at the time, it was him [who provided funds, like the others]'. [AB].

Through extensive description of what the speaker sensed as schemes and tricks of the trade to steer the cooperative's policies away from matters of importance to fishermen and their (blue-collar) functional prerequisites (interests that were actually in line with the white-collar administrators), he recounts what took place within the cooperative and how his kind were pushed out. The source of information here is by no means an abstract context: it plays a strategic role in the rhetorical fight between AB, the fisherman, and the board, as in (4).

(4) [Jhe dis au directeur] *'i counoés oussi beun que toé les cumbines qu'o peut avoér dans ine coopérative !', jhe li redis.* ***Bé alào*** *! Més attensiun ! çh'ét que jhe m'adressoés à li, més jh'avoés oublliai [que] y en avét quatre ou cinq àotres [directeurs] qu'étiant là.*

SF: '[Je dis au directeur] 'je connais aussi bien que toi les combines qu'il peut y avoir dans une coopérative !', je lui redis. *Tu penses bien !* Mais attention ! C'est que je m'adressais à lui, mais j'avais oublié [que] y en avait quatre à cinq autres [directeurs] qu'étaient là'.

'[I said to the chairman] 'I know just as well as you do the tricks that can be played in a cooperative!' I told him again. *Sure!* But watch out! I was speaking to him, but I had forgotten [that] there were four or five others [directors] who were there.'. [AB].

(5) *Ah bé* ***alào*** *! Més fallét qu'o séjhe signai pour les deux, là – çhés deux commissères (...): le secrétère a pris daus notes entre temps, et pis li aproés, bé dame ! Il récapitule tot ce qu'il dét mettre [dans çhau document], quoé.* [AB].

SF: '*Tu penses bien !* Mais fallait que ce soit signé par les deux, là – ces deux commissaires (...) : le secrétaire a pris des notes entre temps, et puis lui après, bon eh bien...! Il récapitule tout ce qu'il doit mettre [dans ce document], quoi'.

'*Yes indeed*! But the minutes of the meeting had to be signed by both clerks – both delegates (...): the secretary took notes in the meantime, and then, you know! He recaps everything he must put [in this report], you know' [AB].

Examples (2) to (5) provide instances of *alào* used as a powerful evidential tool in discourse: in (2) it follows the statement 'you are now giving me plain proof of the way things work over here'. In (3), it anticipates the detailed explanation of why the cooperative society should not be managed according to the whims of the white-collar administrators, since it had initially been funded by the blue-collar workers. He points out that his own father bought his share too, in spite of his extremely modest means, and he saw him work hard to contribute for the benefit of his fellow men. This reminiscence is presented as clear evidence for his claim about the original purpose of the institution. In (4), *alào* dramatically punctuates his demonstration, as he declares that he is aware that, on the basis of the evidence already pointed out as to co-opting voters to the board, he could raise suspicion as to more delicate issues, being unaware that the assembly was also attended by other board members from neighbouring cooperatives. The fear being that the other chairmen could think he is indicating other kinds of intrigue, and that he could be accused of slander. In (5), the narrative follows with an intricate episode, in which a clerk asks one of his sons to sign off on the minutes of the meeting where the speaker mentioned the co-optation scheme. As we will see, the son first signs, then changes his mind and comes back to strike out his signature on the document. In this spot, *alào* highlights the consequences of having all discussions registered in a document, as a kind of resultative evidential. This set of evidentials can be summed up as (2) comprobative (i.e. bringing evidence or proof as to an assertion's reliability), (3) experiential, (4) recapitulative, (5) resultative. These four conceptual structures give finer grain to the notion of source of information: either out of clear evidence (*X* gave me evidence of a scheme); out of a definite lifespan of experience (I know it because I saw how *X* was involved in situation *Y*); as the logical consequence of an enumeration of facts and assessments (as *X* and *Y* happened/were uttered, so *Z* would be expected as a reaction or as an obstacle); or as a source for further active comprobation (*X* will be the source of a further construct – an official report). As suggested by this list, the evidentiality of *alào* transcends truth value: it has much to do with reporting and confirming – in the latter dimension it converges partially with epistemicity, through a continuum. The next set of data will focus on epistemicity proper, in contrast to evidentiality. In this case, the item being examined (*vantér*) will lead us to a continuum integrating a more generic concept – *mirativity*.

3.2 Epistemic *Vantér* (Assumptive-Admirative)

Epistemic *vantér* is a strategic piece of the dialect EEA chessboard under survey. The PS reference dictionary does not say much about this lexeme: '*vantàe, vantér*: adj. Peut-être [maybe]; (*bén*) probablement [probably]' (Pivetea 2006: 764). The Gallo dictionary has *ventiés*, translated as 'peut-être, probablement, sans doute' [maybe, probably, undoubtedly] (Auffray 2007: 533). Data from our Noirmoutier corpus suggest that *vantér* differs notably from 'sans doute' [undoubtedly] and 'peut-être' [maybe], which often alternate with this item with meanings akin to those found in SF. *Vantér* conveys epistemic commitment as to the validity of facts and the degree of accuracy of statements. In (6), AB uses it to give a rough estimate of the periodicity of the cooperative board meetings, and of the rank of a colleague in a queue at the gas pump on the harbour in (7). In (8), AB accounts for the narrative of his elder son, who says that he was afraid that signing the report on the meeting where his father had given away the schemes of the white-collar administrators of the board might turn out dangerous for him – *who knows*.

(6) [A la coopérative maritime] *çhéques foés y at le burèa à renouvelae, te sés. Y a daus mundes qui sunt rendus en bout de mandat. Te doés faere cunsell d'administrasiun. Te fés tant d'an-nées, pis au bout de deux ou troés ans,* ***vantér bai****, fàot en élire d'àotres à la pllace, quoé. [AB]*

SF: '[A la coopérative maritime] quelques fois il y a le bureau à renouveler, tu sais. Il y a des gens qui sont arrivés en fin de mandat. Tu dois convoquer un conseil d'administration. Tu fais tant d'années, et puis au bout de deux ou trois ans *à peu près*, il faut élire de nouveaux membres à la place [des anciens], quoi'.

'[At the maritime cooperative] sometimes the board has to be renewed, you know. There are people who have come to the end of their term. You have to convene the board of directors. You do a certain number of years, then after two or three years, *more or less*, others have to be elected for the spots, you see'

(7) (pour s'approvisionner en fuel sur le port, quand il y avait la queue)
(...) *Jh'étoés le premér, moé. [Le gars de l'Epine] l'at arrivai* ***vantér bai*** *en dizième posiciun. Jh'é dit 'Nun, més çhe vat pas !* [AB]

SF: (...) 'J'étais le premier [arrivé], moi. [Le collègue de l'Epine] est arrivé *plus ou moins* en dixième position. J'ai dit "Non, mais ça ne va pas du tout, ça !" '

(In order to get fuel on the harbour, when fishermen were queuing in their boats, waiting for the clerk to open the gas pump):
(...) 'I was the first in line'. [The guy from L'Epine] was *more or less* in tenth position. I said "No, this will not do!"'.

(8) *Il [mun fils] dit " jh'étoés pas sorti de la coopérative, d'in cop jh'é pensai 'pourvu que j'éjhe poét signai la condamnassiun à mort de mun paere". Il a dit 'si jhamés ils portant pllinte, et si jhamés y avét in procès et que jh'aroés signai çhau truc-là, al alant* ***vantér*** *l'envoér en cabane (rire) !"* [AB].

SF: 'Lui, [mon fils], il dit 'j'étais à peine sorti de la coopérative, quand tout d'un coup j'ai pensé 'pourvu que je n'aie pas signé la condamnation à mort de mon père !'. Il a dit 'si jamais ils portaient plainte, si jamais il y avait un procès et que j'avais signé ce truc-là, ils ***seraient*** tout aussi bien capables de l'envoyer en prison ! (rire) !'

'He [my son] says 'Hardly had I left the cooperative when suddenly I thought 'I hope I haven't just signed my father's death sentence!'. He said 'if ever they filed a complaint, and if ever there were a trial and I had signed this thing, they *might* just be capable of sending him to jail (laughter)!".

In (9), *vantér* has an admirative connotation, as an old woman (MT) remembers her youth, when she visited a farm in Le Vieil soon after World War I, and she was struck by the number of female children who were living in the house. In (10) *vantér bai* also has an admirative flavour, as she remembers how much was demanded from young soldiers during and after World War I.

(9) *Ah oui, bé alors, i étoés surprise, jhustement ; pis totes çhés jheunes feulles qu'étiant là (...), als étiant* ***vantér bai*** *[six ou sept sœurs]. Alors, çh'ét dire que çhe fését ine fourmillère sans parell.* [MT_La Guérinière, born in 1902]

SF: ‘Ah oui, eh bien alors, j’étais surprise, justement ; et puis, toutes ces jeunes filles qu’étaient là (...) *il y avait bien* [six ou sept sœurs dans cette famille] ! Alors, pour ainsi dire, c’était une fourmilière sans pareille’

‘Oh, yes, well I was surprised, indeed; and all these young girls who were there (...), there *must* have been [six or seven sisters]. You know, it was an unparalleled ant-hill [of sisters in this family]’.

(10) *Et pis mun fraere surtout, hein, qui li revenét poét, pasque le cuntinuét. D’otrefoés als fasiant* ***vantér bai*** *sept ou huit ans de service militae. Alors, çhe cumptét pas comme service acunplli a sen ajhe, çheu.* [MT].

SF: ‘Et puis mon frère surtout, qui, lui, ne revenait pas, parce qu’il continuait [à faire son service militaire]. Jadis, ils faisaient *probablement* sept ou huit ans de service militaire. Alors, ça ne comptait pas comme service accompli, ça’

‘And my brother especially, who, as for him, wasn’t coming back because he was continuing [in the army]. It used to be that they did *more or less* seven or eight years of military service. So it didn’t count as part of the service that [his time in the war].’

In (11), epistemicity reaches a climax in merging with the subjectivity of Ego – even though it stems from an indirect narrative, of an old man from Le Vieil trying to trick people into believing there were so many potatoes in a single row that a family of eight or ten people had enough to eat for a whole winter.

(11) *(Ol) ét comme çhèle foés qu’il racuntét que y avét ine tale de pataques le lung d’ine branche; alors al en avét levai yine, pis (ol) étét telement ine bèle effort, que y avét troés nids de pies dedans, dans la tale de pataques ! Avec çhes pataques, quand ils les avunt arrachai, ils étiant* ***vantér bai*** *huit ou neuf dans la famille ; bé l’aviant azu pr tot lutre hivers à manjhae de la récolte de pataques* ! [HG_Le_Vieil].

SF: ‘C’est comme la fois où il racontait qu’il y avait une touffe de patates le long d’une vasière ; alors il en avait voulu arracher un plant, et voilà qu’il avait dû faire un tel effort pour soulever une touffe, [parce]qu’il y avait trois nids de pie dedans, dans la touffe de patates ! Avec ces patates, quand ils les ont arrachées, ils étaient *bien au moins* huit ou neuf dans la famille ; en bien, ils avaient eu de quoi manger pour tout leur hiver rien qu’à manger cette touffe de patates !’

> 'It reminds me of the time he told us that there was a row of potatoes along a salt pan; so he wanted to dig up one of the plants, then he had to make a great effort to dig up a bunch [because] there was a nest with three magpies in the potato row! With those potatoes, once they had dug them up, there *must have been* eight or nine people in the family; well, they had enough potatoes to eat for the whole winter from that one harvest!'

As an epistemic proper, *vantér* can therefore be described as an assumptive-admirative adverb: it covers an array of concepts such as tentative or provisional assessment (*estimative*) in (6, 7), *projective* or *speculative* (8) and *hyperbolic* (11).[9] In contrast, (9) and (10) mingle to some extent estimative and mirative (see Aikhenvald's above quotation). This leads us to a third strategic item in the EEA system in Noirmoutier PS: evidential *vér*, where the continuum runs from assertion and confirmation of the source of the information towards other rhetoric functions, such as iterative assessment. This item is highly dialogic, i.e. less centred on Ego and one's access to the source, or the first-hand versus non-first-hand information, and more focused on the co-construction of discourse. From this point of view, it also differs from a simple modal adverb, as it enhances the role of evidentiality as a co-construction mechanism in discourse, beyond grammar and the lexicon.

3.3 Evidential *Vér* (confirmative-punctuative)

Evidential *vér* (cf. SF 'voire' [indeed, or even]') will be examined separately from evidential *alào* and epistemic *vantér*, as it leads us to a wider domain of discursive resources, which can be qualified as *tags* – among them *dame !*, already mentioned above, and which often combines with *vér* and *alào* (e.g. *dame vér ! dame alào !*). It also differs from *alào* and *vantér* in space and time: it apparently receded from most of the villages during the 20th century. It had so far resisted in the south in the 1980s, when I documented free discourse in PS for my Ph.D. dissertation on sociolinguistic variation. All examples here are from a female speaker aged 81 in Barbâtre, whom we met serendipitously in the old

9 For terms such as *assumptive* and *speculative*, see Palmer (1986/2001) – *speculative* entails resorting to a mental projection, I also suggest the term *projective*, although it might be desirable to avoid further neologisms. *Estimative* here applies to a quantitative estimate, *hyperbolic* refers to a variant of *estimative* – for a rough or bold estimate rather than a cautious one.

people's home of Noirmoutier-en-L'île, where she had arrived one year before. Although example (15) suggests that the tag already had a stereotyped flavour to it, she seemed not to be aware of her own frequent use of it, as the other examples show. In (12), *vér* confirms her assessment of the specific stubbornness of donkeys and mules.

(12) *Més i croés que gn'a daus bàetes pr entreus-màemes qui sunt capricieuses, hein ! Surtout les brdins, les mulets et les ânes. Moéns les chevàos. Més les mulets pis les ânes, çh'ét tot pllin capricieus. Als se feriant putoût tuae que nun pas qu'als marcheriant, n'a daus mouments.* ***Vér***. *Més i vous dis moé, çh'étét énervant ...*

SF: 'Mais je crois qu'il y a des bêtes qui, quant à elles, sont capricieuses, hein ! Surtout les ânes, les mules et les ânes. [C'est] moins [le cas] des chevaux. Mais les mules et les ânes, c'est très capricieux. Ils se feraient plutôt tuer que de se mettre en marche, parfois. *Sans blague.* Mais je vous dis, moi, c'était énervant ...'

'But I do believe that there are animals who are naughty, aren't there! Especially donkeys, mules and asses. Horses less so. But donkeys and asses are extremely naughty. They'd rather get killed than start walking sometimes. *Truly.* I'm telling you, they're really annoying'.

In (13, 14), it confirms what the interviewer has just said, on the basis of the information the speaker had previously made available to him. Furthermore, in (15), *vér* is used iteratively both as an enumerative and assertive tag – a function we call *punctuative*.

(13) – *Et àotrement, çhe fét cumbai d'an-nées que vous àetes içhi, à la mésun de retréte de Noérmoutae ?*
– *Içhi ? Rén que çhéte an-née, hein !*
– *Rén que çhéte an-née ?*
– ***Vér*** *! I sé rén que là de çhète an-née.*

SF: '– Et autrement, ça fait combien d'années que vous êtes ici, à la maison de retraite de Noirmoutier ?
– Ici ? Rien que depuis cette année, hein !
– Seulement depuis cette année ?
– *Oh oui* ! Je suis là seulement depuis cette année'.
'– And otherwise, how long have you been here, in this old people's home?

– Here? Only this year!
– Only this year?
– *Truly*, I've only been here this year (no more)'.

(14) – *Alors, ve me disiez que ves étiez d'ine famille de cultivateurs ?'*
– ***Vêr** !*
– *Alors, que ves aviez daus vaches ...*
– *Daus vaches, **vér**, daus poules, daus canards, **vér**, daus potets et pis daus vaches, **vér**.*

SF: '– Alors, vous me disiez que vous étiez d'une famille de cultivateurs ?'
– *Oui !*
– Alors, que vous aviez des vaches ...
– Des vaches, *oui*, des poules, des canards, *oui*, des canetons et aussi des vaches, *oui*.'

'– So, you were saying that you were from a family of farmers?'
– *Indeed!*
– So, you had cows ...
– Cows, *indeed*, chickens, ducks, *indeed*, ducklings and also cows, *indeed*'.

(15) ***Vér**, mun petit camarade ! Als disiant torjhout "**vér**, **alào** **vér**, mun petit camarade !" Quand als causiant deus hommes ensemblle, "mun petit camarade ! ... "*

SF: '*Oui*, mon petit camarade ! Ils disaient toujours "*oui*, pour sûr, *oui*, mon petit camarade !" Quand ils parlaient, deux hommes ensemble, " mon petit camarade !".'...

'*Indeed*, my little lad! They [old men] always used to say: "*indeed*, for sure, *indeed*, my little lad', when they would talk, two men together, "my little lad!..."'

Examples (16) and (17) are all the more interesting as they strongly contrast sociolinguistically, in terms of style or register. In (16), the interviewer is awkwardly looking for the proper word for 'mating (donkeys)', using 'saillir' [mount] instead of 'prendre' [take] ('faire prendre les bêtes' [have the animals mate]), which triggers a tag answer in SF 'oui' [yes], instead of PS *vér*. As soon as the blunder is repaired in (17), by using the proper verb in the question, the PS tag shows up in the answer, as expected. This glimpse into fine-grained code-switching confirms the sensitivity of the endogenous evidential-epistemic system to diaphasic settings: the EEA system is stronger when deeply embedded in discourse in PS, whereas it is easily displaced by the AAA system of SF in conditions of register mixing.

(16) '– ... *Et i é entendu dire que d'àotrefoés, çh'étét en Brbâtre que le munde de l'île aliant cherchae lutres câgnots pr la culture ...*'
'– ***Oui*** ...'
'– *Y avét daus mundes qui fesiant saillir les bàetes*'
'– ***Oui, oui, oui*** ...'

SF: '– ... Et j'ai entendu dire qu'autrefois, c'était à Barbâtre que les gens de l'île allaient se fournir en bêtes de somme pour la culture ...'
– *Oui* ...
'– Il y avait des gens qui faisaient saillir leurs bêtes'
'– *Oui, oui*, c'est cela ...'

'– And ... I've been told that formerly, people went to Barbâtre to get donkeys for their plots ...'
– *Yes* ...
'– Some people brought their own animals to *be mounted*'
'– *Yes, yes, yes* ...'

(17) '– *çh'étét en Brbâtre qu'o se fesét ?*'
'– ***Vér***. *En Brbâtre, que als fesiant – au respect – prendre les bàetes.*'

SF: '– *C'était à Barbâtre que ça se faisait ?*
'– *C'est cela. [C'était] à Barbâtre qu'ils faisaient – sauf votre respect – s'accoupler les bêtes'.*

'– So it was in Barbâtre that they had it done?
– *Indeed*. In Barbâtre, that is where people had them – with all due respect – mate'.

This survey of the three main endogenous lexemes resorting to an EEA system in North-Western PS (*alào, vantér, vér*), with examples recorded in the 1980s (1982–88) on the island of Noirmoutier, gives but a glimpse of the richness of such a system in an Oïl dialect. Much material transcribed in this period from oral narratives awaits more study – as well as untranscribed material.[10] Most of this interesting EEA system actually lingers below the surface of conversation, and remains inconspicuous as such. An approach anchored in conversational strategies makes this covert system more available for interpretation and thus, for categorisation as an EEA system proper. As we have seen more than once, checking

10 Over 150 hours of tape recordings were deposited in the Archives Sonores de la Bibliothèque Nationale by the author during the period mentioned above.

sources on these adverbs and tags, they tend to be underestimated in reference dictionaries and monographs. One of the reasons for this gap in documentation is due to the difficulty of integrating amateur and academic dialectology into general and typological linguistics (Léonard 2012).

4 Conclusion and Prospects

Disentangling the pragmatic values of the EEA set in Noirmoutier PS highlights how heuristic categories such as evidentiality and epistemicity may prove to be, when applied to data sets we always thought we knew too well, either because of their dialectal status, as in this instance, or because available 'maps' only show already 'discovered islands', as the king answers sincerely to the man who asked for a boat for his search for unmapped territories. This is precisely what one should expect from heuristic concepts: to be as useful as a compass or sextant when revisiting maps or launching expeditions for unknown territories. Indeed, the whole bulk of linguistic theories, especially in the 20th century and the last decades has played a major role in rediscovering language, as a cognitive asset of the species, but also language through the complexity and refinements of unwritten and often endangered languages or dialects – all comparable to the islands yet to be discovered in Saramago's tale. Noirmoutier PS is barely spoken anymore, except in La Guérinière and L'Epine (especially the hamlet of La Bosse), and L'Herbaudière and Le Vieil to a certain extent. It has thoroughly disappeared from the hamlet of La Fosse, and from the small towns of Noirmoutier-en-l'Île and Barbâtre, as I observed in the years 2010–12 when I went back to record new data from a few speakers in order to complete the documentation I had begun in the 1980s. The author of this paper was even mistaken by some younger islanders for one of the last speakers, and was asked on several occasions to show off his skills – a situation which would have seemed absurd or pathetic thirty years earlier. At the time he recorded and transcribed what was to later become an endangered dialect, SF was already mingling with PS, though speakers would cautiously separate both as much as possible – e.g. any reported talk in SF would have been performed in the acrolectal register, whereas any reported conversation in PS would have been inscribed in the basilectal norm.

Nevertheless, although more 'genuine' and less 'contaminated' by SF, local PS had already mingled the EEA and the AAA subsystems, for the sake of pragmatic richness. As already pointed out, SF *peut-être* [maybe] alternated with PS *vantér*, as SF *oui* [yes] or colloquial French *ouais* [yeah] was indeed a good neutral assertive ingredient to mix up with *alào* or *vér* at strategic moments in oral narratives. The situation was the same with negative particles such as SF *pas* [not] and PS *poét* [not], whatever purists may think of this *lectal scrambling*. This mingling can indeed be considered interference, but it should also be grasped as a full house of pragmatic resources, in which the PS items *alào, vér, sia, vantér, dame!* make up the core of the EEA system, not so much in opposition to, as in complementary pragmatic distribution with the AAA system. This repertoire also likely strengthened the local EEA system, many items from this system continue to thrive in regional colloquial French – especially the admirative *dame!* and many syntagmatic calques, like *bé dame, (c'est) bé vrai !* 'Gosh, it sure is true!', *bé dame, oui !* 'Oh my, indeed', *dame non !* 'Oh my, no!'. In contrast, items such as *alào, vér, sia, vantér* are deemed too dialectal to be fully intelligible to outsiders, and are very unlikely to emerge in the currently dominant colloquial French.[11] With the rise of French monolingualism, only the AAA system still thrives, whereas the former EEA system has been lost ... Unless it still looms somewhere in contemporaneous colloquial French speech, as yet undiscovered. Let us hope this paper contributes to fostering research in this domain, in both urban sociolectal and rural dialectal settings. As a matter of fact, any scholar dedicated to Evidentials and Epistemics resembles the man who demanded a boat from the King to search for undiscovered islands – in this case, pragmatic islands of sociocognitive subsystems, highly relevant to the structure of the human mind.[12]

Language consultants

North: HG: Le_Vieil, born in 1908; AB: L'Herbaudière, born in 1925.
Centre: MT: La Guérinière, born in 1902; MJR: L'Epine, born in 1908; South: CP: Barbâtre, born in 1902.
Interviewer: Jean Léo Léonard.

---

11 Needless to say, admirative *dame!* has a much wider areal extension than the former adverbial items – it is to be found in most of Central-Western France, including Bretagne. Epistemic *vantèr*, or more properly *vantiers* < *volontiers* [willingly] was once widespread in the West as well, as documented in dictionaries of 'patois' and regional French in Anjou. In contrast, an item such as evidential *alào* is a singularity and, as far as I know, has never been documented in neighbouring localities. By no means should it be interpreted as cognate to SF *alors* 'then'. Its phonological form points to an etymology of the **ad illum* type, with a low vowel split, rather than *à+lors*, as a *Prep+horam* compound.

12 See Aikhenvald & Dixon (2014), for evidentiality constituting a *grammar of knowledge*.

Abbreviations: AAA – Assertive / Assumptive Adverbs; AGRS – Agreement Subject; EEA – Evidential Epistemic Adverbs; fem – feminine; Pl – Plural; msc – masculine gender; PS – Poitevin-Saintongeais ; SF – Standard French; Sg – Singular.

Acknowledgements: This work is part of the program "Investissements d'Avenir" overseen by the French National Research Agency, ANR-10-LABX-0083 (Labex EFL), in particular PPC11 – Complexity, Geolinguistics & (Morpho)Phonological Patterns (strand 1) and Cross-Mediated elicitation, EM2 (strand 7).

References

Aikhenvald, Alexandra. 2004. Evidentiality. Oxford: Oxford University Press.

Aikhenvald, Alexandra & R. M. W. Dixon (eds.). 2014. *The Grammar of Knowledge: A Cross-Linguistic Typology.* Oxford: Oxford University Press.

Alrahabi, Motasem & Jean-Pierre Desclés. 2009. Opérations de prise en charge énonciative: assertion, médiatif et modalités dans le discours rapporté direct, en arabe et en français. In Krzysztof Bogacki, Joanna Cholewa & Agata Rozumko (eds.), *Methods of lexical analysis, theoretical assumptions and practical applications*. Bialystok: Wydawnictwo Uniwersytetu w Bialymstoku. http://lalic.paris-sorbonne.fr/PUBLICATIONS/2009/pologne.pdf (accessed 10 May 2016).

Auchlin, Antoine. 1981. *Mais heu, pis bon, ben alors voilà, quoi!* Marqueurs de structuration de la conversation et complétude. *Cahiers de linguistique française* 2. 141–159.

Auffray, Régis. 2007. Le Petit Matao. Dictionnaire Gallo-Français / Motier Galo-Françaez, Françaez-Galo. Rennes: Rue des Scribes.

Bally, Charles. 1932. Linguistique générale et linguistique française. Berne: Francke.

Beeching, Kate. 2002. Gender, politeness and pragmatic particles in French. Amsterdam: John Benjamins.

Bouchard, Robert. 2002. *Alors, donc, mais* ..., 'particules énonciatives' et / ou 'connecteurs'? Quelques considérations sur leur emploi et leur acquisition. *Syntaxe et sémantique* 3. 63–73.

Chafe, Wallace L. & Johanna Nichols (eds.). 1986. *Evidentiality. The linguistic encoding of epistemology, Advances in Discourse Processes,* XX. Norwood, New Jersey: Ablex Publishing Corporation.

Devineau, Colette. 2015. *Les parlers de l'Epine et de l'île de Noirmoutier.* La Crèche: Geste Editions.

Ducrot, Oswald. 1980. *Les mots du discours*. Paris: Editions de Minuit.

Gautier, Michel, Freddy Bossy, Jean-Jacques Chevrier, Jean-Loïc Le Quellec & Eric Nowak. 1993. *Grammaire du Poitevin-Saintongeais*. Mougon: UPCP-Geste Paysanne.

Gautier, Pierre & Liliane Jagueneau (ed.). 2002. *Ecrire et parler poitevin-saintongeais du XVIè siècle à nos jours*. Bignoux/La Crèche: Parlanjhe Vivant-Geste Editions.

Hansen, Maj-Britt Mosegaard. 1998. The function of discourse particles: A study with special reference to Spoken Standard French. Amsterdam: John Benjamins.

Hwang, Young-ai. 1992. *Eh bien, alors, enfin et disons, en français parlé contemporain*. Thèse, Université de la Sorbonne Nouvelle.

Léonard, Jean Léo. 1991. *Variation dialectale et microcosme anthropologique: l'île de Noirmoutier (Vendée, France)*. Ph. D. dissertation, Aix-en-Provence, Université de Provence, manuscript.

Léonard, Jean Léo. 1998. Microdialectologie et syntaxe: aspects du pronom neutre poitevin. In *Actes du XXIe Congrès International de Linguistique et de Philologie romane*, vol 2: *Morfologia e sintassi delle lingue romanze*, 543–556. Tübingen: Niemeyer.

Léonard, Jean Léo. 2004. Entre A. Dumas et J. Potocki: retour sur des phénomènes d'allophonie vocalique dans les parlers poitevins nord-ouest, ou 'le transcrupscrit' retrouvé dans une cabane à huîtres. In Tobias Scheer (ed.), *Corpus* 3, *Usage des corpus en phonologie*, 435–503.

Léonard, Jean Léo. 2005. Statut et fonction du poitevin en forme de poire. In Liliane Jagueneau (ed.). Actes du colloque des 5 et 6 nov. 2004, Université de Poitiers, *Le poitevin-saintongeais: images et dynamique d'une langue*, 143–166. Paris: L'Harmatan.

Léonard, Jean Léo. 2012. *Eléments de dialectologie générale*. Paris: Michel Houdiard.

Léonard, Jean Léo & Liliane Jagueneau. 2013. Disparition, apparition et réapparition des langues d'oïl : de l'invisibilisation au nouveau regard, *Bulletin de la Société de Linguistique de Paris* 108/1. 283-343.

Narrog, Heiko. 2005. Review of Aikhenvalt (2004). *SKY Journal of Linguistics* 18. 379–388.

Nichols, Johanna. 1986. The bottom line: Chinese Pidgin Russian. In Wallace L. Chafe & Johanna Nichols (eds.). *Evidentiality: The Linguistic Coding of Epistemology*, 239–257.

Palmer, Franck R. 1986/2001. *Mood and Modality*. Cambridge: Cambridge University Press.

Pivetea, Vianney. 2006. Dictionnaire Français > Poitevin-Saintongeais ; Poetevin-Séntunjhaes > Françaes. La Crèche: Geste éditions.

Pusch, Claus D. 2007. Is there evidence for evidentiality in Gascony Occitan? *Italian Journal of Linguistics* 19:1. 91–108.

Rézeau, Pierre. 1976. Un patois de Vendée. Le parler rural de Vouvant. Paris: Klincksieck.

Rooryck, Johan. 2001. Evidentiality, Part I, *Glot International* 5–4. 125–133.

Adrián Cabedo Nebot & Bert Cornillie

A prosody account of (inter)subjective modal adverbs in Spanish

Abstract: In this article we examine the prosodic values of intersubjective and subjective readings conveyed by Spanish modal adverbs ending in *–mente* and which are used in talk-in-interaction. Our analysis consists of a pragmatic analysis of the adverbs in the dynamic context of speaker hearer interaction as well as of an acoustic analysis of the average, i.e. standardized, F0 values of the different readings. Our data from the CORLEC and Val.Es.Co corpora give an indication of significant differences in the prosodic configuration of subjectivity and intersubjectivity in Spanish talk-in-interaction. In the article we show that the speaker marks prosodically the pragmatic dimension involving shared knowledge with the co-participant. The global pitch of the intersubjective readings of the adverbs is perceived as superior to that of the subjective readings. Moreover, intersubjectivity readings display melodic fluctuation from the second syllable (fall) to the final one (rise). This attracts the attention of the co-participant, whereas the prosody of subjectivity presents a continuous rise. In general, we have not found any cases of *de-accentuation* (Astruc and Nolan 2007a, 2007b) in the prosodic realization of the Spanish adverbs under examination.

Keywords: prosody, modality, (inter)subjectivity, Spanish

1 Introduction

In the pragmatic-linguistic and interactional-linguistic literature, prosody has received a great deal of attention (cf. Barth-Weingarten, Dehé and Wichmann

We would like to thank the anonymous reviewer for his/her constructive criticisms and interesting comments, which have no doubt contributed substantially to the improved version of the present paper. It goes without saying that all remaining problems are our own responsibility.

Note: This study has been funded by the following Spanish Project: "La atenuación pragmática en el español hablado: su variación diafásica y diatópica" (Ministerio de Economía y Competitividad of Spain, ref. FFI2013-40905-P).

Adrián Cabedo Nebot, University of Valencia
Bert Cornillie, University of Leuven

https://doi.org/10.1515/9783110572261-007

2009; Dehé and Wichmann 2010; Barth-Weingarten, Reber and Selting 2010). Prosody is generally seen to function as a focalizing means of linguistic expression (Wennerstrom 2001; Dorta Luis 2008). Hence, the way in which things are pronounced influences the perception of the linguistic message.

Yet, the prosody of modal qualifications is relatively understudied. There is some recent work on discourse markers and grammaticalization (cf. Wichmann, Vandenbergen and Aijmer 2010), on epistemic parentheticals (cf. Dehé and Wichmann 2010) and on tag questions (cf. Dehé and Braun 2013; Kimps, Davidse and Cornillie 2014; Kimps 2016). As far as sentential adverbs are concerned, Astruc and Nolan (2007a, 2007b) and Prieto (2002) studied their prosody for Catalan and Allerton and Cruttenden (1974) did so for English. Yet, so far no study has addressed the prosody of the subjective and intersubjective readings of modal expressions in talk-in-interaction. In this chapter we will examine the question of whether there is a correlation between specific prosodic patterns and subjective versus intersubjective readings of modal adverbs ending in *-mente*. In doing so, we will show that subjective and intersubjective readings have different melodic contours. In the following lines, we will first discuss what we understand by (inter)subjectivity and then pass on to review the previous accounts of the modal adverbs in Catalan and English. At the end of the section we will describe the dataset.

In general, subjectivity refers to the speaker's (pragmatic) attitude to the proposition (Traugott approach) or the speaker's (and co-participants's) subjective construal of some aspect of a linguistic expression (Langacker approach). It is common knowledge that subjectivity and intersubjectivity have been used in several ways in the literature. Most contributions in Athaniasiadou, Canakis and Cornillie (2006) distinguish between an objective and a subjective construal of meaning that is not linguistically coded by a linguistic form. In doing so, they adopt Langacker's (1990) conceptualist semantic view of the notion of subjectivity, which does not leave much room for pragmatics, in general, nor intersubjectivity, in particular. In their overview paper, Davidse, Vandelanotte and Cuyckens (2010) emphasize that the term intersubjectivity should be reserved for encoded semantic meaning, which is seen as the result of a process that involves the semanticization of the pragmatic meaning. Ghesquière (2010) proposes a textual intersubjective function and Narrog (2012a, b) disentangles the points that the above-mentioned approaches have in common from those that make them differ.

With regard to the (inter)subjectivity of modality, Nuyts (2001) and Cornillie (2008) have argued for an intersubjective reading of epistemic and evidential qualifications that can be shared by speaker and hearer, as opposed to a speaker-centered subjective reading of modality. Moreover, Cornillie (2010a, b) also refers to the speaker's hinting at shared knowledge or a shared stance as an intersubjectivity strategy. Traugott (2010: 34) states that such a view is different (she calls it "orthogonal") from her own view of intersubjectivity, which is restricted to (semantically) conventionalized meanings of intersubjectivity. Hence, Traugott (2010) focusses on linguistic expressions that index subjectivity ("speaker attitude or viewpoint") or intersubjectivity ("addressee's self-image"), whereas Nuyts (2001) and Cornillie (2008, 2010) and others deal with contextual, i.e. pragmatic meanings.

In this paper we will have recourse to the notion of (inter)subjectivity from a pragmatic, and more specifically interactional, perspective. Given the changing dynamics of speaker hearer interaction in conversation, we are interested in the different pragmatic, i.e. subjective vs. intersubjective, readings of the epistemic modal and/or evidential meaning expressed by the adverbs. In our analysis, the subjective reading refers to an epistemic or evidential qualification without the speaker making any hint at possible knowledge or opinions shared with the co-participant. Hence, subjective qualifications convey the speaker's own assessment of his/her world, and are not concerned with the interactional organization of the sequence, for instance, in terms of adjacency pairs. By contrast, intersubjective qualifications involve the speaker's assessment of a shared world and express an intention to take into account the co-participant's views.

Our prosody-based study of (inter)subjectivity examines a set adverbs that belong to a specific morpho-syntactic paradigm, namely that of the adverbs in *–mente*. These adverbs are a morphologically very productive class in Romance, also via the Catalan and French suffix *–ment* (Torner 2007). They stem from the Latin ablative case of MENS, MENTIS 'mind', which gives *–mente*. In both form and function, they can be compared with the productive paradigm of English adverbs ending in *–ly*.

In Spanish as well as in English the established class of adverbs consists of learned variants of the naturally grammaticalized adverbial phrases expressing epistemic modality and evidentiality (*a lo mejor* 'perhaps', *quizá* 'maybe', *tal vez* 'perhaps', *por lo visto* 'apparently', *al parecer* 'it seems'). Interestingly, Wierzbicka (2006) distinguishes clearly between subjectively oriented adverbs in *–ly* and what she calls modal particles such as *maybe* and *perhaps*. Yet, this strict separation of subjective and intersubjective functions along the types of adverbs is not what we observe for the adverbs in *–mente* (nor for English adverbs such as *obviously* as a matter of fact). In this study, we will describe in which contexts there is a subjective dimension and which other contexts there is an intersubjective effect.

With regard to the prosody, few studies address the class of adverbs ending in *–mente*. Yet, Astruc and Nolan (2007a; 2007b) have examined the prosodic configurations of these adverbial expressions in Catalan (adverbs ending in *–ment*) and English (adverbs ending in *–ly*). On the basis of a set of examples produced in a phonetics laboratory, in which informants were asked to read 78 utterances with sentential and extra-sentential adverbs, they came to the conclusion that these adverbs show up almost systematically as independent prosodic units. This is in line with what other prosody accounts of sentential adverbs have pointed out (see, for instance, Prieto 2002 for Catalan, or Allerton and Cruttenden 1974 for English).

By contrast, Cabedo's (2014) account of the prosodic contours of the sentential uses of these Spanish adverbs suggests a different distribution. He shows that several adverbs ending in *–mente* (*supuestamente* 'supposedly', *indudablemente* 'undoubtedly', *exactamente* 'exactly'...) present a balanced distribution of prosodically independent units and dependent ones that are part of other, larger prosodic units. Cabedo (2014) explains these prosodic differences in terms of the type of language studied: for instance, colloquially spoken Spanish, which is characterized by communicative immediacy, witnesses a high number of words per minute and has fewer independent units.

Another feature that is frequently mentioned in studies on the prosodic configurations of adverbs is the *de-accentuation* of tokens. Surprisingly, the literature on the prosody of English adverbs systematically mentions the criterion of *de-accentuation* as a phenomenon that characterizes sentential adverbs (Allerton and Cruttenden 1974). However, this is not what Astruc and Nolan (2007) find for Catalan, nor what Cabedo (2014) observes for Spanish. In Astruc and Nolan's (2007a: 255) terms: "Catalan speakers tend to deaccent the sentential adverb less frequently than English speakers do, as was expected from the initial assumption that Catalan, unlike English, is a "non-plastic" language".

Finally, another important element that we have to take into account is the epistemological validity of the previous accounts found in the literature (Allerton and Cruttenden 1974; Astruc and Nolan 2007a, 2007b; Prieto 2002). In most of the above-mentioned studies, the analyses were carried out on corpora which contain non-spontaneous materials, i.e. acoustic materials that were registered in phonetics laboratories where, generally speaking, a group of informants were asked to read a set of sentences or texts. However, a speech situation without spontaneous speech means that the results of the linguistic analysis may be different from what speakers do in natural, interactional environments. It is no wonder that the previous studies did not address the prosody of pragmatic dimensions such as subjectivity and intersubjectivity.

On the other hand, it should be mentioned that the analysis of pitch scales (F0) in real spontaneous speech can only be done on the basis of high quality recordings. Unfortunately, due to the interactional context, clean recordings are not readily available. Yet, it is in this specific speech context that we find additional meaning effects that are a crucial part of the pragmatic analysis. Hence, in this study we have adopted a corpus-based methodology that both relies on the rich interaction in spontaneous speech and warrants the acoustic analysis in terms of high quality recordings.

For the sake of comparability, we limit ourselves to the analysis of the prosodic patterns of five adverbs that end in –*mente*: the evidential adverbs *obviamente* 'obviously' and *evidentemente* 'evidently' and the epistemic adverbs *seguramente* 'certainly', *indudablemente* 'undoubtedly' and *posiblemente* 'possibly'. We have chosen these adverbs because (i) they convey both subjective and intersubjective readings in clear contexts of use, and (ii) they are the most frequent ones in the corpus that we analysed. Yet, we were obliged to exclude from the final analysis many cases that were not suited for the acoustic analysis, as will be shown in Section 2.1.

The remainder of the paper is structured in the following way. In Section 2 we will present the methodology that we have applied to the dataset. Section 3 is the main body of the paper in that it contains the detailed description of the prosodic patterns of the subjective and intersubjective readings of the five adverbs. Finally, in Section 4 we discuss the results and present two conclusions.

2 Methodology

2.1 Data

This paper is based on an acoustic analysis of several corpora containing spontaneous talk-in-interaction from Spain, amongst others, the Corpus Oral de Referencia de la Lengua Española Contemporánea (CORLEC, 269.500 words) and the Val.Es.Co 2.0 Corpus (120.246 words, Cabedo and Pons Bordería 2013). The former corpus stands for a wide array of different spoken genres. Besides a whole range of different spoken activities belonging to the communicative distance (e.g. court, games, teaching), it includes talk-in-interaction stemming from different contexts and settings (e.g. interviews, radio programmes, debates, conversations). By contrast, the latter corpus stands for Valencia Español Coloquial 2.0 and exclusively contains colloquial conversations in Spanish. That is, the speech participants are friends, relatives or neighbours who speak spontaneously with each other in an informal setting.

The study was preceded by filtering out the audio files of which the acoustic quality was not good enough. In total, we found 234 cases in the two corpora, but

Table 7.1: Frequency distribution of the tokens

	Val.Es.Co	CORLEC	Total
Obviamente 'obviously'	4 | 30.7 %	9 | 69.3 %	13
Seguramente 'certainly'	4 | 22.2 %	14 | 77.8 %	18
Posiblemente 'possibly'	2 | 22.2 %	7 | 77.8 %	9
Evidentemente 'evidently'	1 | 8.3 %	11 | 91.7 %	12
Indudablemente 'undoubtedly'	2 | 20 %	8 | 80 %	10
Total number of tokens	13 | 21 %	49 | 79 %	62
Total number of words	120.246 | 31 %	269.500 | 69 %	

we only kept 62 cases in the final set of utterances that were incorporated in the study. Thus, we obtained the following number of tokens. As for the average frequency distribution of the adverbs, 21 % of the adverbs come from the Val.Es.Co-corpus and 79 % of them were found in the CORLEC-corpus. When we take into account the proportion of the two corpora in the combined corpus used for this chapter, the Val.Es.CO-corpus has fewer instances than the CORLEC. Now, it is established knowledge that evidential and epistemic adverbs ending in *–mente* are more frequent in more formal genres (cf. Cornillie 2010a, b; Company Company 2014). As the CORLEC-corpus is seen as a slightly more formal corpus than the Val.Es.Co one, in that it not only includes conversations and interviews but also other genres such as political discourse and journalism (debates, news reports, etc.), it is normal that it contains more adverbs that end in *–mente*.

In the remainder of the paper, we will not be concerned with distinguishing prosodic patterns of the adverbs in terms of different genres, since this is not one of the objectives of this study.

2.2 Method: Melodic stylization

Given that voices are idiosyncratic and susceptible to gender variation, it is imperative to apply a method of melodic stylization, mainly for the sake of the comparability of the sound fragments. The present-day literature offers a series of ways to address this need. The commonly used models assign an absolute value to the rising tones and falling tones that are observable in the subsequent syllables of the phonic group.

The *Tones and Break Indices* (TOBI) model, for instance, describes the different tonal configurations in terms of rises (H) and falls (L) in the pitch scale.

Estebas and Prieto (2009) as well as Prieto and Roseano (2010) have developed the specific TOBI values for their application to Spanish.

Another approach, which is more centred on the acoustic data, argues for an analysis based on relativized units of tonal changes. This way, the unit of semi-tone can be used in the TOBI model (cf. Roseano and Planas 2013) or the rises and falls can be measured in terms of percentages of change across syllables, like the MAS (Melodic Analysis of Speech) method does (cf. Cantero-Serena 2002; Cantero-Serena and Font-Rotchès 2009), so as to obtain standardized Hz contours (FO). These methods of stylization aim at eliminating any subjective appraisal from the analysis of rising and falling tones.

In the present study, we will have recourse to a slightly modified version of this model, in that the percentage of the rise in the first syllable will be taken from the last syllable before the adverb, as proposed in Cantero and Font-Rotchès (2009) model. Instead we will directly calculate the percentual difference between two contiguous syllables. For example, let us imagine that we have an adverb, like *obviamente*, with four syllables; following Cantero-Serena and Font-Rotchès MAS model, the first syllable will have a value of 100 % and the following syllables will take the percentual variation from that point. As we said before, we do not take the first syllable of the adverb to compute 100 %, but the last syllable of the previous word.

Moreover, we take the average pitch scale of all subjective versus intersubjective examples of each adverb. Hence, following the MAS model of acoustic analysis proposed by Cantero-Serena and Font-Rotchès (2009) the tables that represent the results of this study (Figure 7.1–Figure 7.6) contain values of standardized Hz. This means that the examples that we give do not directly correspond to the values of the specific tables. Since we will not examine their pitch scale individually, we do not show the FO curve of each example. Rather, the examples that we reproduce are meant to illustrate the pragmatics and semantics of the adverbs in terms of their subjective or intersubjective reading.

Table 7.2: MAS methodology for standardize pitch

Token	Previous syllable	Ob	via	Men	Te
Hertzs	277	340	320	296	311
%	100	22.7 %	−5.9 %	−7.5 %	5.1 %
Standardized melody	100	123	116	107	112

Source: Cantero-Serena and Font-Rotchès (2009).

3 Analysis of the tonal contours

3.1 Obviamente

The Spanish adverb *obviamente* 'obviously' consists of four syllables, of which the first and the third syllables are stressed. A slow pronunciation of the adverb allows disentangling the bilabial occlusive and the bilabial fricative ['ob-βja-'men-te] and to keep the expected syllabic structure, whereas the most common pronunciation in spontaneous speech is combining the stress in the first [o] with a lengthened bilabial at the beginning of the second syllable ['o-βja-'men-te] (Quilis 1981, 1993).

In our data, 8 cases of the adverb *obviamente* have been labelled as subjective, whereas 5 are intersubjective. In the following examples, we observe an intersubjective reading in (1) and a subjective one in (2).

(1) H2> Sí…
H1>…eh…. hasta cierto punto también sorprendente porque… eh… el primer año en quinientos tampoco… Lo cierto es que nos hacía albergar grandes esperanzas de que se pueden limar esas diferencias… lo que ocurre es que la gente delante va ¡tan deprisa!…
H2> <fático=afirmación>…
H1>…que…<fático=duda> bueno, creo que es… ¡muy fácil!… **obviamente** dentro de las grandísimas dificultades, creo que es muy fácil limar un segundo, segundo y medio…
H2> Exacto…
H1> …pero luego… <fático=duda> limar las tres, cuatro, cinco, seis, siete décimas…

H2> yes…
H1> erm… to a certain extent, it is also surprising because… erm… in the first year, in 500[cubic centimeters] we did not… the truth is, we had reasons to have very high hopes for the possibility of reducing our difference… but the people racing before us, they go so fast!
H2> <phatic=affirmation>…
H1> …that… <phatico=hesitation> well, I think it's… very easy!… **obviously** considering the huge difficulties, I think it is really easy to reduce one second, one and a half seconds…
H2> Exactly…
H1>…but then… <fático=duda> to reduce those three, four, five, six, seven tenths of seconds…

(2) H2> ...Ha sido el reportaje tal vez más extenso de mi vida, pues he tarda(d)>o dos años en... en contar lo que (( )) no en contar lo que sabía, porque... yo he podido... los últimos datos es... los he sabido pues pocos días antes, no he podido publicarlo antes porque he estado... diez días internado en un hospital, ha sido lo único quee pero, vamos, yo he sabido, no es que lo supiera desde antes del juicio, como me han pregunta(d)>o algunas personas, no, yo sabía algunos datos... algunos datos pero que no tenía todavía contrastados. A mí me hacía falta que Dionisio saliera de la cárcel, ver, observar y escuchar algunos... datos y algunos elementos y (( )) y bueno, entonces ahora ha sido el momento... también él... él creo que silencio> a él también le habría gustado contarlo, aunque ahora diga todo lo contrario **obviamente** porque de alguna manera vive un poco... pesaroso porque... sus cómplices no le quieren demasiado bien.
H1> Pues sus cómplices eh... con el... con el dinero que... que falta, ¿qué... qué ha hecho?, ¿qué ha pasado?

H2>...It has probably been the longest report of my life, for it took me two years to... to tell what (( )) not to tell what I knew, because... I have been able... the latest data are... they came to my knowledge few days before, I could not publish them before because I had been... confined in a hospital for ten days, that is the only thing that..., but, anyway, I knew about those facts, it is not that I knew about them before the trial, as some people have asked me, no, I knew [only] some facts... some facts that I knew but that I had not verified yet. I needed Dionisio to be released from prison, I needed to watch, to observe and to hear some... data, some elements and (( )) and well, the moment was right now... he also, I think he <silence> he would have also liked to explain everything, although he now says exactly the opposite **obviously** because in some way he lives a bit... distressed because... his partners do not really like him very much
H1> And his partners.. erm... with the... with the money that... that is missing, what... what did they do? What's happened?

In example (1), the speech participants are talking about a topic that they both know, i.e. motocross. Speaker H1 uses the adverb to introduce an idea which (s)he thinks that co-participant (H2) may be thinking of (cf. Cornillie 2010a). Hence, we have an intersubjective reading of *obviamente*. In this context, it is noteworthy mentioning that speaker H2 confirms the statement made by speaker H1 by means of the adverb *exacto*. By contrast, in example (2), speaker H2 is telling an elaborate story about the publication of a news item, without hinting at shared knowledge or presuppositions. Thus, the adverb *obviamente* is subjectively used, in that it plays a role within the realm of H2's own story, without requesting from H1 any confirmation of shared information.

As for the prosodic configuration of the adverbs in Figure 7.1, one can see the patterns of subjective and intersubjective readings in the framework of standardized melodic contours MAS from all the *obviamente* adverbs gathered in our corpus.

As becomes clear from Figure 7.1, both contours witness an identical final configuration. That is, in both cases there is a rise in the –*men*- syllable followed by a clear fall in the last syllable of the word. The difference between the two pragmatic values is situated in the fall in the second syllable in the case of the intersubjective reading.

Both the fall in the post-stress syllable (with 15 standardized Hz) and the subsequent rise in the –*men*- syllable (25 standardized Hz for the intersubjective value and 15 standardized Hz for the subjective reading) are perceptively discernible. In general, 10 standardized Hz correspond to 1.5 st (semi-tones), which is the value that the literature considers as significant (Roseano and Fernández Planas 2013).

One can observe an important difference in statistical scores for the subjective and intersubjective dimensions: subjective (M = 102, SD = 5.04) and intersubjective (M = 91, SD = 5.93); t (11) = 8.7, p = 0.0002.[1] Subjective *obviamente* shows an expected prosodic configuration: a consistent rising tone from the first

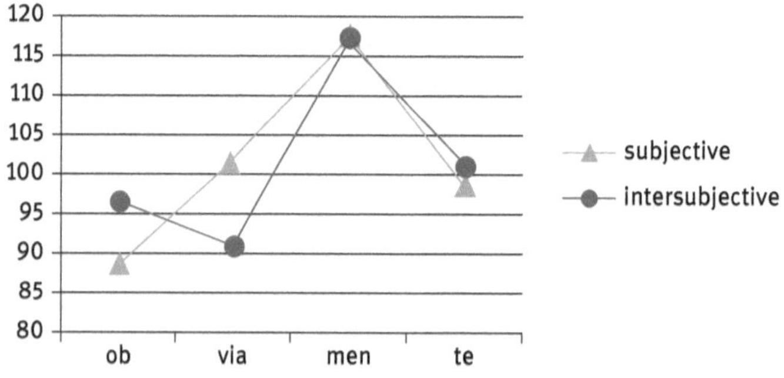

Figure 7.1: Standardized melodic contours of *obviamente*.

1 For the sake of statistical contrast of the syllables we apply the T of Student procedure, according to Field's (2009) proposal.

syllable till the last syllable, where a clear fall takes place. The intersubjective *obviamente*, by contrast, shows a marked melodic pattern: a strong fall occurs in the post-stress syllable, i.e. the one that immediately follows the first stressed syllable. Moreover, another important aspect of the melodic configuration of the two pragmatic values consists in the fact that the first stressed syllable of *obviamente* is characterized by higher pitch when it yields an intersubjective reading than when it expresses a subjective reading.

3.2 Seguramente

The adverb *seguramente* contains five syllables, of which the second and the fourth are stressed. The standard peninsular Spanish pronunciation usually makes explicit all sounds, e.g. [se’ɣura’mẽn̪te], although, due to the articulatory weakening typical of spontaneous talk, the first syllable is sometimes not clearly pronounced.

In our dataset, 12 cases are subjective in nature, whereas the intersubjective values amount to 6, i.e. one third of all cases.

(3) H3> A la extranjero>Coquette/extranjero> (hablante alemán> ¡Ah! Eso . . .)
H3> Es que a esta gente le gustan mucho los extranjero>blues/extranjero>
H2> Ah, pues sí, tío. (hablante alemán> Está cerca de... de... de la ininteligible> y eso, ¿no?. Podemos ir a esas...)
H3> Lo que pasa es que yo no sé si sigue habiendo actuaciones martes, miércoles y jueves.
H2> seguramente/ lo que pasa que hoy estará muy lleno a lo mejor.
H3> No.
H2> ¿No?

H3> To the Coquette (German speaker> Oh! That..)
H3> These people love blues
H2> Oh, yeah, dude (German speaker> It’s close to the... to the... to the ((unintelligible > and that, isn’t it? We could go to that...)
H3> The thing is, I don’t know if there are still shows on tuesdays, wednesdays and thursdays.
H2> Probably there are/ but perhaps today there will be plenty of people.
H3> No.
H2> No?

(4) H2> Una ciudad sit- (( )) situada... sitiada, perdón; un montón de soldados dando vueltas en torno ahí, y obviamente, la prostitución trabajando en torno a la ciudad.
H1> fático=afirmación>
H2> Desde... vacilación> que el tiempo es tiempo. Esta mujer, que seguramente era una prostituta que estaba trabajando en los alrededores del sitio, le ha dado con el... con el mosquetón, por supuesto, y la ha herido. Pero, automáticamente, eso se quiere ver interpretado como la bruja que vuela. Y esa bruja es condenada. Y ante la tortura de la Inquisición, esa mujer confiesa lo que le hagan confesar. simultáneo> La his(( ))
H1> Qué hermosa historia /simultáneo> pero qué triste, ¿no?
H2> La historia de la brujería... está plagada... de seres que en un momento determinado, Consuelo, se vieron obligados a confesar lo que quisieran.

H2> A sit- (( )) situated... besieged city, sorry; a lot of soldiers hanging around, and obviously, prostitutes working around the city
H1> phatic= affirmation>
H2> Since... vacillation> the dawn of time. This woman, who was probably a prostitute working on the outskirts of that place, he hit her... with the musket, of course, and injured her. But, automatically, this fact is interpreted as a flying witch. And that witch is condemned. And, at the prospect of being tortured by the Inquisition, that woman confesses what she is told to confess simultaneous> The his(( ))
H1> What a lovely story / simultaneous> but sad, isn't it?
H2> The history of witchcraft... is filled with... human beings that, in a given moment, Consuelo, they were compeled to confess what others wanted them to.

In examples (3) and (4) we have an intersubjective and a subjective reading, respectively. In example (3), the intersubjectivity of the adverb has to do with speaker H2 confirming the previous assessment made by speaker H3, who introduced the topic of the music concerts and the possibility to attend them. On the other hand, in example (4), speaker H2 tells a piece of history concerning a military siege of a city and the presence of a woman who the speaker considers to be a prostitute. This reading is subjective because it does not engage in a shared space.

Figure 7.2 emphasizes the special prosody of the subjective and the intersubjective readings of *seguramente* on the basis of all *seguramente* tokens found in our corpus.

First, although in the first syllable subjective *seguramente* has a slightly higher pitch value than its intersubjective counterpart, the two following standardized

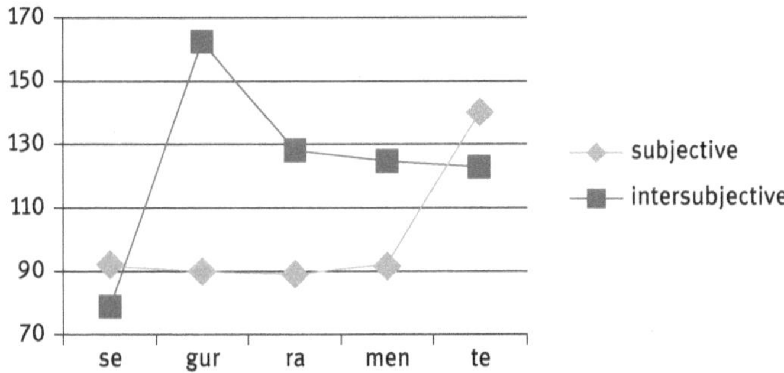

Figure 7.2: Standardized melodic contours of *seguramente.*

syllables of subjective *seguramente* keep similar values till the strong rise of the final syllable (50 Hz rise). On the contrary, most syllables of intersubjective *seguramente* present much higher pitch than its subjective counterpart, with an average of 40 standardized Hz higher; only in the last syllable –*te* is the subjective reading 20 Hz higher than the intersubjective one. Of all syllables, the most striking difference is the stress in the stressed syllable -*gu*- in intersubjective *seguramente*, 70 standardized Hz above subjective *seguramente*.

Finally, whereas intersubjectivity shows a tonal rise in the first syllable and falls in the rest of the prosodic group, subjectivity, as shown in Figure 7.2, displays tonal linearity in all syllables with the exception of the last one, which witnesses a post-stress rise. Such a pattern is common in peninsular Spanish (Llisterri et al. 2003). As far as the statistics are concerned, there is a significant difference between the results for the subjective values ($M = 91$, $SD = 4.69$) and those for the intersubjective ones ($M = 162$, $SD = 10.95$); t (16) = −47.83, p = 0.0001.

Generally speaking we can conclude that the intersubjective reading of the adverb *seguramente* is prosodically marked in two ways: first, the differences in the F0 of the two stressed syllables; second, the general tonal value (the average of all syllables) is much higher than in the subjective reading.

3.3 Posiblemente

Just as with *seguramente*, *posiblemente* 'possibly' consists of 5 syllables; the stressed ones of which are the second and the fourth syllable. In our data, *posiblemente* only shows up 9 times, with 6 subjective readings and 3 intersubjective ones. Hence, in comparison with the other adverbs under examination, *posiblemente* does not seem to have the same representativity. Moreover, the cases of intersubjective *posiblemente*, as in example (5), usually belong to adjacency pairs in which the assessment of the first pair part, i.e. the turn provoking another turn, is confirmed in the second part, by means of additional expressions such as the adverb *sí* or the discourse particle *claro*.

(5) H2> ¿Cómo se sale a la cancha cuando ves que… que nada, que no hay forma de ganar? ¿Se sale ya desmoralizado?
H1> No… se sale… vacilación> con rabia, y esa rabia hace que quizá estés eh… demasiado agarrota(d)>o y… fático=duda> y… fático=duda> que te produce más rabia, con lo cual te agarrotas mucho más… y acabas ininteligible> así… y no puedes mover ni las pestañas.
H2> risas> Ahora que haces ese gesto… ¿un poco de extranjero>Jeckling/extranjero> y extranjero>Mister Hayd/extranjero> sí que es Fernando Romay?
H1> Sí, sí, **posiblemente**.
H2> Sí, ¿verdad?
H1> sí, desde luego… fático=duda>

H2> How does one take the field when you can see there's… no way, no way to win? Are you demoralized beforehand?
H1> No… you take the field… vacillation> with rage, and that rage might make you feel… too stiff… phatic=hesitation> and… phatic=hesitation> that produces more rage, so you get stiffer… and you end up being unintelligible> like that… and you cannot even move your eyelashes
H2> laughter> Now you make that face… Is Fernando Romay not a bit of a Jeckyll and Mister Hyde?
H1> Yes, yes, **he possibly is**.
H2> Yeah, right?
H1> Yes, indeed… phatic=hesitation>

(6) H2>Huy, huy, huy.
H1>fortísimas pero lo cierto es que extranjero>Christian Brando/extranjero> ha sido condenado a diez años de cárcel, no los va a cumplir todos **posiblemente** pero va a cumplir bastantes, porque repito, está también pendiente un proceso penal de un disparo en la cara a un señor que discutió con él cuando extranjero>Christian Brando/extranjero> iba drogado o borracho. Y extranjero>Christian Brando/extranjero> va drogado o borracho con bastante asiduidad desde los catorce años.
H2>Pues eh… ya está. El asunto ha terminado para él por lo que se refiere al procedimiento judicial y ahora de lo que se trata es de su reinserción y de su redención.

H2>Huy, huy, huy.
H1>very strong but the certain thing is that Christian Brando has been condemned to 10 years in prison, he won't do them all **possibly** but he will do a lot of [years], because I insist, there is also a case hanging about a shot in the face of a man who discussed with him when Christian Brando was stoned and drunk. And Christian Brando has been repeatedly stoned and drunk since he was 14 years old.
H2>Well eh... this is over. The issue has come to an end for him as far as the court case is concerned and now the important thing is his reinsertion and his redemption.

Example (5) contains a positive answer by speaker H1 and, hence, is in line with the intersubjective dynamics between speaker and co-participants. Both speaker H1 and speaker H2 share knowledge about Fernando Romay, a basketball player, and his performance on the field. Following the question by speaker H2, speaker H1 confirms his previous assessment. In example (6), by contrast, speaker H1 tells a story about the case of a person in a foreign prison. By means of *posiblemente* the speaker indicates that the complete period of imprisonment will be held. In H2's turn, no shared knowledge is involved.

Figure 7.3 shows the melodic pattern for subjectivity and intersubjectivity calculated from the means of all the *posiblemente* adverbs registered in our database.

In Figure 7.3, the pitch values of subjective *posiblemente* rise slowly with increases of 5 standardized Hz per syllable. At the end of the group, in the final post-stress syllable there is a light tonal rise. Between the first syllable *po-* and the final syllable *–te* a difference of 20 Hz is noticed.

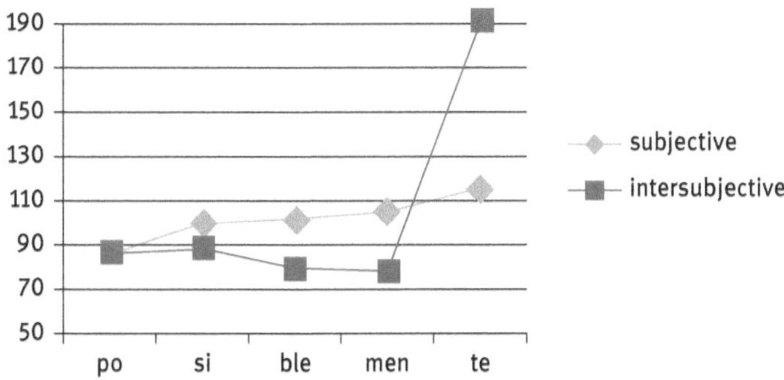

Figure 7.3: Standardized melodic contours of *posiblemente*.

Intersubjective *posiblemente*, by contrast, has a rise of 5 standardized Hz from the first syllable to the stressed syllable *-si-*, but presents a fall of 10 Hz in *–ble-* and in *–men-*. The most striking thing is the rise in the post-stress *-te*, which witnesses a difference with *–men-* of 100 standardized Hz. This emphatic prosody can be explained, as previously mentioned, in terms of confirmation strategies, which commonly have an intersubjective value and in which prosody is combined with other affirmative elements, as, for example, the adverb *sí*.

In contrast with what we have observed for other adverbs, subjective *posiblemente* has higher prosodic values than intersubjective *posiblemente* in all syllables, with a difference of 15 standardized Hz in the first syllable and 25 Hz in the second one. The only difference is found in the last syllable, where the post-stress tonal rise in *–te* is 80 standardized Hz higher than with intersubjective *posiblemente*; this difference is statistically significant since the following scores were obtained: for the subjective reading (M = 105, SD = 4.6) and the intersubjective reading (M = 78, SD = 2.82); t(7) = 20.79, p = 0.0001. Hence, the prosodic configuration of intersubjectivity witnesses more contrasts between syllables, whereas subjectivity has higher F0 values, but in a continuous rising line.

3.4 Evidentemente

The adverb *evidentemente* has 6 syllables; the stressed syllables are the third (*-den-*) and the fifth (*-men-*). In line with the other adverbs, there are no special phonetic characteristics in the pronunciation [eβ̞i'ð̞̆en̪te'mẽn̪te], although the first syllable appears often in a weaker form in spontaneous spoken discourse.

In this paper, we examine 8 intersubjective cases, e.g. (7), and 4 subjective cases, e.g. (8).

(7) H2> O sea, que no publicaste /simultáneo>... No publicaste eso por humanidad...
H3> No...
H2> ... exclusivamente, ¿no? simultáneo> Aunque... aunque...
H3> Sí, ininteligible> muy fuerte /simultáneo>
H2> ... sabías que tenía **evidentemente** una buena noticia en la mano.
H3> Claro, pero... pero imagínate,
H2> fático=afirmación>
H4> fático=afirmación>

H2> hence, you didn't publish /simultaneously>... You didn't publish this for the sake of humanity...
H3> No...

H2> . . . exclusively, ¿no? /simultaneously>. . . Although. . . although. . .
H3> Yes, unintelligible> very strong /simultaneously>. . .
H2> . . . you knew that (s)he had clearly good news in her/his hand.
H3> Yes, but. . . but imagine
H2> phatic=affirmative> (yes)
H4> phatic=affirmative> (yes)

(8) H2> Consientan el renunciar a ese hijo. Y claro, esto no ocurre. esto no ocurre con facilidad. Padres que renuncian a su hijo y que consientan la adopción son casos escasísimos. Y los casos de adopción que se. . . promueven pues son los casos en los que hay un abandono en el momento del nacimiento, prácticamente, y algún caso más de. . . abandono más tardío, pero muy escasos. Entonces, el año pas(d)>o, por ejemplo, en la Comunidad de Madrid, que es una de las comunidades que promueve mayor número de adopciones en toda España, pues se promovieron 121. De esos 121, 103 eran niños recién nacidos, y el resto eran otros casos en los que se había producido un abandono posterior.
H1> <fático=afirmación>
H2> Pero eh. . . ese mismo año, nosotros hemos recibido más de quinientas solicitudes de. . . familias dispuestas a adoptar un niño. Entonces, **evidentemente** no es posible satisfacer a quinientas familias si lo que venimos eh. . . teniendo como niños abandona(d)>os es un número de 121, y además, un número descendiente, porque el año anterior habían sido 127, y el anterior ciento treinta y. . . seis, creo recordar. Eh. . . El año que viene pues en vez de 121 serán 115 o 117 o 112.
H1> <fático=afirmación>
H2> They agree to give up on that child. And of course, this does not happen, this does not happen easily. Parents who give up on their child and who agree to adoption are rare. And these cases of adoption which are being proposed are cases in which there is abandonment at the moment of birth, basically, and some other cases of. . . late abandonment, but very rarely. So, last year, for instance, in the Comunidad de Madrid, which is one of the communities with the highest number of adoptions in Spain, they arranged 121. Of these 121, 103 were recently born children, and the rest were other cases in which later abandonment occurred.
H1> <phatic=affirmative> (yes)
H2> But eh. . . that same year, we have received more than 500 applications from. . . families willing to adopt a child. So, evidently it is not posible to [serve] 500 families if what we currently have as abandoned children is

around 121, and [which is] moreover a decreasing number, because last year they were 127, and the year before 136, I mean to remember. Eh... Next year instead of 121 we will have 115 or 117 or 112.
H1> <phatic=affirmative> (yes)

In example (7), which shows a case of intersubjectivity, the co-participants are journalists who are talking about publishing news in the written press. Speaker H2 mentions the quality of the good news items published in the past and uses the adverb *evidentemente* to look for positive reinforcement and the confirmation by speaker H3. This confirmation is explicitly expressed by means of the adverb *claro* in the following turn. By contrast, example (8) is characterized by subjectivity, in that speaker H2 extensively deals with the adoption system in Spain and uses the adverb *evidentemente* to express the assessment that one cannot satisfy all families who want a child to adopt. The confirmations by H1 are spread over the whole communicative exchange and do not seem to be based on shared knowledge. Instead, it is the speaker's own reasoning which seems to motivate the use of this adverb.

Figure 7.4 shows interesting information about the prosodic configuration of the subjective and intersubjective values of *evidentemente*; as in previous Sections, this Figure comes from the means of the syllables of all the *evidentemente* adverbs included in our corpus.

First, the subjective reading of the adverb has a rising prosodic configuration of about 25 standardized Hz, which is the distance between the lowest pitch, 90 standardized Hz corresponding to the initial syllable and the highest pitch of 115 standardized Hz that characterize the final syllable. The rising tone is usually related to the expression of doubt or the uncertainty about what is said.

Second, the prosodic pattern of the intersubjective reading presents more differences, with a continuous rise from the first stressed syllable, an abrupt

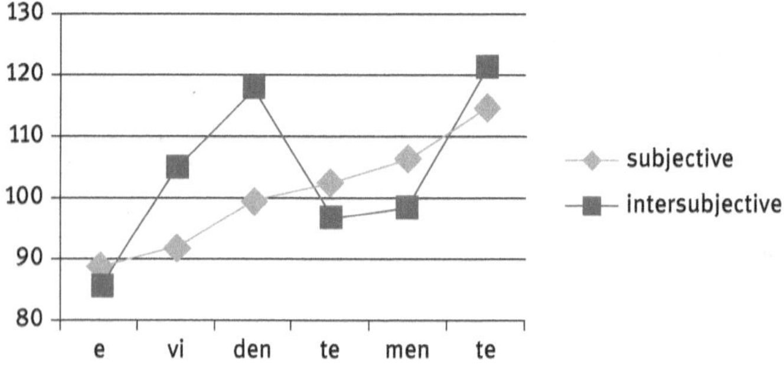

Figure 7.4: Standardized melodic contours of *evidentemente*.

fall of about 20 standardized Hz in the following two syllables and a new rise of again 20 standardized Hz at the final syllable. This 'circumflex' configuration is marked and is used to express different pragmatic values, as argued for in studies on peninsular Spanish (cf. de la Mota and Rodero 2010), or on Mexican Spanish (cf. Martín-Butragueño 2004).

If we compare the subjective and the intersubjective uses, we notice that, in general, the intersubjective use shows higher pitch, as well as a first stressed syllable (-*den*-) with a higher tone (119 standardized Hz) than its subjective counterpart (100 standardized Hz). This difference is statistically significant due to the following scores for the subjective value ($M = 100$, $SD = 3.8$) and the intersubjective value ($M = 118$, $SD = 6.78$); $t(10) = -12.66$, $p = 0.0001$.

Although the subjective reading has a second stressed syllable (–*men*-) with a higher tone than its intersubjective counterpart, the latter has higher pitch in the final syllable. This time, there is a difference of 5 standardized Hz with the subjective value.

In sum, whereas subjective *evidentemente* presents a continuous prosodic inclination and lower pitch values than intersubjective *evidentemente*, the latter shows a discontinuous melodic pattern, with strong falls and rises.

3.5 Indudablemente

The fifth adverb that we address here is *indudablemente*. Just like *evidentemente*, this adverb is formed by six syllables, of which the third and the fifth are stressed ones. The pronunciation [ĩn̪du'ð̞aβ̞le'mẽn̪te] does not show anything particular in peninsular Spanish, with the exception of a possible weakening or elision of the first syllable in spontaneous speech.

In our study we have 6 cases of *indudablemente* with an intersubjective reading and 4 cases with a subjective reading. These values are exemplified in (9) and (10):

(9) H1> . . . porque dice: "Bueno, si por lo menos quien me va a tomar declaración se contiene la risa hasta que yo me vaya. . . " risas>
H2> Hombre, **indudablemente**, es una de. . . es una de las cosas. . . a nosotros no. . . no es que nos. . . nos dé mucha risa, precisamente, porque indudablemente se está cometiendo un. . . delito, y por supuesto, pues. . . Lo que pasa es que. . . es lógico. . . es mucho menos tensa esa denuncia que una denuncia en la que se. . . hace constar pues una agresión sexual, o una. . . un atraco a mano armada. Pero. . . no cabe duda que nosotros le hacemos el mismo caso a esa denuncia que a. . . que a cualquier otra. Lo que sí que es

difícil es que el ciudadano vaya, porque piensa... dice: “Vamos, encima voy a quedar por tonto”.
H1> Claro.
H2> Y la verdad es que en... en un timo puede caer cualquiera.

H1> ... because he says: “Well, if the one who will take the report will suppress his laughter till I am leaving....” laughter>
H2> man, of course, it is one of... is one of the things... to us ... it is not that.... it provokes a lot of laughter to us..., precisely, because undoubtedly there is being committed a... crime, and of course, well... What happens... it’s logical... this complaint is much more problematic than a complaint in which... one reports a case of sexual harassment, or one... an armed hold-up. But... there is no doubt that we pay equal attention to this complaint as to whatever other. What is truly difficult is that the citizen is gonna, because he thinks,... he says: “Okay, so in addition I will give a stupid impression”.
H1> Yes, indeed.
H2> And the truth is that everybody can fall for a fraud.

(10) H2> Ah, puede ser lo del alcalde, entonces.
H1> Sería una... cosa buena.
H2> Padre, para quienes nos están escuchando y nunca han visto la imagen, nunca han visto la talla, descríbanos cómo es.
H1> Pues la imagen es... de un... metro 73 centímetros; es lo que se llama el extranjero>Ecce Homo/extranjero>, cuando... Pilato lo presentó ante el pueblo, con las manos atadas, coronado de espinas y dijo: “He aquí el hombre”
H2> Sí.
H1> Y... después, lleva una túnica muy bonita, vacilación>... Aquí lo más importante es **indudablemente** el rostro, la cara. Es... es impresionante. Es bastante moreno, algunos dicen que... que si es moro... risas> Bastante negro, vamos, no del todo, pero...
H2> O sea, de... tez oscura.
H1> Sí.

H2> Ah, so it may be the thing about the mayor.
H1> That would be a... good thing.
H2> Father, for whom who are listening to us and have never seen the image, have never seen the size, describe a bit how it is.
H1> Well the image is... of a... one meter 73 centimetres; it is what is called Ecce Homo, when... Pilate presented him to to the people, with the hands tied, crowned with thorns and said: “Look here the man ”

H2> Yes.
H1> and... furthermore, he wears a beautiful robe, vacillation>... Here the most important thing is undoubtedly the face, the head. It is... is impressive. He is quite black, some say that... that he is like an African... laughter> Very black, well, not completely, but...
H2> So, with... dark skin.
H1> Yes.

Intersubjectivity is easily observable if, as in example (9), it is part of a confirmation turn following a previous turn. In this example, speaker H1 interviews speaker H2, who is a policeman, and he asks him questions about the way the police deals with strange reports. In this context, speaker H2 says that speaker H1 is *indudablemente* right. In example (10), by contrast, subjectivity is found in the words of speaker H1, who is talking about Jesus Christ. In this context, *indudablemente* shows up in turn-medial position and is not followed by a confirmation turn by speaker H2, but is part of inferential reflections about the colour of Jesus' skin represented in the image.

Figure 7.5 shows the prosodic configurations of subjective and intersubjective *indudablemente*.

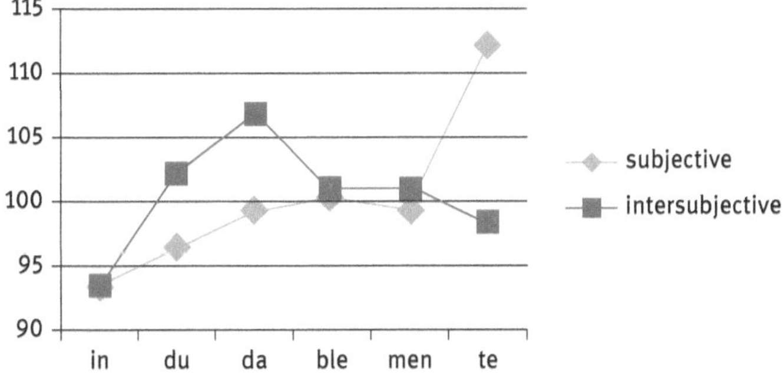

Figure 7.5: Standardized melodic contours of *indudablemente*.

In the case of subjectivity, the tonal rise is continuous till a small fall of 2 standardized Hz in the *–men-* syllable and a clear rise of 14 standardized Hz in the post-stress syllable. Intersubjective *indudablemente*, by contrast, is characterized by a steady rise of 13 standardized Hz from the first syllable (with 94 standardized Hz) till the first stressed syllable (with 107 standardized Hz). Afterwards, there is a tonal fall in the three other syllables.

If we compare both readings, the intersubjective one is prosodically more perceivable than the subjective one. The higher pitch patterns of intersubjectivity are clear in the first stressed syllable, with 8 standardized Hz more than the subjective counterpart. This difference is statistically significant for subjective ($M = 99$, $SD = 3.6$) and intersubjective values ($M = 107$, $SD = 3.36$); $t(8) = -9.62$, $p = 0.0001$.

Finally, the rise in the final syllable of the adverb is striking: 13 Hz more in the subjective than in the intersubjective reading. In other words, whereas the intersubjectivity emphasized the stressed syllable of the adjective –*da*-, subjectivity does the same with the final syllable –*te*.

4 Pitch and (inter)subjectivity: discussion and conclusions

In the previous sections we have presented an analysis of five modal adverbs (*obviamente*, *seguramente*, *posiblemente*, *evidentemente* y *subjetivamente*) in terms of the prosodic configurations of their respective subjective and intersubjective readings. Although most of the adverbs have a different syllabic distribution (4 syllables in *obviamente*, 5 syllables in *seguramente* and *posiblemente*, and 6 syllables in *evidentemente* and *indudablemente*), they have several elements in common, which allows us to compare the results. For instance, the five adverbs, just like the other Spanish adverbs that end in–*mente*, have two stressed syllables.

This fact makes it possible to compare the melodic behaviour of the two stressed syllables. As we wanted to give a general overview based on all tokens analysed, we have taken in consideration the average pitch of the stressed syllables in subjective realizations in contrast with intersubjective realizations among the 62 adverbs included in our study. The results of this test can be observed in Figure 7.6.

On the basis of the data studied we can present two general conclusions about the pitch of intersubjective and subjective readings observed in the adverbs under examination:

1. The global pitch of the intersubjective readings of the adverbs is preceived as superior to that of the subjective readings. The intersubjective reading shows average values that are 15 standardized Hz higher than those of the subjective reading. This way, the speaker marks prosodically the pragmatic dimension involving shared knowledge with the co-participant, which is in line with previous literature on the pragmatic meaning of prosody (Rao 2006). Other authors have reached the same conclusion for other pragmatic values such as (im)politeness (Culpeper 2011).

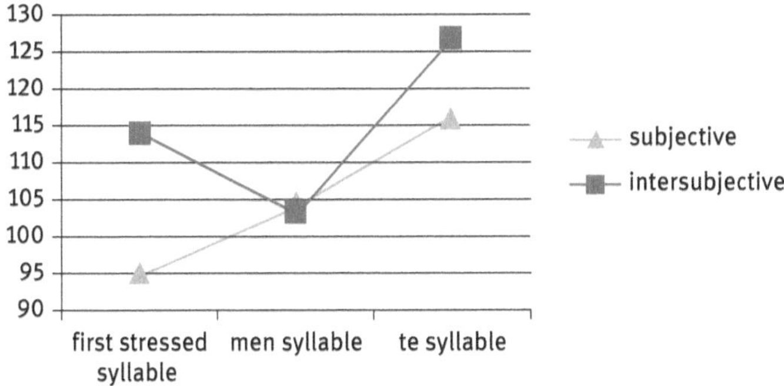

Figure 7.6: Standardized melodic contours of subjectivity and intersubjectivity.

2. The intersubjectivity readings shows a fall in the second stressed syllable (*-men-*), which is then followed by a strong rise in the final syllable of the adverb (*-te*). The melodic fluctuation, which attracts the attention of the co-participant, is situated in the realm of intersubjectivity, whereas the prosody of subjectivity presents a continuous rise. In general, we have not found any cases of *de-accentuation* (Astruc and Nolan 2007a, 2007b) in the prosodic realization of the Spanish adverbs under examination.

In sum, our data give an indication of significant differences in the prosodic configuration of subjectivity and intersubjectivity in Spanish talk-in-interaction. These results corroborate the observation that a pragmatically marked expression, in our case an intersubjective expression which refers to information shared among the speaker and co-participants, is also marked prosodically.

In future research, the data used for this study should be broadened and subsequently analysed for more epistemic and evidential adverbials, taking into account other prosodic factors such as syllable duration or discourse position of the adverbs. It would also be interesting to study the prosodic independence of these structures, as other studies have done for languages such as Catalan or English (cf. Astruc 2005; Astruc and Nolan 2007a, 2007b).

References

Allerton, David & Alan Cruttenden. 1974. English sentence adverbials: their syntax and their intonation in British English. *Lingua* 34. 1–30.

Astruc, Lluïsa. 2005. The form and function of extra-sentential elements. *Cambridge Occasional Papers in Linguistics* 2. 1–25.

Astruc, Lluïsa & Francis Nolan. 2007a. Variation in the intonation of sentential adverbs in English and Catalan. In Carlos Gussenhoven & Tomas Riad (eds.), *Tones and tunes, volume I: Typological and comparative studies in word and sentence prosody*, 233–263. Berlin, New York: Mouton de Gruyter.

Astruc, Lluïsa & Francis Nolan. 2007b. A cross-linguistic study of extra-sentential elements. In Pilar Prieto, Joan Mascaró & Maria-Josep Solé (eds.), *Segmental and prosodic issues in romance phonology*, 85–107. Amsterdam, Philadelphia: John Benjamins.

Athaniasiadou, Angeliki, Costas Canakis & Bert Cornillie. 2006. *Subjectification: Various Paths to Subjectivity*. Berlin, New York: Mouton de Gruyter.

Barth-Weingarten, Dagmar, Nicole Dehé & Anne Wichmann (eds.). 2009. *Where Prosody Meets Pragmatics*. Bingley: Emerald Group Publishinig Limited.

Barth-Weingarten, Dagmar, Elisabeth Reber & Margret Selting (eds.). 2010. *Prosody in Interaction*. Amsterdam, Philadelphia: Benjamins.

Cabedo Nebot, Adrián. 2014. Relación entre el grado de certeza y los valores de F0 y duración silábica en algunos adverbios terminados en -mente. *Revista Signos* 47. 196–216.

Cabedo Nebot, Adrián & Salvador Pons Bordería. 2013. Corpus Val.Es.Co 2.0. Retrieved from http://www.valesco.es

Cantero-Serena, Francisco José. 2002. *Teoría y análisis de la entonación*. Barcelona: Universitat de Barcelona.

Cantero-Serena, Francisco José & Dolors Font-Rotchés. 2009. Protocolo para el análisis melódico del habla. *Estudios de Fonética Experimental XVIII*. 17–32.

Company Company, Concepción. 2014. Adverbios en *-mente*. In C. Company Company (ed.), *Sintaxis histórica de la lengua española. Tercera parte: Adverbios, preposiciones y conjunciones. Relaciones interoracionales*, 3 vols., 459–614. México: Fondo de Cultura Económica y Universidad Nacional Autónoma de México.

Cornillie, Bert. 2008. On the grammaticalization and (inter)subjectivity of Spanish evidential (semi)auxiliaries. In Elena Seoane & Maria José López-Couso (eds.), *Theoretical and Empirical Issues in Grammaticalization*, 55–76. Amsterdam, Philadelphia: Benjamins.

Cornillie, Bert. 2010a. An interactional approach to epistemic and evidential adverbs. In Gabriele Diewald & Elena Smirnova (eds.), *Linguistic Realization of Evidentiality in European Languages*, 309–330. Berlin: Mouton de Gruyter.

Cornillie, Bert. 2010b. On conceptual semantics and discourse functions: The case of Spanish modal adverbs in informal conversation. *Annual Review of Cognitive Linguistics* 8 (2). 300–320.

Culpeper, Jonathan. 2011. "It's not what you said, it's how you said it!" prosody and impoliteness. *Discursive approaches to* politeness, 57–83. Berlin, New York: Mouton de Gruyter.

Dehé, Nicole & Bettina Braun. 2013. The prosody of question tags in English. *English Language and Linguistics* 17 (1). 129–156.

Dehé, Nicole & Anne Wichmann. 2010. Sentence-initial *I think (that)* and *I believe (that)*. Prosodic evidence for uses as main clause, comment clause and discourse marker. *Studies in Language* 34 (1). 36–74.

de la Mota, Carme & Emma Rodero. 2010. La demarcación entonativa y el énfasis en la locución de los editores de boletines informativos radiofónicos. *Actas del XXXIX simposio internacional de la sociedad española de lingüística (SEL)*. Santiago de Compostela: Universidad de Compostela.

Dorta Luis, Josefa. 2008. La focalización prosódica: Funcionalidad en los niveles lingüístico y pragmático. *Estudios de Fonética Experimental* 17. 105–138.

Estebas, Eva & Pilar Prieto. 2009. La notación prosódica en español. una revisión del Sp_ToBI. *Estudios De Fonética Experimental XVIII*. 263–283.

Field, Andy P. 3rd ed. 2009. *Discovering statistics using SPSS: (and sex and drugs and rock 'n' roll)*. London: SAGE.

Ghesquière, Lobke. 2010. On the subjectification and intersubjectification paths followed by the adjectives of completeness. In Kristin Davidse, Liewen Vandelanotte & Hubert Cuyckens (eds.), *Subjectification, intersubjectification and grammaticalization*, 277–314. Berlin: de Gruyter.

Kimps, Ditte. 2016. *English variable tag questions: A typology of their interpersonal meanings*. University of Leuven: Department of Linguistics. Unpublished doctoral dissertation.

Kimps, Ditte, Kristin Davidse & Bert Cornillie. 2014. A speech function analysis of British English tag questions in spontaneous dialogue. *Journal of Pragmatics* 66. 64–85.

Llisterri, Joaquim, María Jesús Machuca, Antonio Ríos, Carme de la Mota & Montserrat Riera. 2003. Algunas cuestiones en torno al desplazamiento acentual en español. In Esther Herrera & Pedro Martín-Butragueño (eds.), *La tonía: Dimensiones fonéticas y fonológicas* (Cátedra Jaime Torres Bodet, Estudios de Lingüística 4), 163–185. México: El Colegio de México, Centro de Estudios Lingüísticos y Literarios.

Martín-Butragueño, Pedro. 2004. Configuraciones circunflejas en la entonación del español mexicano. *Revista de Filología Española* 84. 347–373.

Narrog, Heiko. 2012a. *Modality, Subjectivity, and Semantic Change. A Cross-Linguistic Perspective*. Oxford: Oxford University Press.

Narrog, Heiko. 2012b. Beyond intersubjectification. Textual uses of modality and mood in subordinate clauses as part of speech-act orientation. *English Text Construction* 5 (1). 29–52.

Nuyts, Jan. 2001. *Epistemic Modality, Language, and Conceptualization: A cognitive-pragmatic perspective*. Amsterdam – Philadelphia: John Benjamins.

Prieto, Pilar. 2002. Entonació. In Joan Solà, Maria-Rosa Lloret, Joan Mascaró & Manuel Pérez Saldanya (eds.), *Gramàtica del català contemporani*, 393–462. Barcelona: Editorial Empúries.

Prieto, Pilar & Paolo Roseano (eds.). 2010. *Transcription of intonation of the spanish language*. München: Lincom Europa.

Quilis, Antonio. 1981. *Fonética acústica de la lengua española*. Madrid: Gredos.

Quilis, Antonio. 1993. *Tratado de fonología y fonética españolas*. Madrid: Gredos.

Rao, Rajiv. 2006. On Intonation's relationship with pragmatic meaning in Spanish. In Timothy Lee Face, & Carol A. Klee (eds.), *Selected proceedings of the 8th hispanic linguistics symposium*, 103–115. Somerville: MA. Cascadilla Proceedings Project.

Roseano, Paolo & Ana Maria Fernández Planas. 2013. Transcripció fonètica i fonológica de l'entonació: Una proposta d'etiquetatge automàtic. *Estudios De Fonética Experimental* XXII. 275–332.

Torner, Sergi. 2007. *De los adjetivos calificativos a los adverbios en –mente: semántica y gramática*. Madrid: Visor Libros.

Traugott, Elisabeth C. 2010. (Inter)subjectivity and (inter)subjectification. A reassessment. In Kristin Davidse, Liewen Vandelanotte & Hubert Cuyckens (eds.), *Subjectification, intersubjectification and grammaticalization*, 29–74. Berlin: de Gruyter.

Wennerstrom, Ann K. 2001. *The music of everyday speech: Prosody and discourse analysis*. New York – Oxford: Oxford University Press.
Wichmann, Ann, Anne-Marie Vandenbergen & Karin Aijmer. 2010. How prosody reflects semantic change: a synchronic case study of *of course*. In Kristin Davidse, Liewen Vandelanotte & Hubert Cuyckens (eds.), *Subjectification, intersubjectification and grammaticalization*, 103–154. Berlin • New York: Mouton de Gruyter.
Wierzbicka, Anna. 2006. *English*: *Meaning and Culture*. Oxford: Oxford University Press.

Laurent Gosselin

French expressions of personal opinion: je crois / pense / trouve / estime / considère que p

Abstract: French expressions of personal opinion, like *je crois que* 'I believe that', *je pense que* 'I think that', *je trouve que* 'I find that', *je considère que* 'I consider that', *j'estime que* 'I reckon that', have been studied extensively from different points of view: as parentheticals in a syntactic perspective, as metarepresentational prefixes in a pragmatic and cognitive framework, as evidential markers or as epistemic operators in a logical perspective. We examine in this article a particular characteristic of these expressions which concerns the restrictions they impose on the choice of the predicates in the *that*-clause. The aim of this article is to describe and to explain these restrictions and constraints on the interpretation of utterances containing such expressions of personal opinion, in the framework of the Modular Theory of Modality (Gosselin 2010).

Keywords: personal opinion, epistemic modality, appreciative modality, axiological modality, alethic modality, logic of conviction

1 Introduction

French expressions of personal opinion, like *je crois que* 'I believe', *je pense que* 'I think', *je trouve que* 'I find', *je considère que* 'I consider', and *j'estime que* 'I reckon', have been studied extensively from different points of view – as parentheticals from a syntactic perspective (Blanche-Benveniste 1989; Apothéloz 2003; Blanche-Benveniste and Willems 2007; Avanzi and Glikman 2009; Haßler 2014; Schneider, Glikman and Avanzi 2015), as metarepresentational prefixes in a pragmatic and cognitive framework (Récanati 1981, Récanati 2000), as conventional implicatures from a pragmatic point of view (Jayez and Rossari 2004), as evidential markers (Dendale and Van Bogaert 2007), or as epistemic

Note: I am grateful to Gerda Haßler and an anonymous reviewer for their helpful comments and suggestions.

Laurent Gosselin, University of Rouen-Normandie

https://doi.org/10.1515/9783110572261-008

operators from a logical perspective (Martin 1987; Martin 1988) – while *je trouve que* was analysed by Ducrot (1980) as a marker of *prédication originelle* 'original predication'.

These expressions have the particularity of indicating that the judgement that they introduce falls within *the personal opinion of the speaker* (for a discussion of this notion, see Tuchais 2014). As such, they belong to the general category of expressions with modal values, specifically markers of individual subjectivity (referring to the subjectivity of the speaker, see Martin 1987; Borillo 2004). This class includes not only propositional attitude verbs (*croire*, *trouver estimer* ...), in the first person and present tense, but also prepositional phrases (*selon moi*, *à mon avis*, *à mes yeux*, *pour moi* 'in my opinion', and so on; see Borillo 2004; Coltier and Dendale 2004). These expressions are generally (see Haillet 2004: 3) regarded as expressing epistemic modalities that apply to a propositional content (as part of the *modus* / *dictum* opposition according to Bally, 1932) and as discourse markers of mitigation. This attenuative value is due to a general principle explained by Borillo (2004: 31):

> Pour le locuteur, signaler le point de vue subjectif du propos qu'il énonce est une manière d'en affaiblir la portée. Il manifeste ainsi une certaine prudence, soit par rapport à la vérité de ce qu'il avance, soit par rapport aux jugements évaluatifs qu'il introduit dans son discours.
>
> [For the speaker, to indicate the subjective character of what he states is a way to weaken it. He thus manifests some caution, either with respect to the truth of what he says, or in relation to evaluative judgements he issues in his speech.]

The purpose of this article is to challenge the "unitary view" of the semantic and discursive role of verbal expressions of personal opinion. We want to show (1) that the expressions studied each have a specific meaning and therefore are not always substitutable for one another, (2) that though they all indicate the speaker's personal opinion, they do not systematically operate an attenuative modalization, and (3) that, contrary to what their syntactic similarity suggests, not all of them express an epistemic modality that applies to the propositional content (as it is generally admitted; see Thompson and Mulac 1991: 313; Boone 1996: 48; Apothéloz 2003: 252; Haßler 2014: 6).

The analyses are carried out in the framework of the Modular Theory of Modalities (Gosselin 2010), which will be discussed here informally. We will successively present the theoretical perspective (Section 2), the semantics of *je crois que* and the mechanism that leads to the attenuation effect (Section 3), the semantics of *je trouve que* (Section 4), that of *je considère* / *estime que* (Section 5), and finally that of *je pense que* (Section 6). The conclusion will summarize the differences by means of a table.

2 Modality in a wide sense

We classically distinguish judgements of reality from value judgements. A judgement of reality states what the case is (it describes a situation), while a value judgement consists of speaking well or ill of an individual or situation. A judgement of reality can be objective, in the sense that it is presented as true regardless of the subjective point of view of the speaker (ex. 1), or subjective, i.e. depending on the speaker's point of view (ex. 2).

(1) *Cette table est rectangulaire;*
'This table is rectangular'

(2) *Ce champ est assez grand*
'This field is quite extensive'.

The judgement expressed by (2) is subjective since it assumes a norm of evaluation, which remains implicit, and depends on the speaker.

A value judgement cannot be objective, but depends either on the subjectivity of individuals (e.g. 3) or on a system of conventions (moral, ideology, religion, etc.), as in (4):[1]

(3) *Ce pain est bon*
'This bread is good'

(4) *Cet homme est malhonnête*
'This man is dishonest'.

These phenomena can be analysed in modal terms, provided that it is recognized, following Brunot (1922: 541) and Bally (1965, § 47), that the lexical constituents of the *dictum* can themselves express modalities (taken in a wide sense). In this case, Gosselin (2010: 102–114, 2015) speaks of *intrinsic modalities* (i.e. internal to the *dictum*). In this framework, we will say that (1) illustrates an alethic modality attached to the predicate of the sentence, (2) illustrates an epistemic one, (3) illustrates an appreciative one, and (4) illustrates an axiological one. The alethic modality corresponds to a judgement of reality presented as objective, epistemic modality to a judgement of reality made in a subjective assessment,

1 This distinction corresponds to the opposition between appreciations and judgements (Martin and White 2005: 35–36), and also to the distinction between judgements referring to personal norms and judgements referring to a system of social norms (Asher, Benamara and Mathieu 2009: 283).

appreciative modality to a value judgement about the (un)desirable character of an object or a situation, and axiological modality to a value judgement about the (blame) worthiness of an individual or situation.

These intrinsic modalities may be marked linguistically, as in the examples above, in which they are associated with tokens, or inferred on the basis of background knowledge. For example, statement (2) may have, in some contexts, a positive appreciative value (thus becoming a value judgement in addition to being a judgement of reality). Pragmatically inferred modalities have the specificity of being avoidable in some contexts (unlike linguistically marked modalities).

Intrinsic modalities can be embedded by *extrinsic modalities* (i.e. belonging to the *modus*), as in the statement

(5) *Je crois que Paul est honnête*
'I believe Paul is honest'.

Here an extrinsic epistemic modality, expressed by *je crois que*, applies to an intrinsic axiological modality associated with the predicate in the complement clause (*honnête*).

3 *Je crois que* and the logic of conviction

The expression *je crois que* 'I believe' expresses an extrinsic epistemic modality, which is compatible with all sorts of modalities, intrinsically associated with the predicates: alethic (7a), epistemic (7b), appreciative (7c), or axiological ones (7d)[2]:

(7) a. *Je crois que cette table est rectangulaire*
'I believe this table is rectangular'
b. *Je crois que ce champ est assez vaste*
'I believe this field is quite extensive'
c. *Je crois que ce pain est bon*
'I believe this bread is good'
d. *Je crois que cet homme est malhonnête*
'I believe this man is dishonest'.

2 In order to control rigorously the interaction between modalities, we have constructed examples and we judge their acceptability by introspection. A study based on corpora would be more convincing, but it would have required a far longer discussion.

The role of this expression (*je crois que*) is to introduce the judgements as belonging to the individual subjective opinion of the speaker (her belief). It has long been observed (see Benveniste 1966: 264, Borillo 1982, Vet 1994) that this expression plays the role of mitigator of an assertion (as a rhetoric–pragmatic function). We will try to explain this effect.

Imagine that you are in your office, and you are asked on the phone if your colleague is there. If you answer

(8) *Je crois qu'elle est ici*
'I believe she's here',

your interviewer will think that you are not sure. One might assume that this is because *croire que p* expresses a relatively low degree of belief, but this explanation is not satisfactory. Indeed in this case, statement (9),

(9) *Pierre croit que sa collègue est ici*
'Peter believes his colleague is here',

should imply that Peter is not sure of it. But it is false. This statement is compatible with the assumption that Peter is convinced that his colleague is here. In fact, *croire* is a verb that only indicates that the speaker of the utterance does not presuppose the content of the completive. Moreover, what is remarkable and at first sight paradoxical is that even if the speaker uses expressions that literally mean certainty, it is understood that she is not absolutely sure of what she says:

(10) *Je suis certaine / sûre / convaincue / persuadée qu'elle est là*
'I am confident she is here'.

These phenomena can be explained in the light of the *logic of conviction* (Lenzen 2004). Lenzen (2004: 973) posits that if a subject is convinced that p, if she is really certain of it, she believes that she knows that p.

Principle of conviction: "C (a,p) → B(a,K(a,p))"
a: person; C: "is convinced"; B: "believes"; K: "knows".

It follows that "knowledge and conviction are subjectively indiscriminable in the sense that person *a* cannot tell apart whether she is 'only' convinced that p or whether she really knows that p" (Lenzen 2004: 973).

On the other hand, among epistemic verbs, a distinction is classically made between factive verbs (which presuppose the truth of the propositional contents of the complement clause) and non-factive verbs (which do not presuppose the truth of this content, see Karttunen 1973, Kreutz 1998, Korzen 2001). *Savoir que* 'know', *se douter que* 'suspect', and *ignorer que* 'ignore' belong to the first class and *croire que* 'believe' and *être certain(e) / sûr(e) /persuadé(e) que* 'be confident' to the second.

From all this follows that the speaker who is convinced that p will assert *je sais que p* 'I know that p', or even simply *p* (*p* and *je sais que p* being equipollent; see Gosselin 2014). Therefore, if a speaker uses non-factive epistemic expressions, like je *crois / suis certain(e) / persuadé(e) / convaincu(e) que* 'I believe / am sure / persuaded / convinced that', it triggers an implicature from the utterance. The interpreter will think that if the speaker has used not just *p* or *je sais que p*, it is because she does not believe that she knows that p and therefore she is not really convinced that p, hence the systematic mitigation effect, which may seem contradictory to what the statement says literally (as in the example 10). As Martin notes (1987: 57), it is "impossible de dire sans mauvaise foi *Je crois qu'il est à la maison* si je sais pertinemment qu'il y est" ['impossible to say without bad faith *I believe he is at home* if I know for a fact that he is'].

This very regular inferential mechanism helps to explain why the degree of belief indicated by non-factive belief expressions is not weakened when belief is attributed to a third party (ex. 9): as belief is not attributed to the speaker of the utterance, the inferential mechanism grounded on the principle of conviction does not apply, and there is no implicature.

This inferential mechanism helps also probably to explain the origin of the weakening of epistemic adverbs (which refer to the belief of the speaker): *sans doute* 'probably' (lit. 'without any doubt'), *certainement* 'certainly', and *sûrement* 'surely', which do not involve certainty, in contemporary French. We may assume that in the diachronic evolution of the meaning of these expressions, the implicature, systematically associated with the principle of conviction, has been conventionalized.

4 *Je trouve que* as an indicator of individual subjectivity

As Ducrot (1980) and Blanche-Benveniste and Willems (2007) observe, *je trouve que* 'I find' is not compatible with all sorts of predicates in a complement clause (unlike the expressions studied in the previous section). In terms of intrinsic modalities, we can say that this expression is not compatible with intrinsic alethic modalities, while it combines with epistemic, appreciative, and axiological ones:

(11) a. **Je trouve que cette table est rectangulaire*
'I find that this table is rectangular'
b. *Je trouve que ce champ est assez vaste*
'I find that this field is quite extensive'
c. *Je trouve que ce pain est bon*
'I think that bread is good'
d. *Je trouve que cet homme est malhonnête*
'I find that this man is dishonest'.

Moreover, in discourse, *je trouve que* does not systematically express mitigation of the assertion. Tuchais (2014: 106) observes that, by presenting a judgment as a personal opinion, the speaker may mitigate her position or, conversely, cause other points of view to stand out and thus affirm that she is taking a very strong position. It depends on the situation of speech. One can even say that if a speaker chooses to indicate explicitly that she opposes the common opinion (e.g. *moi, personellement, je trouve que* 'I, personally, I find that'), it is a way of strengthening her position, claiming her refusal to follow the common opinion.

At the semantic level this expression only serves to clarify the nature of the subjectivity intrinsically associated with the predicate by restricting it to the *individual* subjectivity of the speaker. By default, an intrinsically subjective predicate refers to the collective subjectivity, to common opinion: by stating that *ce pain est bon* 'this bread is good', the speaker presents her judgement as referring to a collective subjective evaluation. However, by adding *je trouve que*, she indicates that the subjectivity is not *collective* but *individual*, related to the person of the speaker (it is her personal opinion).

Therefore, we will consider that *je trouve que* does not introduce an additional modality (in addition to the intrinsic subjective modality of the predicate), but serves to make clear the (individual) nature of the subjectivity of the predicate. The predicative lexeme and the phrase *je trouve que* together contribute to building the expression of individual subjectivity. Thus *je trouve que* is fundamentally different from epistemic modal expressions (*je crois / suis certain(e) / persuadé(e) que*). It is because *je trouve que* does not trigger the construction of an extrinsic epistemic modality, like *je crois que*, but specifies the intrinsic subjective modality of the complement clause's predicate, that this expression imposes restrictions on predicates. It is not compatible with alethic ones, because they are objective. This is also why it does not systematically serve as an assertion's mitigator: the mechanism founded on the principle of conviction, described in relation to epistemic modalities, does not apply.

We conclude with an example that illustrates the respective operations of these two types of expressions of personal opinion:

(12) a. *Je crois que cette soupe est bonne*
'I believe the soup is good'

b. *Je trouve que cette soupe est bonne*
'I find this soup is good'.

Statement (12a) expresses an individual belief of the speaker concerning a collective subjective evaluation. The inferential mechanism presented in Section 2 leads to a rhetoric-pragmatic effect of mitigation. This mitigated judgement may correspond to two distinct situations (at least):

- The speaker has not tasted the soup and expresses a personal opinion about the probability that the soup is good (since she knows the cook, the ingredients of the soup, what is said about it, etc.);
- She tasted the soup, but does not consider herself able to deliver a collective subjective evaluation of the soup's flavour, for example, either because she is sick and unable to appreciate it or because this soup belongs to some exotic cuisine for which she does not know the evaluation criteria.

The same does not apply to *je trouve que* (12b), which is only used to restrict the judgement to the speaker's individual subjectivity regarding the appreciative evaluation expressed by the predicate (*bonne*), which otherwise would refer, by default, to the collective subjectivity, to common opinion. According to the state of opinion of the participants in the conversation, this restriction concerning the nature of the subjectivity may correspond to its attenuation (the speaker indicates that she does not seek to impose her personal appreciative evaluation) or, conversely, to its strengthening (she signals, in this way, that she opposes her personal opinion to the common opinion).

5 *J'estime / considère que:* subjectivity and variability of judgements

The expressions *j'estime / considère que* 'I reckon / consider' are similar to *je trouve que*: they do not signal an extrinsic epistemic modality, but specify the nature of an intrinsic subjective modality (associated with the predicate). Consequently, they do not necessarily mitigate the assertion, and they are compatible with epistemic, axiological, and appreciative predicates but with much more difficulty with alethic ones:

(13) a. ??*J'estime / ?? Considère que cette table est rectangulaire*
'I reckon / consider that this table is rectangular'

b. *J'estime / considère que ce champ est assez vaste*
'I reckon / consider that this field is quite extensive'
c. *J'estime / considère que ce pain est bon*
'I reckon / consider that this bread is good'
d. *J'estime / considère que cet homme est malhonnête*
'I reckon / consider that this man is dishonest'.

They differ, however, from *je trouve que* relative to the type of restriction made on the subjectivity of the predicate.

The opposition between subjective and objective judgments is based, according to the Kantian tradition, on the "variability in the validity of judgements" between subjects. If a judgement is true for *any* subject, whatever she may be when she is endowed with reason, it is considered *objective*. It is *subjective* in the opposite case, when its validity varies between subjects. However, this dimension of "variability" has two characteristics that are relevant to our study. On the one hand, there are *degrees* of variability. For example, to say that an axiological judgement (such as 4) refers to a system of conventions implies that it is stable and shared *within this system*, which itself depends on the variability of ethics and ideologies. In other words, the axiological variability of judgements corresponds to an intermediate degree between objectivity of alethic (i.e. objective) judgements and unstable individual subjectivity. On the other hand, variability may concern not only subjects but also temporality, because a subject can change his mind or, on the contrary, remain steady in his convictions. And there are also different degrees of temporal variability of judgements: axiological judgements correspond to an intermediate degree of temporal variability, between alethic judgements and appreciative judgements (which are unstable).

Consider now the phrases *je trouve / considère / estime que*. It appears that *je trouve que* is perfectly compatible with the temporally varying individual subjectivity, while *j'estime / considère que* imply a certain temporal stability of judgement:

(14) *Cette semaine, je suis grippé, et je trouve / ?? estime / ?? considère que le pain est bon et que le fauteuil est inconfortable*
'This week, I am affected by the flu and I find / reckon / consider that the bread is good and that the chair is uncomfortable'.

Conversely, *je considère / estime que*, unlike *je trouve que*, are compatible with some alethic predicates that express a categorization along a continuum (15), or an approximate categorization (17), and are thus on the border between (objective) alethic and (subjective) epistemic predicates. In a situation of *crachin* 'drizzle' in Normandy, (15a) sounds more natural than (15b):

(15) a. *Je considère / estime qu'il pleut*
'I consider / reckon it's raining'
b. ? *Je trouve qu'il pleut*
'I find it's raining'.

Similarly, Tuchais (2014: 324) provides the example:

(16) *Ma chambre, je considère que je l'ai payée* (Cl. Mauriac, *La marquise sortit à cinq heures*)
'My room, I consider that I paid for it'.

In this example, it is possible to replace *considérer* with *estimer*, but much less naturally with *trouver*.

Even more clearly, regarding a table measuring 65 cm by 68 cm, one can say, by approximation,

(17) a. *Je considère / estime qu'elle est carrée*
'I consider / reckon it is square'

but with much more difficulty,

(17) b. ? *Je trouve qu'elle est carrée*
'I find it is square'.

From all this, it follows that *je trouve que* marks a higher degree of variability of the judgement than *je considère / estime que*. This is why *je considère / estime que* are more appropriate for the expression of axiological judgements (based on convention systems, which are relatively stable), while *je trouve que* is more appropriate for appreciative judgements bound to particular time positions, as the contrast between (18a) and (18b) shows:

(18) a. *Je considère / estime / ? trouve qu'il est coupable*
'I consider / reckon / find that he is guilty'
b. *Je trouve / ? considère / ? estime que la soupe est brûlante*
'I find / consider / reckon that the soup is hot'.

It is remarkable that *trouver* becomes acceptable in (18a) in the case of moral culpability, whereas it is excluded in the case of legal guilt. Morality is more akin to collective subjectivity, while legal guilt rests on a system of stable and codified conventions.

As for the difference between *je considère* and *j'estime*, *considérer que* refers to a judgement that can be voluntary and subject to a decision, which is not the case for the expressions *j'estime / trouve que* any more than for *je crois / pense que*.

(19) *J'ai décidé de considérer / ?* estimer / ?* trouver qu'il était responsable de cette situation*
'I decided to consider / reckon / find that he was responsible for this situation'.

6 The dual function of *je pense que*

Just like *je crois que*, *je pense que* 'I think' is compatible with all types of predicates (respectively alethic, epistemic, axiological, and appreciative ones in the following examples):

(20) a. *Je pense que cette table est rectangulaire*
'I think this table is rectangular'
b. *Je pense que ce champ est assez vaste*
'I think this field is quite extensive'
c. *Je pense que ce pain est bon*
'I think this bread is good'
d. *Je pense que cet homme est malhonnête*
'I think this man is dishonest'.

With alethic predicates, this expression has a value very close to *je crois que* 'I believe'. It expresses an epistemic modality, which has a systematic effect of mitigation of the assertion in discourse. In the situation described in Section 3, in which the speaker is asked if her colleague is here, the answer

(21) *Je pense qu'elle est ici*
'I think she is here'

has, at first glance, effects similar to *je crois qu'elle est ici*. However, there are differences between *croire* 'believe' and *penser* 'think' in this construction (see

Martin 1988; Dendale and Van Bogaert 2007). A judgement expressed by *croire* cannot be the subject of a decision (unlike *considérer*, see above), but it may be subject to a desire which is not possible with *penser*:

(22) *Je veux bien croire / ?* penser qu'il ne m'a pas reconnu*
'I want to believe / think that he did not recognize me'.

In this respect, *croire* functions like *considérer*, while *penser* is akin to *trouver*, *estimer*:

(23) *Je veux bien croire / considérer / ?* penser / ?* trouver / ?? estimer qu'elle est belle*
'I want to believe / consider / find / reckon she is beautiful'.

Moreover, the judgement denoted by *je crois que* must be based on knowledge about the situation, which gives positive reasons for belief, while the judgement expressed by *je pense que* may rely only on general knowledge and the absence of arguments against it. For example, if the speaker has not seen someone for a long time, she will use (24a) instead of (24b). The latter utterance would imply that the speaker has grounds, based on her knowledge of recent facts, to believe that her interlocutor remembers her:

(24) a. *Je pense que vous vous souvenez de moi*
'I think you remember me'
b. *Je crois que vous vous souvenez de moi*
'I believe you remember me'.

Consequently, even in the situation described above (in which the speaker is interviewed about the presence of her colleague), the two answers, *je crois / pense qu'elle est ici*, do not have exactly the same value. The first (with *je crois que*) assumes that the speaker has positive reasons to believe in her colleague's presence – that is, for example, the result of an abduction (see Desclés and Guentchéva 2001) based on the observation of the presence of her car in the car park – while the second (with *je pense que*) may be grounded either on positive reasons or on a simple lack of information that would oppose the judgement: as this colleague is usually here and if the speaker has no reason to think otherwise, she says that she thinks (*pense*) she is here.

However, the main specificity of *je pense que* is that this expression works in a way comparable to *je crois que* when combined with an alethic predicate, but may also work like *je trouve / considère / estime que* when combined with an axiological one. Thus, in the statement

(25) *Je pense que cette décision est juste*
'I think this decision is right',

the expression "je pense que", in its most plausible interpretation, does not express an epistemic modality, but simply refers the axiological assessment to the speaker's *personal* opinion, without any effect of mitigation. In that case, *penser que* becomes almost synonymous with *trouver que*, *considérer que*, and *estimer que*.

With epistemic and appreciative intrinsic modalities (and also, to a lesser extent, with some axiological ones), two interpretations may appear, sometimes leading to ambiguity. For example, the utterances

(26) a. *Je pense que ce champ est assez vaste*
'I think that this field is quite extensive'
b. *Je pense que ce pain est bon*
'I think that bread is good'

can be interpreted either as expressions of belief (with a mitigation effect) in a judgement assigned to collective subjectivity (*penser* and *croire* are quasi-synonyms) or as a marker of individual subjectivity, not introducing any mitigation of the assertion. This second interpretation appears more clearly if we consider (26a) and (26b) as responses to the question *Qu'en penses-tu?* 'What's your opinion?'. *Je pense que* becomes almost synonymous with *j'estime / considère que* or *mon avis personnel est que* 'my personal opinion is that'. In other words, the speaker of (26b) either may not have tasted the bread and expresses a belief about its taste quality (with a mitigation effect) or may have tasted it and gives her personal opinion (with no mitigation effect).

We can summarize this analysis with a schema.

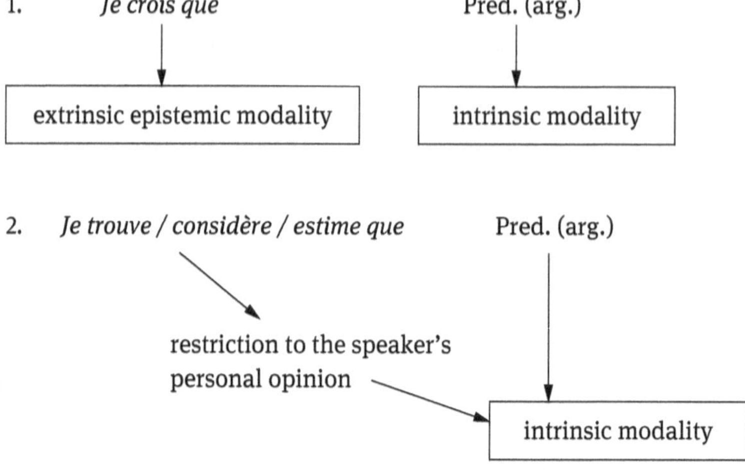

3. *Je pense que* : a) structure 1 with an alethic (objective) predicate
b) structure 1 or structure 2 with a subjective (epistemic, appreciative, or axiological) predicate

Figure 8.1: Modal structures of expressions of personnal opinion

7 Conclusion

The syntactic similarity of expressions of personal opinion is misleading. They are likely to play two distinct roles: either they trigger the construction of an extrinsic epistemic modality (compatible with all sorts of predicates in the complement clause) or they specify the nature of the subjective modality intrinsically associated with the predicate (excluding in the same time objective ones). *Je crois / suis certain(e) / persuadé(e) ... que* belong to the first case and *je trouve / considère / estime que* to the second one. The peculiarity of *je considère / estime que* versus *je trouve que* is the fact that these terms are able to transform some alethic approximate categorization judgements into subjective judgments (e.g. 15–17). The expression *je pense que* may, depending on the context (and in particular on the modality intrinsically associated with the predicate), fulfill either of these two roles: sometimes it expresses extrinsic epistemic modality (in the manner of *je crois que*) and sometimes it restricts the inherent subjectivity of the predicate to the personal opinion of the speaker.

Table 8.2: Properties of expressions of personnal opinion

	Je crois que	*Je trouve que*	*Je considère que*	*J'estime que*	*Je pense que*	
Expresses an extrinsic epistemic modality	+	–	–	–	+	–
Compatible with all sorts of predicates	+	–	–	–	+	–
Always a mitigator	+	–	–	–	+	–
Requires positive reasons	+	Irrelevant	Irrelevant	Irrelevant	–	Irrelevant
Compatible with some alethic predicates	+	–	+	+	+	–
Can be the object of a desire	+	–	+	–	–	–
Can be the object of a decision	–	–	+	–	–	–
Marks a high degree of variability of appreciation	Irrelevant	+	–	–	Irrelevant	–

It is only when they express an extrinsic epistemic modality that these expressions systematically have a mitigating effect on the speaker's commitment. This effect results from a discourse implicature triggered on the basis of a principle of the logic of conviction (Lenzen 2004) saying that a subject who is really convinced that p "believes she knows that p". Accordingly, if the speaker does not use the factive epistemic modality *je sais que p* or does not simply say *p*, but uses a non-factive epistemic modality (*je crois / pense / suis certain(e) / sûr(e) / convaincu(e) ... que p*), the interpreter will infer that, the speaker is, in fact, not really convinced that p.

Within these two subclasses of expressions of personal opinion, every expression has characteristics of its own, as the possibility of referring to a judgement which may result from a desire or decision, or, for epistemic modality, the requirement or not for positive reasons to believe that p.

Table 8.2 summarizes the main modal characteristics of these different expressions.

Finally, let us note also that the contrasts observed concerning the use of these expressions of personal opinion make possible the use of such phrases as tests to identify the intrinsic modal value of predicates (the compatibility test with *je trouve que* can be used to isolate alethic predicates).

References

Apothéloz, Denis. 2003. La rection dite "faible": grammaticalisation ou différentiel de grammaticité. *Verbum* 25. 241–262.

Asher, Nicolas, Farah Benamara & Yannick Mathieu. 2009. Appraisal of opinion expressions in discourse. *Lingvisticae Investigationes* 32 (2). 279–275.

Avanzi, Mathieu & Julie Glikman (eds.). 2009. Entre rection et incidence : des constructions verbales atypiques ? Études sur *je crois*, *je pense* et autres parenthétiques. [Special issue]. *Linx* 61.

Bally, Charles. 1932. *Linguistique générale et linguistique française.* 1st edn. Paris: Leroux.

Bally, Charles. 1965. *Linguistique générale et linguistique française.* 4th edn. Berne: Francke.

Benveniste, Emile. 1966. *Problèmes de linguistique générale* I. Paris: Gallimard.

Blanche-Benveniste, Claire. 1989. Constructions verbales "en incise" et rection faible des verbes. *Recherches sur le français parlé* 9. Aix-en-Provence: Université de Provence, 53–73.

Blanche-Benveniste, Claire & Dominique Willems. 2007. Un nouveau regard sur les verbes "faibles". *Bulletin de la Société de linguistique de Paris* CII-1. 217–254.

Boone, Annie. 1996. Les complétives et la modalisation. In Claude Muller (ed.), *Dépendance et intégration syntaxique. Subordination, coordination, connexion*, 45–52. Tübingen: Niemeyer.

Borillo, Andrée. 1982. Deux aspects de la modalisation assertive: *croire* et *savoir*. *Cahiers de grammaire* 4. 5–38.

Borillo, Andrée. 2004. Les "Adverbes d'opinion forte" *selon moi, à mes yeux, à mon avis, ...* : point de vue subjectif et effet d'atténuation. *Langue Française* 142. 31–40.

Brunot, Ferdinand. 1922. *La pensée et la langue.* Paris: Masson.

Coltier, Danlèle & Patrick Dendale. 2004. La modalisation du discours de soi: éléments de description sémantique des expressions *pour moi*, *selon moi* et *à mon avis*. *Langue Française* 142. 41–57.

Dendale, Patrick & Julie Van Bogaert. 2007. A semantic description of French lexical evidential markers and the classification of evidentials. *Rivista di Linguistica* 19/1. 65–89.

Desclés, Jean-Pierre & Zlatka Guentchéva. 2001. La notion d'abduction et le verbe *devoir* "épistémique". In Patrick Dendale & Johan Van der Auwera (eds.), *Les verbes* modaux (Cahiers Chronos 8), 103–122. Amsterdam & Atlanta: Rodopi.

Ducrot, Oswald. 1980. *Les mots du discours.* Paris: Minuit.

Gosselin, Laurent. 2010. *Les modalités en français* (Chronos studies 1). Amsterdam & New York: Rodopi.

Gosselin, Laurent. 2014. Sémantique des jugements épistémiques: degré de croyance et prise en charge. *Langages* 193. 63–81.

Gosselin, Laurent. 2015. De l'opposition *modus/dictum* à la distinction entre modalités extrinsèques et modalités intrinsèques. *Bulletin de la Société de Linguistique de Paris.* CX-1. 1–50.

Haillet, Pierre-Patrick. 2004. Présentation. In *Procédés de modalisation: l'atténuation*, *Langue Française* 142. 3–6.

Haßler, Gerda. 2014. Étude comparée de l'usage parenthétique des verbes épistémiques dans trois langues romanes. *Discours* 14. URL: http://discours.revues.org/8888

Jayez, Jacques & Corinne Rossari. 2004. Parentheticals as conventional implicatures. In Francis Corblin & Henriette de Swart (eds.), *Handbook of French Semantics*, 211–229. Stanford: CSLI.

Karttunen, Lauri. 1973. Presuppositions of Compound Sentences. *Linguistic Inquiry* IV. 169–193.

Korzen, Hanne. 2001. Factivité, semi-factivité et assertion: le cas des verbes *savoir*, *ignorer*, *oublier* et *cacher*. In Hans Kronning, Coco Norén, Bengt Novén, Gunilla Ransbo, Lars-Göran Sundell & Brynja Svane (eds.), *Langage et référence*, 323–333. Uppsala: Acta Universitatis Upsaliensis.

Kreutz, Philippe. 1998. Une typologie des prédicats factifs. *Le Français moderne* 66. 141–181.

Lenzen, Wolfgang. 2004. Epistemic Logic. In Ilikka Niiniluoto, Matti Sintonen & Jan Woleński (eds.). *Handbook of Epistemology*, 963–984. Dordrecht: Kluwer.

Martin, James R. & Peter R. White. 2005. *The language of evaluation. Appraisal in English*. London & New York: Palgrave Macmillan.

Martin, Robert. 1987. *Langage et croyance*. Bruxelles: Mardaga.

Martin, Robert. 1988. CROIRE QUE p / PENSER QUE p. *Annexes des Cahiers de linguistique hispanique médiévale* 7 (7). 547–554.

Récanati, François. 1981. *Les énoncés performatifs : contribution à la pragmatique*. Paris: éd. de Minuit.

Récanati, François. 2000. *Oratio obliqua, oratio recta: an essay on metarepresentation*. Cambridge, Mass.: The MIT Press.

Schneider, Stefan, Julie Glikman & Mathieu Avanzi. 2015. *Parenthetical Verbs*. Berlin: De Gruyter.

Thompson, Sandra A. & Anthony Mulac. 1991. The discourse conditions for the use of the complementizer *that* in conversational English. *Journal of Pragmatics* 15. 237–251.

Tuchais, Simon. 2014. *Comment dire ce que « je » pense en japonais et en français. Etude contrastive de l'expression de l'opinion personnelle*. Paris: Thèse de doctorat de l'EHESS.

Vet, Co, 1994. Savoir *et* Croire. *Langue Française* 102. 56–68.

Mario Squartini

Mirative extensions in Romance: evidential or epistemic?

Abstract: This chapter reappraises some discourse effects of the Romance Future by interpreting them as 'mirative strategies' connected to the interplay of the epistemic and evidential features that characterizes the modal meaning of the Future. In contrasting different extensions of the inflectional Future in French and Italian, mirativity will be described as a multifarious category that not only derives from indirect evidentiality but might also be linked to epistemic degrees of certainty. The special behaviour of Catalan, whose modal Future neutralizes the differences between French and Italian, confirms that these extensions may all belong to the same mirative domain.

Keywords: mirativity, evidentiality, epistemic modality, Future, Conditional

1 A new "mirative vogue"

The vibrant phase disparagingly considered by Aikhenvald (2003: 19) as a shallow "evidential vogue" has now been followed by an equally fashionable "mirative vogue". Since the early 1990s evidentiality has been gradually expanded from the *exotic* domain where it used to be confined to a more *domestic* dimension in which it has been naturalized by gradually adopting it in the descriptions of Romance languages (pioneering interventions by Dendale and Tasmowski 1994; Guentchéva 1994). A similar upsurge of interest is now affecting the notion of mirativity, which was originally launched as an independent grammatical category by DeLancey (1997). In the discussion that followed DeLancey's seminal work a confrontation arose between a stance defending the independence of mirativity from evidentiality (Aikhenvald 2004) and those who stressed the similarities between the two by grouping them together or suggesting a more general category encompassing indirective evidentiality and mirativity (*médiatif* in Guentchéva 1996 and Lazard 1999). Discussions were more recently refuelled by a monographic debate (*MIR(ative) revisited*) published in *Linguistic Typology*, in which DeLancey (2012) and Aikhenvald (2012) insist on the independence of mirativity

Mario Squartini, University of Turin

https://doi.org/10.1515/9783110572261-009

from evidentiality, while the opposite stance is advocated by Hill (2012), who contends that the existence of markers dedicated to mirativity is not confirmed by uncontroversial data. According to Hill (2012), the data traditionally exploited to show the "essence" of mirativity are in fact side effects of evidentiality, which supports Lazard's (1999) notion of "mediativity" as a general grammatical category having both evidentiality and mirativity within its semantic scope. However, the only point that seems to remain firm in this unsteady landscape is the relationship between mirativity and the semantic branch of evidentiality that is linked to "indirectivity", where the speaker has no direct access to the information and is only deriving information from a varied array of indirect clues (inferences, conjectures and reports). A connection between mirativity and indirect evidentiality is pointed out by Aikhenvald (2004: 195), who notices that inferred and reported evidentials may "acquire a mirative meaning", whereas "[a] firsthand or a visual evidential hardly ever does". In a sense, the very "essence" of what we normally intend as mirativity might be a special overuse of indirective markers in contexts of direct knowledge. This is what derives from well-known *Paradebeispiele* of mirativity. Consider the universally cited Turkish past indirective marker *-mış*, which not only expresses inferences and hearsay, but is also appropriate in (1), assuming a context in which the speaker opens the door and directly sees Ahmet, who pops up as an unexpected visitor (Aksu-Koç and Slobin 1986: 162):

(1) *Ahmet gel*-miş
'Ahmet has arrived!'

The recurrent connection between mirative extensions and markers of indirectivity was unorthodoxly reappraised by Plungian (2010: 48), who suggested that it is the epistemic nature connected to indirect information that might trigger mirativity. Being indirectly acquired, knowledge derived via inferences or second hand is intrinsically less certain and therefore epistemically biased. But, if Plungian's suggestion is correct, the study of mirativity should no longer be restricted to *evidential* systems, being in principle compatible with *epistemic modality*, especially in those cases in which a marker not only expresses an epistemic reduction in the degree of certainty but also signals the mode of knowing through which information is acquired. This point will be elaborated in what follows by describing mirative uses of Romance forms traditionally considered as *epistemic* markers, in which, however, the expression of a reduced degree of certainty is coupled with *evidential* meanings expressing indirect modes of knowing. Romance data are sufficiently varied to provide a complex picture of this tripartite relationship including not only evidentiality and mirativity but also epistemic modality.

2 No "indignation Future" in Italian?

Like many other languages French and Italian display a verb form, often referred to as the *inflectional Future* (e.g. Fr. *sera*, It. *sarà* '(it) will be'), in which temporal and modal uses coexist. The extent to which these forms are productively used in the two languages may be very different, also depending on the competition with other forms (especially the "deandative" periphrases, e.g. Fr. *il va pleuvoir* 'it is going to rain'), whose pace of grammaticalization is very different in the two languages. However, French and Italian coincide in admitting the inflectional Future (henceforth *the Future*) in conjectural uses, in which temporal reference is not futural (in (2) the situation is in fact located in the present) and modality becomes paramount:

(2) (Fr.) *Il* sera *chez lui maintenant / (It.)* Sarà *a casa ora*
'He will be at home now'

In a sense, the following occurrence (3) of the French Future *ils se moqueront* (lit. 'they will be making fun of me'), which also refers to present time (Azzopardi and Bres 2011: 64), might be interpreted as another modal extension parallel to the epistemic Future in (2). But in fact the speaker in (3), who is the main character of one of La Fontaine's *Fables* (17th c.), is not dubitatively conjecturing what is going on. The fox speaking here is rather expressing astonishment with respect to the unexpected resilience of a group of turkeys, who are behaving as if they were able to subvert the well-established predator-prey relationship. As the fox finds out that the turkeys are unexpectedly well equipped to resist his attacks, he shouts:

(3) *Quoi ! ces gens* se moqueront *de moi !*
'What ! These people are making fun of me!'
(La Fontaine, *Fables*, XII / *18. Le renard et les poulets d'Inde*)

In French linguistics this special usage of the Future, which is typically complemented by the discourse marker *quoi* 'what', has been dubbed *Futur d'indignation* 'Indignation Future' (Martin 1981: 82), a label that can now also apply to the discovery of something extremely *new*. Considering what we know from the typological literature on mirativity, the French *Futur d'indignation* might be reappraised by highlighting its function as the expression of surprise, the well-known Aksu-Koç and Slobin's (1986) "speaker's unprepared mind".

An interesting comparative point in this respect is that, despite the similarities between French and Italian, an Italian Future cannot naturally occur in (3). A look at the Italian translators of La Fontaine's *Fables* confirms this intuition.

In two translations compared here the most direct rendering through an Italian Future never occurs and two different modal options are chosen. In (3a) the translator introduces a modal ('want to') followed by the infinitive of the lexical verb 'mock, make fun of' (*si vogliono burlare*), whereas a 19th c. translator (3b) proposes a Conditional (*si farebbero giuoco*) instead of the Future:

(3) a. *Costor, – dicea, –* si vogliono burlare, (Jean de la Fontaine, *Favole,* transl. by E. De Marchi, Torino, Einaudi, 1958: 515)
    b. *Come? queste genti* si farebbero giuoco *di me?* (*Favole* di La Fontaine, Milano, Sonzogno, 1883: 113)

The Spanish translation in (3c), with the Present Indicative (*se burlan*), suggests a consistent behavior of Italian and Spanish vs. French in not accepting the Future:

(3) c. ¿Se burlan *de mí aquellos de quienes podría ser rey?* http://5minutospararereflexionar.blogspot.it/2010/11/el-zorro-y-los-pavos.html [last access 23.8.2017]

Apparently, Italian (and Spanish) seem to be recalcitrant towards Futures in contexts in which non-futural temporal reference combines with the expression of the speaker's unprepared mind. This discrepancy is confirmed by what is traditionally treated as another special use of the French Future, the so called *Futur de bilan*, where a Future Perfect is used to "sum up" a process made of different phases ranging from the past into the future (Wilmet 1976: 48–52, Martin 1981: 82, fn. 6). The 'indignation Future' described above and the *Futur de bilan* are considered as separate uses, but in fact they overlap in contexts where the speaker sums up the process leading to a given result and at the same time expresses surprise:

(4) *« Enfin, c'est incroyable, il* aura fallu *attendre hier pour entendre un président de la République... »*
'So, it is unbelievable, we needed (lit. it will have needed) to wait until yesterday to hear a president of the Republic ...'

(5) *Incroyable, il* aura suffi *que je signale ces deux stations hier soir pour qu'elles soient toutes les deux rétablies aujourd'hui*
'Unbelievable, it was enough (lit. it will have sufficed) that I pointed out those two stations last night for them to be both reconnected today'

The temporal adverbs *hier* 'yesterday' (4) and *hier soir* 'last night' (5) make it clear that these are *modal* Futures, which actually refer to past time, but in what sense are they modal? They do denote verified facts ('The fact is that we had to wait ... / The fact is that it sufficed ...') and therefore can hardly be considered as epistemic conjectures. In these cases the speaker seems to be evaluating the big (4) or minor (5) effort needed to reach a given result, whose process the speaker sums up without casting epistemic doubts on its attainment. By evaluating the effort required to achieve a given result the speaker also expresses surprise, which is reinforced by collocation with lexical items that explicitly express the speaker's unprepared mind (*incroyable* 'unbelievable').

If interpreted as mirative, these uses represent a modern version of La Fontaine's 'indignation Future' and consistently with the translators' difficulties in rendering (3), the Future Perfects in (4–5) cannot be translated by the corresponding forms in Italian, where two Present Perfects are appropriate: *è stato necessario* 'it was necessary (lit. has been necessary)' in (4), *è bastato che* 'it was enough (lit. has been enough)' in (5). My proposal in interpreting these results is that French, unlike Italian (and Spanish), includes modal uses of the Future whose core function is mirative expression of the speaker's surprise. In the next section, these results will be comprehensively interpreted by considering the systematic relationship of the Future with another modal form, the Conditional, which, as suggested by the 19th c. translation of La Fontaine's Future (3b), might play a role among the Romance expressions of mirativity.

3 French vs. Italian: Where else do they differ?

The description presented in section 2 has pinned down a discrepancy in the modal uses of the Future in two languages, French and Italian, which, more generally speaking, appear very similar as far as the combination of temporal and modal features in the semantics of the Future is concerned. Albeit minor, the restrictions in mirative extensions pointed out above might be sensitive to more significant differences. And in fact, Italian and French modal Futures do differ in other respects, especially if one takes into account the paradigmatic relationship between the Future and the Conditional. In particular, a divergence appears when considering the dubitative expression of conjectures in direct questions, where French regularly admits a Conditional, even though the corresponding form in a declarative sentence would normally (but see also fn. 1) be a Future. The contrast between (6), where the Future occurs as a conjectural form in a declarative sentence, and (7), where it is instead the Conditional that has replaced the Future in the interrogative sentence, demonstrates the paradigmatic opposition between the two forms, which can be interpreted in terms of epistemic commitment of the speaker (Dendale 2010, Bourova and Dendale 2013: 184–185):

(6) *Il n'est toujours pas là. Il* aura oublié *le rendez-vous*
'He is not here yet. He will have forgotten our meeting'

(7) *Il n'est toujours pas là.* Aurait-il oublié *le rendez-vous ?*
'He is not here yet. Did he forget (lit. would have forgotten) our meeting?'

Epistemic modality is involved here in its uncontroversial sense, as the expression of different *degrees of certainty* (cf. also Bres and Azzopardi 2012). On the one hand, the switch between the Future and the Conditional is triggered by the morphosyntactic structure that opposes French declarative vs. interrogative sentences (Squartini 2010), which, even though not obligatorily (especially in yes / no questions, cf. Azzopardi and Bres 2014: 3003), allow the Conditional instead of the Future. On the other hand, it can be semantically interpreted as connected to the dubitative nature of interrogative sentences. The speaker in (7) dubitatively proposes a conjecture that might explain a certain state of affairs, whereas in (6) the same conjecture is presented more assertively.

The interesting comparative point now is that this epistemic contrast does not occur in Italian, where it is neutralized by using one and the same form (the Future) in declarative (8) as well as in interrogative sentences (9).

(8) Avrà dimenticato *l'appuntamento*

(9) Avrà dimenticato *l'appuntamento?*

Pointing out the ungrammaticality of an Italian Conditional in (9) is not tantamount to saying that the Conditional is always excluded from Italian interrogative sentences. Take for instance the questions in (10–11), where both French (10) and Italian (11) do admit a Conditional:

(10) *Ce que vous dites est terrible : l'angoisse* serait *le prix à payer pour l'émancipation de l'individu ?* (Haillet 2001: 319)
'What you are saying is terrible: is anguish the price to pay for the individual's emancipation?'

(11) *L'angoscia* sarebbe *il prezzo da pagare per l'emancipazione dell'individuo?*

But (10) radically differs from (9) in terms of evidentiality. While (8) and (9) contain a conjecture, i.e. the product of the speaker's own reasoning, the Conditionals in (10–11) report information the speaker has just acquired from someone else (second-hand information: *What <u>you</u> are saying ...*) and quote it with possible polemical distance (Abouda 2001) and mirative nuances (Kronning 2013: 126).

Putting together the results of the empirical observations made here, we can conclude that the paradigmatic opposition between the Future and the Conditional works on a different semantic basis in the two languages. In French it is based on the epistemic commitment of the speaker with more epistemic confidence expressed by the Future, whereas the Conditional signals less confidence and therefore appears in interrogative sentences.[1]

Instead, Italian bases the distinction on an evidential divide between the speaker's own reasoning as opposed to reports derived from second-hand information. Table 9.1 depicts these results by interpreting the distinction between the Italian Future and the Conditional as a privative opposition of two evidential features: [+ SELF], which represents the Future as a conjectural form expressing the speaker's own conjectures, while the evidential functions of the Conditional are restricted to reports of external sources, i.e. [– SELF] or [+ OTHER]. In French, where conjectural uses of the Conditional are admitted (in questions and elsewhere, see fn. 1), the distinction between the two forms cannot be represented as a privative opposition dividing conjectures vs. reports. There is rather a scalar gradient of dubitativity, where the Conditional occurs in contexts with a lower degree of certainty, such as those in which the source of information is external (reports) or those in which the speaker codifies dubious conjectures by inserting them in direct questions.[2]

Table 9.1: Futures and Conditionals: French vs. Italian

	FUTURE	**CONDITIONAL**
Italian	[+ SELF]	[+ OTHER]
French	– [– > – > DUBITATIVE – > – >] +	

1 As noted by Desclés (2009), the morphosyntactic restrictions connected to the distinction between interrogative and declarative sentences do not tell us the whole story on the distribution of the inferential Conditional, which is also admitted in declarative sentences with a higher degree of epistemic certainty (Provôt and Desclés 2012: 50–51):

(i) Il *aurait* donc *plu* [puisque la route est mouillée]
'It did rain (lit. would have rained), then (since the road is wet)'

Interestingly, this is also a mirative context, in which the speaker is struck by objective data compelling the inferential conclusion (cf. the collocation with the *conclusive* discourse marker *donc* 'then' and the exclamative intonation).

2 In Squartini (2008: 938–939) I had already discussed the peculiarities of the French Conditional with respect to the features [SELF] and [OTHER]. There, I suggested a solution in which I underlined the non-applicability of the feature [+ OTHER] to the French Conditional. Here, I take a more radical stance by totally disposing of the features [SELF] and [OTHER] in the description of the French Conditionals and Futures, which I instead analyze in terms of epistemic scalarity.

The different arrangement of epistemic and evidential features depicted in Table 9.1 might also explain why French and Italian diverge in the development of mirative extensions, which, as shown above, in French are admitted with both forms (Future and Conditional), whereas in Italian only mirative Conditionals occur. The Italian Future is dominated by the feature [+ SELF], which implies that the speaker, in presenting his/her own surmises, might also be asserting the truth of the propositional content of the sentence. What the speaker is doing by using a Future is not reducing the epistemic commitment, but rather insisting that what is asserted has to be attributed to his/her internal reasoning. Due to this internal orientation towards the speaker's own reasoning, the Italian Future cannot be accommodated in the mirative contexts seen above, which contradict any internal orientation towards the speaker's mind. There mirativity is rather the expression of the speaker's surprise with respect to something that comes from outside and is so unexpected that the speaker would never have figured it out as really happening. La Fontaine's fox is outraged at a behavior that he would have never thought possible (considering the subordinate role of his prey). Through mirativity the speaker is expressing a surprised reaction to external reality in a way that might be paraphrased as 'I can't believe it', which cannot be compatible with a form like the Italian Future, whose primary feature is the expression of the speaker's [+ SELF]. This explains why the Italian Future is recalcitrant to mirativity, whereas French Futures, whose distinction from Conditionals is based on a scalar gradient of epistemicity, admit mirative readings, as Conditionals do. Being not based on an evidential opposition [+ SELF] vs. [+ OTHER], they can both express the speaker's distancing effect with respect to unexpected information. This analysis crucially lies in the assumption that the Italian Future is not compatible with mirativity, due to its intrinsic orientation towards the speaker's self as the evidential source. Being self-oriented it cannot be combined with the distancing effect of mirativity, a hypothesis confirmed by the empirical observation that the only possibility of making the Italian Future compatible with mirative contexts involves a change in polarity. What La Fontaine's fox says in (3) might be translated into Italian by inverting polarity (from positive to negative) and implementing the prosodic contour of interrogative sentences:

(12) *Non mi* prenderanno *mica in giro?*
'Are they really making fun (lit. won't they make fun) of me?'

By means of the non-canonical form of negation (postverbal *mica* added to the canonical preverbal operator *non*, Squartini 2017), the speaker stresses a polarity switch with respect to what was expected. This interaction between modality and polarity independently confirms the intrinsic nature of the Italian Future as a grammatical marker that, in its modal functions, emphasizes the role of the speaker as the evidential source of the information. When the speaker wants to keep a distance from the propositional content, as is the case in mirative contexts, a polarity switch is required. In the next section I will discuss other behaviors of the Italian Future that also support an evidential analysis of it, ultimately indicating that mirativity may have more facets than conceived so far.

4 Italian Futures: The speaker as evidential source

Olbertz (2009) scanned the complex boundary between mirativity and illocution, ultimately demonstrating that these two dimensions should not be confused, even though marked expressions of the speaker's surprise are recurrently joined by an equally marked morphosyntax connected to special illocutionary types. This correlation will be confirmed in this section by presenting Italian uses of the Future that typically share exclamative intonational patterns, in some cases supported by special word order and focus. However, the illocutionary type may vary and what all these uses have in common is their *interactional* function as discourse strategies exploited by the speaker to perform various *discursive moves*, e.g. conceding to the interlocutor that something is true, admitting that something must be true or attracting the interlocutor's attention to something which is especially relevant. Some of these uses are intrinsically dialogical and allow the speakers to perform acts that are face-threatening for the interlocutor, e.g. when the speaker responds to an insult.

The best known representative of these uses is the *concessive Future*, which is extremely common in Italian as well as in other Romance languages (e.g. Spanish). (13) represents a typical occurrence of the Italian concessive Future, which is used to perform a conceding move, followed (*but*...) by a second move, in which the speaker cancels a derogatory implicature apparently derived from her socio-regional background (Piedmont, North-West Italy):

(13) Sarò *piemontese, ma mica scema!* (Berretta 1997: 8)
'I may be (lit. will be) from Piedmont, but I am not stupid!'

The existence of a concessive Future is at odds with its definition as an epistemic form. If epistemicity is intended as involving a reduction of the speaker's commitment to the truth of the propositional content, one can hardly define as epistemic the Future in (13), where the speaker is not tentatively doubting something but rather presenting a state of affairs that is undoubtedly true. Squartini

(2012) suggested that this incongruity can be circumvented once we assume that the Future is not *per se* epistemic, being rather evidential (Escandell Vidal 2010). Through the Future the speaker signals that the source of information has to be found in the speaker's self, which does not exclude a reduction of the commitment to the factuality of the situation, but is also compatible with a situation that is definitely factual, as is the case with the concessive Future in (13). The speaker who performs the concessive move also reasserts his/her authoritative role as the evidential source by singling out information that is shared with the interlocutor. This prepares the background for the second move, in which possible implicatures are canceled. The emphasis put by the speaker on (his/her role as the information source is effectively expressed by using a form (the Future), whose semantics can be reduced to the feature [+ SELF]. This is not tantamount to saying that any occurrence of the Italian Future is necessarily factual, which is obviously not the case. A concessive Future may even occur in contexts in which the speaker does not vouch for the factuality of the situation (*Sarà anche come dici tu, ma io non ci credo* 'It may be (lit. will be) as you say, but I don't believe it'). The speaker may be more or less convinced of the factuality of a situation, which, however, does not affect his/her role as the primary evidential source in cases of indirect knowledge.

Interestingly, the different behavior of French and Italian seems to support these conclusions. As suggested above, French and Italian modal Futures differ as far as the interplay of evidentiality and epistemicity is involved, which might suggest that the discursive extensions of the Future towards concessivity should be barred because of the evidential role of the speaker as the authoritative source of the information that is particularly foregrounded in concessive contexts. In fact, this is the case in French, where concessive Futures are not documented (Rocci 2000).

Other *interrogative* or *exclamative* uses confirm these conclusions, as is apparent in the inferential interpretation of the Italian Future in (14), which has a direct counterpart in Spanish (Bolón Pedretti 1999: 837), while similar cases are not described among the modal functions of the French Future:

(14) SARÒ *scema!? Mi sono dimenticata le chiavi!*
'I must be (lit. will be) stupid! I forgot my keys!'

These are inferential contexts, in which the speaker derives *abductive* consequences (she must be stupid!) out of external evidence (the fact that she forgot her keys). At the same time, the inferential conclusion refers to a subjective evaluation (*modalité appreciative* in Gosselin 2010) and is expressed in a marked contour with focus on the verb form that signals to what extent the speaker is impressed by her own behavior, being, albeit reluctantly, ready to admit a fault.

All in all, what these marked uses of the Italian Future have in common is their interactional nature as a means of expressing that the speaker concedes or admits that something must be or is more or less likely to be true, even what the speaker would have not, in principle, been inclined to accept. The interactional context of these uses also allows the speaker to reverse concessivity and admittance into their opposites, as in the following dialogue, in which the Italian Future is used by speaker B to retort to an insult that speaker A has just uttered (a parallel use of the Spanish Future is described by Bolón Pedretti 1999: 837):

(15) A. *Stupido! B. Stupido* sarai *tu!*
A. 'Stupid!' B. 'YOU ARE (lit. will be) stupid!'

Interestingly, all the uses considered here can be accommodated within an evidential interpretation, once we realize that what is expressed is the illocutionarily marked response of the speaker, who reacts to external evidence by conceding or admitting that something may or must be true. In (15) the external evidence is what has just been said by another speaker, which suggests that this might be considered as a very marked and interactional occurrence of a report. In (15) speaker B is repeating ('reporting, citing') what has just been said by reversing the target and responding to the offense with the same lexical items used by speaker A. Reportivity is also connected to the concessive use seen above, where the propositional content interactionally conceded by the speaker, is often a reportative quote of what another speaker has just said.

Inferentiality (14) and reportivity (15) involved in these marked uses of the Future suggest a link to evidentiality, which, again, seems to disconfirm the traditional interpretation of the Italian Future as an epistemic form. As concluded above, an epistemic interpretation is applicable rather to the French Future, which might explain why French does not admit all these exclamative uses where the speaker not only expresses an evaluative stance but also reacts to an external source, thus reasserting his/her role as the final and authoritative source of the information. Such a marked implementation of the feature [+ SELF] is particularly apparent in the provocative uses in (15), in which the speaker is reacting to external evidence by citing the offence but at the same time attributing it to a different target. In switching the target the speaker makes a complex dialogical move, in which an external source is quoted but also corrected by the speaker, who thus reasserts his evidential authority. Obviously, this can only be possible with a form like the Italian Future that, as independently demonstrated above (see Table 9.1), is based on the speaker's self as an evidential source.

The link to evidentiality is even more directly confirmed by the following occurrence of the Italian Future (16), in which the speaker draws the interlocutor's attention to a state of affairs that is perceivable as direct evidence: the whole town of Parma and its province covered by the shields of the local football team. In this case, the speaker is not expressing a conjecture or any other type of inferential reasoning, neither is this a report. What is described by the speaker is patently visible ('*seeing* a crossed heart every five meters *pleases my eye* so much') and is not proposed as uncertain. By using a gradable adjective ('beautiful') the speaker is not only evaluating what can be seen by the interlocutors but is also drawing their attention to that situation.

(16) *Ma* sarà *poco bella Parma (e anche la provincia a dire il vero) tappezzata di manifesti con il cuore crociato ???? [...] poi magari sarà anche poco ultras, però vedere ogni 5 metri un cuore crociato mi allieta l'occhio mica da ridere* [from www.]
'Isn't (lit. won't be) it beautiful Parma (and its province as well) wallpapered with crossed heart posters??? then perhaps it may be (lit. will be) not 'hooligan' enough, but, seeing a crossed heart every five meters pleases my eye so much'

Interestingly, (16) also contains another Future ('it may be (lit. will be) not hooligan enough') of the concessive type seen above ('I admit that this might be not hooligan enough'), which confirms the similarity between the different uses of the Future discussed together in this section. At the same time, when collocated together these two Futures demonstrate the different dialogic move that they produce. Whereas the first Future in (16) attracts the interlocutor's attention to a given state of affairs, the second one performs the concessive move. The interesting point from my perspective, which is more oriented to find out the common semantic features from which the two discursive uses independently stem, is that they can all be interpreted as expressions of the speaker's self as a primary source, which authoritatively reasserts this evidential function in contexts that are discursively marked in terms of the relationship between the speaker and the hearer(s). All these uses can hardly be explained as epistemic strategies to lower certainty, as is especially apparent in (16), where the speaker is so convinced of the truth of what is asserted that the Future here becomes a strategy to convince the interlocutors by attracting their attention to a state of affairs that is explicitly visible.

The link to evidentiality poses the question whether these uses of the Future can be interpreted as mirative extensions. The issue is particularly relevant with respect to (16), where the Future denotes direct evidence by means of a form that more generally expresses indirect knowledge (assumptions and conjectures). This reminds us of the behavior of languages in which markers of indirect evidence may also denote direct perceptions, provided that they are presented as mirative discovery of new information (see (1) above). Actually, in (16) the speaker has not necessarily discovered something new, but a look at languages with evidential markers traditionally described as provided with well-attested mirative extensions seems to suggest interesting parallels to the Italian use of the Future in (16). By asserting the speaker's own evaluation of something that is patently true and perceivable to all interlocutors, the Future in (16) is also a way to praise a situation that can directly affect the interlocutor's world. Interestingly, compliments are among the pragmatic extensions of the Turkish evidential marker of indirectivity *-mış*. As pointed out by Aksu-Koç and Slobin (1986: 182), the speaker's surprise with respect to new information is pragmatically exploited as a strategy to express admiration:

(17) *kız-ınız* *çok* *iyi* *piyano* *çal-ıyor*-muş
daughter-your very good piano play-PRS-MIŞ[3]
'Your daughter plays the piano very well!'

One might contend that here we are dealing with pragmatic strategies only indirectly connected to mirativity. However, we do find more directly comparable cases, as in the following use of the same Turkish marker *-mış* (18), which testifies to a mirative extension from indirect knowledge (inferentiality). Interestingly, this context is very similar to the Italian (14) inferential use seen above:

(18) *meğer* *ne* *aptal*-miş-*im*
apparently what fool-MIŞ-1SG
'What a fool I am /I've been' (Perry 2000: 234, Zeyrek 1994)

From the parallel behavior of the Italian (and Spanish) data with respect to the Turkish evidential marker *-mış* two different observations derive. On the one hand, these data indicate that I might be on the right track in interpreting all these uses of the Italian and Spanish Futures as evidential. Otherwise, we might have difficulties in demonstrating why they show a behavior similar to a typical evidential (mediative) marker such as Turkish *-mış*. On the other hand, these

3 Abbreviations: PRS = present; 1SG = first person singular

Turkish-Romance pragmatic correlations invite us to consider the Romance uses as mirative extensions, as plausibly seems to be the case in Turkish. But if these are mirative extensions of the Romance Future attested in Italian and Spanish, how should we dub the expressions of surprise of the French Futures discussed in section 2? Do they all belong to mirativity? If this is so, the contrast between French and Italian / Spanish suggests that Romance mirativity admits two different subtypes. First of all, the data discussed above have allowed me to detect the French mirative use, which is connected to the gradient of epistemic commitment characterizing the opposition between the French Conditional and Future. Secondly, I have identified another mirative subtype, typical of Italian and Spanish Futures, where it is the speaker's self-assertion as primary evidential source that is marked by the Future.

5 Evidentiality, mirativity and epistemicity

When trying to draw general conclusions from the data discussed above, the question arises whether these empirical results on a possible intra-Romance distinction between two different subtypes of mirativity might be capitalized on in order to address the question posed at the outset of this work regarding the semantic connections of mirativity to the boundary between evidentiality and epistemicity. As described in section 1, evidentiality and mirativity are so strictly interwoven that their very independence has been questioned (see especially Hill's 2012 radical position). But the recurrent connection between indirect evidentiality and mirativity, which has suggested the proposal of a macrocategory in terms of "mediativity" (Lazard 1999), has also pushed Plungian (2010) to hypothesize a possible connection from indirect evidentiality to mirativity through the reduction of the degree of certainty intrinsically connected to indirect knowledge. In this respect, the results derived from our Romance data indicate that mirativity is in fact a Janus-faced category, which can be fed either by epistemic or by evidential content. As concluded above, the French Future is a form that can be accommodated in an epistemic continuum and is therefore consistent with a mirative reading that can be glossed as 'I can't believe it'. In this case the speaker expresses his/her own surprise upon sudden discovery of a state of affairs that does not even belong to his/her expectations and is therefore presented as non-factual in the speaker's cognitive frame. The observation that the Italian Future only admits this interpretation if inserted within the scope of a negative operator is very telling in this respect: the speaker cannot believe that something has just turned out to be true and therefore presents it as a non-fact through the switch to negative polarity. This connection to non-factuality allows us to consider this interpretation of mirativity as connected to the speaker's degree of certainty, which makes it indisputably epistemic. On the other hand, the mirative readings of the Italian and Spanish Futures are derived from evidential modes of knowing and are therefore applicable to inferences (the prototypical case can be glossed 'I must / may be stupid but ...') but also include those cases in which the speaker draws the interlocutor's attention to direct evidence visibly perceivable to everybody. In all these cases what counts is the role of the speaker as authoritative source of the information, who manipulates different modes of knowing.

Now, it might be counter-argued that the French and Italian data discussed above are too diverse to be arranged in a complementary distribution of different values within one and the same functional domain generally covered by mirativity. In other words, the problem might be that the data presented above and extracted from different languages have not enough in common to be compared and this might explain why they are not found together in the same language. But we do have a Romance language where the same inflectional Future covers the whole domain that in French and Italian is split into two subdomains. This is what happens in Catalan, where the Future occurs in contexts in which the speaker attracts the interlocutor's attention to some self-evident facts:

(19) *N'*arribaràs *a dir, de beneitures!* (Wheeler *et al.* 1999: 351)
'You really do come out with (lit. you will get to say) some stupid things!'

Even though here there is a derogatory judgment and not a compliment, (19) is comparable to the Italian use mentioned above in (16), in which the speaker emphasizes his/her authoritative role as evidential source, at the same time expressing surprise. But, unlike Italian, Catalan also admits the same inflectional form of the Future in contexts like (20) where the speaker takes epistemic distance from the propositional content, producing the effect 'I can't believe it', which is not grammatical in Italian (unless you switch to negative polarity). As noticed by Pérez Saldanya (2002: 2637–2638), (20) is uttered just after another speaker has denied something, and not before it, as would be more consistent with the temporal meaning of a Future:

(20) *¡T'*atreviràs *a negar-ho!* (Pérez Saldanya 2002: 2637–2638)
'You dare (lit. you'll dare) deny it!'

Interestingly, the coexistence of these two exclamative uses of the Future occurs in Catalan, a language where the modal uses of the Future in conjectural and inferential contexts (i.e. the typical "epistemic Future" that can be found in the other Romance languages) either do not exist at all or are very restricted (for a discussion cf. Pérez Saldanya 2000, 2002). Having none of the typical modal values of the Romance Future, the Catalan form is apparently free to develop all the other discursively marked uses, without distinguishing between the typical *Italian* self-assertion of the speaker as the evidential source (19) and the *French* epistemically distancing effect 'I can't believe it' (20).

The uniform treatment provided by Catalan, in which one and the same form (the inflectional Future) covers the different pragmatic extensions in (19) and (20), indicates that these two have something in common. On the other hand, the varied behavior of Italian / Spanish vs. French had led me to investigate the different semantic contents of (19) vs. (20). My analysis above has suggested that what (19) and (20) have in common can be assigned to mirativity, whose general umbrella explains the uniform behavior of Catalan. Instead, what keeps the distinction between (19) and (20), thus explaining the different behavior of Italian vs. French, is due to the interaction of mirativity with the two independent parameters of evidentiality and epistemicity, respectively.

Along the lines suggested by Olbertz (2009), more research on the interaction between these mirative extensions and the illocutionary features connected to them is now needed in order to show whether my conclusions here are only due to a superficial mirative vogue or are based on a more solid characterization of the role of mirativity in Romance, which might eventually demonstrate its autonomy as a semantic dimension independent from illocutionary types. Another point that should be further investigated is the relationship between mirativity and Gosselin's (2010) "appreciative modality", which pops up in some (but not all!) of the uses discussed above. However, what remains certain from the Romance data, as well as from recent analyses (Aikhenvald 2012, 2014; Hengeveld and Olbertz 2012), is that mirativity turns out to be a category much more multifaceted than the sheer notion of "speaker's surprise" would suggest. More generally, the speaker's "knowledge status" and his or her "expectation of knowledge" (Aikhenvald 2014: 31–32) seem to be influenced by the interaction not only with the source of knowledge (evidentiality) but also with the subjective management of different degrees of certainty (epistemic modality).

References

Abouda, Lotfi. 2001. "Les emplois journalistique, polémique, et atténuatif du conditionnel. Un traitement unitaire." In Patrick Dendale & Liliane Tasmowski (eds.), *Le conditionnel en français*, 277–294. Paris: Klincksieck.

Aikhenvald, Alexandra Y. 2003. "Evidentiality in typological perspective." In Alexandra Aikhenvald & Robert M. W. Dixon (eds.), *Studies in evidentiality*, 1–31. Amsterdam & Philadelphia: John Benjamins.

Aikhenvald, Alexandra Y. 2004. *Evidentiality*. Oxford: Oxford University Press.

Aikhenvald, Alexandra Y. 2012. "The essence of mirativity". *Linguistic Typology* 16: 435–485.

Aikhenvald, Alexandra Y. 2014. "The grammar of knowledge: a cross-linguistic view of evidentials and the expression of information source." In Alexandra Aikhenvald & Robert M. W. Dixon (eds.), *The grammar of knowledge. A cross-linguistic typology*, 1–51. Oxford: Oxford University Press.

Aksu-Koç, Ayhan & Dan I. Slobin. 1986. "A psychological account of the development and use of evidentials in Turkish." In Wallace Chafe & Johanna Nichols (eds.), *Evidentiality: The linguistic coding of epistemology*, 159–167. Norwood (NJ): Ablex.

Azzopardi, Sophie & Jacques Bres. 2011. "Temps verbal et énonciation. Le conditionnel et le futur en français : l'un est dialogique, l'autre pas (souvent)". *Cahiers de praxématique* 56: 53–76.

Azzopardi, Sophie & Jacques Bres. 2014. "Futur, conditionnel et effets de sens de *conjecture* et de *rejet* en interrogation partielle." *Congrès Mondial de Linguistique Française 2014 SHS Web of Conferences* 8: 3003–3013.

Berretta, Monica. 1997. "Sul futuro concessivo: riflessioni su un caso (dubbio) di de/grammaticalizzazione". *Linguistica e Filologia* 5: 7–40.

Bolón Pedretti, Alma. 1999. "Pasivos serán los de antes: apuntes discursivo-enunciativos sobre el valor del futuro". *Hispania* 82: 830–840.

Bourova, Viara & Patrick Dendale. 2013. "Serait-ce un conditionnel de conjecture ? Datation, évolution et mise en relation des deux conditionnels à valeur évidentielle". *Cahiers Chronos* 26: 183–200.

Bres, Jacques & Sophie Azzopardi. 2012. "On aurait oublié les clés du dialogisme sur la porte de l'analyse ? *De l'effet de sens de conjecture du futur et du conditionnel en français.*" In Jacques Bres, Aleksandra Nowakowska, Jean-Marc Sarale & Sophie Sarrazin (eds.), *Dialogisme : langue, discours* (Gramm-R 14), 137–149. Bern: Lang.

DeLancey, Scott. 1997. "Mirativity: The grammatical marking of unexpected information". *Linguistic Typology* 1: 33–52.

DeLancey, Scott. 2012. "Still mirative after all these years". *Linguistic Typology* 16: 529–564.

Dendale, Patrick. 2010. "Il serait à Paris en ce moment. Serait-il à Paris ? À propos de deux emplois épistémiques du conditionnel. Grammaire, syntaxe, sémantique." In Camino Álvarez Castro, Flor M. Bango de la Campa & María Luisa Donaire (eds.), *Liens linguistiques. Études sur la combinatoire et la hiérarchie des composants*, 291–317. Bern: Lang.

Dendale, Patrick & Liliane Tasmowski (eds.). 1994. *Les sources du savoir et leurs marques linguistiques* (Langue française 102). Paris: Larousse.

Dendale, Patrick & Liliane Tasmowski (eds.). 2001. *Le conditionnel en français*. Paris: Klincksieck.

Desclés, Jean Pierre. 2009. "Prise en charge, engagement et désengagement". *Langue française* 162: 29–53.

Escandell Vidal, María Vitoria. 2010. “Futuro y evidencialidad”. *Anuario de lingüística hispánica* 26: 9–34.
Gosselin, Laurent. 2010. *La validation des représentations. Les modalités en français*. Amsterdam / New York: Rodopi.
Guentchéva, Zlatka. 1994. “Manifestations de la catégorie du médiatif dans les temps du français.” In Patrick Dendale & Liliane Tasmowski (eds.), *Les sources du savoir et leurs marques linguistiques*, 8–23. Paris: Larousse.
Guentchéva, Zlatka (ed.) 1996. *L'énonciation médiatisée*. Louvain and Paris: Peeters.
Haillet, Pierre Patrick. 2001. “A propos de l'interrogation totale directe au conditionnel.” In Patrick Dendale & Liliane Tasmowski (eds.), *Le conditionnel en français*, 295–330. Paris: Klincksieck.
Hengeveld, Kees & Hella Olbertz 2012. “Didn't you know? Mirativity does exist”. *Linguistic Typology* 16: 487–503.
Hill, Nathan W. 2012. “Mirativity does not exist: *ḥdug* in “Lhasa” Tibetan and other suspects”. *Linguistic Typology* 16: 389–433.
Kronning, Hans. 2013. “Il condizionale epistemico di attribuzione in italiano”. *La lingua italiana* 9: 125–142.
Lazard, Gilbert. 1999. “Mirativity, evidentiality, mediativity, or other?”. *Linguistic Typology* 3: 91–109.
Martin, Robert. 1981. “Le futur linguistique: temps linéaire ou temps ramifié ? A propos du futur et du conditionnel français”. *Langages* 64: 81–92.
Olbertz, Hella. 2009. “Mirativity and exclamatives in functional discourse grammar: Evidence from Spanish.” In Evelien Keizer & Gerry Wanders (eds.), *Web Papers in Functional Discourse Grammar* 82. *The London papers* I. 66–82.
Pérez Saldanya, Manuel. 2000. “Naturalitat, cognició i variació morfològica.” In *Jornades de la secció filològica de l'Institut d'estudis catalans a Elx i a la Universitat d'Alacant*, 21–33. Barcelona / Elx: Institut d'estudis catalans.
Pérez Saldanya, Manuel. 2002. “Les relacions temporals i aspectuals.” In Joan Solà, Maria-Rosa Lloret, Joan Mascaró & Manuel Pérez Saldanya (eds.), *Gramàtica del català contemporani*, 2567–2662. Barcelona: Empúries.
Perry, John R. 2000. “Epistemic verb forms in Persian of Iran, Afghanistan and Tajikistan.” In Lars Johanson & Bo Utas (eds.). *Evidentials. Turkic, Iranian and neighbouring languages*, 229–256. Berlin and New York: Mouton de Gruyter.
Plungian, Vladimir A. 2010. “Types of verbal evidentiality marking: an overview.” In Gabriele Diewald & Elena Smirnova (eds.), *Linguistic realization of evidentiality in European languages*, 15–58. Berlin and New York: Mouton De Gruyter.
Provôt, Agnés & Jean-Pierre Desclés. 2012. “Existe-t-il un ‘conditionnel médiatif’ en français ?”. *Faits de langues* 40: 46–52.
Rocci, Andrea. 2000. “L'interprétation épistémique du futur en italien et en français: une analyse procédurale”. *Cahiers de Linguistique Française* 22: 24–274.
Squartini, Mario. 2008. “Lexical vs. grammatical evidentiality in French and Italian”. *Linguistics* 46(5): 917–947.
Squartini, Mario. 2010. “Where mood, modality and illocution meet: the morphosyntax of Romance conjectures.” In Martin G. Becker & Eva-Maria Remberger (eds.). *Modality and Mood in Romance: Modal interpretation, mood selection, and mood alternation* (Linguistische Arbeiten 533), 109–130. Berlin/New York: De Gruyter.
Squartini, Mario. 2012. “Evidentiality in interaction: The concessive use of the Italian Future between grammar and discourse”. *Journal of Pragmatics* 44: 2116–2128.

Squartini, Mario. 2017. “Italian non-canonical negations as modal particles: information state, polarity and mirativity.” in Andrea Sansò & Chiara Fedriani (eds.). *Discourse Markers, Pragmatic Markers and Modal Particles: New Perspectives* (Studies in Language Companion Series 186), 203–229. Amsterdam / Philadelphia: Benjamins.

Wheeler, Max W., Alan Yates & Nicolau Dols. 1999. *Catalan: A comprehensive grammar.* London/New York: Routledge.

Wilmet, Marc. 1976. *Etudes de morphosyntaxe verbale.* Klincksieck, Paris.

Zeyrek, Deniz. 1994. “The function of *mış* in Turkish folktales”. *Journal of Turkology* 2: 239–303.

Part III: **Baltic and Slavonic languages**

Anna Bonola

The Italian epistemic future and Russian epistemic markers as linguistic manifestations of conjectural conclusion: a comparative analysis

Abstract: In this article I propose a contrastive comparison between epistemic Italian future and some Russian linguistic markers of conjectural inferential conclusion from a sign. The main focus of the article is on Russian. First, I give an interpretation of the epistemic Italian future (Bertinetto 1979; Rocci 2000, Rocci 2005, Squartini 2004) within Congruity theory as described in Rigotti 2005 and Rocci 2005. Then I will show on the basis of a corpus analysis that in similar communicative situations in Russian we may use some discourse particles, usually defined as evidential markers (such as *vidimo, vidno, po-vidimomu* and *pochože, kažetsja, kak budto*).

From my analysis, it results that the Russian markers that most often combine indirect inferentiality, conclusion and conjecture, are *vidno* and *po-vidimomu* (which are also stylistically different) and so they appear to translate the Italian inferential epistemic future in a more unequivocal way. The markers of the second group (*kak budto, kažetsja, pochože*) mainly signal an imperceptive evidential, while *kažetsja* signals the reportive one.

Keywords: Epistemic future, evidential markers, conjectural conclusion, Russian language, Italian language

The theoretical frame of our research is Congruity theory (CTh), which provides an integrated semantic and pragmatic approach. Within CTh all conditions imposed by predicates[1] on their arguments – those entailed by the lexical meaning of the predicate as well as those associated with the real referents in the communicative situation – are treated as presuppositions which must be present

1 A *predicate* is conceived ontologically as a possible mode of being, a general notion that subsumes more specific ontological distinctions such as those between properties and relations, states and events, actions and non-actions (Rigotti 2005: 78).

Anna Bonola, Catholic University of the Sacred Heart

https://doi.org/10.1515/9783110572261-010

in the common ground[2] of communicative interaction. In other words, presuppositions depend on the predicate, imposing conditions on its arguments, as well as on real arguments, and must be respected in the common ground of the communicative situation.

In Rigotti-Rocci 2001 it is argued that it is possible to treat coherence in terms of predicates and presuppositions not only of a single sentence, but of entire texts. In order to do this, the hypothesis of congruity must be extended well beyond lexical predicates by admitting into the semantic structure of texts *high-level pragmatic abstract predicates* which, on occasion, have no linguistic manifestation at all. For these predicates Rigotti uses the term *connective predicate* (CP) (Rigotti 2005: 81). Within this theoretical frame texts are represented as a "hierarchy of predicate-argument relations holding between the text sequences at different levels and connecting each sequence to the whole text" (Rigotti 2005: 76).

Let us consider the following example:

(1) U_{-1}: *My son doesn't drive.*
U_0: *He is five!*

The utterance U_0 "He is five!" is understood as respondent to the task of *giving a reason* for the state of affairs stated in the first utterance U_{-1} "My son doesn't drive". This task can be defined through a relational CP including among its arguments the two utterances (text sequences) and imposing certain presuppositional constraints (preconditions) on them, which must be respected in order to ensure congruity at the textual level, that is, the coherence of the text. We can say that in (1) congruity is ensured by a CP of *causal explanation of a fact*. Besides utterance U_0 and, if it is the case, other utterances before (U_{-1}) or after (U_{+1}) U_0, logically depending on U_0, the speaker and the hearer (addresser and addressee) must also figure among the arguments of the CP; the presuppositions that the CP imposes on them are comparable to the felicity conditions imposed by Searlian illocutions (Searle 1969), which typically involved the speaker and the hearer.

The CP is thus pragmatic in nature and characterizes the utterance by specifying what the speaker does to the addressee with his utterance (Rigotti 2005: 82).

2 By *common ground* we mean all the propositions which addresser and addressee know when they are producing an utterance (Clark 1996).

1 Italian epistemic future as marker of a CP

In (1) the CP of *causal explanation of a fact* has no linguistic manifestation. Nevertheless the CP may have linguistic manifestations and, what is more, of very different kinds. These linguistic markers of the CP are referred to using different terms: *pragmatic connectives* (Jayez and Rossari 1998), *discourse markers* etc. Rigotti calls them *predicative connectors*.

The fact that the CTh provides a very general definition of CPs, independent from linguistic markers, enables us to define more precisely the semantics of predicative connectors; in fact, in every language there are many different ways of marking CPs, depending on which aspects of the CP are manifested and which conditions and contexts are involved: "The connectors can differ from language to language, or within the same language, depending on the arguments of the CP they signal and on the requirements (i.e. the presuppositions) imposed on its arguments" (Rocci 2005: 317).

Therefore, let us consider now how the semantics of the Italian *epistemic future* (EF) can be explained as a linguistic marker of a CP, i.e. as a predicative connector. We will refer to Rocci 2005, where the Italian EF is analyzed within the CTh.

Concerning the basic semantics of the EF, Rocci states that the Italian future is the logical consequence of a certain conversational background (i.e. a set of propositions) which must be identified within the context of the utterance by means of a saturation.[3] This conversational background is the combination of two sets of propositions belonging to two different domains: C (context-conditions) + N (usual circumstances).[4] The basic semantics of the Italian future can be described as follows: $(\{ C \cup ! N\} \rightarrow p)$ (Rocci 2005: 311).

Starting from this basic semantics, Rocci suggests his classification for the Italian future, according to the different kinds of saturations. Within the EF, he distinguishes between a *concessive* and *inferential* future. Our focus will be on the inferential epistemic future (IEF).

Rocci (2005: 275–285) identifies five different kinds of Italian IEF:

3 "It is not about choosing the more contextually suitable value among a series of predefined systematic semantic values, but rather saturating a certain variable X – argumentative or even predicative – through context. [...]" (Rocci 2005: 46).

4 We must pay attention to the fact that the union between C and N is submitted to the restriction of compatibility, i.e. there must be compatibility between usual circumstances and context conditions.

IEF1: *The* inference is based on the usual course of events:

(2) *La questione è che sono passati molti anni,* ***saranno***$_{\text{FUT.3PL.EVID}}$ *tutti cambiati.*
'The fact is that many years have passed since then; ***they'll all have*** changed.'

IEF2: Quantity estimate[5]:

(3) *Saranno*$_{\text{FUT.3PL.EVID}}$ *più di 100 metri*
'It ***must be*** more than 100 meters.'

IEF3: Epistemic future in the apodosis of a conditional construction:

(4) *Se quella è l'avanguardia, l'esercito intero* ***sarà***$_{\text{FUT.3SG.EVID}}$ *enorme.*
'If that is *the* advance guard, the whole army ***must be*** huge.'

IEF4: Epistemic future in interrogative sentences:

(5) ***Sarà***$_{\text{FUT.3SGG.EVID}}$ *già a casa?*
'Do you think ***he'll be*** home yet?'

IEF5: Inferential-conjectural epistemic future:

(6) U_{-1} *Non vedo la macchina di Luigi nel parcheggio.*
'I can't see Luigi's car in the parking lot.'
U_0 ***Sarà***$_{\text{FUT.3SG.EVID}}$ *già andato a casa.*
'***He must*** have already gone home.'

Our analysis focuses on this fifth kind of epistemic future, which in Italian is very common and typical (Bozzone Costa 1991); within the CTh it has been interpreted as a textual connector manifesting a CP of *conclusion of a non-demonstrative inference made by the speaker* (Bonola and Gatti 2013).

Let us consider example (6) from Rigotti (2005: 84): in this case, the future of the Italian text ("sarà andato") marks the second of the two utterances as a *conclusion of a non-demonstrative inference made by the speaker*. U_{-1} provides a premise, a piece of evidence – a sign[6] – from which this conclusion (U_0) arises. We note that if the argument is based on a sign, the premise U_{-1} is not sufficient to account for the inferential process involved. To obtain the conclusion we need a second implicit premise stating the regular occurrence of the sign and its denotatum: "generally, if L's car isn't in the university parking lot, he is not at university".

5 We need to bear in mind that an *estimate* is not an *approximation*: an approximation is a statement about an imprecise quantity (maybe I could quantify exactly, but for some reason, I do not want to); an estimate is a *conjecture* about a quantity which, at the moment, cannot be measured. So the Italian future here is not synonymous with "about".

6 We use *sign* here in the Aristotelian sense of the word: when something regularly occurs in concomitance with something else, it is the case that something is the sign of the occurrence of something *else*. We call this "something else" *denotatum*: the sign is the better known fact, and the *denotatum* is less accessible.

According to the CTh, the CP of the text we are analyzing has 5 argument places:

i) The speaker (S): s/he wants to show that an inferential process is leading her/him to the conclusion (evidential component) and that the conclusion is probable;
ii) U_{-1}: explicit premise (sign), which is supposed to be factual;
iii) Xcg: implicit major premise (*common ground*): the information shared by the speaker and hearer (generally, if Luigi's car isn't in the university parking lot, he is not at university);
iv) U_0: conclusion, which has not yet been accepted by the hearer.
v) The hearer (H): he is supposed to share the *common ground* Xcg with the speaker, but not yet the conclusion U_0.

We notice that the inferential conclusion marked by the IEF5 has the status of a hypothesis, aiming to explain a sign. So, considering the epistemic-inferential elements marked in this case by the Italian IEF5, we can observe:

(a) An *explaining inference* going back from the *consequent* (I can't see Luigi's car in the parking lot) to the *antecedent* (He has already left university) through a syllogism.[7]
(b) An unnecessary and ampliative *hypothetical conclusion*, whose probability can be graduated.
(c) An evidential component, in so far as the addresser suggests to the addressee that the source of knowledge is an inference (it is then a case of inference conveyed in a non-propositional way).[8]

Unlike Pietrandrea (2004: 17–19), who describes the Italian epistemic future as a pure epistemic marker which can occur in inferential contexts, we consider there to be also an evidential component in IEF5. This evidential component, as Giannakidou and Mari (2013) stressed, arises not so much from indirectness of evidence,

---

7 We must pay attention to the fact that what follows (consequent) may be a consequence of what comes before (antecedent), but not necessarily, like in the following example, where we have a combination of circumstances but not a cause-effect relationship between them:
– *Il tizio che hai incontrato ha dei lunghi baffi?* [The person you met has a long moustache?]
– *Sarà*$_{\text{FUT.3SG.EVID}}$ *il portinaio* [It must be the concierge]. (Rocci 2005: 305)

8 The inferences made by the addressee on the basis of the hints in the text or context are called *communicative*, whereas those made by the addresser are *communicated*; the latter, in particular, are the foundation of argumentative texts (Rigotti and Cigada 2004: 50); for more on the distinction between an inference communicated in a propositional way and another in a non-propositional way within a communicated inference see Rocci (2005: 324).

but from incompleteness of knowledge, i.e. we have an inferential reasoning with indirect premises, which works also in case of direct visual perception of a sign.

In conclusion, the three epistemic-inferential elements (a, b, c) in example (6) form a preferential combination of the Italian IEF5, but not all of them are actualized during use.[9]

The studies of the Italian epistemic future within CTh provide us with a general definition of the CP of *conclusion of a non-demonstrative inference made by the speaker from a sign*, which is independent from its specific linguistic manifestation by connectors. This general definition enables us now to make a contrastive comparison among different linguistic markers (connectors) of the same CP in Italian and in Russian; in fact, as stated above, in every language there are many different ways of marking the same CP, depending on which aspects of the CP are manifested and which conditions and contexts are involved. The aim of our comparison is to point out these aspects and conditions in order to show how on the basis of a contrastive analysis of the same CP in different languages we can better define the semantics of some Russian evidential markers and of the Italian IEF5 as well.

2 Our research

Our first problem was to have a list of Russian markers that may possibly mark a CP similarly to those marked with the IEF5, considering that epistemic use of future in contemporary Russian is either obsolete or stylistically marked (Bonola and Gatti 2013). In order to obtain this list, we proceeded in the following way:

a) We asked 4 native-speaker collaborators to translate a corpus of examples of the IEF5 from Italian to Russian; our collaborators always used *naverno/oe*, and more rarely *verojatno*, *pochože*. Nonetheless the first two connectors – *naverno/oe*, *verojatno* – usually just modalize the sentence without specific evidential meaning (the research is presented in Bonola and Gatti [2013])

9 The inferential connective of conclusion expressed by the Italian IEF5 can also have an *argumentative* component. In this case, besides the presupposition that S and H do not share the conclusion yet, there is the intention of S to show to H his inferential process with the aim to argue for the plausibility of the conclusion expressed in U_0 (Rocci 2005: 324, 327, Gatti 2010: 166). Note though that the inferential connectives and the argumentation do not completely overlap. For example, in the sentence "Il sole sta tramontando. *Devo aver dormito* [must-1.SG sleep] molto" [The sun is setting. I *must* have slept a lot] (Rocci 2005: 327), we use the inference of a fact (*ho dormito molto*) [I slept a lot], signaled by the epistemic modal verb *dovere* originating from a sign (*il sole sta tramontando*) [the sun is setting], but we do not have any argumentative move.

b) Considering that the CP marked by the IEF5 has an evidential component referring to the inference, we examined some Russian evidential markers,[10] and more precisely, according to Plungian 2001, inferential indirect evidentials marking reflected evidence.[11] In fact, according to the linguistic descriptions of these evidential markers, they seem to be suitable as connectors of the CP of conjectural conclusion from a sign, marked by IEF5, as they are used to communicate knowledge by inference on the basis of:
   - perceptive elements such as symptoms or signs (*perceptivanaja evidencial'nost'*)
   - general conditions (the distinction between perceptive elements and general conditions recalls the distinction between context-conditions (C) and usual circumstances (N), on which Rocci (2005) based the basic semantics of the Italian future (see section 1));
   - speculative (*umozritel'nye*) operations (*prezumptivnaja evidencial'nost'*), i.e. various inferential and logical operations.

After obtaining a list of Russian markers in this way, we chose the following Russian evidentials, which seem to occur in contexts similar to those of the IEF5 (*knowledge by a sign*):
- *vidimo/vidno/po-vidimomu* (apparently, evidently);
- *pochože* (it is likely that), *kažetsja, kak budto* (as though, as it were, it seems).

Možet byt', vozmožno, navernoe/naverno (maybe, probably), already discussed in (Bonola: 2014), do not appear in our list.

Then we analyzed how these connectors are used in a subcorpus of private oral conversations and mini-dialogues or quarrels (*nepubličnaja ustnaja reč': razgovor, mikrodialog, spor*) which we selected from the National Corpus of Russian language (NKRJa). We obtained a subcorpus of 175,329 propositions and 1,080,271 words; within it, we first defined which CPs are manifested by each connector mentioned above, using the conceptual apparatus of CTh. We considered at least 25 examples for each connector (if available), searching for those cases in which they mark a *conclusion of a non-demonstrative inference made by the speaker from a sign*. In each example the marker can occur more than once, thus the total amount of occurrences can be more than 25. We considered

10 Usually evidentials in Russian have no systematic morphological markers, but rather a lexical expression (adverbs or particles, deriving from reflexive verbs; Wiemer 2008: 15).

11 Studies on evidentiality distinguish two types of Russian indirect evidentials: *quotational* and *inferential* ones (Wiemer 2008: 335–336).

not only signs directly perceived by the speaker (what Kronning [2001] called *prémisses in praesentia*) but also *prémisses in absentia* (Kronning 2001: 75–76; Dendale 1999: 21).

Lastly, we submitted our Russian examples to translational substitutions from Russian to Italian. We checked whether it was possible to translate the Russian inferential marker with an Italian IEF5, in order to identify similarities and differences between the Italian IEF5 and the Russian connectors, when they occur as a marker of the same CP.

We shall now report the results of our analysis. Since space is limited, we will focus on a few examples for each Russian connector, the clearest and most revealing ones.

2.1 *Vidimo*

Usually, *vidimo,*[12] in communicative contexts of a conclusion on the basis of a non-demonstrative inference made by the speaker, introduces an inferential evidential component of the CP, as shown in a rather classical example like (7).

(7) *Na* *ulice,* *luži*
on road.LOC.SG puddles.NOM.PL
Vidimo, *noč'ju* *šel* *dožd'*
EVID night.INS.SG go.PST.3SG rain.NOM.SG

In (7) the inferential process on the basis of a sign and of the common knowledge Xcg (we know that when it rains it will be wet outside) leads to clear evidence inferred from the visible consequences of the rain; also, the lexical root of the particle *vidimo* stresses the perceptive, visual basis of the inference. So, here *vidimo* can be translated in Italian with *chiaramente/si vede/deve* (in English *evidently, must*) and marks a CP of *conclusion on the basis of an inference*. Considering the fact that *vidimo* is translated into English like in Italian with adverbs and expressions such as *apparently, evidently, a quanto pare, pare che, evidentemente, chiaramente*, etc., we can say that *vidimo* may mark the inference of

12 *Vidno* and *vidimo* historically are both adverbs related to the verb *videt'* (to see), but in contemporary Russian they are discourse markers (particles); as we are analyzing them from a semantic point of view, we will gloss them simply with EVID, i.e. evidential.

something probable or of something necessary, unless the context regulates one of the two possibilities.

In our subcorpus *vidimo* has been found in 108 documents and has 185 entries. Out of 25 examples analyzed in our subcorpus, in 33 occurrences (among which 5 were elliptical constructions) *vidimo* marks an indirect inference (but only one with a clear reportive meaning, i.e. as a marker of someone else's words). Instead, in 4 cases it is difficult to attribute a precise inferential value to *vidimo*, like in (8), where it is used to suggest the blatancy of what is being said and it could be translated into Italian with the adverb "chiaramente":

(8) A: *Ty, glavnoe, familiju ne nazyvaj…*
you.NOM.SG important.N surname.ACC.SG NEG mention.IMP
A: *L'importante è che non dici il cognome…*
'The important thing is not to mention the surname…'
B: *Mne v ponedel'nik idti so vsemi ètimi*
I.DAT.SG in Monday.ACC.SG go.INF with all.INS.PL these.INS.PL
dokumentami, i sobstvenno, napečatannymi,… sobstvennoručno
documents.INS.PL and, in-fact, printed.INS.PL by hand
Ja budu pisat' kak est', to biš', Kanda,
I.NOM.SG be.FUT.1SG write.INF as be.PRS.3SG that mean.1SG Kanda
Linali… [smech]. Ja ***vidimo****… ja*
Linali [laughters] I.NOM.1SG apparently.EVID I.NOM.1SG
vidimo *tak že… budu pisat'*
apparently.EVID so-as be.FUT.1SG write.INF
B: *Lunedì mi tocca andare con tutti questi documenti, e stampati da me, stampati di mia mano… Scriverò come è, come… Kanda, Linali… [risate] Io,* ***chiaramente***$_{\text{EVID}}$*… io,* ***chiaramente***$_{\text{EVID}}$ *scriverò così com'è…*
'On Monday I have to go in with all these documents and, well, all printed by me, actually printed by hand… I'll write it as it is, how… Kanda, Linali… [laughters] **evidently… evidently**, I will write it like this…' (www.ruscorpora.ru, last accessed in July 2015)

Among the indirect inferential examples, *vidimo* can be translated into Italian with *dovere* or with the IEF5, although there are some differences between the two: *dovere* usually marks an epistemic necessity and therefore conveys a certain inference and a strong judgment (Pietrandrea 2004: 4). Moreover, according to Rocci (2005: 310), the inference of the modal verb *dovere* as a matter of fact is not only based on elements belonging to the general common ground of the interlocutors, but it also leans on the personal experience of the speaker, not shared with the interlocutor[13]; for this reason it often has a higher strength of thesis[14] than the epistemic future,[15] i.e. the commitment of the speaker about the level of truth of what she/he states is higher.

In our corpus, the contexts in which the IEF5 seems preferable are those in which the speaker tries to interpret a sign in praesentia (9) or when she/he is describing an event (10). In these two cases the person who is speaking is trying to interpret the detected (9) or reported (10) sign on the basis of her or his general understanding, while the comprehension is under way, so the conclusion drawn by the sign is in its early stages, therefore conjectural, and the strength of thesis is not very high, thus the use of the IEF5 is a good solution. In (9) the use of *dovere* seems possible as well, but it conveys a higher degree of certainty:

(9) B: *Vot èti dve sinie palki, oni*
here these.NOM.PL two blue.NOM.PL sticks.NOM.PL they.NOM.PL
javno suščestvujut dlja ob"javlenija… Samo ob"javlenie,
evidently be.PRS.3PL for sign.GEN.SG itself sign.NOM.SG
***vidimo** ležit gde-to gluboko v Moskva-*
apparently.EVID be.PRS.3SG somewhere deep.ADV in Moskva-
reke…
river.LOC.SG

13 This is how one of the differences between the IEF5 and the epistemic use of the modal verb *dovere* in Italian can be explained: both actually originate from available hints in the context (signs), which work as a minor premise for a conclusion, but the conjectural feature of the IEF5 asks for a shared stereotypical common ground (Xcg). Should this be missing, it would be impossible to use an epistemic-inferential future to replace the Italian epistemic *dovere*, which, on the contrary, does not necessarily impose the requirement of stereotype on the common ground, as shown in the sentence: "Poi svolti a sinistra dopo cento metri ci *deve* essere una pizzeria o qualcosa di simile" [Then if you turn left after 100 meters there must be a pizzeria or something similar]. In this case, the poor strength of the thesis and the conjectural feature of the IEF5 would be in contrast with the non-stereotypical and certain knowledge expressed by the addresser, which is the result of personal experience, and therefore the following sentence would not be possible: "Poi svolti a sinistra dopo centro metri **ci sarà* una pizzeria o qualcosa di simile" [Then if you turn left after 100 meters there *should* be a pizzeria].

14 The graduation of certainty within an inferential conclusive process has also been called «strength of thesis» (Snoek-Henkemans 1997: 108, 117; Rocci 2005: 333–337). This indicates the level of certainty of whoever is proposing the thesis, distinguishing among the weak (*possibly, maybe*), strong (*must, certainly*) and moderate modalities (*probably*). In regards to the degrees of modality, Palmer 1986 speaks of *degree of commitment*: "any modal system that indicates the degree of commitment by the speaker to what he says" (Palmer 1986: 5).

15 Concerning the degree of certainty, Pietrandrea (2004: 5, 17) considers the Italian epistemic future unmarked.

B: *Ecco, questi due bastoni blu, chiaramente sono per un cartello... Il cartello* ***sarà*** FUT.3SG.EVID */****deve*** MUST.EVID *essere da qualche parte in fondo alla Moscova...*
'Okay so, these two blue sticks, *evidently* they're part of a sign... The sign must be somewhere at the end of the Moskva River...' (www.ruscorpora.ru, last accessed in July 2015)

(10) A: *V Kolomenskoe? [smech] Dima Pigasov*
in Kolomenskoe.LOC.SG [laughters] Dima.NOM.SG Pigasov.NOM.SG
s kakogo tam?
what on earth there?
A: *A Kolomenskoe? [risate] Dima Pigasov cosa cavolo ci faceva lì?*
'In Kolomenskoe? [laughter] What on earth was Dima Pigasov doing there?'
B: *Ja ne znaju, čë on tam*
I.NOM.SG NEG know.PRS.1SG why he.NOM.1SG there

zatesalsja. ***Vidimo,*** *emu nečego bylo*
sneake.in.PST.3SG EVID he.DAT.SG nothing.GEN.SG be.PST.3SG
delat', rešil poechat'.
do.INF decide.PST.3SG go.INF
B: *Non so perché si sia intrufolato. Non* ***avrà avuto*** HAVE.FUT.3SG.EVID *niente da fare e ha deciso di andare.*
'I don't know why he sneaked in. He ***can't*** have had much to do/ ***apparently*** *he had* nothing to do and he decided to go.' (www.ruscorpora.ru, last accessed in July 2015)

Instead when the strength of thesis is high, then the translation with *dovere* seems better; this happens especially in some examples in which the inference is anticipated before the sign, which is named right after, and the sign is presented as a consequence of the inferred element. For example, in (11) it is said that Natasha *must* have known the cost of the trip (inference), and for this, she kept quiet (sign) and did not want to participate anymore.

(11) *Tam sidit Nataša Pavlova, kotoraja*
there seat.PRS.1SG Natasha.NOM.SG Pavlova.NOM.SG who.NOM.SG
vrode kak sobiralas', no uznala cenu,
apparently, mean.PST.3SG [to come] but find-out.PST.3SG cost.ACC.SG
vidimo, *ona n-ne zachotela, voobšče otmolčalas'.*
EVID she.NOM.SG NEG want.PST.3SG in-the-end keep-quiet.PST.3SG

Nu potomu čto dorogo s… na samom dele.
well because expensive.ADV actually

C'era Natascia Pavlova che, a quanto pare, aveva intenzione di venire, ma ***deve***~MUST.PRS.3SG.EVID~ *aver saputo il costo e non ha voluto, è stata zitta. Beh perché è caro in effetti…*
'There was Natasha Pavlova who, apparently, wanted to come, but she ***must have found out*** the cost (of the trip) and she didn't come (in the end), she kept quiet. Well, it is actually quite expensive…' (www.ruscorpora.ru, last accessed in July 2015)

As a matter of fact, example (11) lacks one of the fundamental requirements of the previously mentioned CP of conjectural conclusion deriving from a sign, which, during the process, calls for the consequent (sign: keep quiet) to come before the antecedent (cause: the excessive cost). In fact, the modal verb *dovere* in Italian seems to be more suitable in case of deductive logical processes, going from antecedent to consequent (Pierandrea 2004: 12).

In (12) the inference is based on the experience of the speaker and the strength of the conclusion is very high, thus in this case *dovere* is more appropriate; if the IEF5 were used, it would imply that the speaker wants to make the conclusion a conjecture:

(12) *On menja za ruku vzjal, a ja*
he.NOM.SG I.ACC.SG by hand.ACC.SG held.PST.3SG but I.NOM.SG
tak byla fil'mom uvlečena, čto kak-to krivo
so be.PST.3SG film.INS.SG catch up.PTCP.PASS.SG that sort-of askew
ruku schvatila daže ne ruku, a prosto
hand.ACC.SG grab.PST.1SG actually NEG hand.ACC.SG but simply
tupo za palec za bol'šoj i ***vidimo*** *každyj*
stupidly by finger.ACC.SG by big.ACC.SG and EVID every.NOM.

raz, kogda byli v fil'me kakie-to momenty,
time.NOM.SG, when be.PST.3PL in film.LOC.SG some.NOM.PL moments
strašnye momenty, ja tak sil'no ego
terrible.NOM.PL moments.NOM.PL I.NOM.SG so bad.ADV he.GEN.SG
palec sžimala i dergala čto čut' i ne
finger.ACC.SG squeeze.PST.1SG and twist.PST.1SG that nearly NEG
slomala.
brake.PST.1SG

Mi ha preso per mano, e io ero così presa dal film che gli ho afferrato malamente la mano; anzi, nemmeno la mano, gli ho preso stupidamente il dito, il pollice, e ogni volta che il film faceva paura, ***devo***$_{\text{must.PRS.1SG.EVID}}$ *avergliello stretto e girato così forte, che per poco non gliel'ho rotto.*
'He held my hand, and I was so caught up in the film that I sort of grabbed his hand too; actually, I didn't grab his hand, I stupidly went straight for the finger, the thumb, and every time I got scared during the film, I ***must*** have squeezed it and twisted it so badly, that I nearly broke it.'
(www.ruscorpora.ru, last accessed in July 2015)

2.2 *Vidno*

In our corpus the marker *vidno* has approximately 60 occurrences, since it was necessary to remove all the adverbial and predicative uses from the initial automatic search results (267 entries), so as to have only the discourse particles, in order to establish if they had evidential function or not.

In more than half of the cases, *vidno* marks indirect inference, but not in situations of knowledge from a sign. In these cases the inference is based on the usual course of events and we can use what Rocci called IEF1 (see section 1), i.e. a simple inferential epistemic future:

(13)

Tipa	*prodjuser.*	*Vot*	*on*	*ee*	*snačala*
sort.GEN.SG	producer.NOM.SG	here	he.NOM.SG	she.ACC.SG	at-first

chotel	*raskrutit'.*	*kak*	*pevicu*	*Vot.*	*U*	*nego*	*tam,*
want.PST.3SG	launch.INF	as	singer.ACC.SG	so	by	he.GEN.SG	there

vidno,	*ničego*	*ne*	*polučalos'…*
EVID	nothing.GEN.SG	NEG	manage.PST.3SG

E' una specie di produttore. E all'inizio voleva lanciarla come cantante. Ecco. Ma non ***sarà riuscito***$_{\text{MANAGE.FUT.3SG.EVID}}$/***deve***$_{\text{MUST.PRS.3SG.EVID}}$ ***essere riuscito*** a combinare niente…
'He is a sort of producer. At first he wanted to launch her as a singer, so. But ***evidently*** he can't have managed to do anything.' (www.ruscorpora.ru, last accessed in July 2015)

However, in our corpus *vidno* is also used to mark an inferential conclusion from a sign (12 times). Besides the use of *evidentemente*, or of the locution *si vede che*, *vidno* can be translated with *dovere*; in our examples the use of the IEF5 is acceptable as well, but it weakens the strength of thesis:

(14) *Vot oni segodnja v Kervu poechali. V*
here they.NOM.PL today to Kerva.ACC.SG go.PST.3PL in
Kerve [...] uže dačnye učastki stojat,
Kerva.LOC.SG already dacha's.ADJ.NOM.PL land.NOM.PL stay.PRS.3PL
uže voda est', est' èlektričestvo.
already water.NOM.SG be.PRS.3SG be.PRS.3SG electricity.NOM.SG
*Nu, **vidno** doplačivali.*
well, **EVID** pay.PST.3PL

Oggi sono andati a Kerva. A Kerva [...] ci sono già le dace con la terra/ c'è già l'acqua, l'elettricità. Beh, ***evidentemente***$_{\text{ADV.EVID}}$ / ***si vede***$_{\text{SEE.PRS.3SG.EVID}}$ *che hanno finito di pagare/**devono***$_{\text{MUST.PRS.3PL.EVID}}$ aver finito di pagare/***avranno finito***$_{\text{FINISH-FUT.3PL}}$ di pagare.
'Today they went to Kerva. In Kerva [...] there are already dachas with some land/there's already water, electricity. Well, **evidently/it seems** that they ended up paying /they **must** have ended up paying/ they **will have** ended up paying.' (www.ruscorpora.ru, last accessed in July 2015)

2.3 *Po-vidimomu*

In our corpus the use of *po-vidimomu* is much less frequent, it occurs only 7 times (probably because it is now obsolete and therefore not commonly used in the daily spoken register).[16]

Po-vidimomu, in all our examples, signals a conclusive inference, but not always from a sign: in (15) *po-vidimomu* signals that the conclusion is inferred, but we don't know on what basis. Nevertheless the speaker makes a certain inference (as the adverb *certamente* [certainly] signals), so the use of IEF1 does not seem possible:

(15) *Èto byla det... detskaja peredača. I s*
this be.PST.3SG children's program.NOM.SG and from
ètogo značit vot oni načali. No
this.GEN.SG mean.PRS.3SG so they.NOM.3PL start.PST.3PL but
èto po-vidimomu bylo dlja bolee staršich uže
this *clearly*EVID be.PST.3SG for much older.GEN.PL already

16 From a stylistic point of view, *vidimo* appears not to be marked, whereas *vidno* is marked as typical of the spoken register, and *po-vidimomu* belongs to the official register (Kiseleva and Paillard 2003: 52).

konečno rebjat.
certainly child.GEN.PL

Era una trasmissione per bamb... bambini. E così hanno iniziato da quello. Ma era ***evidentemente***$_{\text{ADV.EVID}}$ */****doveva***$_{\text{MUST.PST.3SG.EVID}}$ *essere per bambini certamente più grandi.*
'It was a child ... children's program. And so they started from that one. But it was ***clearly*** a program for much older children/it ***must*** have been a program for certainly much older children.' (www.ruscorpora.ru, last accessed in July 2015)

In (16), on the contrary, the addresser provides a sign to prove how exceptional it was for her, as a child, when her dad would go to pick her up. In order to communicate such certainty, she adds a series of evidences, among which is the fact (sign) that all the details of those distant recollections are still in her memory today; moreover, the precision of these details is confirmed by an external witness, her mother. In this case we have a certain conclusion and so the uncertainty conveyed by the IEF5 is inappropriate, whereas *dovere* is certainly more suitable:

(16) *Mne bylo tri goda. Vot ja*
I.DAT.SG be.PST.3SG three years.GEN.SG here I.NOM.SG
pomnju kak papa nas vstrečal.
remember.PRS.1SG when dad.NOM.SG we.ACC.SG pick-up.PST.3SG.
Ja mame nedavno rasskazyvala. Ona
I.NOM.SG mum.DAT.SG not-long-ago tell.PST.1SG she.NOM.SG
govorit: "ty absoljutno pravil'no vse govoriš'".
say.PRS.3SG you.NOM.SG absolutely correctly all.N.SG say.PRS.2SG".
Po-vidimomu dlja menja uže èto bylo vot
clearly for I.ACC.SG already this be.PST.3SG here
kakoe-to bol'šoe sobytie.
such.ADJ.INDF.SG important.NOM.SG event.NOM.SG

Avevo tre anni. E mi ricordo quando papà veniva a prenderci. L'ho raccontato poco tempo fa alla mamma, e lei mi ha detto: "Quello che dici è assolutamente corretto". Si ***vede***$_{\text{SEE.PRS.3SG. EVID}}$ *che* per me era/per me ***doveva***$_{\text{MUST.PST.3SG.EVID}}$ *essere/**per me ***sarà***$_{\text{BE.FUT.3SG.EVID}}$ *stato* un grande avvenimento.
'I was three years old. And I remember when dad would come and pick us up. I told mum about this not long ago and she told me: "What you tell me is absolutely correct". It was ***clearly*** an important event for me/it ***must*** have been an important event for me/**it* ***should*** have been an important event for me.' (www.ruscorpora.ru, last accessed in July 2015)

2.4 *Kak budto (by)*

In our corpus, *kak budto* (*by*) occurs in 134 documents and has 206 entries. In 23 out of 25 cases, this marker does not indicate a conjectural conclusion. In (17), for example, the speaker gives an approximate description of the physical appearance of the person he is looking at, as if it were the result of a supposed loss of weight; the aim of her/his statement however is not to infer the conclusion that the person has lost weight, but rather to describe what he is seeing by a comparison, which is the dominant meaning of *kak budto* (Letučij 2008: 222). Thus, the indirect evidential has the aim of approximately describing the perception of who is looking. We can say that in (17) congruity is ensured by a CP of *description of a state*, since in the context we have no elements allowing us to suppose other communicative aims (like a polemical reply and so on). Such cases are explained as *imperceptive* indirect evidential (Letučij 2008, Padučeva 2012), conveying an imprecise perception. In this case we translate *kak budto* into Italian with the subjunctive form of the verb:

(17)	A:	*Krasavec.*			
		handsome-boy.NOM.SG			
	A':	*E' un bel ragazzo.*			
		'He is a handsome boy'.			
	B:	*Takoe*	*čuvstvo,*	***kak budto***	*on*
		Such.ADJ.NOM.SG	feeling.NOM.SG	as if	he.NOM.SG
		pochudel.			
		slim.down.PST.3SG			
	B':	*Si ha l'impressione che* ***sia dimagrito***$_{\text{SLIM DOWN-SBJV.3SG}}$			
		'He looks ***as if*** he has lost a lot of weight.'			

(www.ruscorpora.ru, last accessed in July 2015)

The value of approximation of *kak budto* often hedges the responsibility of the statement of the speaker. In the following example (18), taken from our corpus, this is rather clear: the first speaker uses the expression *kak budto* to describe the behavior of a third person, and his interlocutor answers back, precisely because of this use of *kak budto* that is intended to hedge the statement and the speaker's responsibility for it.

(18)	A:	*U*	*nas,*	*govorjat,*	*paniku*	*navodjat*	***kak budto***
		by	we.GEN.PL	SAY. PRS.3PL	panic.ACC.SG	create.PRS.3PL	as if

special'no. [. . .]
on-purpose [. . .]

A': *Da noi, dice, creano il panico* ***come se lo facessero*** do.SBJV.3SG *apposta.*
'It is said that they create panic here ***as if they were doing*** it on purpose. [. . .]'

B: *Počemu* **kak budto**? *Počemu* **kak budto**-*to? Ne* **kak budto**, *a*
why *as if?* why *as if?* NEG *as if,* but
special'no.
on purpose.

B': *Perché* **'come se'**? *Perché* **'come se'**"? *Non* **'come se'**, *ma apposta.*
'Why **as if**? Why ***as if***? It's not ***as if***, but on purpose.' (www.ruscorpora.ru, last accessed in July 2015)

In our corpus there are only 2 cases in which *kak budto* could be interpreted as a connector of a CP of inferential conclusion in situations in which the speaker sees signs that s/he tries to interpret; here *kak budto* could be translated with an Italian IEF5 and, in this case, the Italian translation would unequivocally express the conjectural-conclusive value of the CP.

In (19), for example, the speaker is describing a device which is not working and not reacting to the commands, and seemingly responding as if it were unplugged (inferred fact):

(19) *On voobšče daže otklika ne prinimaet*
It.NOM.SG generally even confirmation.GEN.SG NEG receive.PRS.3SG
ot platy. On na nee voobšče nikak
from motherboard.GEN.SG It.NOM.SG to it.ACC.SG actually at all
ne reagiruet, voobšče nikak. Kak budto by on voobšče
NEG react.PRS.3SG actually at all as if it.NOM.SG generally
ne podključen k nej.
NEG plug.PTCP.NOM.SG to it.DAT.SG

Comunque non riceve nemmeno il segnale della scheda madre. Non reagisce proprio, proprio zero. ***Sembra*** SEEM-PRS.3SG *che non* ***sia*** BE-SBJV.3SG /***è come se*** AS IF ***non fosse*** BE-SBJV.3SG /***sarà*** BE.FUT.3SG.EVID scollegato.
'It's not even receiving confirmation from the motherboard. It's not actually reacting at all. *It* ***appears to be/it's as if it were/it*** *must be* unplugged.' (www.ruscorpora.ru, last accessed in July 2015)

The third Italian translation, with the IEF5, is not good, as the conjectural conclusive value is certainly stronger than in the Russian text.

2.5 *Kažetsja*

This term occurs in 283 documents with 482 entries, but the number drastically drops – 35 – if the cases in which it was used as a discourse particle are selected. In 15 out of 25 cases, *kažetsja* has the function of making the statement uncertain, with the aim of hedging the responsibility of the speaker in regards to what he is stating. Here, *kažetsja* is a doxastic marker (it seems that), and for this reason, in most of the cases in Italian, it can be translated using *pare* (*che*)/*sembra* (*che*) [it seems] or with probability modal markers such as *forse*, *può essere* [perhaps, maybe] and it does not express a CP of inferential conclusion.

(20) *Ty* *znaeš'*, *ja* ***kažetsja***, *načinaju*
you.NOM.SG know.PRS.2SG I.NOM.SG *maybe* begin.PRS.1SG
ponimat' *alkogolikov...*
understand.INF... alcoholics.ACC.PL
*Sai, io, **forse**$_{ADV}$ inizio a capire gli alcolizzati ...*
'You know, ***maybe***, I'm beginning to understand alcoholics...' (www.ruscorpora.ru, last accessed in July 2015)

In 7 cases, *kažetsja* is reportive, but its function is often that of hedging the epistemic responsibility of the speaker who hides his statement behind what is said by others.

In (21) the speaker C reports the words of interlocutor B to a third interlocutor A, who seems not to have understood; here *kažetsja* signals the reported speech as well as the uncertainty of the speaker:

(21) A: *Galja,* *kakoj* *nomer* *doma*
Galja.NOM.SG which.ADJ.NOM.SG number.NOM.SG house.GEN.SG
nado?
need
A: *Galja, a che numero dobbiamo andare?*
'Galja, which house number is it?'
B: *Vos'm...* *vos'moj* *po-moemu.*
Eig... eight.ADJ.NOM.SG to-my-mind.
B: *Ott... Otto secondo me.*
'Eig... eight I think.'
A: *Vos'moj?*
Eight.ADJ.NOM.SG
A: *Otto?*
'Eight?'

C: ***Kažetsja*** *vosem'*...
seem.PRS.3SG.QUOT eight ...
C': **Pare**$_{\text{PRES.3SG.QUOT}}$...*otto*...
'It ***seems*** to be eight...' (www.ruscorpora.ru, last accessed in July 2015)

In (22) instead, it signals the connection to a common opinion about fashion, in order to reply to the negative attitude of the interlocutor about the jeans they are talking about, and thus it is used to justify one's own positive opinion:

(22) A: *Mne èti džinsy ponravilis' srazu.*
I.DAT.SG these.NOM.PL jeans.NOM.PL like.PST.3PL from-the-beginning
A: *Questi jeans mi sono piaciuti subito.*
'I liked these jeans from the beginning.'
B: *Nu, mne ne očen'.*
well I.DAT.SG NEG very-much.
B: *Beh, a me non molto.*
'Well, I don't really like them.'
A: *Oni modnye, kažetsja.*
they.NOM.PL fashionable.NOM.PL seem.PRS.3SG.QUOT
A: **Pare**$_{\text{SEEM-PRS.3SG.QUO}}$ che siano di moda.
'They ***seem*** to be fashionable.' (www.ruscorpora.ru, last accessed in July 2015)

In our corpus, *kažetsja* marks a CP of conjectural conclusion from a sign only in 3 cases, and in all these cases the translation with the IEF5 is not only possible, but preferable to the use of *dovere*, since we are in the initial phase of the reasoning and the conjectural element has a weak strength of thesis:

(23) A: *Nu-nu vpered s pesnej!*
come on, on with song.INS.SG
A: *Su, su, avanti con la canzone!*
'Come on, on with the song!'
B: *A čto èto u tebja s golosom? Ty*
and what this.NOM.SG by you.ACC.SG with voice.INS.SG you.NOM.SG
zabolela čto li?
get-ill.PST.3SG *what or?*
B: *Cosa ti succede alla voce? Ti sei ammalata?*
'What's happening to your voice? Are you ill or what?'
C: *Čto-to v gorle peršit, kažetsja,*
something in throat. LOC.SG tickle.PRS.3SG seem.PRS.3SG.EVID
nasmork načinaetsja.
cold.NOM.SG begin.PRS.3SG

C': *C'è qualcosa che mi raschia; mi* ***starà venendo***$_{\text{COME-FUT.3SG. PROG.EVID}}$ / ***a quanto pare***$_{\text{SEEM-PRS.3SG.EVID}}$ *mi sta venendo* il raffreddore.
'There's something itchy; I ***must*** *be* coming down with a cold/*it* ***seems*** that I'm coming down with a cold.' (www.ruscorpora.ru, last accessed in July 2015)

2.6 *Pochože*

Pochože occurs in 51 documents with 62 entries. In 15 out of 25 cases it does not indicate conclusion, but a statement with modal value: the speaker predicts something probable. It can then be translated with modal markers such as *forse*, *probabilmente*, etc.:

(24) A *Nu značit, čto vse ostaetsja na*
well mean.PRS.3SG that everything.NOM.SG remain.PRS.3SG in
svoich mestach
their.LOC.PL place.LOC.PL
A: *Dunque significa che tutto rimarrà al suo posto.*
'Well it means that everything stays in place.'
B: *Poka da.*
for-the-moment yes.
B: *Per il momento sì.*
'For the moment, yes.'
A: *Da tak i budet* ***pochož*** *vsegda.*
Yes, so be.FUT.3SG maybe forever.
A: *Sì, sarà così,* ***probabilmente/forse*** *per sempre.*
'Yes, it will be like this, **probably/maybe** forever.'
B: *I mne tak kažetsja.*
also I.DAT.SG so seem.PRS-3SG
B: *Anche a me pare così.*
'I think so too.' (www.ruscorpora.ru, last accessed in July 2015)

Like *kažetsja*, *pochože*, on occasion, is reportive (in our corpus there are 3 cases), such as case (25), in which interlocutor B reports what he heard his wife say about the separation of their daughter from her husband:

(25) A: *Poka deti est', skol'ko b ni*
as-long-as child.NOM.PL be.PRS.3SG how-much doesn't matter
zarabatyval, vse ravno est' kuda potratit'.
earn.SBJV.2SG in-any-case be.PRS.3SG where spend.money.INF

A: *Finché hai i figli, per quanto tu possa guadagnare, c'è sempre da spendere.*
'As long as you have children, it doesn't matter how much you can earn, you're always going to spend money.'

B: *Da. I vot mladšej pomogaju, čto-to s*
yes. and here the-little-one.DAT.SG help.PRS.1SG something with
mužem u nee neladno za poslednee vremja.
husband.INS.SG by she.GEN.SG badly lately.

B: Sì. La più piccola la aiuto io, negli ultimi tempi ha avuto problemi col marito.
'Yes. I'm helping the little one, she's been having problems with her husband lately.'

A: *Ona razobralas' s nim?*
she.NOM.SG separate.PST.3SG with he.INS.SG

A: *Si è separata?*
'Have they separated?'

B: *Da razobralas'* ***pochože*** *uže.*
yes separate.PST.3SG **likely.**QUOT already

B: *Pare* SEEM-PRS.3SG.QUOT *che sia già separata.*
'It **seems** they are already separated.'

A: *Ona vam čto, ne soobščaet?*
she.NOM.SG you.DAT.PL why NEG tell.PRS.3SG

A: *Perché? Non le dice niente?*
'Why? Isn't she telling you anything?'

B: *Materi-to soobščaet.*
mother.DAT.SG tell.PRS.3SG

B: *Lo dice alla madre.*
'She talks to the mother.' (www.ruscorpora.ru, last accessed in July 2015)

In (26) the individual who is speaking reports having witnessed a murder. In this case, *pochože*, as *kak budto*, is used to describe something on the basis of a similarity in an inductive context:

(26) *I takoj načinaju prismatrivat'sja. Smotrju,*
and this.NOM.SG start.PRS.1SG look-closely.INF watch.PRS.1SG
snačala oni ***pochože*** *emu na*
at-the-beginning they. NOM.SG **likely.**EVID he.DAT.SG on
golovu èto svetili.
head.ACC.SG this.NOM.SG shine.PST.3PL

Inizio a scrutare. Guardo, all'inizio c'è stata una luce, ***sembra*** SEEM.PRS.3SG.EVID
sulla testa [...]
'So I'm starting to look closely. I'm watching, at the beginning *it* ***seems*** that there has been light, on his head [...].' (www.ruscorpora.ru, last accessed in July 2015)

With indirect inferential value, in 5 examples *pochože* indicates a CP of conclusion from a sign:

(27)

2–3 nedeli	*prošlo.*	*Nu,*	*ja*	*tože*	*ne*
2–3 weeks.NOM.PL	pass.PST.3SG	well	I.NOM.SG	either	NEG

stal	*emu*	*zvonit'.*	*A*	*on,*	***pochože,***
begin.PST.1SG	he.DAT.SG	call.INF	and	he.NOM.SG	**likely**.EVID

pozvonil	*dlja*	*togo,*	*čtoby*	*ja*	*den'gi*
call.PST.3SG	for	that.GEN.SG	in-order-to	I.NOM.SG	money.NOM.PL

prines	[...].
bring.PST.1SG	

Sono passate 2–3 settimane. Beh, nemmeno io l'ho chiamato. E lui ***deve*** *aver chiamato* MUST-PRS.3SG.EVID CALL */* ***avrà chiamato*** CALL-FUT3.SG.EVID *perché gli portassi dei soldi* [...].
'It's been 2–3 weeks. Well, I haven't called him either. And he ***must*** *have* called to get me to bring him some money [...]' (www.ruscorpora.ru, last accessed in July 2015)

3 Conclusions

To conclude, we can state that there is a certain difference among the markers whose semantics refer to seeing (*vidimo, vidno, po-vidimomu*) and the markers of the second group (*kak budto, kažetsja, pochože*), whose semantics are based on the concept of appearance and similarity.

1) *vidimo, vidno, po-vidimomu* mark a CP of conjectural inferential conclusion from a sign more often than the markers of the second group; moreover, the highest number of this type of CP is marked by *po-vidimomu* and *vidimo*, while *vidno*, in approximately half the cases, marks an indirect inference from common knowledge or the usual course of the events (corresponding to IEF1), but does not express a CP of conclusion from a sign. The reportive value has never been found in our corpus, but this does not mean it should be excluded. Certainly though, it is not frequent.

2) The markers of the second group (*kak budto, kažetsja, pochože*) seldom only mark a CP of inferential conclusion from a sign: in 2 of 25 cases for *kak budto, kažetsja*, and 5 for *pochože*. *Kak budto* mainly marks an imperceptive evidential, while *kažetsja* marks the reportive one. However, both have the principal function of blurring the epistemic responsibility of the speaker. Instead, *pochože* is

mainly found with modal assertions, whereas in other cases it can have different functions. Among these are the reportive and imperceptive evidential functions, and in 5 cases it marks mark a CP of inferential conclusion.

As far as the Italian translations of these markers with the IEF5 or with the epistemic modal *dovere* are concerned, in conjectural inferential conclusion from a sign they are often both possible as markers of inferential reasoning, but not as markers of modal graduation. In fact, the Italian language, unlike Russian, marks modal graduation by the opposition between IEF5 and the modal verb *dovere*, so that when the context requests a high degree of epistemic certainty (i.e. the speaker is inferring a necessary conclusion) IEF5 isn't a possible translation of the Russian markers.

With regards to the graduation of the epistemic modality, the markers of the first group generally occur in statements with a higher strength of thesis than those in the second group, especially *kak budto* and *kažetsja*.

Finally, as far as the type of logical operation at the basis of the inferential conclusion (deduction, induction and abduction) is concerned, surely, the most frequent is also the most common in daily reasoning, that is, abduction. In only a few cases did we find purely inductive or deductive processes: in the first case, translation with IEF5 is better, in the second, the use of the modal *dovere* seems more suitable.

To sum up, the Russian markers that most often combine indirect inferentiality, conclusion and conjecture, are *vidno* and *po-vidimomu* (which are also stylistically different) and so they appear to translate the Italian IEF5 in a more unequivocal way.

The comparison among Russian markers on the basis of the Italian IEF5 thus leads to the conclusion that for the Russian language, the distinction among evidential markers seems to actually reflect, within the group of indirect evidentials, the distinction between imperceptive, inferential and reportive evidentials.

Abbreviations: 1 – first person; 3 – third person; ACC – accusative;
ADJ – adjective; ADV – adverb(ial); CP – connective predicate; DAT – dative;
EF – epistemic future; EVID evidential; FUT – future; GEN –genitive;
IEF – inferential epistemic future; INF – infinitive; INS – instrumental;
IMP – imperative; LOC – locative; N – neuter; NEG – negation, negative;
NOM – nominative; PASS – passive; PL – plural; PRS – present; PST – past;
PTCP – participle; QUOT – quotative; SBJV – subjunctive; SG – singular;
U0, 1 . . . – Utterance0, 1

References

Bertinetto, Pier Marco. 1979. Alcune ipotesi sul nostro futuro (con alcune osservazioni su potere e dovere). *Rivista di grammatica generativa* 4 (1–2). 77–138.

Bonola, Anna. 2014. Connettori di conclusività in russo e in italiano. In Olga Inkova, Marina di Filippo & François Esvan (eds.), *L'architettura del testo. Studi contrastivi slavo-romanzi*, 103–117. Alessandria: Edizioni Dell'orso.

Bonola, Anna & Maria Cristina Gatti. 2013. Modal'nye glagoly i atemporal'noe upotreblenie buduščego vremeni kak pokazateli argumentativnosti v ital'janskom jazyke v sopostavlenii s russkim [Modality and atemporal use of the future as an argumentative marker in Italian and Russian]. In Olga Inkova (ed.), *Du mot au texte. Ot slova k tekstu. Études slavo-romanes. Slavjano-romanskie razyskanija*, 73–89. Bern: Peter Lang.

Bozzone Costa, Rossella. 1991. L'espressione della modalità non fattuale nel parlato colloquiale (con particolare riferimento agli usi del futuro). *Quaderni del dipartimento di linguistica e letterature comparate* 7. 25–73.

Clark, Herbert. 1996. *Using Language*. Cambridge: Cambridge University Press.

Dendale, Patrick. 1999. "Devoir" au conditionnel: valeur evidentio-modale et origine du conditionnel. In Svetlana Vogeleer, Andrée Borillo, Marcel Vuillaume & Carl Vetters (eds.), *La modalité sous tous ses aspects* (Cahiers Chronos 4), 7–28. Amsterdam-Atalanta: Rodopi.

Gatti, Maria Cristina. 2010. Soedinitel'nye elementy v argumentativnom diskurse i pokazateli argumentativnosti v russkom jazyke [Relational elements in argumentative discourse in Russian]. *L'analisi linguistica e letteraria* 18 (2). 161–172.

Giannakidou, Anastasia & Alda Mari. 2013. Epistemic weakening with future and must: non veridicality, evidentiality, and partial knowledge. In Joanna Blaszczack, Dorota Klimek-Jankowska. Krzystof Migdalski & Anastasia Giannakidou (eds.), *Tense, mood and modality: New perspectives on old questions* (Studies in Generative Grammar). Boston: University of Chicago and Institut Jean Nicod. http://ling.auf.net/lingbuzz/001836/current.pdf (accessed 01 August 2015).

Jayez, Jacques & Corinne Rossari. 1998. Pragmatic Connectives as Predicates. The case of inferential connectives. In Patrick Saint-Dizier (ed.), *Predicative Forms in Natural Language and in Lexical Knowledge Bases*, 285–239. Dordrecht: Kluwer Academic Publishers.

Kiseleva, Ksenja & Denis Paillard. 2003. Mechanizmy semantičeskogo var'irovanija na primere gruppy ednic s kornem -vid-: vidimo, po-vidimomu, vidno [Mechanisms of Semantic Variation exemplified by Linguistic Units with the root *-vid: vidimo, po-vidimomu, vidno*]. In Ksenja Kiseleva & Denis Paillard (eds.), *Diskursivnye slova russkogo jazyka: kontekstnoe var'irovanie i semantičeskoe edinstvo* [Discourse words in Russian: an essay in context-semantic description], 50–79. Moskva: Azbukovnik.

Kronning, Hans. 2001. Pour une tripartition des emplois du modal devoir. In Patrick Dendale & Johan van der Auwera (eds.), *Les Verbes Modaux* (Cahiers Chronos 8), 67–84. Amsterdam & Atlanta: Rodopi.

Letučij, Aleksander. 2008. Sravnitel'nye konstrukcii, irrealis i evidencial'nost' [Comparative constructions, irrealis and evidentiality]. In Björn Wiemer (ed.), *Lexikalische Evidentialitäts-Marker in Slavischen Sprachen. Wiener Slawistischer Almanach* 72. *Special issue*, 215–238.

Padučeva, Elena. 2012. Evidentiality in Russian. Paper presented at the International Conference on the nature of evidentiality, Leiden, 14 June. http://lexicograph.ruslang.ru (accessed July 2015).

Palmer, Frank. 1986. *Mood and Modality*. Cambridge: Cambridge University Press.
Pietrandrea, Paola. 2004. L'articolazione semantica del dominio epistemico dell'italiano. *Lingue e Linguaggio* (2). 171–206.
Plungian, Vladimir. 2001. The place of evidentiality within the universal grammatical space. *Journal of pragmatics* 33. 349–357.
Plungian, Vladimir. 2008. O pokazateljach čužoj reči i nedostovernosti v russkom jazyke: *mol, jakoby* i drugie [On Russian markers of citation and lower certainty *mol, jakoby* and others]. In Björn Wiemer (ed.), *Lexikalische Evidentialitäts-Marker in Slavischen Sprachen*, 285–311. Wiener Slawistischer Almanach (72). Special issue.
Rigotti, Eddo. 2005. Congruity theory and argumentation. In Marcelo Dascal, Frans H. van Eemeren, Eddo Rigotti, Sorin Stati & Andrea Rocci (eds.), *Argumentation in Dialogic Interaction* (Special issue of Studies in Communication Sciences), 75–96.
Rigotti, Eddo & Sara Cigada. 2004. *La comunicazione verbale*. Milano: Apogeo.
Rigotti, Eddo & Andrea Rocci. 2001. Sens, non-sens, contresens. *Studies in Communication Sciences* 1. 45–80.
Rocci, Andrea. 2000. L'interprétation épistémique du futur en Italien et en Français: une analyse procédurale. *Cahiers de Linguistique Française* 22. 241–274.
Rocci, Andrea. 2005. *La modalità epistemica tra semantica e argomentazione*. Milano: ISU.
Searle, John R. 1969. *Speech acts: An essay in the philosophy of language*. Cambridge: Cambridge University Press.
Snoek-Henkemans, Francisca. 1997. *Analysing complex Argumentation* Amsterdam: SicSat.
Squartini, Mario. 2004. Disentangling evidentiality and epistemic modality in Romance. *Lingua* 114. 873–895.
Wiemer, Björn. 2008. *Lexikalische Evidentialitäts-Marker in Slavischen Sprachen*, Wiener Slawistischer Almanach (special issue of Wiener Slawistischer Almanach 72).
Wiemer, Björn. 2008, Pokazateli s citativnoj i inferentivnoj funkcijami v russkom i pol'skom jazykach – kommunikativnye mechanizmy semantičeskogo sdviga [Reportative and inferential markers in Russian and Polish – communicative triggers of a semantic shift]. In Björn Wiemer (ed.), *Lexikalische Evidentialitäts-Marker in Slavischen Sprachen* (special issue of Wiener Slawistischer Almanach 72). 336–374.

Axel Holvoet

Epistemic modality, evidentiality, quotativity and echoic use

Abstract: The purpose of the article is to shed light on the mutual relationships between three distinct but related domains of linguistic marking. Whereas the first two, epistemic modality and evidentiality, are now firmly established in the linguistic literature, the third, interpretive use, originally formulated in the framework of linguistic pragmatics (Sperber & Wilson 1986), is still waiting for recognition as a sui generis type of linguistic marking. Interpretive use of utterances is defined by Sperber and Wilson as the use of utterances to refer to other utterances rather than to states of affairs. They distinguish two subtypes: quotations and echoic interpretations. A discussion of echoic use in grammar can be found in Holvoet & Konickaja (2011). Lexical interpretive use markers can be divided into quotative and echoic use markers; the differences are discussed in the article. Instances of polyfunctionality covering the different domains of marking mentioned here invite us to pause at the mutual relationships between them, and at the possible ways of diachronic development.

Keywords: epistemic modality, evidentiality, interpretive use, quotatives, echoic expressions

1 Introduction

The relationship between modality and evidentiality is a vexed question in the linguistic literature. We can distinguish two questions here: on the one hand, whether the two categories are distinct, as claimed by De Haan (1999) and others, or whether they are notionally related and can be subsumed under a common supercategory, as argued by Boye (2012) (an alternative possibility being that evidentiality can be subsumed under modality, as assumed in Palmer 2001); and, on the other hand, how the two categories interact in discourse. It is well known that

Note: My thanks are due an anonymous reviewer for constructive criticism, to Bernard Comrie for his useful editorial comments, and to Wayles Browne for checking my English and providing valuable observations and suggestions. I remain, of course, solely responsible for the shortcomings of the article.

Axel Holvoet, Vilnius University

https://doi.org/10.1515/9783110572261-011

the use of an evidential marker may be a device allowing the speaker to distance her/himself from a claim and thus indirectly to express an epistemic stance. It is only to this second aspect of the modality-evidentiality relationship that I will be referring in this article.

As I will attempt to show, epistemic modality interacts not only with evidentiality but also with other domains of linguistic marking that show a certain affinity with (one subtype of) evidentiality through the notion of quotation and, more generally, reference to other people's utterances. In what follows I will introduce the notions of quotative and echoic marking, arguing that they should be viewed as distinct from evidentiality. I will attempt to set these two notions apart from evidentiality by means of a definition that is canonical rather than formulated in terms of necessary and sufficient conditions, as the borderlines between types are fuzzy. Apart from examples of markers that are specialized in one of the functions mentioned above, I will discuss a Lithuanian marker that covers them all. This will be an occasion to discuss the relationships between the different types of marking, and possible paths of diachronic development.

2 Quotatives and Echoic use

The categories of modality and evidentiality are well established in the literature, even though mutual relationships and demarcation are debated. Grossly simplifying, we could formulate both in terms of modulation. Modality takes a proposition and modulates it in terms of possibility and necessity, desirability etc.; evidentiality modulates it in terms of information source. In the case of evidentiality there is, say, a report (or evidence of another kind) mediating between the state of affairs referred to and the speaker's utterance (which is aptly reflected in the term *médiatif*, used in the French linguistic tradition, cf., e.g., Guentchéva 1996). The important thing is, however, that a statement of the type *Mary reportedly arrived yesterday* does not refer to the report, but to the arrival.

One may, however, imagine linguistic markers focusing on the report rather than on the state of affairs to which this report refers. This possibility is explored by Sperber & Wilson (1986), who introduce the notion of interpretive use. They define it as follows:

> Any representation with a propositional form, and in particular any utterance, can be used to represent things in two ways. It can represent some state of affairs in virtue of its propositional form being true of that state of affairs; in this case we will say that the representation is a description, or that it is used descriptively. Or it can represent some other representation

> which also has a propositional form – a thought, for instance – in virtue of a resemblance between the two propositional forms; in this case we will say that the first representation is an interpretation of the second one, or that it is used interpretively.
>
> (Sperber & Wilson 1986, 228–229)

Sperber & Wilson distinguish two subtypes of interpretive use: one is quotation, the other is what the authors call *echoic interpretations*. The latter “achieve relevance by informing the hearer of the fact that the speaker has in mind what so-and-so said, and has a certain attitude to it” (Sperber and Wilson 1986, 238). Here the authors do not have in mind a specific utterance by a specific person: an imputed thought may also be involved, or something said by people in general.

That canonical quotation, set apart by such means as quotation marks, should be an instance of linguistic form reproducing linguistic form rather than referring to an extralinguistic state of affairs, and therefore also of interpretive use as defined by Sperber and Wilson, does not seem controversial. But what about hearsay marking, which also crucially involves utterances in addition to states of affairs? A few authors (Blass 1990; Blakemore 1999) have suggested that languages may develop dedicated markers of interpretive use, and have pointed to evidentials or, more specifically, hearsay markers as an instance of this. That hearsay markers could be interpretive use markers is an idea that has not been taken seriously by investigators of evidentiality: the proposal is not even mentioned in Aikhenvald (2004). Perhaps deservedly so, for hearsay markers represent just one type out of a cluster of evidential meanings, of which many (say, inferential or mirative meaning) have, in principle, nothing to do with verbal communication, or even with verbal representations of anything. What is worse, the hearsay function often occurs jointly with “non-verbal” forms of evidentiality, e.g. both in the Balkan languages and in Lithuanian the evidential expresses reportive, inferential and mirative meanings (Kehayov 2008, 36).

The notion of interpretive use seems, however, to be an adequate tool in the description of other types of marking, first of all for those which we will call quotatives.

The term “quotative” appears in two different meanings in the literature. On the one hand, it is used to refer to a subtype of reported speech, i.e. “a reported evidential which involves exact indication of who provided the information” (Aikhenvald 2004, 25). This is also the meaning in which Aikhenvald herself uses the term (Aikhenvald 2004, *passim*), but the glossary added to her book also lists the meaning “a verbal form or a particle introducing a verbatim quotation of what someone else has said” (Aikhenvald 2004, 394). Apart from this glossary entry,

Aikhenvald does not refer to this use of the term, evidently assuming – correctly in my opinion – that it does not belong to the domain of evidentiality.

It is in the sense just mentioned, however, that the term "quotative" is used in Buchstaller & Van Alphen (2011). The articles in this volume deal with linguistic units used to mark the fact that whatever follows (or precedes, as the case may be[1]) is a rendition of speech rather than a statement on reality. Quotatives introduce or in some way creatively reproduce something that was said, and this something need not be a statement with a truth value; it can be a question, or an expressive exclamation, or just anything:

(1) *And she is like "what do you mean?"*

Here *what do you mean* is an expression of indignation without a propositional content to which the notion of "information source", crucial for evidentiality (cf. Aikhenvald 2004, 1), could be applicable. Sequences like this are not among those which would typically be combined with evidential markers. An utterance of the type **Reportedly/Allegedly wow!* would be unexpected.

It is obviously useful to have a term to refer to markers like English *he is like*, German *und er so*, and similar units discussed in Buchstaller & Van Alphen. Nothing better than "quotative" suggests itself here, whereas for "speaker-identifying reportives" some alternative term could probably be devised. I will henceforth use the term "quotative" in the sense in which it is used in Buchstaller & Van Alphen, that is, in the sense of a type of marking that is related to, but does not belong to the domain of evidentiality.

Quotatives need not reflect exactly what was said. The speaker referred to in (1) is sure to have vented her indignation, but if she did so using other expressions and expletives, the rendering in (1) may still be accurate in the sense of giving the addressee a general idea of the purport of the utterance referred to as well as of its stylistic features and the non-verbal behaviour accompanying it. In Aikhenvald's definition "a verbal form or a particle introducing a verbatim quotation of what someone else has said", the element of verbatim quotation should probably be relaxed.

Though the rendering of the utterance may be approximate, some kind of utterance is obviously presupposed when a quotative marker is used. We will now turn to markers that are, in a way, similar but do not presuppose an utterance.

---

1 An instance of a marker following the sequence it has in its scope (pointed out to me by Wayles Browne) would be ... *or words to that effect.*

An example is Russian *mol*, a particle that, according to the dictionary, marks an utterance as "a rendering of some other person's speech or thought" (this characterization is taken from the "Smaller Academy Dictionary of Russian", ed. Evgen'eva, *sub voce*). In the following example (from the dictionary just mentioned) it serves as a characterization of people's non-verbal behaviour:

(2) *Ne puskajut i posmatrivajut na nas: nu kak, mol?*
NEG let.in.PRS.3PL and cast.looks.PRS.3PL at 1PL.ACC well how PRT
'They won't let us in and cast looks at us [as if they wanted to say] well, what now?'

One could object that this is just an extended use of quotative marking, there being no difference of principle between quoting real and imaginary utterances. This seems more or less adequate in situations where non-verbal behaviour is being verbalized, and languages not having specialized markers will insert *as if (s)he wanted to say.* The range of situations for which we need descriptive notions is much wider, however, and, as further examples below will illustrate, we would have to stretch the notion of quotative beyond what we would be prepared to if we wanted to maintain it. I will therefore introduce a third term in addition to hearsay and quotative, viz. echoic use marking. By this I mean the marking of what Sperber & Wilson call 'echoic interpretations'.

In Holvoet & Konickaja (2011) the category of "interpretive deontics" is introduced, a notion referring to deontic forms such as imperatives and hortatives used "echoically" in order to refer to what other people expect from the speaker. The Russian echoic imperative, for instance, refers to demands laid upon the speaker and evaluated as unreasonable by the latter:

(3) *On sdela-l ošibk-u, a ja za nego otvečaj.*
he make-PST.M.SG mistake-ACC and I for him.ACC answer.IMP.2SG
'He made a mistake and I am expected to answer for it!'

The unreasonable demand is rendered in the form of an imperative, a form that could have been used by an imaginary interlocutor telling the speaker to feel responsible. Of course the sentence refers to a broader situation and it would be impossible to pinpoint a speech act situation in which such a demand would actually have been uttered and a particular speaker who would have uttered it. Are we prepared to speak of a quotative when there is nobody to quote, and no situation that would at least have provided the non-verbal behaviour that could be translated into a quotative? Perhaps, but I would like to suggest that it is worth while introducing a third notion for situations in which there is no utterance. What is the case is that reference is made to a type of utterance in order to characterize a type of situation, a type of behaviour or a certain mentality. In (3) we have an echoic reference to a type of directive sentences, used here to convey that the speaker (or some other person) is under an obligation which (s)he resents. There are more examples of this; for instance, it is common in several languages to use a hortative form (normally used for the third person) in order to express a request for permission. This speech act is performed by referring echoically to a type of utterances used to express permission. This can be illustrated from Polish:

(4)	*Niech*	*tylko*	*usiądę,*	*zaraz*	*wszystko*	*opowiem.*
	HORT	only	sit.down.FUT.1SG	presently	everything	recount.FUT.1SG

'Just allow me to sit down, I'll tell you everything in a moment.'

Compare *niech usiądzie* 'let her/him sit down'. Sentences like (3) and (4) get the regular echoic interpretations they get in virtue of being grammaticalized. Russian has grammaticalized the echoic use of the imperative illustrated in (3) in a way that Polish has not, whereas Polish and Slovenian, among other languages, have grammaticalized the echoic use of a hortative particle to express requests for permission in a way that Russian has not.

This grammaticalization of an echoic use of an imperative or hortative (the demarcation of these two notions is largely a matter of terminology, cf. Van der Auwera, Dobrushina & Goussev 2004) is made possible by the fact that directives can normally contain only 2nd and 3rd person forms; an imperative or hortative combined with 1st person markers is therefore easily identified as something special, viz., an echoic directive. In this sense, imperative-hortatives are particularly well suited to develop peripheral echoic types of use which require no additional marking. Non-directive utterances, on the other hand, usually contain indicative forms that cannot be as easily identified as echoic, so that additional marking is necessary. This is why we find a segmental marker in a sentence like (2).

The term "echoic" seems appropriate because linguistic form is here used in a specific way that contrasts both with primary, descriptive use and with metalinguistic use. Whereas metalinguistic use refers specifically to linguistic form with the aim of saying something about it (with the aim of commenting on some detail of grammar or style), echoic use refers to linguistic form with the aim of illustrating the kind of thing that is usually done with it, and of commenting on this kind of thing.

3 Problems with demarcation

In introducing the notion of "echoic use marker" alongside that of "quotative marker" I am fully aware that there is no way of rigorously setting apart these two types of marking. We can certainly identify the prototypical cases. For quotatives, this will be the *and she's like* type, where we have a reference to a particular situation with identified interlocutors. For echoic use markers, we could give (3) as a prototype: we have no identified speaker here, nor do we have an identified speech situation; we just understand reference is being made to a situation which one could characterize by imagining some person uttering a sentence like *You should answer for this*. Between these two extremes, there will be many intermediate situations.

On the other hand, though quotative markers are distinct in principle from evidential markers, it will presumably not always be easy to keep these two things apart either. If a reported evidential involves exact indication of who provided the information, it could also incorporate elements from this person's utterance, just as, say, indirect speech may incorporate elements of direct speech.

As the three types of marking under discussion overlap, a classical definition based on necessary and sufficient conditions is difficult to give, and it is preferable to define the clear and undisputable instances. We thus arrive at a canonical definition as advocated in Brown, Chumakina & Corbett, eds. (2013) and attempted for direct and indirect speech in Evans (2013):

- hearsay marking accompanies a rendering of the propositional content of an utterance; quotative marking does not entail propositional content – a purely expressive utterance devoid of propositional content may also be involved, and this also holds for echoic use marking;
- hearsay marking is therefore typically found in affirmative clauses whose content is asserted rather than presupposed (a feature already emphasized by Anderson 1986, 277); quotative marking shows no such preferences, neither does echoic use marking;
- hearsay marking does not involve the use of the linguistic substance used in conveying the content of the utterance to which reference is made; quotative marking implies that what is in its scope at least bears a resemblance to the linguistic substance of the quoted utterance, and so does echoic use marking;
- hearsay markers presuppose a real utterance, but usually contain no reference to the author, time and circumstances of the utterance; quotative markers presuppose a real utterance, produced at a certain time by a certain person; echoic use markers do not presuppose this, but typically render the kind of thing somebody (often a representative of a certain group of people) could have said, as a means of characterizing a situation, or the mentality of a certain group of people.

4 Evidential, quotative and echoic marking and epistemic meanings

It is widely known that it is often difficult to draw a line of division between evidentiality and epistemic modality. Not only because the two could be said to be different aspects of one more general phenomenon, which Palmer (2001) calls "propositional modality", or Boye (2012) "epistemic meaning", but also because evidential marking can develop strong epistemic overtones.

Epistemic modality and evidentiality are probably in some way related through a notion of "epistemic support" as argued by Boye (2012). This seems to be reflected in the development of many individual markers, such as Polish *podobno*, which, as late as the 19th century, had an undifferentiated meaning of epistemic support which could be interpreted modally ('probably') or evidentially ('allegedly, reportedly'), whence, though a process of specialization, a purely hearsay function in modern Polish.

On the other hand, we find markers that are at some stage purely evidential but acquire secondary epistemic meanings. This can be illustrated with the example of Lithuanian *esą*, a lexical evidential marker originating as a neuter participial form of the verb *būti* 'be' (the use of participial forms instead of finite verb forms is the main morphological means of expressing evidentiality in Baltic; it is traditionally known as the oblique mood, cf. Ambrazas, ed. (1997, 262–266)). We find a typical hearsay use in (5):

(5) *Net ir naujausi-ais laik-ais žmon-ės esą kartais*
even newest-INS.PL.M time-INS.PL person-NOM.PL EVID sometimes
susiduria su šiomis būtyb-ėmis.
hit.upon.PRS.3 with DEM.INS.PL.F being-INS.PL
'It is said that even in the most recent times people have sometimes been confronted with such beings.'[2]

In (6) the evidential marking is embedded – it occurs in a complement clause with the noun *teiginys* 'claim':

(6) *Nuvalkiot-as teigin-ys, kad esą ekonomik-a*
hackneyed-NOM.SG.M claim-NOM.SG that EVID economics-NOM
nagrinėja materiali-as žmog-aus
investigate.PRS.3 material-ACC.PL.F man-GEN.SG

2 http://priekavos.lt/ar-egzistavo-legendiniai-zmones-su-sunu-galvomis/

gyvenim-o *sąlyg-as,*
life-GEN.SG condition-ACC.PL
yra *visiškai* *klaiding-as.*
be.PRS.3 absolutely erroneous-NOM.SG.M
'The hackneyed claim that economics allegedly investigates the material conditions of human life is absolutely wrong.'[3]

In principle, *esą* can still be interpreted evidentially ('the claim that – as many people say...') but at this stage it has acquired epistemic overtones, which is shown by the fact that it cannot be used if the complement-taking predicate expresses a positive evaluation:

(7) ?*Teigin-ys,* *kad* *esą* *ekonomik-a* *nagrinėja*
claim-NOM.SG that EVID economics-NOM investigate.PRS.3
materiali-as *žmog-aus* *gyvenim-o* *sąlyg-as,*
material-ACC. PL.F man-GEN.SG life-GEN.SG condition-ACC.PL
yra *visiškai* *teising-as.*
be.PRS.3 absolutely correct-NOM.SG.M
?'The claim that economics allegedly investigates material conditions of human life is absolutely correct.'

It is often difficult to state at which point a hearsay marker loses its evidential status and becomes epistemic. A hearsay marker may acquire the secondary epistemic meaning 'contrary to what somebody has said' or 'contrary to what some people say'. Hence we may arrive at a meaning like 'contrary to what some people think' or 'contrary to what somebody might think'. At what point the meaning changes is hard to tell because the existence of an alternative point of view is usually revealed by the fact of somebody having expressed it.

The epistemic meanings arising from hearsay marking are different from typical epistemic markers like *perhaps* or *probably*. The latter do not refer to alternative judgements and in this sense could be called "first-level" epistemics. For epistemic markers constrasting two different epistemic judgements we could then use the notion of "second-level" epistemics. *Probably* would thus be a first-level epistemic and *supposedly* a second-level epistemic.

How do second-level epistemic markers arise? The question whether quotatives and echoic use marking could also provide a source for them will be posed in the following sections.

---

3 http://mokslai.lt/referatai/ekonomika/ekonomikos-teorijos-objektas.html

5 A case study: Lithuanian *atseit*

I will here illustrate some of the problems adumbrated above, availing myself of the example of the Lithuanian particle *atseit*. It arose from the verbal form *atsieiti* 'it costs so-and-so much, it comes down to'. None of the functions hereinafter discussed can be found in the Academy Dictionary, where its meaning is defined as 'that is, therefore'.

First of all, *atseit* may be a hearsay marker. This is illustrated in the following example, where the clause containing the marker is introduced by the complement-taking verb *atrodo* 'it seems', which expresses epistemic stance. This epistemic stance is underspecified, that is, it may be of a deductive kind or result from information supplied by other persons; this is disambiguated by the marker *atseit* in the complement clause, which supports the latter of the two interpretations mentioned here.

(8) *Ten* *man* ***atrodo*** ***kad*** ***atseit*** *naujausi-os*
there 1SG.DAT seem.PRS.3 that PRT newest-NOM.PL.F
technologij-os *ir* *gali* *su* *kazkoki-u*
technology-NOM.PL and be.able.PRS.2SG with some-INS.SG.M
prietais-u *ak-yse* *užfiksuoti,* *matyti* *prieš-us* *ir kt.*
device-INS.SG eye-LOC.PL fix.INF see.INF enemy-ACC.PL etc.
'It seems (that's what I've heard), that the newest technologies [are used] there [sc. in that computer game] and that with the aid of some device in your eyes you can locate and see enemies etc.'[4]

This example is interesting in that there are not the slightest epistemic overtones here. Rather, epistemic stance is expressed in the complement-taking verb, so that the only function remaining for the particle is to specify the subtype as hearsay.

In simple clauses it is usually difficult to establish whether *atseit* is evidential or whether the epistemic nuance of doubt predominates:

(9) *Tai* *dary-dam-as,* *širvintišk-is* ***atseit*** ***ne-žinojo,*** *kad*
this do-CVB-M.SG Širvintos.dweller-NOM.SG PRT NEG-know.PST.3 that
į *jo* *sąskait-ą* *perves-t-i* *pinig-ai.*
into 3.GEN.SG.M account-ACC.SG transfer-PPP-NOM.PL.M money-NOM.PL

4 http://www.games.lt/g/game.naujiena/26964

'In doing this the dweller of Širvintos allegedly did not know money was being transferred to his account.'[5]

In the following example *atseit* seems to be quotative. There is a clearly located situation in which a clearly identified person is referred to as producing an utterance. There is a speech act verb (*sako* 'they say'), which would lead us to expect either a speech act complement or a direct quotation. Instead, we get a quotative marker after which the grammatical markers switch to those of direct speech (1st and 2nd person pronouns are used as in direct speech), and indeed the whole utterance that follows could have been an authentic quotation:

(10) *Policinink-ai* *sako* *kad* *atseit* *mes* *nieko* *prieš* *kad*
policeman-NOM.PL say.PRS.3 that PRT 1PL.NOM nothing against that
jus *čia* *plaukio-tumėt,*
2PL.NOM here boat-IRR.2PL
[*bet gavom iškvietima (iš prokuroro) ir turim į jį kaip nors reaguot*].
'The policemen say something like 'We haven't got anything against your boating here [but we got a notification (from the prosecutor's office) and we have to react to it somehow].'[6]

Many uses of *atseit* are, however, in the domain of what I have characterized above as echoic marking. Some uses are in a way reminiscent of the quotative use but for the fact that there is no actual utterance. What is involved can be, for instance, the verbalization of non-verbal behaviour, as illustrated for Russian *mol* in (2). The following example illustrates this: as in the case of quotation, there is a specific communicative situation and a specific discourse participant, but no actual verbal utterance:

(11) *Jis* *tik* *papurtė* *galv-ą,* *atseit* *ne-trauk,* *o*
3.NOM.SG.M only shake.PST.3 head-ACC.SG PRT NEG-pull.IMP.2SG but
po *to* *apsižiūri,* *kad* *danči-o* *nėra.*
after that realize.PRS.3 that tooth-GEN.SG be.PRS.3SG.NEG
'He only shook his head as if he wanted to say 'don't pull', but then realized that the tooth was already out.'[7]

---

5 http://www.sirvinta.net/teisetvarka/apmulkintos-vilnietes-pinigai-atsidure-sirvintiskio-saskaitoje/

6 http://forum.modelis.lt/archive/index.php/t-568.html (2015-06-04)

7 http://www.supermama.lt/forumas/lofiversion/index.php/t374-100.html

The distance with regard to quotative marking increases when no reference is made to a specific communicative situation or to an utterance imputed to somebody in a specific situation, but rather to what somebody *could* have said. This is seen in (12), where a certain way of thinking, illustrated by a certain type of utterance, is as it were held up for inspection and then rejected by the speaker:

(12) *Ne-sakau,* *kad* *viską* *galima* *nupirkti* *už*
NEG-say.PRS.1SG that everything.ACC be.possible buy.INF for
pinig-us – ***atseit,*** *duokit* *mums* *pinig-ų,* *ir*
money-ACC.PL **PRT** give.IMP.2PL us.DAT money-GEN.PL and
kit-as *numer-is* *bus* *fantastišk-as.*
next-NOM.SG.M number-NOM.SG FUT.3 fantastic-NOM.SG.M
'I'm not saying you can buy everything for money – {atseit} just give us money and the next issue will be fantastic.'[8]

There is clearly no actual utterance here. A certain mentality or way of thinking is characterized by referring echoically to a possible utterance of the type 'Just give us money and everything will be fine'.

After having illustrated three types of use of *atseit* that would satisfy the above definitions of evidential, quotative and echoic marking, we turn to the uses in which we can discern epistemic overtones. They will, of course, occur in contexts where we have some propositional content which can be the object of epistemic evaluation. In (13), *atseit* can probably best be characterized as epistemic in the sense of what was characterized above as second-level epistemic marking: the meaning is 'contrary to what some say':

(13) *O* *ta* *mint-is,* *kad* ***atseit*** *apmokestin-us* *žmon-ės* *mažiau*
but that thought-NOM that **PRT** tax-CVB people-NOM less
važiuos *savo* *auto,* *o* *daugiau* *vieš-uoju,* *yra*
drive.FUT.3 RPO car[INS] but more public-INS.SG.M.DEF be.PRS.3
nesąmon-ė.
nonsense-NOM
'But the notion that if a tax were introduced people would allegedly drive about less in their cars and make more frequent use of public transport is nonsense.'[9]

8 http://eia.libis.lt:8080/archyvas/viesas/20111219122211/http://www.culture.lt/lmenas/?leid_id=3140&kas=straipsnis&st_id=10643
9 *http://m.delfi.lt/verslas/article.php?id=58928375&com=1&no=0&top=1*

The function of *atseit* in this example is not immediately clear. One could imagine an evidential function: *atseit* could point to the fact that the opinion rejected by the speaker has been uttered by some person or is regularly uttered publicly. Such a marking would be rather redundant but that does not mean it could not occur. The substitution test illustrated above for *esą* helps us out again. If we replace the word *nesąmonė* 'nonsense', which implies a clearly negative view of the content of the complement clause, with some predicate implying a positive view, the use of *atseit* becomes impossible:

(14) **Mint-is,* *kad* ***atseit*** *apmokestin-us* *žmon-ės* *daugiau*
thought-NOM that **PRT** tax-CVB people-NOM more
važiuos *vieš-uoju* *yra* *teising-a.*
drive.FUT.3 public-INS.SG.M.DEF be.PRS.3 correct-NOM.SG.F
Intended meaning: 'The notion that if a tax were introduced people would allegedly make more frequent use of public transport is correct.'

The condition for such second-level epistemic meanings to arise is syntactic embedding. In this connection it is interesting to note that the ability of expressing a negative epistemic stance (a nuance of doubt concerning the accuracy of a statement) has been noted for complementizers, cf. Noonan (2007, 58) on the Jakaltek complementizer *tato* as opposed to *chubil*; from Russian we could add *jakoby* as opposed to *čto*. Actually *atseit* can also occasionally acquire the function of a complementizer marked for negative epistemic stance (implying the content of the complement clause is at variance with the facts):

(15) [*Naują straipsnį kritikavo ir vadinamoji nevalstybinė žiniasklaida,*]
teig-dam-a *atseit* *jis* *sugrąžin-si-ąs*
claim-CVB-SG.F COMPL 3.NON.SG.F take.back-FUT-EVID.SG.M
šal-į *į* *1937* *met-us.*
country-ACC.SG to year(PL)-ACC
'[The so-called non-governmental media also criticized the article], claiming it would take the country back to 1937.'[10]

10 http://www.bernardinai.lt/straipsnis/2005-11-30-vadzimas-vileita-kodel-man-patinka-dabartine-baltarusija/5648

6 Sources of epistemic meaning

The conjunction of all four functions mentioned until now and illustrated for Lithuanian *atseit* is, at first glance, easy to account for. The oscillation between evidential and epistemic function is a well-attested fact, and the evidential, or more specifically reportive function is, on the other hand, functionally related to quotative use, as both involve utterances. It seems reasonable to assume that quotative marking can lead to echoic use marking through an extension of the notion of quoting. A semantic map would thus look as follows:

Here the notion of "epistemic" meaning refers to what was described above as "first-level" epistemic meanings. "Second-level" epistemic nuances, however, should probably be assigned a different position. They may arise just as well from quotative or echoic marking. As we saw above, echoic use is a device often used to characterize a certain way of thinking, a certain mentality or a certain state of mind; and verbatim quotation may serve the same purpose. When the aim is to characterize, say, a certain type of expectations, as in (12), there is no obvious path to second-level epistemic marking, as expectations are not truth-valued. But echoic marking characterizing a certain type of evalution can be embedded in complementation constructions with speech act verbs, as in (16):

(16) *Pensinink-ų atstov-ai skambiai prabilo,*
pensioner-GEN.PL representative-NOM.PL loudly protest.PST.3
kad atseit mums girt-ų pinig-ų
that PRT 1PL.DAT drunk-GEN.PL money-GEN.PL
ne-reikia ir kaip čia bus, kad mūsų
NEG-be.needed.PRS.3 and how here be.FUT.3 that 1PL.GEN
vaik-ai turės gerti daugiau tam, kad
child-NOM.PL have.to.FUT.3 drink.INF more in order that
didė-tų pensij-os.
increase-IRR.3 pension-NOM.PL
'The pensioners' representatives protested loudly [saying] we don't need drunk money and how is it that our children will have to drink more in order to increase our pensions.'[11]

11 http://blaivus.blogspot.com/2014/11/gersim-ne-i-savu-o-i-danijos-pensininku.html

Here *atseit* is not evidential: there is no assertion that could be modified by a hearsay marker; rather an attitude is referred to, and the strategy is quotative, that is, an approximative rendering of what the pensioners themselves say is offered (with retention of 1st person forms and other features of direct speech). In order to show the contrast, I will give an example where *atseit* occurs in a similar complement clause selected by a speech act verb but its basic function is evidential (as a claim is involved), and evidentiality is also marked in the verb form: an active participle is used instead of a finite verb form, which, as mentioned above, is the morphological means of marking evidentiality in Baltic. There are no elements of quotation – we have the regular 3rd person forms we would expect here:

(17) *Jie* [...] *vis-ą* *laik-ą* *atkakliai* *teigė,*
3.NOM.PL.M whole-ACC.SG time-ACC.SG stubbornly claim.PST.3
kad *atseit* *jie* *psichiatrij-a* *ne-piktnaudžiav-ę.*
that PRT 3.NOM.PL.M psychiatry-INS.SG NEG-abuse-PST.EVID.PL.M
'They [sc. Lithuanian psychiatrists] kept stubbornly claiming that they (allegedly) hadn't abused psychiatry.'[12]

We see, then, that the construction 'X says that *atseit* ...' can, in principle, form a context for two types of marking. The complement clause can contain some propositional content, the veracity of which is doubted by the speaker, as in (17). Or it can contain an evaluative statement that is not truth-valued, as in (16). Are these discrete paths of development that don't intersect at any point? Probably not. Many embedded utterances are evaluations that are nonetheless truth-valued as the speaker may agree with the evaluation or not. Compare the following:

(18) *Ir* *kodėl* *jie* *sako,* *kad,* *atseit,* *labai* *sveik-a*
and why 3.NOM.PL.M say.PRS.3 that PRT very wholesome-N
šeim-oje *išsirėkti* *ir* *pasibarti?*
family-LOC.SG shout.one's.fill.INF and quarrel.INF
'And why do they say it's wholesome to shout one's fill and fight it out in the family?'[13]

12 http://www.tv3.lt/m/naujiena/620584/saugumo-rusiuose-ir-psichiatrinese-ligoninese-iii
13 http://www.delfi.lt/gyvenimas/meile/olapinas-tikra-scena-ar-netikra-laime.d? id=6093060

Whether *atseit* is, in this particular case, a hearsay marker with epistemic overtones ('that is what they say but I doubt it') or a quotative or echoic marker ('this is an approximative rendering of what kind of things people would say'), is hard to establish. It is also hard to establish what exactly gives rise to the epistemic overtones we note in such sentences. Echoic renderings are seldom neutral, as Sperber and Wilson suggest in their characterization of echoic use as "achieving relevance by informing the hearer of the fact that the speaker has in mind what so-and-so said, and has a certain attitude to it". Views, attitudes, states of mind etc. which the speaker endorses and with which (s)he identifies require no echoic rendering. The speaker's negative attitude, or at least her/his distancing her/himself from the state of mind reflected in a real or imaginary utterance, may be reinterpreted as doubt about the well-foundedness of a claim contained in this utterance. It is conceivable, therefore, that a direct connection is established between quotative or echoic marking and epistemic modality. This would mean that the interaction of those types of marking with epistemic modality need not be mediated by evidentiality. It is also far from certain that it must be unidirectional. At discourse level, shifts between evidential, quotative, echoic and epistemic function can probably go in any direction.

7 Concluding remarks

As I hope to have shown in this article, the affinity and interaction of epistemic modality with evidentiality and related domains of linguistic meaning has two aspects that deserve to be set apart. On the one hand, there is arguably a semantic affinity between epistemic modality and evidentiality. On the other, epistemic modality interacts, at discourse level, with a number of types of linguistic marking that are concerned with other people's utterances; these include, apart from evidentiality, quotative and echoic marking, which have to be set apart from evidentiality. They all tend to develop what I have called "second-level" epistemic meaning, i.e. they are used to contrast divergent epistemic stances.

Abbreviations: ACC – accusative; COMPL – complementizer; CVB – converb; DAT – dative; DEF – definite; DEM – demonstrative; EVID – evidential; F – feminine; FUT – future; GEN –genitive; HORT – hortative; IMP – imperative; INF – infinitive; INS – instrumental; IRR – irrealis; LOC – locative; M – masculine; N – neuter; NEG – negative; NOM – nominative; PL – plural; PPP – past passive participle; PRS – present; PRT – particle; PST – past; RPO – reflexive possessive; SG – singular

References

Aikhenvald, Alexandra. 2004. *Evidentiality.* Oxford: Oxford University Press.

Ambrazas, Vytautas (ed.). 1997. *Lithuanian Grammar*. Vilnius: Baltos lankos.

Anderson, Lloyd B. 1986. Evidentials, paths of change, and mental maps: Typologically regular asymmetries. In William Chafe & Johanna Nichols (eds.), *Evidentiality: The Linguistic Coding of Epistemology, Advances in Discourse Processes*, XX, 273–312. Norwood & New Jersey: Ablex Publishing Corporation.

Blakemore, Diane. 1999. Evidence and modality. In Keith Brown & Jim Miller (eds.), *Encyclopedia of Grammatical Categories*, 141–145. Amsterdam, etc.: Elsevier.

Blass, Regina. 1990. *Relevance Relations in Discourse. A Study with Special Reference to Sissala*. Cambridge: Cambridge University Press.

Boye, Kasper. 2012. *Epistemic Meaning. A Crosslinguistic and Functional-Cognitive Study*, Berlin: De Gruyter Mouton.

Brown, Dunstan, Marina Chumakina & Greville G. Corbett (eds.). 2013. *Canonical Morphology and Syntax*. Oxford: Oxford University Press.

Buchstaller, Isabelle & Ingrid van Alphen. 2011. *Quotatives. Cross-Linguistic and Cross-Disciplinary Perspectives*. Amsterdam-Philadelphia: John Benjamins.

De Haan, Ferdinand. 1999. Evidentiality and epistemic modality: Setting boundaries. *Southwest Journal of Linguistics* 18 (1). 83–101.

Evans, Nicolas. 2013. Some problems in the typology of quotation: a canonical approach. In Dunstan Brown, Marina Chumakina & Greville G. Corbett (eds.), *Canonical Morphology and Syntax*, 66–98. Oxford: Oxford University Press.

Guentchéva, Zlatka. 1996. Introduction. In Zlatka Guentchéva (ed.), *L'énonciation médiatisée*, 11–18. Louvain: Peeters.

Holvoet, Axel & Jelena Konickaja. 2011. Interpretive deontics. A definition and a semantic map based on Slavonic and Baltic data. *Acta Linguistica Hafniensia* 43 (1). 1–20.

Kehayov, Petar. 2008. *An Areal-Typological Perspective to Evidentiality: The Cases of the Balkan and Baltic Linguistic Areas*. Tartu: Tartu University Press.

Noonan, Michael. 2007. Complementation. In Timothy Shopen (ed.), *Language Typology and Syntactic Description*. Vol. II: *Complex Constructions* (2nd edn), 52–150. Cambridge: University Press.

Palmer, Frank R. 2001. *Mood and Modality* (2nd edn). Cambridge: Cambridge University Press.

Sperber, Dan & Deirdre Wilson. 1986. *Relevance: Communication and Cognition*. Cambridge MA: Harvard University Press.

Van der Auwera, Johan, Nina Dobrushina & Valentin Goussev. 2004. A semantic map for imperatives-hortatives. In Dominique Willems, Bart Defrancq, Timothy Colleman & Dirk Noël (eds.), *Contrastive Analysis in Language. Identifying Linguistic Units of Comparison*, 44–66. Basingstoke: Palgrave Macmillan.

Daniel Petit

Evidentiality, epistemic modality and negation in Lithuanian: revisited

Abstract: In the typological literature, evidentiality is often defined as the negative counterpart of reality. Strikingly enough, this negative conception has not yet led the scholars to investigate whether there can be a formal proximity between evidentiality and negation. The aim of this article is to determine the origin of the Lithuanian evidential particle *nevà*, which is apparently cognate with the negative particle *ne-* 'not'. A thorough analysis of the philological data, combined with a typological approach, shows that the particle *ne-* in *nevà* does not reflect a negative meaning, but more convincingly must be traced back to a 'comparative' meaning of the same particle ('like'), this in turn being an archaism of the Baltic languages. The derivation of an evidential particle from a comparative structure is itself cross-linguistically trivial and may reasonably account for the origin of the particle *nevà*.

Keywords: evidentiality, Baltic, particle, etymology

1 Introduction

In the typological literature, the notion of 'evidentiality' has been much debated during the last years.[1] As is well known, the technical term 'evidentiality' refers to the linguistic means used by a speaker to 'indicate something about the *source* of

1 E.g. Chafe and Nichols (1986); Guentchéva (1996); Guentchéva and Landaburu (2007); Johanson and Utas (2000); Aikhenvald and Dixon (2003); Aikhenvald (2004) and more recently Diewald and Smirnova (2010), among many others. In the English-speaking literature (e.g. Aikhenvald and Dixon 2003, Aikhenvald 2004), the terms *evidential* and *evidentiality* have become traditional. In France, at least since Lazard (1956: 149, footnote 2) and Guentchéva (1996, 2007), the terms *médiatif* and *médiativité* have been chosen to express the same notion – in order to do justice to the specific semantic content of the word *évidence* in French (cf. Guentchéva 1996: 13, Lazard 2000: 209–210). Other terms have been proposed, such as *médiaphorique* (Hagège 1995: 15) or *indirective* (Johanson and Utas 2000: 61).

Note: This paper is a revised English version of a paper first published in German in 2008: 'Zum Ausdruck der Evidentialität im Baltischen: Die litauische Partikel *nevà*' (in *Acta Linguistica Lithuanica*, 59, pp. 33–56). I was invited to provide an English translation by Zlatka Guentchéva (Paris).

Daniel Petit, Ecole Normale Supérieure

https://doi.org/10.1515/9783110572261-012

the information in the proposition', according to Bybee's (1985: 184) classic definition. Evidential markers make clear how the speaker was informed about the event described in the sentence, in particular whether experienced directly or not.

Recent debates on evidentiality have focused on two issues. The first one was the delimitation of 'grammatical' vs. 'lexical' evidentiality: whereas some scholars restrict evidentiality to grammar, others regard it as a more comprehensive category, including lexical expressions as well. The former view was defended by Aikhenvald (2003: 19), who significantly wrote that 'one of the current misconceptions concerning evidentiality is to do with a gratuitous extension of this term to cover every way of expressing uncertainty, probability and one's attitude to the information, no matter whether it is expressed with grammatical or with lexical means.' The latter view is explicitly defended by Boye (2010: 291): 'evidentiality is not reserved for grammatical expressions and their meanings. Rather, it is taken to cover both lexically and grammatically expressed meanings'.[2] The second issue that has been subject to much controversy is the distinction between evidentiality and epistemic modality. For a long time, the two notions were not regarded as distinct one from the other, which still appears in Joseph's definition (2003: 97): 'Evidentiality can be defined as the indication of the source of a speaker's information, of the modality by which that information was gained, and/or of the speaker's stance (i.e., attitude) towards the truth of the information'. Several recent works (e.g. Squartini 2004, de Haan 2009) have drawn attention to the necessity to separate evidentiality (referring to the source of the information) and epistemic modality (referring to its subjective validation). According to Diewald and Smirnova (2010: 6), 'while evidentiality indicates the source of evidence a speaker has for making a statement, without necessarily accompanying that with a factuality judgment, epistemic modality is concerned exactly and exclusively with the latter, i.e. with the degree of factuality a speaker attributes to a proposition'. There is, of course, a close relationship between the two notions, sometimes resulting in the fact that the same formal markers may assume the two functions. Wiemer (2007: 173) rightfully notes that 'evidential markers cannot be accounted for without also taking into consideration the actual speaker's attitude toward the proposition expressed'. One possible option could be to use 'evidentiality' as a cover symbol for every kind of qualification of the nature of the evidence and to add the adjectives 'objective' (event-centred) or 'subjective' (speaker-centred) to refer to the source of the information versus to the position of the speaker, if their distinction is made necessary in a given language. This would avoid the use of 'epistemic' for something that has in fact not much in common with the notion of *epistḗmē* (ἐπιστήμη) itself, at least

2 See also Wiemer (2007: 174).

in its primary meaning given by Ferrier (1854: 75 sq.). For the sake of simplicity, in this paper, I will use the term 'evidential' in a broad meaning, both in reference to indications on the source of the information (evidentiality proper) and to the speaker's validation of the content of the utterance (epistemic modality), and I will make a distinction between the two levels only when necessary.[3]

Building on this inclusive definition, some approaches to 'evidentiality' limit their scope to the description of how a speaker keeps his/her distance from the content of his/her utterance; sometimes, 'evidentiality' is even regarded as the negative counterpart of reality. Guentchéva, for example, defines the 'médiatif' as *non-prise en charge du contenu informationnel* 'disengagement on the propositional content' (1996: 13). Strikingly enough, this negative conception of 'evidentiality' has not yet led the scholars to investigate whether there can be a *formal* proximity between its formal expression and negative markers. In fact, most evidential markers are clearly different from negative markers, whether they are expressed by the verbal forms themselves (e.g. the Albanian admirative, or the Estonian *modus relativus*) or by independent particles added to the verbal forms (e.g. German *angeblich* 'allegedly'; French *apparemment* 'apparently', *prétendument* 'supposedly'; English *like*, Russian *budto* 'as if, apparently', Polish *rzekomo* 'allegedly'). None of these particles seems to be connected with the expression of negation. They usually derive from verbs of 'saying' (German *angeblich* < *angeben* 'to state', French *prétendument* < *prétendre* 'to claim', Polish *rzekomo* < *rzec* 'to say') or from the lexical field of 'appearance' (French *apparemment* < *apparent* 'apparent', English *like*), more rarely from the existential verb 'to be' (Russian *budto* < *byt'* 'to be'). There is, however, one evidential particle that seems to be connected with the expression of negation: the Lithuanian evidential particle *nevà* 'allegedly', apparently cognate with the negative particle *ne-* 'not'. The aim of my paper is to determine the origin of the particle *nevà* in order to confirm whether there can be a link between evidentiality and negation.

2 Philological description

The etymology of the Lithuanian particle *nevà* 'allegedly' has not yet been paid the attention it deserves. A brief description may be found in Fraenkel (LEW

3 Note, in passing, that this view corresponds to one of Ferrier's fundamental propositions about epistemology, that 'the objective part of the object of knowledge, though distinguishable, is not separable in cognition from the subjective part, or the ego' (1854: 101).

I 498), but no mention of *nevà* is made in the etymological dictionary of the Lithuanian language by the Polish scholar Smoczyński (2007). Even the philological data have not really been investigated so far.

As far as I know, the particle *nevà* is not attested in Old Lithuanian (16th–18th centuries). Its first occurrence goes back to the beginning of the 19th century. It is found in the Lithuanian dictionary by Christian Gottlieb Mielcke (1800: 564), where it is associated with another particle *būk* (< imperative of *būti* 'to be'):

(1) Mielcke, Ch. *Littauisch-deutsches und Deutsch-littauisches Wörter-Buch* (1800: 564)
Neva *būk* *nekaltas* *esąs*
PCLE PCLE innocent.NOM.SG being.PTCP.NOM.SG
'as if he would be innocent, allegedly innocent'

More instances of *nevà* begin to emerge in the course of the 19th century. Interestingly enough, they first occur in informal uses or in familiar texts. The use of *nevà* in fairy tales is particularly noteworthy. We find it attested, for example, in the 'Lithuanian fairy tales' (*Lietuviškos Pasakos*) by Jonas Basanavičius (1898: I 178)[4]:

(2) Jonas Basanavičius, *Lietuviškos Pasakos* (1898: I 178)
O *tas* *vaikinas* *ir* ***neva*** *nusidavė* *girtu,*
and the.NOM.SG boy.NOM.SG also **PCLE** feign.PAST.3 drunk.INSTR.SG
atsigules *ant* *lovos* *kelinę* *tą* *užsismaukė*
lying on bed.GEN.SG trousers.ACC.SG the.ACC.SG put.PAST.3
ir ***neva*** *miegti*
even **PCLE** sleep
'And the boy feigned to be drunk, lying on the bed, he put his trousers as if he would sleep.'

In the 20th century, the particle *nevà* becomes more frequent in Lithuanian literature, especially in stories and novels that seek to reproduce the spoken language, e.g. in the works of writers such as Sruoga, Tumas-Vaižgantas, or even Mykolaitis-Putinas. An illustrative example can be taken from a fiction story by Juozas Tumas-Vaižgantas (1869–1933):[5]

4 Another instance occurs in the *Litauische Märchen und Erzählungen* by Ch. Jurkschat (1898: 124). Cf. LKŽ VIII 749.
5 Cf. LKŽ VIII 749.

(3) Juozas Tumas-Vaižgantas (1869–1933)

Saviški, tušti Aleksio įrodymai
peculiar.NOM.PL empty.NOM.PL Alexis.GEN.SG explanations.NOM.PL
labiau įtikindavo Jokūbą, negu labia išmintingi
more convince.PAST.3 Jacob.ACC.SG than very reasonable.NOM.PL
*ir **neva** mokslingi privedžiojimai.*
and **PCLE** scientific.NOM.PL deception.NOM.PL
'Alexis' peculiar and empty explanations convinced Jack more than very reasonable and allegedly scientific deceptions.'

Another genre in which the use of *nevà* seems to have been frequent since the 19th century is private writing, i.e. private letters or memoirs, often characterized by an informal or even familiar style. An instance of the particle *nevà* is found, for example, in the autobiography of the East Prussian Lithuanian Vilius Gaigalaitis (1870–1945):[6]

(4) Vilius Gaigalaitis (1870–1945)

*Buvome į blogą garsą įklampyti, **neva***
were.PAST.1PL in bad.ACC.SG reputation.ACC.SG involved.NOM.PL **PCLE**
neištikimi esanti ?
unfaithful.NOM.PL being.NOM.PL
'Did we enjoy a bad reputation as if we would be unfaithful?'

It is to be noted that until the 1930s the particle *nevà* was still rejected by some purists. In 1911, the distinguished Lithuanian linguist Jonas Jablonskis (1860–1930) wrote in a letter that the particle *nevà* with the meaning 'as' (= *lýg*) should be avoided.[7] In the Lithuanian-Russian dictionary by Sereiskis (1933: 511), *nevà* is rendered by Russ. *budto, kak-budto, budto-by* 'allegedly' and illustrated by the following example:

(5) Sereiskis, *Lietuviškai-rusiškas žodynas* (1933)

*Jie sako, **neva** aš sutrukdžiau visą*
they say.PRS.3 **PCLE** I impeded.PAST.1SG whole.ACC.SG
dalyką.
matter.ACC.SG
'They say that I have allegedly impeded the whole matter.'

---

6 Cf. Kaukienė (1997: 323).

7 Cf. Piročkinas (1986: 164). Cf. also *Jablonskio laiškai*, ed. Piročkinas, Vilnius (1985: 28, 29).

Sereiskis explicitly states that *nevà* with the meaning 'that...allegedly' is less correct than the standard construction *kàd* 'that' (followed by the *modus relativus*, i.e. by the evidential use of participles). A few years later (1935), the linguist Juozas Balčikonis reproached the great Lithuanian writer Vincas Mykolaitis-Putinas for having used *nevà* in a sentence of his novel *Altorių šešėly*.[8] He considers *nevà* to be a Slavic loanword; he expressed the same view on several occasions (cf. RR I 148 and 331). Only in recent dictionaries is the particle *nevà* described as neutral. In the Lithuanian dictionary by Niedermann, Senn, Salys and Brender (1951: II 180), we find numerous examples such as (6) and (7):

(6) Niedermann, Senn, Salys and Brender (WlS II 180)

žinios	***neva***	*apie*	*einančias*	*derybas*
news.NOM.PL	**PCLE**	about	going on.ACC.PL	negotiations.ACC.PL

'news about allegedly current negotiations'

(7) Niedermann, Senn, Salys and Brender (WlS II 180)

vaistai,	*kurie*	***neva***	*palengvina*	*kentėjimą*
medicines.NOM.PL	that.NOM.PL	**PCLE**	soothe.PRS.3	pain.ACC.SG

'medicines that are said to soothe pain'

In the standard dictionary of the Lithuanian language (*Dabartinės lietuvių kalbos žodynas*, DŽ [4]2000: 423), the particle *nevà* is paraphrased *tarsi*, *lyg* 'as if, though' and illustrated by two examples, among which we may quote the following one, which provides a good illustration of the construction of *nevà* in the modern language:

(8) *Dabartinės lietuvių kalbos žodynas*, DŽ [4]2000 (cf. LKŽ VIII 749)

Atrodo,	***neva***	*serga.*
it seems.PRS.3.	**PCLE**	he is sick.PRS.3

'It seems that he is sick.'

The particle *nevà* is nowadays frequent in Standard Lithuanian. Roszko (1993: 53–54) and Wiemer (2007) provide us with numerous instances, particularly with instances taken from mass media production. For example:

(9) Roszko (1993: 54)

Kiti	*astronautai,*	*nusileidusieji*	*Mėnulyje,*
other.NOM.PL	astronauts.NOM.PL	having landed.NOM.PL	mond.LOC.SG

8 The incriminated sentence is attested in the following context: *jausdamasis* **neva** *kaltas* 'feeling allegedly guilty' (*Altorių šešėly*, I 233, 6).

juokiasi *iš* *pasakų,* *kuriose* ***neva*** *susitikę*
laugh.PRS.3 at stories.GEN.PL in which.LOC.PL **PCLE** having met.NOM.PL
su *ateiviais* *iš* *kitų* *pasaulių.*
with newcomers.INSTR.PL from other.GEN.PL worlds.GEN.PL
'Other astronauts, having landed on the Moon, laugh at the stories in which, allegedly, they should have met newcomers from other worlds.'[9]

It is not surprising that the particle *nevà* is frequently used in the Lithuanian dialects, which provide us a faithful picture of the spoken varieties of the Lithuanian language. For example, in the so-called 'Kapsian' or 'Zanavykian' dialects, which belong to the High Lithuanian area (close to the river Novà), the particle *næ̀va* (*nèva*) is often attested. Since those dialects have lost the relative mood, the particle *næ̀va* (*nèva*) is usually linked with indicative forms:

(10) Zanavykian dialect of Griškabudis (ZŠŽ II 270)
Næ̀va *g´æ.rt* *karẽĩvei* *prã·šo·* *ale_iš_tìkro·* *i*
PCLE drink.INF soldier.NOM.PL ask.PRS.3. but actually at
mærgà[s] *ž'ũ·ri.*
girls.ACC.PL look.PRS.3.
'The soldiers allegedly ask for a drink, but actually they look at the girls'.

The contrast between *nèva* 'allegedly' and *iš tìkro* 'actually' is to be noted. In the same dialect, *næ̀va* (*nèva*) sometimes display a broader meaning ('so to speak, like, as'), denoting an approximation:

(11) Zanavykian dialect of Griškabudis (ZŠŽ II 270):
Jìz *dẽ·ši[m]* *mæ̃·tu·* ***næ̀va*** *gã·vo·.*
he ten years.GEN.PL **PCLE** receive.PAST.3.
'He reached roughly ten years'.

A variant *næ̀vago.s* (*nèvagos*) is also known in the same dialect,[10] for example:

(12) Zanavykian dialect of Griškabudis (ZŠŽ II 270)
Næ̀vago.z *bãñdo·* *stùba·* *pasistatí.t.*
PCLE try.PRS.3 house.ACC.SG build.INF
'Allegedly he tries to build a house.'

9 Cf. Roszko's Polish translation: *Inni astronauci, którzy wylądowali na Księżycu, śmieją się z opowieści, w których niby się spotkali z przybyszami z innych światów.*
10 Cf. also Senkus (KD 130) and LKŽ VIII 749.

There is thus ground for assuming that the particle *nevà* 'allegedly' belongs to the spoken language and was only recently introduced into the written language, sometimes even reluctantly. This can also explain why there is no instance of *nevà* in Old Lithuanian literature, exclusively limited to religious documents. Any attempt at providing an etymological explanation of *nevà* must account for the fact that it was rejected by some sticklers for scrupulous purity of the language or even considered to be a Slavic loanword. Obviously, it was (and still is to some extent) a familiar word.

3 Etymology of the particle nevà

Before tackling the problem of the etymology of *nevà*, a preliminary remark must be made about its syntactic functions. *Nevà* can have two functions: it can be used either as an adverb ('allegedly', e.g. 13a = German *angeblich*, Polish *rzekomo*) or as a complementizer ('that…allegedly', e.g. 13b = German *daß…angeblich*, Polish *jakoby*). Compare the following two examples taken from Roszko (1993: 53):

(13) a. Roszko (1993: 53)

Pateikiama	*ano*	*meto*	*statistika,*
furnish.PTCP.PASS.NOM.SG	that.GEN.SG	time.GEN.SG	statistics.NOM.SG

kuri	***neva***	*turi*	*parodyti,*	*kaip*	*entuziastingai*
which.NOM.SG	**PCLE**	must.PRS.3	show.INF	how	enthusiastically.ADV

balsavo	*Lietuva.*
vote.PAST.3	Lithuania.NOM.SG

'A statistics of that time is made, which must allegedly show how enthusiastically Lithuania has voted.'[11]

b. Roszko (1993: 53)

Ėmė	*sklisti*	*gandai,*	***neva***	*nedirbs*
begin.PAST.3.	go round.INF	rumour.NOM.PL	**PCLE**	NEG=work.FUT.3

M. M. Mažvydo	*nacionalinė*	*biblioteka.*
M.M. Mažvydas.GEN.SG	national.NOM.SG	library.NOM.SG

'Rumours began to go round, according to which the National Library of Mažvydas will not work.'[12]

---

11 Roszko: *Przytaczana jest statystyka z tamtego okresu, która ma rzekomo pokazać, jak entuzjastycznie głosowała Litwa.*

12 Roszko: *Poczęły rozchodzić się plotki, jakoby biblioteka narodowa imienia M. Mažvydasa miała nie pracować.*

This syntactic ambivalence can be accounted for by assuming the reanalysis of original paratactic constructions. In the example 8 (*atrodo, neva serga* 'it seems that he is sick'), both interpretations are actually open: *nevà* can be seen as an adverb in an asyndetic structure ('it seems, allegedly he is sick') or as a complementizer ('it seems that he is sick'). It is precisely in such contexts that the use of *nevà* as a complementizer may have arisen. It is likely that *nevà* was originally only an adverb.

In order to determine the etymology of the particle *nevà*, some crucial points must be taken into account.

First, the position of stress. In Modern Lithuanian, *nevà* is regularly end-stressed, but a dialectal variant with stem stress (*nèva*) is known as well. Such a variation is unexpected. Moreover, the dialectal form *nèva* is at variance with a typically Lithuanian phonetic law, according to which the vowels *e* and *a* are lengthened in non-final position in open syllables and receive a circumflex tone. Instead of *nèva*, one would thus expect **nẽva* (as in Lith. *kẽvalas* 'shell', *klẽvas* 'maple', *drẽvę* acc. sg. 'hollow of a tree', etc.), not *nèva* with a short vowel (and a grave accent, denoting short vowels in stressed position).

A further problem is that a sequence **-ev-* before back vowel is expected to yield **-av-* in Lithuanian; **-ev-* is preserved only before front vowels. This phonetic rule explains the difference between Lith. *sãvas* 'one's own' (< Proto-Indo-European **sew-o-*, Gr. ἑός) and *devynì* 'nine' (< **dev-in-* < Proto-Indo-European ***h_1*new-n̥*, Lat. *nouem*, with secondary lengthening to **dev-yn-* after *aštuonì* 'eight'). The preservation of **-ev-* before the back vowel **-a* in *nevà* needs further explanation.[13]

In order to resolve all these problems, the best solution could be to argue that *nevà* was originally a compound of two independent words **nè* + **và*. This would explain why the vowel *è* was not lengthened in non-final position: it did not stand in non-final position, but in final position in an independent word (**nè*) and in that position the lengthening *è* > *ẽ* did not take place. The reconstruction of two independent words can also explain why the sequence **ev* did not undergo the change to **av* before back vowel: it can be assumed that the univerbation of **nè* and **và* took place after this phonetic change. Finally, the stress variation *nevà* / *nèva* might reflect the position of stress either on the first member of the compound or on its second member. From all this, one may conclude that *nevà* represents the recent univerbation of two independent words **nè* + **và*.

Following this line of thought, it is more than likely that the first element of *nevà* is identical to the Indo-European negative particle **nè*, which is still preserved in the Lithuanian proclitic negation *nè*. Some of the most striking features

13 A variant *navà* is very rare.

of *nevà* may find parallels in the negative particle *nè*: lack of lengthening of *e* in non-final position (e.g. Lith. *nèkalba* 'he does not speak / they do not speak'), lack of the phonetic change **-ev- > *-av-* before back vowel (e.g. Lith. *neválgo* 'he does not eat / they do not eat'), stress mobility (e.g. *nèkalba / neválgo*). The idea that the negative particle inherited from Indo-European was originally independent from the verb is not new; the regular univerbation (e.g. *nèkalba / neválgo*) must be seen as secondary.[14] The question arises how a negative particle could have played a role in the formation of the particle *nevà*. It is precisely at that point that typological difficulties begin to appear.

Other particles may display a similar meaning in Lithuanian: their basic meaning is 'allegedly'; sometimes, they appear weakened as approximation markers. Some of them belong to the lexical field of 'saying' (e.g. *sãko* < 'one says' from *sakýti* 'to say', *tar̃si* < 'you will say', *tar̃tum* or *tarýtum* < 'you would say' from *tar̃ti* 'to say, to pronounce'), others are derived from the existential verb 'to be' (*bū́ti*) in the relative mood (*esą̃* < neuter of the active participle) or in the imperative (*bū́k*, or *bū̃k*). The same meaning can also be expressed by particles of comparison, such as Lith. *lýg* 'like' (cf. also *lýgtai*). The difference between *nevà* and *esą̃* still needs to be determined more precisely, but it seems likely that *nevà* presupposes a bigger distance of the speaker towards the content of the information than *esą̃*; it seems to be more epistemic than evidential. A thorough study on this point is needed.

As already said at the beginning of this paper, the same lexical fields underlie the formation of evidential particles in other languages of the world. But, strikingly enough, I have found no language in which an evidential particle may be traced back to a negative particle. And this is probably not an accident. What evidentiality does actually express, including the speaker's attitude toward the content of the utterance, is a strategy of distantiation of the speaker from the truth of the information, not necessarily the complete negation of that information. A derivation of the Lithuanian evidential particle *nevà* from the negation *ne-* would be, at best, typologically very uncommon.

A further typological difficulty is the explanation of the second element *-và*. Given the fact that it must represent an originally independent word, it is likely to be identical to the deictic particle *và* 'here ! look over there !'. The particle *và*, often used in the spoken language, is typical of the familiar style. It is not attested in Old Lithuanian; its first occurrences go back to the end of the 19th century (cf. Būga RR

---

14 In the prehistory of the Baltic languages, the negative particle was still an independent word. This is shown by relics of tmesis in Old Prussian (OPr. *neggi* 'and not' < **ne-gi* + verb, III 3_{14}, 33_{10}, 45_{9}, 85_{6}, 109_{14}) and in Lithuanian (e.g. Lith. *nesidúoda* 'he does not give himself' < **ne-si-dúoda*, with interposition of the reflexive particle *-si-*).

I 328, II 47). Functionally it belongs to a subclass of deictic particles for which the name 'presentative particles' has been coined by some scholars, e.g. Russ. *vot*, Lat. *ecce*, Fr. *voici*, *voilà*, etc. The function of such particles is to draw the attention of a speech partner to a given reality.[15] In most instances, the particle *và* may be translated by the French particle *voici* / *voilà* or by the Latin particle *ecce*. Examples:

(14) a. Jan Otrębski (GJL III 371)
Và, *ką* *aš* *radau.*
PCLE what.ACC.SG I find.PST.1SG
'Look what I have found!' (Fr. *Voici ce que j'ai trouvé !*)
b. High Lithuanian dialect of Pivašiūnai (cf. LKŽ XVII 763)
Dabar ***và*** *laiko* *y[ra].*
now PCLE time.GEN.SG is.PRS.3.
'Now, look, we have time' (Fr. *Voilà, il y a du temps.*)
c. High Lithuanian dialect of Pivašiūnai (cf. LKŽ XVII 763)
Aš ***và*** *pinigų* *turiu.*
I PCLE money.GEN.PL have.PRS.1SG
'Look, I have money!' (Fr. *Voilà, j'ai de l'argent.*)
A variant *vã* (with lengthening) is more rarely attested:

(15) High Lithuanian dialect of Miežiškiai (cf. LKŽ XVII 763)
Vã *keturi* *arkliai* *–pasigauk*
PCLE four.NOM.PL horses.NOM.PL take.IMP.2SG
katrą *nori.*
which one.ACC.SG want.PRS.2SG
'Look ! Here are four horses — take the one you wish!' (Fr. *Voici quatre chevaux – prends celui que tu veux !*)

Assuming an etymological connection between *và* and *nevà*, one gets an explanation for the familiar connotation of the second form, because the presentative particle *và* itself is characterized by the same connotation. Both particles are not attested before the 19th century, both first occur in texts based on the spoken language or seeking to reproduce the spoken language. I assume that the particle *và* is responsible for that connotation and that *nevà* owes its familiar character to its second element *và*.

The analysis of *nevà* as a Slavic loanword probably derived from the idea that *và* is borrowed from Russian *vot* 'look here!'. This is unlikely. Būga (RR II 46, III 826) rightly considers *và* a genuinely Lithuanian word (*savas žodis*). A loanword from

---

15 See Petit (2010a, 2010b).

Russian would not have yielded *và*, but *vàt*. There is actually such a form *vàt* in some Lithuanian dialects,[16] but it is obviously a different word than *và*. One could perhaps argue that *và* and *vàt*, due to their synonymy and their phonetic similarity, were conceived of as free variants of the same particle, but their origin is clearly different. Interestingly enough, there is no corresponding pair *nevà* / **nevàt*.

Beside *và*, variants are also found with further deictic, resp. emphatic particles, e.g. *vàge* (LKŽ XVII 814), *vàgi* (LKŽ XVII 815), etc. On the analogy of *niekadà* / *niekadõs* 'never', a lengthened form *võs* was created on *và* (cf. LKŽ XIX 957).[17] Similarly, on **neva-gà* (with a particle *-gà*), a variant *nèvagos* was created, for example in the dialects of Šakiai, Geistarai and Žalioji (near to Vilkaviškis). Other variants could be classified here, e.g. *vaĩ* (LKŽ XVII 831), *vaigi* (LKŽ XVII 847), *vajè* (LKŽ XVII 980), *vajaĩ* (LKŽ XVII 979), even if we cannot be sure whether this is really the same particle, since the meaning is not exactly the same: *vaĩ* and *vajè* are used as interjections expressing a movement of surprise. Some dialects (mostly in the Low Lithuanian area) also present a particle *vè* (LKŽ XVIII 460) with the same meaning as *và* ('look! look over there!'); a further variant *vègi* (LKŽ XVIII 502) is attested very rarely. Given the morphological instability of particles in the grammar of any language, it is hard to determine whether the prototype must be reconstructed as **và* or **vè*.

The origin of the particle *và* is problematic. Originally, it was probably some kind of deictic particle. Other Indo-European languages display deictic or anaphoric particles that belong to a stem **wo-*, e.g. Russ. *eva*, Serbo-Croatian *ȅvo* 'there, look over there!' (from **e-wo*). One could assume that *và* reflects the neuter of this stem used adverbially, that is, Indo-European **wo(d)* 'so, this way' (or with a locative meaning 'here'). Further pronominal forms based on **e/o-wo-* can be mentioned here: Slavic **ovo-* (OCS. *Ovъ ... ovъ* οἱ μέν, οἱ δέ, Russ. *ovyj*, Serb.-Croat. * òvȁj*, Sloven. *óv*, Cz. *ov*, Pol. *ów* 'that', cf. also OPol. *owo* 'ecce') and Indo-Iranian **ava-* (Avest. *auua-*, OPers. *ava-* 'that', OInd. *avóḥ* gen. dual 'of these two').[18] A connection with the Old Indic emphatic particle *vā̂vá* 'certainly, just' (with reduplication and double accent) is likely. Whether OInd. *vái* 'indeed' (cf. Avest. *uōi* 'certainly' Y 36, 3) is cognate with the preceding forms (or even with Lith. *véi* 'look over there !'), is a possibility that cannot

16 Cf. LKŽ XVIII 391.

17 This form is very rare (probably because of the homonymy with the widespread particle *võs* 'hardly').

18 Trautmann (BSW 20), Fasmer (III 116–117), Hoffmann and Forssman (1996: 167), Kent (1953: 85). Russian *vot* does not belong to the same stem, since it represents **v-oto* (with a prothese **v-*), cf. Pol. *oto* 'id.'.

be definitively ruled out, but must remain doubtful as long as the structure of the particle is not accounted for. Besides, it should be noted that the Old Indic particle *vái* can be negated, cf. *ná vái* 'certainly not, not at all' (Rigveda+), cf. also Avest. *na-uua* 'not at all'.

There is thus ground for assuming that *nevà* consists of two parts, a negative particle *nè* followed by a presentative particle *và*. Here again we are facing a typological difficulty. It is well-known that presentative particles are unable to be negated. In Modern French, for example, a presentative construction such as *voici / voilà des fleurs* 'here are flowers' cannot be changed into **voici / voilà pas des fleurs* 'here are no flowers'.[19] Similarly, there is no negative counterpart of *ecce* in Latin (†*non ecce*), *vot* in Russian (†*nevot*) or *štaĩ* in Lithuanian (†*neštaĩ*). R. Forest (2000: 21–31) has convincingly shown that this constraint on the use of presentative particles must probably be seen as a universal throughout the world's languages. In the Fula language (Niger-Congo, West and Central Africa), for example, a sentence such as *pədao i* 'look over there a field / the field!' (Fr. *voilà un / le champ*) cannot be negated. The reconstruction of a negative structure **ne-và* in Lithuanian, based on the negation of the presentative particle *và*, would be, at best, a typological incongruity.

Such a situation is exemplary of the type of problems that the modern practice of Indo-European linguistics has to deal with. What are we supposed to do when an etymological reconstruction is at variance with typological requirements? It has nowadays become impossible to accept typological contradictions uncomplainingly as if they would be insignificant. Typology must be paid as much attention as the evidence of historical phonology or morphology. In our case study, this means that, if the reconstruction of *nevà* as a compound of the negative particle *nè* and the presentative particle *và*, is shown to be typologically implausible, it must be verified again and probably replaced by another explanation.

Obviously, there is a problem with the reconstruction of a negation *nè* in *nevà*. The question is whether it is really a negation or could bear another function which still needs to be determined.

---

19 In Classical French, the presentative particle *voilà* could be negated, but only in rhetorical questions: *voilà-t-il pas*, cf. *Voilà-t-il pas Monsieur qui ricane déjà ?* 'Here is Mister who is already snickering' (Molière, *Tartuffe*, I 1), *Voilà-t-il pas de quoi pousser des cris sinistres !* 'Is there any reason to scream out awfully?' (Victor Hugo, *Ruy Blas* III 5). Cf. also Grevisse ([12]1986: 642, § 387). This does not mean, however, that the presentative particle *voilà* as such can be negated.

4 Negation and comparison in Lithuanian

It is well-known that the negative particle **nè* in the Baltic languages may also function as a comparative particle. This use has already received the attention of several scholars; I refer in particular to an insightful paper by G.-J. Pinault about negation and comparison in Old Indic (1985), where the Baltic material is abundantly presented and discussed (cf. pp. 131–132).[20] In Modern Lithuanian, the use of **nè* as a particle of comparison is almost exclusively restricted to introduce standards of comparison, with enlarged forms such as *neĩ* or *negù* (more rarely *nekaĩp*) 'than'. Instances may be found in Old Lithuanian (16a) and in Modern Lithuanian (16b):

(16) a. Jonas Bretkūnas, *Postilė* (1591: 37, 17–18)[21]

Tassai	*daug*	*geresnis*	*ira*	***nei***	*wissu*
that.NOM.SG	much.ADV	better. NOM.SG	is.PRS.3	**than**	all.GEN.PL

praraku	*Seno*	*Sokano.*
prophets.GEN.PL	old.GEN.SG	testament.GEN.SG

'That one is much better than that of all the Prophets of the Old Testament'

b. High Lithuanian dialect of Naujamiestis (LKŽ VIII 621)

Geriau	*duoti,*	***negu***	*prašyti.*
better	give.INF	**than**	ask.INF

'It is better to give than to ask.'

In the modern use, only *neĩ* or *negù* (more rarely *nekaĩp*) can be used in that function, but in older texts or in dialects the simple particle *nè* can still occur with comparatives, for example:

(17) Jakob Brodowski, *Lexikon Germanico-Lithvanicum et Lithvanico-Germanicum* (1713–1744: I 153)[22]

Kétures	*Akkis*	*daugiaus*	*máta*	***ne***	*wiena.*
four.NOM.PL	eye.NOM.PL	more	see.PRS.3.	**than**	one.NOM.SG

(German: *Vier Auge fehen mehr als ein.*)

'Four eyes see more than only one.'

20 Cf. also Pinault (1989: 53–74) and Būga (RR I 470–471).

21 Cf. Leskien (1903: 111).

22 Cf. LKŽ VIII 596.

Apart from the comparative structures, in which the negation *nè* bears the function of a particle of comparison (cf. the parallel construction: comparative + *kaĩp* 'like'), a free use of *nè* with a general meaning 'like' sporadically occurs in Old Lithuanian.[23] We find it attested, for example, in the first Lithuanian dictionary:

(18) Konstantynas Sirvydas, *Dictionarium trium linguarum* (^{3}1643: 84, s.v. *jakoby*)

Ne	*zerkałas*	*żiba.*
like	mirror.NOM.SG	shine.PRS.3.

'Like a mirror it shines.'

Another instance is found in the 18th century dictionary by Jakob Brodowski (1713–1744):

(19) Jakob Brodowski, *Lexikon Germanico-Lithvanicum et Lithvanico-Germanicum* (1713–1744: I 151)

Auga	*waikai*	***ne***	*Girroj'*	*Médʒei.*
grow up.PRS.3	children.NOM.PL	**like**	forest.LOC.SG	tree.NOM.PL

(German: *Kinder wachsen auff wie die Bäume im Walde.*)
'Children grow up like trees in a forest.'

Enlarged forms of the negative particle *nè* may also express the same comparative function, for example:

(20) High Lithuanian dialect of Suvalkų Naumiestis (Būga RR III 826)

pìktas	***néi***	*velnias*
cross.NOM.SG	**like**	devil.NOM.SG

'as cross as the devil'

The polysemy of the particle *nè* ('not / like') is likely to reflect an archaism of the Lithuanian language. A similar use is attested in Old Indic (Vedic Sanskrit), where the particle *ná* may function either as negation[24] or as comparative particle, regularly postponed. In the Rigveda, the comparative use of *ná* is even more

23 Cf. LKŽ VIII 597.
24 E.g. RV IV 30, 19: **ná** *tát te sumnám áṣṭave* 'this thy kindness cannot be reached [by words]'. Cf. Pinault (1985: 115).

frequent than its negative use; in that meaning *ná* stands in competition with *iva* 'like' (roughly: *iva* after vowels, *ná* after consonants).[25] It can be argued that the comparative function has secondarily developed from the negative function, through the reanalysis of what G.-J. Pinault called *comparaisons négatives* 'negative comparisons'. Let us take from Pinault (1989: 64) the following example:

(21) Rigveda VI 10, 2

Ghr̥tám	***ná***	*śúci*	*matáyaḥ*	*pavante.*
butter.NOM.SG	**like**	pure.NOM.PL	thought.NOM.PL	clarify.PRS.3PL

'Pure like sacred butter, my thoughts become clear.'

The original meaning was the following one: 'not the butter is pure, my thoughts become clear'. At a more recent stage, the sentence was reanalyzed as 'pure like butter, my thoughts become clear'. This figure of speech, 'negative comparison', is particularly widespread in the Lithuanian folk poetry, the so-called *dainos* (folk songs). An instance of the late 19th century, collected by the famous linguist August Leskien in Wilkischken (East Prussia, nowadays Vilkyškiai):

(22) August Leskien and Karl Brugmann, *Litauische Volkslieder und Märchen* (1882: 16)

Neí	*vė̃jes*	*púte,*	'Not the wind was blowing,
nor	wind.NOM.SG	blow.PST.3	
neí	*sódai*	*úže,*	not the gardens were rumbling,
neither	garden.NOM.PL	rumble.PST.3.	
tìk	*aužulaí*	*lingáva.*	only the oaks were moving.'
only	oaks.NOM.PL	move.PST.3	

with the following meaning:

> 'Just in the same way as the wind was blowing, as the gardens were rumbling, so were the oaks moving.'

It is likely that reanalysis of negations as comparative particles already took place in Indo-European. In most languages, relics of the original polysemy have been preserved only in the expression of degrees of comparison, e.g. Engl. *than* (< *þat* + negation *ne*), Serbo-Croatian *nego* (< negation *ne* + particle -*go*).

My claim is that the existence of a comparative meaning in the negative particle *nè* directly explains the formation of the epistemic particle *nevà* in

25 Cf. Pinault (1995–1996, 1997, 2004).

Lithuanian. Only such a view is likely to account for the typological difficulties we have listed above in this paper. An etymological connection between evidential and comparative particles is cross-linguistically something very common, as shown for example by Lith. *lýg* 'like', sometimes used with the meaning 'allegedly'. The analysis of *nevà* as **nè* 'like' + **và* 'here, look' is not really new; it was already advocated by Fraenkel (LEW I 498), who translated *nè* in *nevà* as 'gleichsam, wie', but without providing any semantic motivation. The formation of *nevà* would be practically identical to that of *kaĩp và*, attested in some Lithuanian dialects with the meaning 'as for example' (= Standard Lithuanian *kaĩp antaĩ*). In contrast to the presentative particle *và*, which describes immediate reality ('exactly as I see it, *hic et nunc*'), the comparative particle *nè* in *nevà* conveys a semantic nuance of indefiniteness ('approximately as I see it, only roughly corresponding to reality'), and it is not surprising that it was used to introduce a distance between the content of the information and the standpoint of the speaker. For linguistic typology, the etymology of *nevà* appears to be relatively instructive: it shows how an evidential effect can derive from distancing oneself from a presentative particle. No doubt that this can shed some light on the deep meaning of evidentiality.

Abbreviations

General abbreviations

ACC – accusative; ADV adverb; FUT – future; GEN – genitive; INF infinitive; INSTR – instrumental ; LOC – locative; NOM – nominative; PAST – past tense; PCLE – particle; PL – plural; PRS – present tense; PTCP – participle; SG – singular

Bibliographical abbreviations

BSW Trautmann, R., 1923.
DŽ *Dabartinės lietuvių kalbos žodynas*, [4]2000.
GJL Otrębski, J., 1956–1965.
KD Senkus, J ;, 2006.
LEW Fraenkel, E., 1955–1965.
LKŽ *Lietuvių kalbos žodynas*, 1941–2001.
RR Balčikonis, J., 1978–1982.
RR Būga, K., 1958–1961.
WlS Niedermann, A., Senn, M., Salys, A., Brender, F., 1932–1968.
ZŠŽ *Zanavykų šnektos žodynas* 2003–2004.

References

Aikhenvald, Alexandra & Robert Malcom W. Dixon (ed.). 2003. *Studies in Evidentiality*. Amsterdam: John Benjamins Publishing Co.

Aikhenvald, Alexandra. 2004. *Evidentiality*. Oxford: Oxford University Press.

Balčikonis, Juozas. 1935. Kelios pastabos dėl V. Mykolaičio-Putino romano "Altorių šešėly" kalbos. *Gimtoji kalba*, 3 = RR I. 144–146.

Balčikonis, Juozas. 1978–1982. *Rinktiniai raštai*, I-II, Vilnius, Mokslas.

Barnes, Janet. 1984. Evidentials in the Tuyuca verb. *International Journal of American Linguistics* 50. 255–271.

Basanavičius, Jonas, 1898. *Lietuviškos pasakos*, I Band. Chicago.

Boye, K.asper. 2010. Evidence for what? Evidentiality and scope. *Sprachtypologie und Universalienforschung (STUF)* 63 (4). 290–307.

Bretkūnas, Jonas. 1591. *Postilla, Tatai esti Trumpas ir Prastas Ischguldimas Euangeliu*, Königsberg. In Ona Aleknavičienė (ed.), 2005. *Jono Bretkūno Postilė*. Vilnius: Lietuvių kalbos institutas.

Brodowski, Jacob. 1713–1744. *Lexicon Germanico-Lithvanicum et Lithvanico-Germanicum*. Manuskript.

Būga, Kazimieras. 1958–1961. *Rinktiniai raštai (RR)*. Zigmas Zinkevičius (ed.), I 1958, II 1959, III 1961. Vilnius: Valstybinė politinės ir mokslinės literatūros leidykla.

Bybee, Joan L. 1985. *Morphology: A Study of the Relation between Meaning and Form*. Amsterdam: John Benjamins Publishing Co.

Chafe, Wallace & Johanna Nichols (eds.). 1986. *Evidentiality: The Linguistic Coding of Epistemology* (Advances in Discourse Processes 20). Norwood, New Jersey: Ablex Publishing Corporation.

Dabartinės lietuvių kalbos žodynas (DŽ), 4th edn. 2000. Vilnius: Mokslas.

Dendale, Patrick & Jean Nuyts. 1994. Bibliographie sélective de l'évidentialité. *Langue française* 102. 121–125.

Diewald, Gabbriele & Elena Smirnova. 2010. *Evidentiality in German: Linguistic Realization and Regularities in Grammaticalization*. Berlin, New York: de Gruyter.

Fasmer, Maks. [3]1996. *Etymologičeskyj slovar' russkogo jazyka*. Moskva, 4 volumes.

Ferrier, James Frederick. 1854. *Institutes of Metaphysic, The Theory of Knowing and Being*. Edinburgh & London: William Blackwood and Sons.

Forest, Robert. 2000. Ce qui ne se nie pas dans les langues. *Mémoires de la Société de linguistique de Paris, N.S., La négation : une ou multiple ?* 4. 21–31.

Fraenkel, Ernest. 1962–1965. *Litauisches etymologisches Wörterbuch (LEW)*, I. Band, A-privekiuoti ; II. Band, privykėti-žvolgai. Göttingen: Vandenhœck und Ruprecht..

Grevisse, Maurice. [12]1986. *Le bon usage*. Bruxelles: Duculot.

Guentchéva, Zlatka (ed.). 1996. *L'énonciation médiatisée* (Bibliothèque de l'Information Grammaticale 35). Louvain, Paris: Peeters.

Guentchéva, Zlatka & Jon Landaburu (eds.). 2007. *L'énonciation médiatisée, II* (Bibliothèque de l'Information Grammaticale 63). Louvain, Paris: Peeters.

Haan, Ferdinand de. 2009. Evidentiality and epistemic modality: setting boundaries. *Southwest Journal of Linguistics* 18. 83–101.

Hagège, Claude. 1995. Le rôle des médiaphoriques dans la langue et le discours. *Bulletin de la Société de Linguistique de Paris* 90. 1–19.

Hoffmann, Karl & Bernhard Forssman. 1996, ²2004. *Avestische Laut- und Flexionslehre* (Innsbrucker Beiträge zur Sprachwissenschaft 115). 2nd edition. Innsbruck: Institut für Sprachen und Literaturen. .

Holvoet, Axel. 2007. *Mood and Modality in Baltic*. Kraków: Wydawnictwo Uniwersytetu Jagiellońskiego.

Johanson, Lars & Bo Utas (eds.). 2000. *Evidentials. Turkic, Iranian and Neighboring Languages*. Berlin: Mouton de Gruyter.

Jones-Bley, Karlene, Martin E. Huld, Angela Della Volpe & Miriam Robbins Dexter (eds.). 2003. *Proceedings of the Fourteenth Annual UCLA Indo-European Conference, Los Angeles, November 8–9, 2002* (Journal of Indo-European Studies Monograph Series 47). Washington DC: Institute for the Study of Man.

Joseph, Brian D. 2003. Evidentiality in Proto-Indo-European? Building a Case. In: Karlene Jones-Bley, Martin E. Huld, Angela Della Volpe & Miriam Robbins Dexter (eds.), *Proceedings of the Fourteenth Annual UCLA Indo-European Conference, Los Angeles, November 8–9, 2002 (Journal of Indo-European Studies Monograph Series* 47), 96–111. Washington DC: Institute for the Study of Man.

Jurkschat, Christoph. 1898. *Litauische Märchen und Erzählungen*. Heidelberg.

Kaukienė, Audronė. 1997. *Klaipėdos krašto vakarų aukštaičių tarmė*. Klaipėda.

Kent, Roland G. 1953. *Old Persian, Grammar, Texts, Lexicon*. New Haven, Connecticut: American Oriental Society.

Lazard, Gilbert. 1956. Caractères distinctifs de la langue tadjik. *Bulletin de la Société de Linguistique de Paris* 52. 117–186.

Lazard, Gilbert. 2000. Le médiatif : considérations théoriques et application à l'iranien. In Lars Johanson & Bo Utas (ed.), *Evidentials. Turkic, Iranian and Neighboring Languages*, 209–228. Berlin: Mouton de Gruyter.

Leskien, August & Karl Brugman. 1882. *Litauische Volkslieder und Märchen*. Strassburg: Trübner.

Leskien, August. 1903. Litauische Partikeln und Konjunktionen. *Indogermanische Forschungen* 14. 89–113.

Lietuvių kalbos žodynas (LKŽ), 1941–2001, Vilnius, Mintis (I–II: 1968–1969, 2nd edn), Valstybinė enciklopedijų, žodynų ir mokslo literatūros leidykla (III-VI: 1956-1962), Mintis (VII–IX: 1966–1973), Mokslas (X–XX: 1976–2001), Juozas Balčikonis (ed.), Kazys Ulvydas and Jonas Kruopas (ed.).

Mielcke, Christian Gottlieb. 1800. *Littauisch-deutsches und Deutsch-littauisches Wörter-Buch*. Königsberg: Hartung.

Niedermann, Anton, Max Senn, Alfred Salys & Franz Brender. 1932–1968. *Wörterbuch der litauischen Schriftsprache (WlS)*. Heidelberg: Winter.

Otrębski, Jan. 1956–1965. *Gramatyka języka litewskiego (GJL)*. Warszawa, Państwowe Wydawnictwo Naukowe, 3 volumes.

Petit, Daniel. 2010a. On presentative particles in the Baltic languages. In Nicole Nau & Norbert Ostrowski (ed.), *Particles and Connectives in Baltic* (Acta Salensia 2), 151–170. Vilnius: Vilniaus Universitetas.

Petit, Daniel. 2010b. Old Lithuanian *añskat, šìskat, tàskat* and cognates. *Acta Linguistica Lithuanica* 62–63. 11–25.

Pinault, Georges-Jean. 1985. Négation et comparaison en védique. *Bulletin de la Société de linguistique de Paris* 80. 103–144.

Pinault, Georges-Jean. 1989. Les voies de la comparaison védique. In Paul Valentin (ed.), *La Comparaison, Actes du colloque tenu les 23 et 24 septembre 1984 par le Département de linguistique à l'Université de Paris-Sorbonne* (*Linguistica Palatina*, Colloquia III), 53–74. Paris: Presses de l'Université Paris-Sorbonne.

Pinault, Georges-Jean. 1995–1996. Distribution des particules comparatives dans la R̥k-Saṃhitā. *Bulletin d'Études Indiennes* 13–14. 307–367.

Pinault, Georges-Jean. 1997. Distribution de la particule négative *ná* dans la R̥k-Saṃhitā. *Bulletin d'Études Indiennes* 15. 213–246.

Pinault, Georges-Jean. 2004. On the usages of the particle *iva* in the Rgvedic Hymns. In Arlo Griffiths & Jan E. M. Houben (ed.), *The Vedas: Texts, Language and Ritual, Proceedings of the Third International Vedic Workshop, Leiden, 2002*, 285–306. Groningen: Forsten.

Piročkinas, Arnoldas. 1986. *Jono Jablonskio kalbos taisymai*. Kaunas: Šviesa.

Ramat, Paolo. 1996. « Allegedly John is ill again »: stratégies pour le médiatif. In Zlatka Guentcheva (ed.), *L'énonciation médiatisée* (Bibliothèque de l'Information Grammaticale 35), 287–298. Louvain, Paris: Peeters.

Roszko, Roman, 1993. *Wykładniki modalności imperceptywnej w języku polskim i litewskim*. Warszawa: Polska Akademia Nauk, Instytut Slawistiki.

Senkus, Juozas. 2006. *Kalbotyros darbai (KD)*. Vilnius: Lietuvių kalbos institutas.

Sereiskis, Benjaminas. 1933. *Lietuviškai-rusiškas žodynas*. Kaunas.

Sirvydas, Konstantinas. 1642. *Dictionarium trium linguarum (DTL³)*. Vilnius. 3rd edn, Jonas Kruopas (ed.), 1979. *Pirmasis lietuvių kalbos žodynas*. Vilnius. Mokslas.

Smoczyński, Wojciech. 2007. *Słownik etymologičny języka litewskiego*.Vilnius.

Squartini, Mario. 2004. Disentangling evidentiality and epistemic modality in Romance. *Lingua* 114/7. 873–889.

Trautmann, Reinhold. 1923. *Baltisch-Slavisches Wörterbuch (BSW)*. Göttingen: Vandenhœck und Ruprecht.

Wiemer, Björn. 2006. Evidencialumo kategorija lietuvių kalboje. *Baltistica* 41/1. 33–49.

Wiemer, Björn. 2007. Lexical markers of evidentiality in Lithuanian. *Rivista di Linguistica* 19/1. 173–208.

Zanavykų šnektos žodynas (ZŠŽ), 2 volumes. 2003–2004. Vilnius: Mokslas.

Part IV: **Non Indo-European languages**

Ferenc Kiefer

Two kinds of epistemic modality in Hungarian

Abstract: The article provides an overview of epistemic expressions in Hungarian. The bulk of the article is devoted to the discussion of the meaning of the possibility suffix, which may express plain possibility but may also have an evidential use in which case it expresses probability rather than plain possibility. The two meanings correlate with two different sentence structures. In the first case the modal verb (i.e. the suffixed verb form) carries main stress and is followed by the complement(s) of the verb, in the second case the modal verb is unstressed and is preceded by a focused constituent. It will be shown that the second meaning is evidential. The two meanings will be termed *epistemic possibility* and *evidential probability*, respectively. Epistemic necessity is expressed by a verb whose meaning, however, is not very different from epistemic possibility. The last section of the article discusses some aspects of the uses of modal particles and modal adverbials.

Keywords: possibility, probability, modal suffix, modal verb, modal particle, modal adverbial

1 Introduction

In most well-known languages expressions of 'can' and 'must' are notoriously ambiguous. Depending on context they can receive, among others, an epistemic, deontic, circumstantial, dispositional or boulomaic reading – to mention just the most frequent types of modality. Moreover, nothing prevents us from distinguishing several readings for one type of modality. In Hungarian epistemic possibility is normally expressed by the verbal suffix *-hat/-het*[1] or by the verb *lehet* (the contamination of

1 The choice between the two forms is determined by vowel harmony.

Note: I have published several papers on modality earlier. Cf. Kiefer 2000 and the cited works therein.

Ferenc Kiefer, Hungarian Academy of Sciences

https://doi.org/10.1515/9783110572261-013

the verb *lesz* 'become' and the possibility suffix –*het*), and epistemic necessity by the defective verb *kell* 'must', which also occurs as a full verb meaning 'be needed' (cf. German *brauchen*). The modal verb *kell* is only used in 3SG and Present Tense (*kell* 'it is necessary'), Past Tense (*kellett* 'it was necessary'), Present Conditional (*kellene* 'it would be necessary'), and Past Conditional (*kellett volna* 'it would have been necessary'). The verb *kell* has two further features which are worth noting: (a) the subject must take the dative (*Péter-nek* ... *kell* 'Peter must ...') and (b) the infinitive is inflected, in the present case it gets a 3P personal suffix (*Péter-nek menni-e kell* 'Peter must go'.[2] In colloquial Hungarian the verb *kell* is often replaced by the German loan *muszáj*, which, however, has only dynamic uses, i.e. it cannot be used epistemically.

Both the suffix *-hat*/*-het* and the verbal form *kell* are multiply ambiguous. A simple modal sentence such as *Bill dolgozhat a könyvtárban* 'Bill may be working in the library' may mean that – according to what we know about Bill and the world – Bill may be working in the library (epistemic reading), but it may also mean that Bill is allowed to work in the library (deontic reading), or that the circumstances in the library are such that Bill is able to work there (circumstantial reading). This is equally true of expressions of necessity. Take, for example, the sentence *Billnek a könyvtárban kell dolgoznia* 'Bill must be working in the library', which may mean that in view of what is known about the relevant aspect of the world Bill must be working in the library (epistemic reading), or according to the rules he is forced to work in the library (deontic reading), or that the circumstances are such that the only place where he can work is the library (circumstantial rading). Without knowing the context in which a modal sentence is uttered it is quite impossible to know what exactly the utterance means. In contrast to modal verbs, modal particles and adverbials such as *talán* 'perhaps', *valószínűleg* 'probably' or *feltehetőleg* 'supposedly' have an epistemic reading only.

Note that the possibility suffix *-hat*/*-het*, which is attached to the verbal base, is not a derivational suffix, at least not a prototypical one,[3] since it never produces new words and suffixed words normally do not get lexicalized. If we disregard inflectional suffixes, it is the last suffix which a verbal form can take. From this we must conclude that this suffix is neither derivational nor inflectional. Consider, for example, the verb *nyit* 'open' and some of its derived forms: -(V)*gat*/-(V)*get* is the iterative suffix, -(V)*dik* the middle voice suffix, and *-tat*/*-tet* the factitive suffix.[4]

2 The full paradigm is: *menn-em kell, menn-ed kell, menn-ie kell, menn-ünk kell, menn-etek kell, menn-iük kell*. The reason that the inflected infinitive must be used can be explained by the fact that the modal verb *kell* is non-conjugable.

3 See Dressler (1989).

4 In Hungarian most suffixes appear in more than one form and the choice of the correct suffix is determined by vowel harmony. 'V' denotes an epenthetic vowel.

(1) a. *nyit-hat* 'may/can open'
b. *nyit-ogat-hat* 'may/can open repeatedly, frequently'
c. *nyit-ód-hat* 'may/can open (itself)'
d. *nyit-tat-hat* 'may/can let open'
e. *nyit-tat-gat-hat* 'may/can let open frequently'

The example (1e) shows the following order of suffixes: factitive – iterative – possibility.

2 Epistemic modality and the inferential use of modals

On its epistemic reading the modal verbal forms can be paraphrased as 'in view of what I know it is possible that V'.[5] Consider the following examples:

(2) *Péter játsz-hat a kert-ben.*
Peter play-can the garden-in
'Peter can be playing in the garden'

(3) *Anna le-het az iskolá-ban.*
Ann be-can the school-in
'Ann can be at school'

(2) asserts that on the basis of what the speaker knows it is not excluded that Peter is playing in the garden but other possibilities, too, may exist. Similarly, (3) asserts that it is not excluded that Ann is at school but, once again, other possibilities are not excluded either. In fact, the speaker may enumarate all the possibilities which may come to his mind.

(4) *Ann can be at school but she can also be at home, or in the cinema, or in the university book store, etc.*

Note that the possibility put forward by the speaker can easily be negated by a third person with a different knowledge background.

5 This is comparable to Hintikka's K (knowledge) operator. See also Kratzer 1978.

(5) a. *Péter nem játsz-hat a kertben, mert néhány perccel ezelőtt találkoztam vele az iskolá-ban.*
'Peter cannot be playing in the garden because a couple of minutes ago I met him at school.'
b. *Anna nem le-het az iskolában, mert éppen most ment a boltba.*
'Ann cannot be at school because she went to the shop just now.'

Notice the order of the constituents in (2) and (3): Subject – Modal – Complement. Furthermore, it is important to note that in (2) and (3) the modal verb form is contrastively stressed. Since the modal suffix is not an independent constituent it can only be stressed by stressing the modal verb form containing this suffix.

In Hungarian grammar the position immediately preceding the verb is often referred to as Focus Position (=FP). If a nominal complement is moved into this position it gets contrastively stressed (henceforth contrastive stress will be indicated by bold letters).

(6) *Péter a **kert-ben** játsz-hat.*[6]
'It is in the garden where Peter may be playing'
(7) *Anna az **iskolá-ban** le-het.*
'It is at school where Ann can be'

In this case the modal does not admit other possibilities. The place where Peter can be playing or where Ann can be represents the only possibility. How can the difference between (2)–(3) and (6)–(7) be explained? One possible explanation runs as follows. It was noticed very early in the literature that contrastive focus has the property referred to as 'exhaustive listing'.[7] According to this property the focused constituent denotes the set of entities for which the predicate holds. The garden is thus the only place for which Peter's playing may hold and Ann's school is the only place where she can be. In other words, (6) and (7) express probability rather than just possibility. As we shall see immediately, sentences expressing epistemic possibility and those expressing probability differ in a considerable number of properties.

6 Alongside of (6) also the following sentences are possible: ***Péter** játsz-hat a kert-ben* 'It is Peter who may be playing in the garden', ***Játsz-hat** Péter a kert-ben* 'It is not excluded that Peter is playing in the garden', etc.
7 See Szabolcsi 1981.

2.1 Negation

Though the above interpretation comes very close to how speakers of Hungarian interpret these sentences, it is not the whole story. Sentences such as (2) and (3) can easily be negated, as we saw above. On the other hand, this is not the case with (6) and (7), which admit external negation only.

(8) *Nem igaz, hogy Péter a* ***kert-ben*** *játsz-hat.*
'It is not true that Peter may be playing in the garden.'

(9) *Nem igaz, hogy Anna az* ***iskolá-ban*** *le-het.*
'It is not true that Ann may be at school.'

By using internal negation we question the validity of the original hypothesis and we put forward our own hypothesis.

(10) *Péter nem a* ***kert-ben*** *játsz-hat, hanem a szobá-já-ban.*
'Peter may be playing in his room rather than in the garden.'

The speaker of (10) may have good reasons to believe that the place where Peter is playing is not the garden but his room. If asked she is expected to mention these reasons as evidence for her belief. In other words, it would seem that what we called probability above is rather an evidential (inferential) meaning. The speaker has evidence for (10) but not for (6).

The situation is different if the focussed constituent lies outside of the scope of the negation and the negative particle precedes the modal verb, as in (11).

(11) *Péter a kert-ben nem játsz-hat.*

The sentence (11) negates plain epistemic possibility: (11) says that it is out of the question that Peter is playing in the garden, in other words, (11) does not negate probability either, it negates the state-of-affairs which might give rise to the inferential meaning 'Peter is very likely playing in the garden'.

2.2 Interrogation

(12a) is the interrogative form of (2): the speaker wants to know if the given state-of-affairs is possible. On the other hand, by asking (12b) the speaker would be questioning his interlocutor's inference, which does not seem to be possible.

(12) a. *Péter játsz-hat a kert-ben?*
'Can Peter be playing in the garden?'
b. **Péter a kert-ben játsz-hat?*[8]
'May Peter be playing in the garden?'

2.3 The premise of a conclusion

A similar difference can be observed if we want to use inferential possibility as a premise in a conditional. In (13a) the premise expresses plain epistemic possibility and the conditional is a grammatical sentence. In contrast, if the premise is an inferential, the conditional becomes ungrammatical. In other words, an inferential cannot be the premise of a conclusion. Compare (13a) and (13b).

(13) a. *Ha Péter* játsz-hat *a kert-ben, akkor biztosan nem esik az eső.*
'If Peter can be playing in the garden, it is surely not reaining
b. **Ha Péter a kert-ben játsz-hat, akkor nem esik az eső.*
'If Peter may be playing in the garden then it is surely not raining.'

2.4 Embedding under the verb 'know'

A sentence expressing epistemic possibility is certainly something which can be known. In contrast inferential probability has to do with the speaker's assumptions and beliefs. This difference manifests itself by allowing a sentence expressing epistemic possibility to embed under the verb 'know' which is excluded in the case of inferential possibility. Compare (14a) and (14b).

(14) a. *Anna tudja, hogy Péter játsz-hat a kert-ben.*
'Ann knows that Peter can be playing in the garden'
b. **Anna tudja, hogy Péter a kert-ben jåtsz-hat.*
'Ann knows that Peter may be playing in the garden.'

Since any proposition can be negated and questioned, and any proposition can be the premise of a conclusion and can be known, we must conclude that inferential possibility is not propositional.[9]

---

8 (11) is possible as an echo-question.
9 Similar things were noted by John Lyons in connection with the meaning of the English modals (Lyons 1977). Lyons used the terms 'objective possibility' and 'subjective possibility' for

On the basis of the above discussion we may thus conclude that two types of epistemic modality must be distinguished: epistemic possibility, which is propositional, and inferential possibility, which advances the speaker's hypothesis about a state-of-affairs, and which is not propositional. In Hungarian, epistemic possibility and inferential possibility can be kept apart structurally. In the case of epistemic possibility main stress is carried by the modal form containing the possibility suffix; on the other hand, in the case of inferential possibility a complement of the verb is contrastively stressed. This complement must precede the verb, i.e. it must occupy the focus position of the sentence.

Before concluding this section let me adduce two sentences representing a minimal pair: given an appropriate epistemic background sentence (15) expresses epistemic possibility, sentence (16) inferential possibility. As can be seen, the two sentences differ in word order and with respect to the place of contrastive stress.

(15) *János* ***me**-het-ett* *mozi-ba.*
John go-can-Past cinema-to
'John could have gone to the cinema' (nothing excluded this possibility)

(16) *János* ***mo**ziba mehetett.*
'John may have gone to the cinema' (his habits and some other indication suggest that)

What about future events? As in many other languages, in Hungarian future is normally expressed by present tense forms. In order to make the future reference more explicit very often the temporal adverbial *majd* is used, as in (17).

(17) *János majd mehet moziba.*
John Adv go-can cinema-to
'John may go to the cinema'

However, (17) can in no way express epistemic possibility, though in an appropriate context it may have a deontic interpretation ('It will be permitted for John to go to the cinema') and a circumstantial interpretation ('The circumstances will be such that it will be possible for John to go to the cinema'). On the other hand, if we change the word order in (17) in order to get the structure typical of inferential possibility the sentence will become ungrammatical:

---

what I termed in the present paper 'epistemic possibility' and 'inferential possibility'. In contrast to English, Hungarian has the advantage that the difference between the two meanings is also reflected structurally (word order, emphasis).

(18) **János majd moziba mehet.*
John Adv cinema-to go-can

The reason for the ungrammaticality is the future temporal reference expressed by the adverbial *majd* and the Present Tense form of the verb. Inferencing must be based on facts and future events are not facts. Consequently, inferential possibility can only refer to past or present events.

To be sure, there are events which normally do not depend on the actions of an intentionally acting agent. Timeless events, if modalized, can only have an epistemic reading, that is, modal sentences such as (19)–(21) normally express epistemic possibility only.[10]

(19) *Télen befagy-hat a Duna.*
in winter freezing-over-maybe the Danube
'In winter the Danube may freeze over'

(20) *A zsíros étel árt-hat az egészségnek.*
the fat food harm-may the health
'Fat food may harm health'

(21) *Egy jó auto is tönkremehet.*
a good car even break-down-may
'Even a good car may brake down'

The events described in (19)–(21) are not controlled by an agent, nor are they due to certain circumstances. They are just compatible with what we know about the world. Hence they express simple epistemic possibility. Even the inferential reading seems to be excluded. On the other hand, the preferred reading of the sentences (22) and (23) is inferential probability. Note, however, that – depending on context – other readings, too, are possible. For example, (22) may also express circumstantial possibility.

(22) *A lány nagyon mélyen alhatott.*
the girl very deeply sleep-may
'The girl may have slept very deeply'

(23) *Anna hasonlíthatott anyjára.*
Ann resemble-may mother-her
'Ann may have resembled her mother'

The verb *kell* 'must', too, can be used to express inferential possibility, as exemplified by the following sentences.

10 These sentences do not tolerate the temporal adverbial *majd*.

(24) *Pistinek otthon kell lennie.*
Steve at-home must be
'Steve must be at home'

(25) *Péternek a kertben kellett játszania.*
Peter the garden-in must-Past play
'Peter must have been playing in the garden'

Sentence (24) is interpreted in the following way: since Steve cannot be found outside of his home the speaker concludes that he must be at home. Similarly, seeing, for example, Peter's dirty shoes, the speaker concludes that he must have been playing in the garden. Once again, however, other interpretations of (24)–(25) are not excluded either. Note that there is no structural difference (word order, stress) between the expression of necessity and that of inferential possibility; consequently without contextual help it is normally impossible to decide which reading is at stake. Furthermore, there is no essential difference between the inferential meaning expressed by means of 'must' and that rendered with the help of 'can', the former is slightly stronger than the latter ('x is more possible than y'). That is, both (25) and (23), as well as (26) and (24) mean inferential possibility but the speaker by choosing (24) and (25) instead of (26) and (27) must have stronger evidence in support of (24) and (25) than in support of (26) and (27).

(26) *Pisti otthon lehet.*
Steve at-home can-be
'Steve can be at home'

(27) *Péter a kertben játszhat.*
Peter the garden-in play-can
'Peter may be playing in the garden'

Two conclusions may be drawn from the above observations: (i) epistemic possibility is a scalar phenomenon: a certain state of affairs can be more possible than another one; (ii) in Hungarian modality is possibility based.

3 On the semantics of modal particles and modal adverbials

Hungarian has a considerable number of particles; some of them express the speaker's attitudes toward a state-of-affairs (e.g. *sajnos* 'unfortunately'), some others may have a logical function, often in addition to a pragmatic function (e.g. *csak* 'only'), and yet others carry a modal meaning. In the majority of cases the modal meaning is epistemic and inferential, but there are two modal adverbials which express boulomaic possibility (*remélhetőleg* 'hopefully', *lehetőleg* 'as far as possible'). The set of modal particles includes the particles *aligha* 'hardly', *alighanem* 'most likely, presumably', *állítólag* 'supposedly', *bizonnyal* 'certainly, surely', *esetleg* 'perhaps, possibly', *kétségkívül* 'undoubtedly', *nyilván* 'evidently' , *talán* 'perhaps' and *tényleg* 'really'; the adverbials *biztosan* 'surely, certainly', *feltehetően* 'presumably, supposedly', *kétségtelenül* 'undoubtedly', *nyilvánvalóan* 'evidently, obviously', *természetesen* 'naturally', *valószínűleg* 'probably', *vitathatatlanul* 'unquestionably' belong to the set of modal adverbials, which are derived from adjectives. As can be seen, modal particles and modal adverbials are different as to their morphological make-up but, as we shall see immediately, not so much with respect to their semantics. They are like the expressions of inferential epistemic possibility with which they share the properties discussed in 2.1.–2.4. Without exception all modal particles and modal adverbials are non-propositional.

(28) a. *Péter ma nyilván otthon dolgozik.*
Peter today evidently at-home works
'Evidently, Peter is working at home today.'
'Peter must be working at home today'
b. *Péter ma nyilván nem otthon dolgozik.*
Peter today evidently not at-home works
'Evidently, Peter is not working at home today'
c. *Péter ma nyilván nem dolgozik otthon.*
'Evidently, Peter is not working at home today'

As shown by (28b, c) the modal particle lies outside of the scope of negation. It is also worth noting that there is no difference in meaning between the sentences (b) and (c). This holds also true for modal adverbials as well, as shown in (29a–c).

(29) a. *Péter ma valószínűleg otthon dolgozik.*
Peter today probably at-home works
'Peter is probably working at home today'
b. *Péter ma valószínűleg nem otthon dolgozik.*
'Peter is probably not working at home today'

Both the modal particle *nyilván* 'evidently' in (28b) and the modal adverb *valószínűleg* 'probably' in (29b) lie outside of the scope of negation. We saw in section 2.1. that sentences expressing inferential possibility cannot be negated.

Since sentences (28a) and (29a), too, express inferential possibility, our observations can be generalized as in (30a,b).

(30) a. *NEG(Mod p)
b. Mod(NEG p)

where p is the propositional content of the sentence, NEG stands for negation and Mod for the modalizing operator.

The meanings of the modal particles and adverbials are notoriously vague. Only a detailed analysis of each individual modal can reveal their typical uses, though – as testified by the analyses proposed thus far – even such analyses cannot do justice to the full range of possible uses of the modal.[11]

It is worth noting that not all modal particles and modal adverbials have an evidential meaning. For example, the particles *aligha* 'hardly' and *talán* 'perhaps' do not seem to have any evidential meaning. The same is true of the modal adverbials *természetesen* 'naturally' and *nyilván* 'evidently'. On the other hand, some particles and adverbials have an evidential meaning but lack any modal meaning. E.g. *állítólag* 'supposedly', *látszólag* 'seemingly', *tudvalevően* 'as known', *lényegében* 'essentially', *esetleg* 'by accident, incidentally', etc.

It would seem that, in general, the modal value expressed by a modal particle or modal adverbial is weaker than the one expressed by a modal verb. Kratzer (1991: 644–645) has illustrated this using the following examples.

(31) a. *Michl must be the murderer.*
b. *Michl is probably the murderer.*
c. *There is a good possibility that Michl is the murderer.*
d. *Michl might be the murderer.*
e. *There is a slight possibility that Michl is the murderer.*
f. *There is a slight possibility that Michl is not the murderer.*
g. *Michl is more likely to be the murderer than Jakl.*

11 The difficulties that may arise in analyzing the meaning of a modal particle or a modal adverbial are clearly demonstrated by the analysis of the modal particle *biztosan* 'surely' proposed in Kugler (2002: 141–144). Some modal adverbials are derived from adjectives. Such is the case with *biztosan* 'surely', which is derived from *biztos*' sure. However, the sentence *Péter biztosan otthon van* 'Peter is surely at home' may have two different meanings. One is equivalent with *Biztos, hogy Péter otthon van* 'It is sure that Peter is at home', the other is evidential and means something like 'certainly, no doubt'. If the speaker wants to make sure that his message is properly understood she will have to add the modifier *egész(en)* 'quite'. Cf. *Péter egész biztosan otthon van* 'Peter is at home with absolute certainty'.

Kratzer argues that in (31a–g) the following implicational relations hold. (a) implies (b), (b) implies (c) and (c) implies (d). At this point the implication relation is reversed: (e) implies (d). Moreover (f) is not compatible with (a) though it is compatible with (b), (c), (d) and (e). However, the problem with this proposal is that representations of inferential modal expressions are not propositions, hence the implications illustrated by (31a-g) cannot be logical implications. Intuitively it seems to be clear that modal particles and adverbials may express various degrees of probability but it seems to be impossible to establish a possibility scale based on objective criteria.

Consider the sentences (32a–e). Each contains a modal adverbial or particle which evaluates the propositional content in a certain way.

(32) a. *A város legfontosabb ipara vitathatlanul a cipőgyártás.*
the city most-important industry indisputably the shoemaking
'The city's most important industry is indisputably shoe production'
b. *A város legfontosabb ipara alighanem a cipőgyártás.*
'The city's most important industry is most likely shoe production'
c. *A város legfontosabb ipara feltehetőleg a cipőgyártás.*
'The city's most important industry is supposedly shoe production'
d. *A város legfontosabb ipara talán a cipőgyártás.*
'The city's most important industry is perhaps shoe production'
e. *A város legfontosabb ipara aligha a cipőgyártás.*
'The city's most important industry is hardly shoe production'

Intuitively, it would seem that on the basis of sentences such as (32a–e) the following possibility scale can be established:

(33) *vitathatatlanul > alighanem > feltehetőleg > talán > aligha*
'indisputably' 'most likely' 'supposedly' 'perhaps' 'hardly'

The adverbial *vitathatalanul* p 'indisputably p' excludes the possibility of *neg* p, *alighanem* p 'most likely p' means that p is more likely to be the case than neg p, *feltehetőleg* p 'supposedly p' means that p is probably the case, *talán* p 'perhaps p' means that p may be the case but non-p is not excluded either, and finally *aligha* p 'hardly p' means that p is almost excluded. That is, *vitathatatlanul p* seems to express necessity rather than possibility, *alighanem p weak* necessity, *feltehetőleg p* strong possibility, *talán p* accidental possibility, and *aligha p* means that *p* is almost completely excluded. It should be made clear, however, that these characterizations are extremely approximative and far from being precise, yet they may show that modal adverbials and particles do reflect a possibility scale.[12]

Contrary to expectation, the various modal adverbials and particles are not always interchangeable, which shows that they do not differ in the degree of possibility only.

(34) a. *A városnak vitathatatlanul hatalmas értelmiségi gárdája van.*
the city-Dat without-any-doubt important intellectual guards has
'Without any doubt the city must have an important intellectual class'
b. *A városnak talán hatalmas értemiségi gárdája van.*
'The city has perhaps an important intellectual class'
c. **A városnak aligha hatalmas értelmiségi gárdája van.*
'The city has hardly an important intellectual class'
d. *A városnak aligha van hatalmas értelmiségi gárdája.*

As shown by (34c, d), the modal particle *aligha* 'hardly' must occupy the position immediately preceding the verb (the predicate) while this is not required by the other particles. The particle *aligha* has a negative meaning, it almost implies the negation of the existence of a certain state-of-affairs, and, like the negative particle, it occupies the focus position in the sentence.

The adverbial *esetleg* 'by chance, incidentally, by accident, perhaps', too expresses possibility. Consider

(35) a. *Ez a beszédzavarokkal, bénulással, esetleg hirtelen hallálal*
this speech disorder paralysis perhaps sudden death
járó gutaütés.
consequence stroke

'Stroke is accompanied by speech disorder, paralysis and perhaps sudden death'

The adverbial *esetleg* differs from most of the modal adverbials by occurring in the premise of a conditional, in questions, and it can also be embedded under the verb 'know'.

12 For a more detailed discussion based on corpus examples cf. Kiefer 2005.

(36) a. *Ha esetleg megtalálnád az idézet helyét, szóljál.*
'If you find by chance the source of the citation, inform me'
b. *Te is velünk tartanál esetleg?*
'Would you also come with us by any chance?'
c. *Tudom, hogy a pénz esetleg még megjöhet.*
'I know that the money may still arrive'

From the above examples we may draw the conclusion that the adverbial *esetleg* cannot express evidential possibility though it does express the speaker's evaluation of the given state-of-affairs.

The above discussion has also shown that what modal adverbials have in common is the adverbial function and the epistemic meaning but they may (and they do) differ from each other in quite a few other aspects.

4 Conclusion

The aim of the present paper was to provide an overview of epistemic expressions in Hungarian. We saw that in Hungarian possibility and necessity can be expressed by verbs, by a verbal suffix, by adverbials and particles. As far as adverbials and particles are concerned Hungarian does not have any particular features that would distinguish it from Standard Average European (Haspelmath 2001). The fact that possibility is expressed by a verbal suffix is, no doubt, a feature which is not part of Standard Average European and it is not shared by the other Ugric languages, in fact, it does not even occur in the languages of the larger Finno-Ugric family. More interesting is the systematic distinction made between plain epistemic possibility and inferential possibility (probability). This is made possible by the fact that word order in Hungarian is relatively free and that the focused constituent must normally occupy the position immediately preceding the verb.

References

Dressler, Wolfgang U. 1989. Prototypical differences between inflection and derivation. *Zeitschrift für Phonetik, Sprachwissenschaft und Kommunikationsforschung* 42. 3–10.

Haspelmath, Martin. 2001. The European linguistic area: Standard Average European. In Martin Haspelmath, Ekkehard König, Wulf Oesterreicher & Wolfgang Raible (eds.), *Language Typology and Language Universals*, 1492–1510. Berlin & New York: Mouton de Gruyter.

Hintikka, Jaako. 1962. *Knowledge and Belief.* Ithaca: Cornell University Press.
Kiefer, Ferenc. 2000. Modality. In Jef Verschueren, Jan-Ola Östman, Jan Blommaert & Chris Bulcaen (eds.), *Handbook of Pragmatics*, 1–36. Amsterdam & New York: John Benjamins: Amsterdam.
Kiefer, Ferenc. 2005. *Lehetőség és szükségszerűség. Tanulmányok a nyelvi modalitás köréből.* Budapest: Tinta Könyvkiadó.
Kratzer, Angelika. 1978. *Semantik der Rede. Kontexttheorie – Modalwörter – Konditionalsätze.* Kronberg: Scriptor.
Kratzer, Angelika. 1991. Modality. In Arnim von Stechow & Dieter Wunderlich (eds.), *Semantik/Semantics*, 639–650. Berlin & New York: Mouton de Gruyter.
Kugler, Nóra. 2002. *Módosítószók a magyar nyelv szófaji rendszerében*. Budapest: Osiris Kiadó.
Lyons, John. 1977. *Semantics* Vols. I–II. Cambridge: Cambridge University Press.
Szabolcsi, Anna. 1981. The semantics of topic-focus articulation. In Jeroen Groenendijk, Theo Janssen & Martin Stokhof (eds.), *Formal Mehods in the Study of Language*, 513–541. Amsterdam: Mathematisch Centrum.

Zuzana Vokurková

Epistemic modalities in spoken Tibetan

Abstract: This article will discuss the main means of expressing epistemic modalities in spoken Tibetan and will demonstrate that these are not expressed by modal verbs, as is the case with many languages of the world but by other lexical and grammatical means. These lexical means include, in particular, epistemic adverbs. The chief grammatical means to be found in the spoken language are morpho-syntactic, consisting of a system of epistemic verb endings, which will be discussed in detail in this article from a formal and functional point of view. It will further illustrate the use of epistemic verb endings in different syntactic structures, i.e. their compatibility with various verb constructions and verb classes, including their use with secondary verbs (modal, aspectual and directional).

Keywords: epistemicity/epistemic modalities, epistemic verb endings, epistemic adverbs, evidentiality

1 Introduction

In various languages, epistemic modalities are expressed by different lexical and grammatical means, e.g. modal verbs and affixes. As regards the lexical expression, apart from modal verbs, epistemic meanings may also be encoded in the lexicon by means of epistemic verbs (verbs of cognition, such as believe, guess, be sure, doubt, think), epistemic adverbs (e.g. probably, likely, maybe, possibly) (Givón 1984: 318) or by other epistemic expressions. In Tibetan,[1] possibility and probability are not conveyed by modal verbs but by other lexical and grammatical means. The most frequent lexical means of conveying epistemic meanings in Tibetan is the use of epistemic adverbs but other lexical means are also common in the spoken language (see Section 2).

1 In this paper, the term Tibetan corresponds to the dialect of Lhasa and its neighbourhood, which is a variety of central Tibetan (*dbus.skad*). It is used as the *lingua franca* in the Tibetan autonomous region and in the Tibetan diaspora (India, Nepal, U.S.A., Europe). It is spoken by about one and a half million people, 130 000 of whom live in the diaspora.

Note: I base this paper on my research work done in Tibet, the results of which are summarized in my PhD. dissertation "Epistemic modalities in spoken Standard Tibetan" (Vokurková 2008) and in *Epistemic modality in standard spoken Tibetan: Epistemic verbal endings and copulas* (Vokurková 2017). Most examples in this paper originate from my research work in Tibet.

Zuzana Vokurková, Charles University in Prague

https://doi.org/10.1515/9783110572261-014

The world's languages also use various grammatical means for conveying modality, whether morphological and syntactic, such as modal particles, verb affixes, or word order. The most characteristic means of expressing epistemic meanings in Tibetan are verb affixes that I designate "epistemic verb endings". In Tibetan, there are two groups of verb endings:

1. Evidential verb endings, which principally express an evidential meaning and certain information, i.e. the speaker presents her/his utterance as certain (example 1).[2]
2. Epistemic verb endings, which principally convey an epistemic meaning. By using these endings, the speaker expresses different degrees of certainty of the actuality of her/his utterance (example 2).[3]

(1) *mo.rang* *lha.sa- r* *'gro-gi.red*
she Lhasa-OBL go (PRS)-FUT+FACT
'She will go to Lhasa.'

(2) *mo.rang* *lha.sa- r* *'gro-gi.yod.kyi.red*
she Lhasa-OBL go (PRS)-IMPF+EPI 2+FACT
'In all likelihood, she will go to Lhasa.'

2 Lexical expression of epistemic meanings

2.1 Epistemic adverbs

Epistemic adverbs are the most important lexical means of expressing epistemic modalities in spoken Tibetan. They may appear either with evidential or epistemic verb endings. The co-occurrence of epistemic adverbs with evidential verb endings is a common way of expressing epistemic modalities (ex. 3a with the epistemic adverb *phal.cher* and the evidential verb ending *gi.red*). Nonetheless, Tibetans often utter sentences with an epistemic verb ending either combined with an epistemic adverb, as in example (3c) with both the epistemic adverb *phal.*

2 For evidentiality see: Aikhenvald 2004, 2011; Aikhenvald and Dixon 2003; Barnes 1984; Chafe and Nichols 1986; Guentchéva 1996; Guentchéva and Landaburu 2007; Johanson and Utas 2000; Tournadre and LaPolla 2014; for evidentiality in Tibetan see: Hu 1989; Garrett 2001; Mélac 2014; Oisel 2013; Tournadre and Sangda Dorje 2003; Wang 1994; Zhou and Xie 2003.

3 For epistemicity, see: Boye 2006; Choi 1995; Nuyts 2001; for epistemicity in Tibetan see: Hu 1989; Tournadre and Sangda Dorje 2003; Tournadre and Shao [to be published]; Vokurková 2008, 2009, 2011, 2017; Wang 1994; Zhou and Xie 2003.

cher and the epistemic ending *gi.yod.kyi.red*, or without it as in example (3b) with the epistemic verb ending *gi.yod.kyi.red*.

(3) a. *mo.rang* *phal.cher* *yong-gi.red*
she probably come-FUT+FACT
'She will probably come.'
b. *mo.rang* *yong-gi.yod.kyi.red*
she come-IMPF+EPI 2+FACT
'She will probably come.'
c. *mo.rang* *phal.cher* *yong-gi.yod.kyi.red*
she probably come-IMPF+EPI 2+FACT
'She will probably come.'

As a matter of fact, in epistemic contexts Tibetans often prefer uttering a sentence that includes an epistemic adverb than without it to stress that they are not certain about what they say as in (3a) and (3c). They tend to use epistemic adverbs, no matter whether the verb ending is evidential[4] or epistemic. In sentences containing both an epistemic adverb and an epistemic ending (as in example 3c), the use of the epistemic adverb depends on the type of epistemic verb ending employed and more importantly, on the speaker's degree of certainty. It is true that the epistemic adverb is often the primary means for determining the degree of probability of an utterance, but epistemic meaning as a whole is also influenced by other linguistic and pragmatic indicators (for example, intonation or the speaker's idiolect). Furthermore, in example (3a), Tibetan consultants suggest that the degree of the speaker's certainty is higher than in examples (3b) and (3c). This is due to the fact that example (3a) contains an evidential ending, which generally conveys the speaker's certainty (100%).

4 They are, however, not used with sensory evidentials (direct evidentials in Garrett's terminology, see Garrett 2001: 87):
a) *khyed.rang- gi* *deb* *ga.par* *yod.red/'dug*
you+H -GEN book where exist (FACT/SENS)
'Where is your book?'
b) *gcig.byas.na* *nyal.khri* *sgang- la* *yod/yod.red/* 'dug*
maybe bed top-OBL exist (EGO/FACT/SENS)
gcig.byas.na *sa* *sgang- la* *yod/yod.red/* 'dug*
maybe floor top-OBL exist (EGO/FACT/SENS)
'Maybe it's on the bed, maybe it's on the floor.'

Epistemic adverbs differ in the degree of certainty they convey: some adverbs express possibility (close to 50%) such as *gcig.byas.na* 'perhaps', 'maybe', others convey a stronger degree of probability such as *phal.cher* 'possibly' or 'probably' and some adverbs that are used in epistemic contexts express near-absolute certainty (close to 100%) such as *gtan.gtan* 'certainly' or 'surely'. Compare the examples below:

(4) *gcig.byas.na mo.rang lha.sa- r 'gro-gi.red*
perhaps she Lhasa-OBL go (PRS)-FUT+FACT
'She will perhaps go to Lhasa.'

(5) *mo.rang gtan.gtan lha.sa-r 'gro-gi.red*
she certainly Lhasa-OBL go (PRS)-FUT+FACT
'She will certainly go to Lhasa.'

The following epistemic adverbs are common in spoken Tibetan:

gcig.byas.na: 'perhaps', 'maybe' or 'possibly' (bKrashis Tsering, Liu 1991, example 4)
phal.cher: 'possibly', 'maybe' or 'perhaps' (bKrashis Tsering, Liu 1991), 'most probably, most likely' (Goldstein 2001, examples 3a and 3c).
spyir.btang: 'in general', 'generally' or 'usually' (Goldstein 2001, example 6).
yang.na: This adverb is usually used in the disjunctive function of 'or' (Goldstein 2001) but may also convey an epistemic meaning of 'perhaps' or 'maybe' (example 7).
ha.lam: 'nearly, 'more or less', 'approximately', 'roughly' (Goldstein 2001)
yin.cig.min.cig: 'in any case', 'without fail' (Goldstein 2001), 'necessarily' or 'absolutely'
gtan.gtan: 'certainly' or 'surely' (Goldstein 2001, example 5).
brgya.cha brgya: Its literal translation is 'one hundred percent' (Goldstein 2001) and it can be translated in English as 'definitely'.

(6) *spyir.bstang nga chu.tshod gnyis.pa tsam-la nang-la slebs-song*
in general I hour second about- home-OBL arrive-PFV+SENS
'I must have got back home by two o'clock.'

(7) *bstan.pa yang.na rgya.nag-la 'gro-gi.yod.kyi.red*
Tenpa maybe China- OBL go (PRS)-IMPF+EPI 2+FACT
'Maybe, Tenpa will go to China.'

As can be seen in the above examples (3) – (7), epistemic adverbs precede or follow the subject of the sentence. Some of them may be used in both positions, some not. They are usually stressed when used at the beginning of a sentence.

2.2 Epistemic verbs and epistemic nominal constructions

In spoken Tibetan, there are various other lexical means than epistemic adverbs that convey an epistemic meaning, such as verbs of cognition, nominal constructions having an epistemic meaning, etc. As for epistemic verbs, note the following example with the epistemic verb *bsams* 'think' (8):

(8) *nga-s cog.tse-'i sgang-la bzhag- yod bsams-byung*
I-ERG table-GEN top-OBL put-PERF+EGO think-PFV+EGO
'I thought I left it on the table. (Context: An answer to the question where the key is. The speaker believes that the key is on the table but is not sure.)'

Furthermore, there are nominal constructions containing a noun or an adjective that have an epistemic meaning, such as the expression with the adjective *'dra.po* 'similar' and the existential copula *'dug/mi.'dug*, meaning literally 'It seems/doesn't seem to be like this...' as in (9), and the expression with the noun *nyen.kha* meaning 'danger' (10) and an existential copula. These expressions are frequently used in the spoken language:

(9) *nyi.ma-la dgongs.pa rag-pa 'dra.po mi.'dug*
Nyima-OBL vacation get-NOM similar exist (NEG+SENS)
'It doesn't seem like Nyima got vacation. (The speaker guesses from the expression on Nyima's face. Nyima looked annoyed as he left the boss's office.)'

(10) *khong-tsho spo.lo thob-yag-gi nyen.kha yod.red*
s/he (H)-PL ball gain-NOM-GEN danger exist (FACT)
'They risk winning the match. Or: They will probably win the match. (Lit.: 'There is a danger of their winning the ball.' Context: While talking about an upcoming match, the speaker thinks so because they are a strong team.)'

Another example of an expression having an epistemic meaning is a conditional clause *nga-s byas-na* which corresponds to the English 'I think' or 'My opinion is' (literally 'If I do it'), as shown in example (11):

(11) *nga-s byas-na kho.rang nang-la yod.ma.red*
I- ERG do (PAS)-if he home-OBL exist (FACT+NEG)
'I don't think he is at home.'

3 Grammatical expression of epistemic meanings

As stated above, epistemic modalities are in spoken Tibetan often conveyed by epistemic verb endings. These verb endings have two fundamental functions: they express the tense-aspect and epistemic modality (Tournadre & Sangda Dorje 2003: 175–176; Vokurková 2008, 2017). This paper will concentrate on the system of these verb endings because they are the most characteristic means for expressing epistemic modalities in spoken Tibetan. The use of epistemic verb endings is illustrated by the following sentences with the epistemic endings *pa.'dra* (12) and *yod.pa.yod* (13). Example (13) expresses a similar meaning as the above example (8):

(12) *nga-r* *yi.ge* *'byor-pa.'dra*
I-OBL letter get-PERF+EPI 2+SENS
'It seems that I got a letter. (Context: The speaker can see a letter on the table.)'

(13) *nga-s* *cog.tse-'i* *sgang-la* *bzhag-yod.pa.yod*
I- ERG table-GEN top-OBL put-PERF+EPI 2+EGO
'I thought I left it on the table. Or: I must have left it on the table. (Context: A reply to the question where the key is.)'

3.1 Formal analysis of epistemic verb endings

There are several different types of epistemic verb endings that are used fairly frequently in spoken Tibetan.[5] Some of these types are paradigmatic, i.e. they are comprised of three different endings, each of them referring to a different tense-aspect (e.g. *yod.kyi.red*),[6] and others are not (e.g. *pa.yod*).[7] These are: *yod.pa.'dra, yod.kyi.red, yod.sa.red, yod.'gro, a.yod, yod.pa.yod, yod-mdog.kha.po-red/'dug, yong.nga.yod, pa.'dug, pa.yod, mi.yong.ngas.*

Consisting of nominalizers and verb auxiliaries, most of the epistemic verb endings were diachronically formed by a process of 'double suffixation'. Tense-aspect is often expressed by the first morpheme and epistemic modality by the second morpheme. During the process of double suffixation a new modal meaning (epistemic

5 In literary Tibetan, there are also several ways of expressing epistemic modality. The most common means in spoken Tibetan, epistemic copulas and epistemic verb endings, occur in literary Tibetan as well (see *Bod-rgya tshig-mdzod chen-mo* 1993, Goldstein 2001, *Bod-kyi-dus-bab* [Tibet Times]). Some of the endings are common for literary and spoken Tibetan, but the majority of them are only used either in literary or in spoken Tibetan.

6 I choose the perfective past form to represent each type of endings.

7 See Section 3.2.1.

modality) developed and this meaning is mainly conveyed by the second part of the new suffix (e.g. *gi.yod.pa.'dra*, *yod.sa.red*). For example, consider the epistemic verb ending *gi.yod-pa.'dra* where the first morpheme *gi.yod* corresponds to the imperfective and the second morpheme *pa.'dra* expresses probability. Nevertheless, this morphemic analysis does not work for all epistemic verb endings, e.g. *mi.yong.ngas*, *pa.yod*, which cannot be divided in two morphemes. As a result, epistemic endings are treated as non-analysable units in this paper, i.e. they are written with dots between syllables, not with a hyphen showing the morphemic structure. The synchronic representation of epistemic verb endings is, therefore, TA+EPI+EVI (tense-aspect + epistemic modality + evidentiality), and not TA-EPI(+EVI).

Epistemic verb endings may be classified according to the parameter of polarity into affirmative and negative endings.[8] In general, affirmative epistemic endings convey positive polarity and negative epistemic endings[9] negative polarity. As a rule, whenever it is possible to use an affirmative verb ending, it is also possible to use its negative counterpart. Diachronically, negative polarity is frequently expressed by the second morpheme of the epistemic ending as illustrated in example (14): (14a) with the affirmative ending *gi.yod-sa.red* is positive and (14b) with the negative ending *gi.yod-sa.ma.red* is negative. However, there are exceptions, e.g. the type *kyi.yod-pa.'dra*, as this type expresses negative polarity in the first morpheme: compare example (15a) with the affirmative ending *kyi.yod-pa.'dra*, and (15b) with the negative ending *kyi.med-pa.'dra*:

(14) a. *kho.rang* *slob.grwa-r* *'gro-gi.yod.sa.red*
he school-OBL go (PRS)-IMPF+EPI 2+SENS
'He probably goes to school. (Context: A reply to the question whether he goes to school. The speaker can observe that the person in question is a child.)'

b. *kho.rang* *slob.grwa-r* *'gro -gi.yod.sa.ma.red*
he school-OBL go (PRS)-IMPF+EPI 2+SENS+NEG
'He probably doesn't go to school. (Context: A reply to the question whether he goes to school. The speaker can observe that the person in question is a nomad.)'

8 There are differences in acceptability concerning certain negative endings between the Tibetans living in Tibet and those in the diaspora. The latter admit some negative forms that are rejected in Lhasa, e.g. *gi.med.sa.red*. The form used in Lhasa is *gi.yod.sa.ma.red*.

9 Diachronically, negative endings are formed by adding the negative morphemes *ma* or *mi* to the affirmative ending, or by using the negative auxiliaries *med*, *min* instead of their affirmative counterparts.

(15) a. *khong mo.Ta btang shes-kyi.yod.pa.'dra*
s/he+H car VBZ know-IMPF+EPI 2+SENS
'It seems he knows how to drive. (Context: The speaker can see the person's behaviour before starting the car.)'

b. *khong mo.Ta btang shes-kyi.med.pa.'dra*
s/he+H car VBZ know-IMPF+EPI 2+SENS+NEG
'It seems he doesn't know how to drive. (Context: The speaker can see the person's behaviour before starting the car.)'

Some types are formally negative (positive) but semantically positive (negative), for example the formally negative endings *med.'gro'o* (pronounced with a rising intonation, *med.'gro'o* has positive polarity while negative polarity is expressed by the formally positive ending *yod.'gro'o*)[10] and *mi.yong.ngas* (containing the negative particle *mi* but having positive polarity, example 17). See the example below, in which (16a) is formally negative (diachronically containing the negative auxiliary *med*) but semantically positive; and (16b) formally positive (diachronically containing the affirmative auxiliary *yod*) but semantically negative (it is sometimes used in a similar way as questions):

(16) a. *las.ka 'di khong-gis byed-kyi.med.'gro'o*
work this s/he+H-ERG do (PRS)-IMPF+EPI 1+FACT
'She probably does this work. (Context: A reply to the question who does the work.)'

b. *las.ka 'di khong-gis byed-kyi.yod.'gro'o*
work this s/he+H-ERG do (PRS)-IMPF+EPI 1+FACT+NEG
'She probably doesn't do this work. Or: Does she (really) do this work?'

(17) *nga cham.pa brgyab-mi.yong.ngas*
I a cold VBZ-FUT+EPI 1+EGO
'It feels like I am catching a cold. Or: I might be catching a cold. (Context: The weather is cold and the speaker is not feeling well.)'

3.2 Functional analysis of epistemic endings

In this section, epistemic verb endings will be discussed from a semantic and functional point of view. These endings can be principally classified according to the tense-aspect they refer to, the degree of probability and the evidential

10 In these endings, the rising intonation is marked by *'o*. With a falling intonation, *yod.'gro* is both formally and semantically positive. For a detailed analysis see Vokurková (2017: 101–111).

meaning (see Sections 3.2.1 – 3.2.3). This is illustrated by the following examples with the epistemic endings *gyi.yod.'gro* and *yod.pa.'dra*. In example (18), *gyi.yod.'gro* is interpreted as the imperfective future, epistemic degree 1 and the factual evidential. In example (19), *yod.pa.'dra* corresponds to the present perfect, epistemic degree 2 and the sensory evidential.

(18) *zla.ba rang-la spo.lo gyar-gyi.yod.'gro*
Dawa you-OBL ball lend-IMPF+EPI 1+FACT
'Dawa might lend you the ball. (Context: A reply to the question whether Dawa will lend the ball to the person asking this question. The speaker infers from the fact that, for example, friends, in general, lend things to each other.)'

(19) *nyi.ma phyin tshar-yod.pa.'dra*
Nyima go (PAS) finish-PERF+EPI 2+SENS
'It seems Nyima has already left. (Context: A reply to the question where Nyima is. The speaker cannot see Nyima's coat so she/he thinks that Nyima has probably left.)'

The relation of epistemic verb endings to the category of person will be analysed in Section 3.2.4. Furthermore, epistemic verb endings may also be characterized according to the degree of frequency with which they are used and the parameter of geographic variation, which is closely connected to this issue (Section 3.2.5.). Last but not least, epistemic endings may also convey other (secondary) meanings: deontic and other modal meanings such as hope, surprise, obligation, disagreement, and regret.[11] In determining these meanings, one has to consider illocutionary modalities and speech acts (Palmer 1986).[12] For example, some epistemic endings used in spoken Tibetan diachronically consist of the nominalizer *rgyu* and an essential (stative) epistemic auxiliary (e.g. *yin.sa.red*), for example *rgyu.yin.sa.red* in (20). These are used in future-tense contexts. Apart from the epistemic and evidential meanings, they also have the deontic meaning of obligation.

(20) *las.ka 'di rang-gis byed-rgyu.yin.sa.red*
work this you-ERG do (PRS)-FUT+EPI 2+SENS+DEO

11 They also mark the speaker's non-engagement or non-commitment with respect to the actuality of her/his utterance (see Oisel 2006).

12 Prosody also has an influence on the semantic interpretation of sentences containing an epistemic ending.

'It seems you have to do the work. (Context: The speaker bases herself/himself on a visual observation that someone is the only person left in the office. All the others left.)'

3.2.1 Markers of tense-aspect

In spoken Tibetan, there are several types of epistemic endings that are fairly frequently used. The majority of these types are paradigmatic, i.e. they are comprised of three different endings, each of them referring to a different tense-aspect.[13] Formally, all these endings consist of two morphemes. The first morpheme is always identical for those endings that express the same tense-aspect (e.g. *gi.yod* for all imperfective endings, i.e. *gi.yod.pa.'dra*, *gi.yod.sa.red*, *gi.yod.bzo.'dug*). The second morpheme differs (e.g. *pa.'dra*, *sa.red*, *bzo.'dug*). The epistemic paradigm is presented in the tables below and illustrated by example with the type *yod.kyi.red* (21).[14]

1 The perfective ending with the first morpheme *pa.yin* is used with the past perfective.
2 The perfect ending with the first morpheme *yod* is used with the past, with past events having relevance to the present, and at times with the immediate present.
3 The imperfective ending with the first morpheme *gi.yod* (or *kyi.yod, gyi.yod*)* is used with the imperfective past, the long-term present and the future.

13 For some contexts, combinations of the nominalizer *mkhan* and the essential (stative) auxiliaries are used in the spoken language. These combinations show the process of incorporation of a nominalizer and an auxiliary in one suffix and the process of development of a new meaning of the combination, in this case "a planned action". This process of grammaticalization has, however, not yet been concluded and generalized for these combinations (See Vokurková 2007).

Moreover, some native speakers living in the diaspora accept other (future) endings than those mentioned in the following table, but these are considered ungrammatical by the Lhasa informants. Diachronically, these endings consist of the nominalizer *gi* and the auxiliary *yin* followed by a second morpheme, e.g. *gi.yin.'gro* (see Vokurková 2017:64).

14 The paradigmatic epistemic endings which are frequently used in the spoken language and form the same paradigm as the type *yod.kyi.red* are: *yod.'gro* (i.e. *pa.yin.'gro, yod.'gro, gi.yod.'gro*) + the ending *'gro; yod.pa.'dra* (i.e. *pa.yin.pa.'dra, yod.pa.'dra, gi.yod.pa.'dra*) + the perfect ending *pa.'dra; yod.sa.red* (i.e. *pa.yin.sa.red, yod.sa.red, gi.yod.sa.red*) + the future ending *sa.red; yod.pa.yod* (i.e. *pa.yin.pa.yod, yod.pa.yod, gi.yod.pa.yod*), the type *a.yod* differs in that the morpheme *a* is placed between the nominalizer and the auxiliary (i.e. *pa.a.yin, a.yod, gi.a.yod*) + the future ending *a.yong*. There is also an epistemic construction with the epistemic suffix *mdog.kha.po*, e.g. *yod-mdog.kha.po-red/'dug* (for more details see Vokurková 2008, 2017).

Some epistemic endings used in spoken Tibetan are not part of the above paradigm. Non-paradigmatic epistemic endings are: *pa.'dug, pa.yod, yong, mi.yong.ngas*. For more details see Vokurková 2008, 2017.

1	Perfective past	*pa.yin.gyi.red*
2	Present perfect and the immediate present	*yod.kyi.red*
3	Imperfective (past, long-term present and future)	*gi.yod.kyi.red*

Note: **Kyi*, *gi* and *gyi* are allomorphs. Their use depends on the word preceding them. In the spoken language, they are all pronounced in the same way: [*ki*]. See e.g. Kesang Gyurme (1992); Tournadre and Sangda Dorje (2003).

(21) a. *khong rgya.gar-la phyin- pa.yin.gyi.red*
s/he+H India-OBL go (PAS)-PFV+EPI 2+FACT
'Most likely, it is to India that she went. (Context: A reply to the question where the person has gone or whether she went to China or India. The speaker knows that she left. Basing her/his statement on the fact that many Tibetans go to India, she/he states that she went to India.)'

b. *khong rgya.gar-la phyin-yod.kyi.red*
s/he+H India-OBL go (PAS)-PERF+EPI 2+FACT
'She has most probably gone to India. (Context: A reply to the question where the person is. The speaker may know that she has left but not necessarily.)'

c. *khong mgyogs.po rgya.gar-la 'gro-gi.yod.kyi.red*
s/he+H soon India-OBL go (PRS)-IMPF+EPI 2+FACT
'Most likely, she will soon go to India. (Context: A reply to the question when she is going to India. The speaker knows that she planned to go in September. It is the end of August now. So the speaker infers that she will probably leave soon.)'

3.2.2 Markers of epistemic modalities

In this paper, epistemic modality is defined in terms of the degree of the speaker's certainty of the actuality of her/his utterance. The various types of epistemic verb endings differ in this degree of certainty. They can be classified in at least three degrees: EPI 1, EPI 2 and EPI 3. EPI 1 corresponds to weaker probability (>50%); EPI 2 to stronger probability (+–75%); and EPI 3 to the highest probability (<100%).[15] Compare the three degrees of certainty expressed by epistemic verb endings in

15 This classification is based on the author's fieldwork in Tibetan communities (for details see Vokurková 2008, 2017).

the following examples: EPI 1 (22), EPI 2 (23), and EPI 3 (24). All types of epistemic endings are classified according to their degree of probability as follows:

EPI 1, weak probability, >50%: *yod.'gro* and *med.'gro'o, mi.yong.ngas, mdog. kha.po+red/'dug*

(22) *khong-gis* *ja srub.ma* *btungs-yod.'gro*
s/he+H-ERG Tibetan tea drink (PAS)- PERF+EPI 1+FACT
'Maybe, she drank Tibetan tea. (Context: A reply to the question: "What did she drink?" The speaker bases her/his statement on the fact that this is a common drink in Tibet. She is Tibetan. So it is probable that she drank it.)'

EPI 2, strong probability, +/–75%: *yod.kyi.red, yod.sa.red, yod.pa.'dra, yod. pa.yod, yong, yong.nga.yod, yod.bzo.'dug.*

(23) *khong-gis* *ja srub.ma* *btungs-yod.kyi.red*
s/he+H-ERG Tibetan tea drink (PAS)-PERF+EPI 2+FACT
'She probably drank Tibetan tea. (Context: A reply to the question: "What did she drink?" She usually drinks it. So the speaker assumes that it is more probable than not that she drank it this time too.)'

EPI 3, high probability, <100%: *pa.yod, pa.'dug, a.yod*

(24) *khong-gis* *ja srub.ma* *btungs-pa.yod*
s/he+H- ERG Tibetan tea drink (PAS)-PFV+EPI 3+FACT
'She must have been drinking Tibetan tea. (Context: A reply to the question as to what beverage she was drinking. The speaker knows that she loves Tibetan tea. So she/he is almost completely positive that that's what she was drinking.)'

3.2.3 Markers of evidentiality

Although it is not their main function, epistemic verb endings also convey an evidential meaning (see Tournadre and Sangda Dorje 2003: 176, 307 for the types *yod.pa.'dra, yod.kyi.red*, and *pa.yod*). Evidentiality is a characteristic feature of Tibetan (DeLancey 1986; Garrett 2001; LaPolla 2000, 2001; Mélac 2014; Sun 1993; Tournadre and Konchok Jiatso 2001; Tournadre and LaPolla 2014; as well as Tournadre and Sangda Dorje 2003). A complex system of evidentials has developed particularly in the spoken language. Its function is mainly to indicate the *source of information, access to the information*, the *time of acquisition* and the *volitionality* (or *controllability*) of the given action.

There are several classifications of the evidentials employed in spoken Tibetan differing in the terminology. In one classification (Tournadre 1994, 1996; Tournadre and Sangda Dorje 2003; Mélac 2014), the Tibetan evidential system is comprised of two main evidential types: indirect and direct. The indirect type is formed by hearsay, as, for example, when the speaker has obtained information from somebody (or something) else. It is expressed by the quotative marker *za*. This morpheme can follow either a copula or a verb ending but never directly a lexical verb. The direct type of evidential is used when the speaker herself/himself is an essential channel for the information in question. This type consists of four evidentials, each of them highlighting the kind of access to information that the speaker bases her/his utterance on: factual, sensory, inferential, and egophoric. They are expressed by various verb endings. As regards epistemic verb endings, for example, *yod.'gro, yod.kyi.red* and *mdog.kha.po-red* convey a factual meaning; *pa.'dug, yod.pa.'dra* and *mdog.ka.po+'dug* a sensory meaning; and *pa.yod, yod. pa.yod* and *a.yod* an egophoric meaning. Compare the differences in evidentiality in examples (25), (26) and (27) below:

(25) *phru.gu slob.grwa-r phyin-yod.kyi.red*
child school-OBL go (PAS)-PERF+EPI 2+FACT
'The child probably went to school. (Context: A reply to the question as to where the child is. The speaker bases herself/himself on a logical inference, e.g. from the fact that it is Monday morning.)'

(26) *dmag.mi-s lam.khag bkag-yod.pa.'dra*
soldier-ERG road block-PERF+EPI 2+ SENS
'Soldiers most likely blocked the road. (Context: A comment to the question: "Why are there no cars today?" The speaker bases her/his statement on the visual perception that there are no cars in the street.)'

(27) *mo.rang-gis chang bzos-a.yod*
she-ERG Tibetan alcoholic drink make (PAS)-PERF+EPI 3+EGO+NEG
'I doubt she made *chang*. (Context: A reply to the question: "Did she make *chang*?". The speaker bases her/his statement on personal knowledge. She/he knows that she doesn't know how to make it.)'

3.2.4 Participant perspective and epistemic verb endings

Epistemic verb endings are neutral regarding the category of person. They can be used with all persons. But since epistemic verb endings are used to express the speaker's uncertainty in relation to the content of her/his utterance, the agent is usually the third or the second person; the speaker is usually less sure about other persons than about herself/himself. Nonetheless, it is sometimes possible to use an epistemic verb ending with the first person as in examples below. First person sentences often convey other (secondary) meanings than the speaker's mere doubts or hesitation, as is the case of sentences with the third person. Thus they sometimes imply non-voluntary actions, disagreement as in (28), the deontic meaning of wish or hope as in (29), etc.

(28) *gza'.zla.ba-r nga khrom-la phyin- yod.'gro'o*
Monday-OBL I market-OBL go (PAS)-PERF+EPI 1+FACT+NEG
'I do not think I went to the market last Monday. Or: Did I go to the market on Monday? (Context: A comment to someone's saying: "I saw you in the market on Monday.")'

(29) *nga 'gro thub-pa*
I go (PRS) be able-FUT+EPI 3+SENS
'Hopefully, I will be able to walk. Or: I must be able to walk. (An ailing woman comments on her attempts to get up from her seat.)'

There are also restrictions on the use of the first person as the agent of the action with certain epistemic verb endings. In these sentences, the secondary verb *myong* 'to have an experience'[16] is usually inserted after the lexical verb as in example (30b). It is rather rare to combine directly the lexical verb and the present perfect ending, as shown in (30a):

(30) a. ? *nga-s bzas- yod.'gro*
I-ERG eat (PAS)-PERF+EPI 1+FACT
'I think I ate it. (Context: A reply to the question whether the speaker has eaten it before. The speaker does not remember exactly.)'

b. *nga za myong yod.'gro*
I go (PRS) have an experience AUX (EPI 1+FACT)
'I think I have eaten it. (Context: A reply to the question whether the speaker has eaten it before. The speaker does not remember exactly.)'

3.2.5 Geographic variation and frequency

Epistemic verb endings can further be classified according to the parameters of geographic variation and frequency. Native speakers of Lhasa and central Tibet tend to use different types of epistemic verb endings from those located in the

16 See Section 4.3 for details on secondary verbs.

diaspora (for the most part India and Nepal). In the diaspora, the epistemic verb endings with the morpheme *sa* (e.g. *yod.sa.red* in 31a) are the most frequent epistemic type but they are less frequent in central Tibet. Instead, other types of epistemic verb ending are preferred, as in (31b):

(31) a. *pa.sangs-la* *dngul* *rag-yod.sa.red*
Pasang-OBL money get-PFV+EPI 2+SENS
'It seems Pasang got [some] money. (The speaker saw Pasang in the shop buying many items.)'

b. *pa.sangs-la* *dngul* *rag-yod.pa.'dra*
Pasang-OBL money get-PFV+EPI 2+SENS
'It seems Pasang got [some] money. (The speaker saw Pasang in the shop buying many items.)'

Concerning the degree of frequency, some epistemic verb endings are very frequent, e.g. *yod.kyi.red*, *yod.'gro* or *a.yod*, others are less common or rare, e.g. *yong.nga.yod* or *yod.bzo.'dug*. Below are sentences with the frequently used ending *yod.'gro* (32) and the rare ending *pa.yin.bzo.'dug* (33):

(32) *khong-gis* *bod.skad* *rgya.gar-nas* *sbyangs-yod.'gro*
s/he+H-ERG Tibetan l. India-ABL learn- PERF+EPI 1+FACT
'He probably learnt Tibetan in India. (Context: A reply to the question where the person learnt Tibetan. The speaker knows that people often learn Tibetan in India.)'

(33) *khong-gis* *rgya.skad* *pe.cin-nas* *sbyangs-pa.yin.bzo.'dug*
s/he+H-ERG Chinese l. Beijing-ABL learn-PFV+EPI 2+SENS
'It seems it is in Beijing that he learnt Chinese. (Context: A reply to the question where the person learnt Chinese. The speaker thinks so because the person speaks with a Beijing accent.)'

From the point of view of the tense-aspect paradigm, certain verb endings differ in frequency, for example, past epistemic verb endings: since perfective past endings and perfect endings differ in the scope of epistemic modality, they also differ in frequency. Regarding the scope, the use of epistemic perfective past endings (e.g. *pa.yin.gyi.red*) is subject to more constraints than epistemic perfect endings (e.g. *yod.kyi.red*), which are unmarked. Only these can relate to the whole sentence (sentence scope in 34a). On the contrary, the perfective past endings have a more restricted (focused) scope, highlighting one part of the sentence (e.g. the agent, the adverbial, the predicate in 34c). They are not used for sentence scope (34b). As a result, they are infrequent in the spoken language:

(34) a. *mo.rang slebs-a.yod*
she arrive-PERF+EPI 1+EGO+NEG
'I doubt she has arrived. (Context: A reply to the question whether she has arrived.)'

b. **mo.rang slebs-pa.a.yin*
she arrive-PFV+EPI 1+EGO+NEG
Intended: I doubt she arrived.

c. *mo.rang lha.sa-r slebs-pa.a.yin*
she Lhasa-OBL arrive-PFV+EPI 1+EGO+NEG
'I doubt it is in Lhasa that she arrived. (Context: A comment to the statement that she has arrived in Lhasa. The speaker knows that she is on her way but she/he thinks that she has not got as far as Lhasa.)'

4 Use of epistemic verb endings in different syntactic structures

4.1 Compatibility of epistemic verb endings with verb constructions and verb classes

This section is a syntactic analysis of the use of epistemic verb endings in spoken Tibetan. Epistemic endings appear in the same syntactic structures as evidential endings and they usually are combined with verbs of different verb classes. Below are examples with the following verb classes: monovalent (intransitive verbs) as in (35); ergative as in (36), possessive (verbs expressing possession: with the first argument, the semantic owner, marked in the dative and the second argument in the absolutive) as in (37); or affective (verbs of feeling: with the first argument, the semantic receiver, marked in the absolutive and the second argument in the dative) as in (38). Consider the following examples with epistemic verb endings:

(35) *nyi.ma na-pa.yod*
Nyima be ill-PFV+EPI 3+EGO
'Nyima must have been ill. (The speaker knows that Nyima was not feeling well last night. A reply to the question on why Nyima left early last night.)'

(36) *kha.lag 'di khong-gis phal.cher za-gi.yod.kyi.red*
meal this s/he+H-ERG probably eat (PRS)-IMPF+EPI 2+FACT

'She will probably eat this food. (Context: The speaker bases herself/himself on the fact that she usually eats this kind of food.)'

(37) *khong-la* *phru.gu* *skyes-pa.'dra*
s/he+H -OBL child give birth (PAS)-PFV+EPI 2+SENS
'It seems she's had a baby. (Context: A reply to the question where she is. She was about to have a baby and she was in front of her house all the time. Today, she is not there.)'

(38) *khong* *gdon.'dre-la* *zhed-kyi.yod.kyi.ma.red*
s/he+H ghost-OBL be afraid-IMPF+EPI 2+FACT+NEG
'Most likely, she won't be afraid of ghosts. / She is most likely not afraid of ghosts. (Context: A reply to the question whether she is afraid of ghosts. The speaker knows that she is not superstitious.)'

4.2 Restrictions to the use of epistemic verb endings

Unlike evidential verb endings, epistemic verb endings are generally only used in affirmative sentences. They are not employed in interrogative sentences, as shown in example (39a). When forming a question, the speaker generally uses an evidential ending instead of the epistemic ending. This is illustrated by the following example in which only the question in example (39b) with the evidential verb ending *song* and the interrogative particle *ngas* is grammatical:[17]

(39) a. * *khong* *phyin-yod.pa.yod-pas*
s/he+H go (PAS)-PERF+EPI 2+EGO-Q
Intended: Is it likely that he left?

b. A: *khong* *phyin-yod.pa.yod* B: *phyin-song-ngas*
s/he+H go (PAS)-PERF+EPI 2+EGO go (PAS)-PFV+SENS-Q
A: 'It is likely that he left.' B: 'Did he (leave)?'

Epistemic verb endings may appear at the end of a complex sentence but they are normally not used in dependent clauses, as shown in (40). This is also the case

17 Nonetheless, it is possible to employ an interrogative particle with those epistemic verb endings or copulas containing the sensory auxiliary *'dug* as their final element, for example *yod.bzo.'dug*, the construction *mdog.kha.po-'dug* and the ending *pa.'dug*. This type of question is very rare in the spoken language.

of many evidential verb endings, for example **yod.red-tsang*, **red-na*. See the following examples with the conjunctions *tsang* "because" and *na* "if":

(40) a. * *khong* *phyin-pa.yod-tsang...*
s/he+H go (PAS)-PFV+EPI 3+EGO-because
Intended: Since he must have gone ...

b. * *char.pa* *btang -gi.yod.pa.'dra-na...*
rain VBZ -IMPF+EPI 2+SENS-if
Intended: If it looks like rain ...

In complex sentences, epistemic verb endings are often used in the apodosis of conditional sentences. From the point of view of the tense-aspect paradigm (see 3.2.1), certain epistemic verb endings are frequently used (perfect and imperfective), whereas others are not (perfective). The perfect epistemic endings (for example *yod.kyi.red*) are usually used in past conditionals (past counterfactuals) and the imperfective epistemic endings (present-future or future, for example *gi.yod.kyi.red*) in present conditionals (factuals and counterfactuals).

Although conditionals including an epistemic verb ending resemble conditionals with evidential verb endings, the epistemic verb endings partially preserve their epistemic meaning. As can be seen from the English translation, there is a slight difference in the degree of certainty between the sentence containing the epistemic verb ending *pa.yod* (41a) and the evidential verb ending *yod.red* (41b). The difference is between an epistemic verb ending with certainty of <100%, as opposed to an evidential verb ending with a certainty of 100%:

(41) a. *rang-gis ci.ni tog.tsam mang.tsam brgyab-yod-na ja 'di*
you-ERG sugar a little bit more put-PERF-if tea this
zhim.po chags-pa.yod
good become-PFV+EPI 3+EGO
'If you had put just a little bit more sugar into the tea, it almost certainly would have tasted good. (Context: The speaker has just tasted the tea but is not completely certain of her/his own utterance.)'

b. *rang-gis ci.ni tog.tsam mang.tsam brgyab-yod-na ja 'di*
you-ERG sugar a little bit more put-PERF-if tea this
zhim.po chags-yod.red
good become-PERF+FACT
'If you had put a little bit more sugar into the tea, it would have tasted good. (Context: The speaker has just tasted the tea. Unlike (39a), she/he is very certain about what she/he is saying.)'

Furthermore, epistemic verb endings, just as evidential verb endings, may be used in sentences with direct and indirect speech. In these sentences, the epistemic verb ending precedes the 'quotation' particle *ze* as in example (42):

(42) *khong sgo phye dgos-med.'gro'o ze lab-pa.yin*
s/he+H door open need-PERF+EPI 1+FACT RepS say -PFV+EGO
'I said that he might need to open the door. (Context: A reply to the question: "What have you said?")'

4.3 Use of epistemic verb endings with secondary verbs

In Tibetan, between the lexical verb and the verb ending, there is a syntactic position corresponding to that of a 'secondary verb'. The secondary verb specifies the meaning of the lexical verb. In spoken Tibetan, there are about twenty secondary verbs that are frequently used. They include modal, aspectual and directional verbs. There are two types of secondary verbs. The first type (Sec 1) behaves syntactically as a lexical verb and is followed by TAM (tense-aspect-modality) verb endings as in (42) and (44). The secondary verbs of the other type (Sec 2) function like nominalizers and as such can only be followed by verb auxiliaries that are identical to copulas (Vokurková 2002, 2007, 2010, 2017; Heine 1993) as in (43a). From a semantic and syntactic viewpoint, many of the secondary verbs demonstrate a particular characteristic: for example, some are limited to one tense, or some are used to convey more than one meaning.

Since secondary verbs follow the lexical verb in a sentence, they are often combined with verb endings, evidential or epistemic. Their use with verb endings is subject to several restrictions:

Firstly, as stated above, some secondary verbs behave as nominalizers or predicative adjectives that can only combine with auxiliaries, not with verb endings. The verb *'dod* 'want', for example, does not usually combine with an epistemic verb ending, as shown in (43b); it is compatible with epistemic verb auxiliaries as in (43a). Another example is the secondary verb *myong* 'to have an experience' as in (30b) above.

(43) a. *khong slob.grwa chen.mo-r slob.sbyong byed 'dod yod.kyi.red*
s/he+H university-OBL study do (PRS) want AUX (EPI 2+FACT)
'She most probably wants to study at university. (Context: A reply to the question whether she wants to study at university.)'

b. * *khong rgya.skad sbyangs 'dod-kyi.yod.kyi.red*
s/he+H Chinese l. learn want- IMPF+EPI 2+FACT
Intended: 'Most probably, she wants to learn Chinese.'

Second, from a semantic viewpoint and the point of view of the tense-aspect paradigm, each secondary verb combines only with certain lexical verbs and certain epistemic verb endings. As a result, some of the combinations are only applicable for some verb classes and the use of secondary verbs with epistemic verb endings is conditioned by the tense-aspects of the sentence (logical, epistemological, and pragmatic). Let us take the example of the secondary verb *'gro* 'go':

The secondary verb *'gro* 'go' has a variety of grammatical functions. It marks the inchoative and progressive aspects, expresses direction away from the speaker after verbs of movement, and conveys other meanings as well.[18] As an aspectual verb, *'gro* can only combine with non-volitional verbs and imperfective verb endings. It functions as an indicator of the inchoative, progressive and iterative aspects. It is thus compatible with imperfective epistemic endings (e.g. *gi.yod.sa.red*), and it does not combine with present perfect endings (e.g. *yod.sa.red*) as illustrated below:

(44) *zla.ba bcu.pa-'i nang-nas grang.mo chags*
month tenth-GEN inside-ABL cold become
*'gro-gi.yod.sa.red / * phyin-yod.sa.red*
go(PRS)-IMPF+EPI 2+SENS / go (PAS)-PERF+EPI 2+SENS
'It seems it begins to be cold in October. (Context: A reply to the question when the weather gets cold.)' / * 'It seems it began to be cold in October.'

5 Conclusion

The paper has demonstrated that possibility and probability are in spoken Tibetan conveyed both by lexical and grammatical means, and that these two means may be combined. As regards the lexical expression, epistemic meanings are primarily conveyed by epistemic adverbs although there are various other lexical means used in the spoken language (nominal constructions, verbs). However, the most characteristic means of expressing epistemic modality is grammatical. It is a complex system of epistemic verb endings which imply different meanings, the main ones being tense-aspect, epistemic modality and evidentiality.

Since epistemic verb endings are the most complex way of expressing epistemicity in spoken Tibetan, the aim of this paper has been to study these endings

18 For more detail, refer to Tournadre and Konchok Jiatso (2001: 89–96).

from a formal, functional and syntactic viewpoint. From a formal viewpoint, epistemic verb endings can be classified into several epistemic types. From a functional viewpoint, epistemic verb endings are employed to mark the tense-aspect, the epistemic degree and the evidential meaning. As regards the tense-aspect paradigm, most of the epistemic types consist of a perfective ending, a perfect ending and an imperfective ending. Furthermore, the epistemic types can also be classified into three epistemic degrees and they differ in the evidential meaning (factual, sensory, egophoric).

From a syntactic viewpoint, epistemic verb endings are used with different verb classes and in different syntactic structures. They can appear at the end of a complex sentence but they are usually not used in dependent clauses. Moreover, they are, in general, not used in interrogative sentences either. Concerning complex sentences, epistemic verb endings are used in the apodosis of conditional sentences. The perfect epistemic endings (e.g. *yod.pa.'dra*) are used in past conditionals (past counterfactual) and the imperfective epistemic endings (e.g. *gi.yod.pa.'dra*) are used in present conditionals.

This paper has also looked at the possibility of combining secondary verbs (modal, aspecto-temporal and aspecto-directional) with epistemic verb endings in spoken Tibetan. There are several criteria influencing the compatibility of secondary verbs with epistemic verb endings. The main ones are the syntactic and semantic properties of the secondary verb, tense-aspect, the verb class of the preceding lexical verb, the evidential meaning of the verb ending, and the participant perspective.

Abbreviations: ABL – ablative; AUX – auxiliary; DEO – deontic; EGO – egophoric evidential; EPI – epistemic; ERG – ergative; FACT – factual evidential; FUT – future; GEN – genitive; H – honorific; IMPF – imperfective (past, present, future); NEG – negative; OBL – oblique; PAS – past; PFV – perfective past; PERF – perfect; PRS – present; Q – interrogative particle; RepS – reported speech particle; SENS – sensory evidential; VBZ – verbalizer

References

Aikhenvald, Alexandra Y. 2004. *Evidentiality*. Oxford University Press, Oxford.
Aikhenvald, Alexandra Y. 2011. *Evidentials*. Oxford Bibliograpies Online.
Bod-rgya tshig-mdzod chen-mo [Great Tibetan-Chinese Dictionary]. 1993. Two volumes. Minzu chubanshe, Beijing.
Boye, Kasper. 2006. *Epistemic meaning: A cross-linguistic study*. University of Copenhagen: Ph.D. dissertation, ms.

Chafe, Wallace & Johanna Nichols (eds.). 1986. *Evidentiality: The Linguistic Coding of Epistemology*. Norwood, NJ: Ablex.
Garrett, Edward J. 2001. *Evidentiality and assertion in Tibetan*. University of California, Los Angeles: Ph.D. dissertation, ms.
Goldstein, Melvyn (ed.). 2001. *The New Tibetan-English Dictionary of Modern Tibetan*. Berkley, Los Angeles, London: University of California Press.
Guentchéva, Zlatka & Jon Landaburu (eds.). 2007. *L'Énonciation médiatisée II: Le traitement épistémologique de l'information: illustration amérindiennes et caucasiennes*. Louvain-Paris: Éditions Peeters.
Givón, Talmy. 1984. *Syntax. A functional-typological introduction* (two volumes). Amsterdam/Philadelphia: John Benjamins Publishing Company.
Heine, Bernd. 1993. *Auxiliaries. Cognitive Forces and Grammaticalization*. Oxford: Oxford University Press.
Hu, Tan et al. 1989. *Lasa kouyu duben* [A Textbook of Lhasa Dialect]. Beijing: Minzu chubanshe.
Johanson, Lars & Bo Utas (eds.). 2000. *Evidentials: Turkic, Iranian and Neighbouring Languages*. Berlin: Mouton de Gruyter.
Kesang Gyurme. 1992. *Le Clair Miroir*. Translated by Heather Stoddard & Nicolas Tournadre. Paris: Prajna [Translation of skal-bzang 'gyur-med 1981].
bKrashis tsering & Liu Dejun. 1991. *English-Tibetan-Chinese Dictionary*. Beijing: Minzu chubanshe.
LaPolla, Randy John (ed.). 2000. *Linguistics of the Tibeto-Burman Area*. University of California. Volume 23.2.
LaPolla, Randy John (ed.). 2001. *Linguistics of the Tibeto-Burman Area*. University of California. Volume 24.1.
Mélac, Eric. 2014. *L'évidentialité en anglais. Approche contrastive à partir d'un corpus anglais-tibétain*. Université de la Sorbonne nouvelle-Paris 3: Ph.D. Dissertation, ms.
Nuyts, Jean. 2001. *Epistemic Modality, Language, and Conceptualization*. Amsterdam: John Benjamins Publishing Comp.
Oisel, Guillaume. 2006. *Emplois particuliers des suffixes médiatifs non-égophoriques dans le tibétain parlé de Lhassa* (The Particular usages of evidential non-egophoric suffixes in Lhasa Tibetan). Université Paris 8 – Vincennes-Saint-Denis: Master 2 – Linguistique, ms.
Oisel, Guillaume. 2013. *Morphosyntaxe et sémantique des auxiliaires et des connecteurs du tibétain littéraire: étude diachronique et synchronique*. Université de la Sorbonne Nouvelle – Paris 3: PhD. Dissertation, ms.
Palmer, Frank Robert. 1986. *Mood and modality*. Cambridge: Cambridge University Press.
Sun, Jackson Tianshin. 1993. Evidentials in Amdo-Tibetan. *Bulletin of the Institute of History and Philology, Academia Sinica* 63–4. 945–1001.
Tournadre, Nicolas. 1994. Personne et médiatifs en tibétain. *Faits de langues* 3. 149–158.
Tournadre, Nicolas. 1996. Comparaison des systèmes médiatifs de quatre dialectes tibétains (tibétain central, ladakhi, dzongkha et amdo). In Zlatka Guentchéva (ed.). *L'Énonciation médiatisée*, 195–213. Louvain/Paris: Peeters.
Tournadre, Nicolas & Konchok Jiatso. 2001. Final auxiliary verbs in literary Tibetan and in the Dialects. *Linguistics of the Tibeto-Burman Area* 24.1. 49–111.
Tournadre, Nicolas & Randy John LaPolla. 2014. Towards a new approach to evidentiality. Issues and directions for research. *Linguistics of the Tibeto-Burman Area* 37:2. 240–262.
Tournadre, Nicolas & Sangda Dorje. 2003. *Manual of Standard Tibetan. Language and Civilization*. Ithaca, New York: Snow Lions Publications.

Vokurková, Zuzana. 2002. *La modalité en tibétain standard: Compatibilité des verbes secondaires avec les auxiliaires finaux.* Université Paris 8–Saint-Denis: D.E.A. Dissertation, ms.
Vokurková, Zuzana. 2007. The process of grammaticalization of nominalizing morphemes and auxiliaries in spoken Standard Tibetan. In Jaroslav Vacek & Alena Oberfalzerová, *Mongolica Pragensia '07,* Ethnolinguistics and Sociolinguistics in Synchrony and Diachrony. 115–130.
Vokurková, Zuzana. 2008. *Epistemic modalities in spoken Standard Tibetan*. Charles University, Prague: PhD. Dissertation, ms.
Vokurková, Zuzana. 2009. The lexical and grammatical expression of epistemic meanings in spoken Tibetan. In Jaroslav Vacek & Alena Oberfalzerová, *Mongolo-Tibetica Pragensia '09.* Ethnolinguistics, Sociolinguistics, Religion and Culture 2/2. 59–76.
Vokurková, Zuzana. 2010. Epistemic modality in Tibetan: The use of secondary verbs with epistemic verbal endings. In Jaroslav Vacek & Alena Oberfalzerová, *Mongolo-Tibetica Pragensia '10. Ethnolinguistics, Sociolinguistics, Religion and Culture* 2/2. 35–58.
Vokurková, Zuzana. 2011. Evidential and epistemic modality in Standard spoken Tibetan. In Tanja Mortelmans, Jesse Mortelmans & Walter de Mulder (eds.), *In the Mood for Mood, Cahiers Chronos* 23. 117–139.
Vokurková, Zuzana. 2017. *Epistemic modality in standard spoken Tibetan: Epistemic verbal endings and copulas*. Prague: Karolinum.
Wang, Zhijing. 1994. *Zangyu Lasa kouyu yufa*. [A Grammar of Spoken Lhasa Tibetan]. Beijing: Zhongyang minzu daxue chubanshe.
Zhou Jiwen & Xie Houfang (eds.). 2003. *Zangyu lasahua yufa* (*bod kyi lha.sa'i skad kyi brda. sprod*) [A Grammar of Lhasa Tibetan]. Beijing: Minzu chubanshe.

Henrik Bergqvist

Intersubjectification revisited: a cross-categorical perspective

Abstract: The article offers three illustrations of how the process of "intersubjectification" (Traugott & Dasher 2002) can be observed in the development of time deictics, person markers and sentence-type markers to encode aspects of the speaker's assumptions concerning the addressee's epistemic access to an event. First-hand data from Lakandon Maya (Yukatekan, Mexico), Kogi, and Ika (Arwako-Chibchan, Colombia) is discussed in order to offer a potentially more nuanced view of intersubjectification in language. While suggested in previous accounts of intersubjectification, the article argues that this process of language change only involves categories and expressions definable as "shifters" (Jespersen 1922), i.e. expressions that at the same time refer to aspects of the speech situation and the proposition.

Keywords: intersubjectivity, time deictics, person markers, sentence-type, grammaticalization

1 Introduction

Some forms of epistemic marking signal knowledge (a)symmetries between the speech participants (Bergqvist 2011, 2012, 2016, 2017). Such markers encode the speaker's assumptions about the addressee's epistemic access to some event. These may be viewed as markers of (epistemic) intersubjectivity and constitute distinct sub-systems in some languages, parallel to other forms of epistemic marking, such as evidentiality and epistemic modality (e.g. Bergqvist 2016, Landaburu 2007; cf. Evans 2005). Evans et al. (2017a) follows Landaburu (2007) and calls this categorical expression "engagement". Example (1) from Kogi (Arwako-Chibchan, Colombia) illustrates the semantic contrast between shared and exclusive access to an event:

(1) a. *uba* *na-kwĩ* ***ni***-*Ø-gua-täw*
eye 1O-have.PRTC SPKR.SYM-3S-do-PROG
'I'm getting tired.' (Context: said yawning, late at night; BUN_090822)

Henrik Bergqvist, Stockholm University

https://doi.org/10.1515/9783110572261-015

b. *uba* *na-kwĩ* ***na**-Ø-gua-täw*
eye 1O-have.PRTC SPKR.ASYM-3S-do-PROG
'I'm getting tired.' (Context: said as a reason for wanting to go to bed; BUN_090822)

In (1), the 'symmetrical' *ni-* and the asymmetrical *na-* encode a contrast between the speaker's assumption that the addressee is aware of the speaker's tiredness (1a) and the speaker's assumption that the addressee has failed to notice, or alternatively has no reason to think, that the speaker is tired (1b). In both forms, the speaker's commitment is entailed and the forms only contrast in terms of whether the addressee's assumed commitment overlaps with the speaker's, or not. If this form of epistemic marking may indeed be regarded as distinct from more familiar forms of epistemic marking, such as epistemic modality and evidentiality, it raises the question of how such systems develop.

Intersubjectification is a grammaticalization process where forms that include the point of view of the addressee (intersubjective) develop from subjective forms that focus on the perspective of the speaker (subjective; see Traugott & Dasher 2002). This process is potentially applicable to constructions from various semantic domains. The present paper specifically discusses such developments using first hand data from Lakandon Maya (Yukatekan, Mexico), Ika, and Kogi (Arwako-Chibchan, Colombia). In these languages, intersubjectification involves time deictics (Lakandon), sentence-type markers, and person markers (Ika and Kogi). The common denominator for these categorical expressions is their status as "shifters" (Jespersen 1922), elements in language that at the same time signal aspects of the speech situation and the proposition (cf. *speech event* and *narrated event*; Jakobson 1990 [1957]).

In Lakandon Maya, a time deictic, *uúch*, has developed from marking a "distant past event" to marking an event as exclusively accessible to the speaker, and as such, unknown to the addressee. While the temporal meaning dimension in *uúch* is still present, the primary use of the marker is to distinguish (past) events that the speaker assumes that the addressee does not know about from those that are assumed to be familiar to the addressee (Bergqvist 2008, forthcoming).

Ika has developed a version of egophoric marking, also called conjunct/disjunct (see Bickel & Nichols 2007; Hale 1980). The egophoric marker *-w*, is cognate to the first person subject marker *-ku* in Kogi and the closely related language Damana. It interacts predictably with a set of epistemic suffixes, *-in*, *-e*, and *-o*, which developed from sentence-type markers to encode different (a)symmetry configurations between the speech participants in terms of 'epistemic authority' (see Bergqvist 2012). The egophoric *-w* occurs in contexts where the speaker claims epistemic authority of a publicly observable event that involves (at least) one of the speech participants. The speaker‘s epistemic authority can either be exclusive to the speaker (*-in*) or shared with the addressee (*-e*) (Bergqvist 2012: in press).

In Kogi, the declarative sentence-type marker *-in/ni* has come to signal 'knowledge symmetry' between the speaker and the addressee, marking events that are equally accessible to both speech participants in an epistemic sense. It is paradigmatically contrasted with the marker *na-*, which signals knowledge asymmetry (from the speaker's perspective) and arguably originates with the first person object marker *na-* (see above; Bergqvist 2016).

The intersubjectification of time deictics, person, and sentence-type markers to include the perspective of the addressee as epistemic markers is an underexplored development that partly may be attributed to the amorphous nature of shifters in language (see Section 2, below). Intersubjectification as a general process of language change may be favourably applied to account for such changes.

2 On intersubjectivity

While the term intersubjectivity purportedly originates with Husserl (1931), it has since acquired technical uses that are only weakly connected to Husserl's initial formulation. For Husserl, intersubjectivity solved the problem of how the 'self' can relate to the 'other', as an alternative to "solipsism", where nothing exists outside the consciousness of the subject. In this context, intersubjectivity is conceived of in terms of empathy (empathic intentionality) and regarded as a requisite for human consciousness, thus possible to equate with human 'experience'. As pointed out by readers of Husserl (e.g. Crossley 1996), this formulation of intersubjectivity fails to account for phenomena like 'community' and language, which were explicit concerns for some of Husserl's followers, such as Maurice Merleau-Ponty and the sociologist Alfred Schutz. Part of the critique against Husserl's notion of intersubjectivity is that it begins and ends with "the constitutive operations of a solitary consciousness" (Crossley 1996: 7) and that the 'other' is created by means of ego's imagination. Husserl's subject "observes" the world and does not engage or interact with it, thus ignoring the role of language and communication in human consciousness (ibid: 8). Failure to consider language and communication as meaning-producing makes an account of 'community' very difficult. Schutz argues that the notion of 'self' automatically produces the 'other' and that these are relational terms, where one is meaningless without the other. Self-knowledge entails knowledge of the other, thus making the notion of a "monadic psyche" obsolete (ibid: 10). Schutz also criticizes the (asymmetric) perception of self and other from the inside-out and outside-in point of view in terms of analogical apperception and pairing – these are not the same. Perception is something that we cannot experience in itself.

In the field of linguistics, the notion of intersubjectivity was first discussed by Emile Benveniste (1971 [1958]) who considered the properties of shifters in language in an effort to illustrate the inherently (inter)subjective nature of language. Roman Jakobson's exploration of shifters in grammar (Jakobson 1990 [1957]) is almost simultaneous to Benveniste's formulation of subjectivity. Jakobson compares linguistic categories that make reference to the event talked about (e.g. aspect) to ones that require explicit reference to the speech situation (e.g. tense). Benveniste discusses the categories of person (I, you), tense (present, as opposed to preterit and future), epistemic modality (in the form of complement taking predicates; *I think that, I suppose that*), as well as speech-acts (e.g. performatives; *I swear*) to illustrate how such constructions must be analysed from the point of view of the speaker uttering them. The following quote elegantly formulates the inherent intersubjectivity of language as seen in the referential properties of shifters:

> Language is possible only because each speaker sets himself up as a *subject* by referring to himself as *I* in his discourse. Because of this, *I* posits another person, the one who, being, as he is, completely exterior to "me", becomes my echo to whom I say *you* and who says *you* to me. This polarity of persons is the fundamental condition in language of which the process of communication, in which we share, is only a mere pragmatic consequence. It is a polarity, moreover, very peculiar in itself, as it offers a type of opposition whose equivalent is encountered nowhere else outside of language. This polarity does not mean either equality or symmetry: "ego" always has a position of transcendence with regard to *you*. Nevertheless, neither of the terms can be conceived of without the other; they are complementary, although according to an "interior"/"exterior" opposition, and, at the same time, they are reversible. If we seek a parallel to this, we will not find it. The condition of man in language is unique. (Benveniste 1971 [1958]: 225)

It is worth noting Benveniste's explicit claim that I holds a unique position against you, a position that he conceptualizes in terms of (in)equality and (a) symmetry. We will have reason to return to this original insight in our discussion of the language data in Sections 4 and 5. The notion of 'knowledge (a)symmetry' appears key to analysing different intersubjective constructions that specify configurations of epistemic access between the speech participants (e.g. *I know, but you don't* vs. *we both know*; Introduction, above; cf. Bergqvist 2012, 2017, in press).

On the level of grammatical categories, it has been long since been noted that the subjective point of view of the speaker is present in well-known categories like tense, epistemic modality and evidentiality (Jakobson 1990 [1957]; see above). The layered meaning of such categories is reflected by their placement vis-à-vis each other where a category like tense is placed closer to the verbal stem than epistemic modality, which in turn is followed by evidentiality (e.g. Bybee 1985; Cinque 1999). This hierarchical placement has also been argued to correspond to an increasing attention to the perspective of the addressee (Narrog 2012; Section 2, below), i.e. categorical expressions featuring intersubjective meanings are commonly placed at the edge of the verbal complex. This placement aligns with the wide scope properties of such forms and their interaction with e.g. speech-act markers. We will have reason to return to this last point in our discussion of data from Lakandon, Ika, and Kogi in Sections 3 and 4.

3 Intersubjectivity and intersubjectification in language

Grammaticalization, according to Hopper & Traugott (2003: 1) "refers to that part of the study of language change that is concerned with such questions as how lexical items and constructions come in certain linguistic contexts to serve grammatical functions or how grammatical items develop new grammatical functions." It has been proposed as a cyclical, unidirectional, and semantically driven process where different stages of grammaticalization are achieved. The development of *will/'ll* ('future') in Modern English exemplifies this process. Historically, *will* was a verb of volition (OE *willan* 'want', 'wish'), still discernible in the somewhat archaic phrase, *do what you will*. It then acquired the status of an auxiliary with modal semantics ('intention') overlapping with tense meaning ('future'). In a still later stage of development, *will* has been reduced to the clitic *'ll* encoding future tense.

The stages of change outlined by the development of *will* are conditioned by sub-processes such as "semantic bleaching", "morphological reduction", "obligatorification", and "phonetic erosion". Semantic bleaching involves the loss of "concrete", lexical content in a morpheme that is becoming grammaticalized; morphological reduction and obligatorification, respectively, account for the shortening and changed grammatical status of a morpheme, and phonetic erosion can be seen in how a morpheme loses the possibility of taking stress. These stages of grammaticalization are not realized at every stage of the grammaticalization process, nor with every morpheme subject to it (see Hopper and Traugott 2003).

The notion of semantic bleaching is accompanied by the acquisition of a new function, which may be semantically less concrete than its previous lexical meaning, but often predictably related to the original meaning of the form (e.g. volition to (future) intention). Cross-linguistic tendencies have been observed for the development of members of categories such as tense, aspect, mood/modality, and evidentiality. A common origin for these is with verbs, e.g. *say* may become grammaticalized to signal 'reported speech' and finish express the function of 'perfect'.

A particular grammaticalization process is discussed in Traugott and Dasher (2002), namely the "intersubjectification" of modal adverbs and forms of social deixis (e.g. Fr. *tu/vous*). This process details how a 'subjective' expression that encodes some aspect of the speaker's point-of-view becomes 'intersubjective' by including the addressee's point-of-view in that of the speaker: "[i]ntersubjectivity crucially involves SP/W's attention to AD/R as a participant in the speech event, not in the world talked about ", it is "the explicit, coded expression of SP/W's [speaker/writer] attention to the image or "self" of AD/R [addressee/reader] in a social or an epistemic sense" (Traugott & Dasher 2002: 22). This development is specifically discussed with respect to how epistemic adverbs (*well, let's*) acquire intersubjective discourse functions and develop into discourse markers. The intersubjective meaning attributed to such forms is thus contingent on their function to relate aspects of the speech situation and the perspectives of the speech participants in discourse.

The process of intersubjectification is a subspecies of the well-known process of cross-categorical reanalysis of forms where e.g. an aspect marker like the 'perfect' may become a past tense marker or an inferential evidential (e.g. Aksu-Koç & Slobin 1986 for Turkish *-mış*). Aspects of this categorical transfer may be attributed to the fuzziness of categories in an analytical sense, but there are cross-linguistic tendencies with regard to the way markers may acquire characteristics outside of their category membership resulting from the "conventionalization of implicatures" (Levinson 2000; cf. "invited inferences", Traugott & Dasher 2002). Implied meaning thus becomes encoded in forms from conventional patterns of use, depending on language specific circumstances. The cross-categorical transfer of meaning and more specifically the intersubjectification of expressions of subjectivity are central to the proposal put forward here. In Sections 4 and 5, below, we will detail how intersubjectification occurs with different kinds of shifters (Jakobson 1990 [1957]; see Section 1, above).

4 Time deictics in Lakandon Maya

In Lakandon Maya, the time deictic *uúch*, ('previously', 'long ago') has grammaticalized from a one-place predicate to an adverbial. The accompanying change in meaning that has occurred in *uúch* is from subjective 'time' to intersubjective 'knowledge'. This process was aided by a grammatical mapping onto the forms *kuúch/ka'ch* ('previously', 'a while ago'; see below), which are cognate to forms found in Colonial and Modern Yukatek. More precisely, the semantic contrast between *uúch* and *kuúch/ka'ch* is between events that are exclusively known to the speaker (*uúch*) and those that are assumed to be shared with the addressee (*kuúch/ka'ch*).

In Yukatek, *uúch* is an intransitive verb meaning 'to happen', but also a temporal-modal (TM) marker with the grammatical status of an auxiliary that is placed directly before the inflected verb. The TM-marker *uúch* is restricted to combine with the dependent status and cannot be inflected by proper verb morphology (see Bohnemeyer 1998; Vapnarsky 1999). These differences are illustrated in the examples below where (2) features the intransitive verb and (3) contains the TM-marker:

(2)	*bíin*	*wa*	*uúch-uk-Ø*	*tuka'ten-é*
	FUT	HYP	happen-DEP.IV-3S.B	again-TOP

'(One day) maybe it will happen again.' (Vapnarsky 1999, p. 113 [my translation and glossing/orthographic adjustments])

(3)	*le'*	*iglèesya*	*yàan*	*te´*	*Sàanta Krùus-o',*	*uúch*	*men-t-ak-Ø*
	DET	church	exist	LOC	PL.N-TD.DIST	REM	build-TR-DEP 3S.B

'The church in Santa Cruz, was built long ago.' (Vapnarsky 1999, p. 143 [my translation and glossing/orthographic adjustments])

In example (2), *uúch* is a fully inflected verb, whereas in (3) it modifies the verb *me(e)n* 'to build'. A further development of *uúch* in Yukatek is as an adverbial that is not restricted to occur before the verbal core.

(4)	*Aa*	*le'l-o*	*k-in-ts'oon*	*uúch-e'*	*pixàan!*
	EXCL	DEM-TD.DIST	INC-1S-shoot	before-TD.ANA	soul

'Oh yes, I was shooting (at it) then, my soul!' (Vapnarsky 1999, p. 5 [tome 2; my translation and glossing/orthographic adjustments])

In Lakandon, a cognate to the Yukatek *uúch* is no longer present in the form of an intransitive verb. Given that *uúch* in the form of an intransitive verb is found in all other Yukatekan languages, this must be regarded as a special development in Lakandon. Only the TM-marker and the adverbial *uúch* are attested. Example (5) shows the TM-marker *uúch* and (6) features the adverbial:

(5) *uúch-ik* *saj-ak* *ma'* *mahk* *k-u-na'k-ar*
REM-ADV.FOC scare-DEP.IV NEG1 person INC-3S.A-go.up-PLN.IV
ich *uy-atooch* *ik-nuukir-o'*
LOC 3S.A-house 1PL.A-ancestors-TD.DIST
'Long ago, they were afraid, no one entered the house of the ancestors' (HB040922_1EChK_4)

(6) *uúch-ik* *k-u-tzikb'a-t-ik-Ø* *in-miim*
before.EXCL-ADV.FOC INC-3S.A-tell-TR-PLN-3S.B 1S.A-grandmother
'My grandmother used to tell (me)' (HB040922_1EChK_4)

While the placement and the actual form of *uúch* (with the adverbial focus marker *-ik*) is identical in (5) and (6), a differentiation can be made from the status marking that *uúch* combines with. In (5) the dependent status marker *-Vk* prompts an analysis of *uúch* as a TM-marker, while in (6), the plain status marker *-ik* motivates an analysis of *uúch* as an adverbial along with the fact that a Lakandon verb only permits one tense/aspect/mood-marker at a time (cf. Vapnarsky 1999: 142, for Yukatek).

The change in grammatical status from (full) predicate to adverbial corresponds to an increasing abstraction of meaning, where 'to happen' becomes 'long ago' and ultimately (in Lakandon) a 'past event (assumed to be) unknown to the addressee' (i.e. 'knowledge asymmetry'). This development is sketched in Figure 15.1.

Clues to the proposed analysis of *uúch* as marker of a past event that is (assumed to be) unknown to the addressee come from the distribution and frequency of *uúch* in various forms of speech. In Lakandon, *uúch* is frequently attested in some speech genres, such as personal narratives. In comparable Yukatek personal narratives, the adverbial *uúch* occurs with much lower frequency. A quick comparison between Lakandon and Yukatek reveals that *uúch* is present in 82 per cent of the lines (73) in one Lakandon narrative, whereas it is found in only 3 per cent of the lines of a Yukatek personal narrative (139 lines; cf. Bergqvist 2008: 331–332). While this comparison admittedly is impressionistic, statistically, it aligns well with other observations regarding differences in grammatical status of *uúch* in the two languages.

Evidence for the proposed analysis relies partly on manipulating the context of an utterance to see how contextual changes affect the congruent use of *uúch*, but also on speaker judgements that emphasize an unknowing addressee as a

Form: *intransitive verb → tense-mood marker → free standing adverbial*
Meaning: *event description → temporal meaning → knowledge asymmetry*

Figure 15.1: The grammaticalization of *uúch* (after Bergqvist still forthcoming).

requirement for the appropriate use of *uúch*. More importantly, the semantic change from temporal operator to a marker of knowledge asymmetry becomes visible from a paradigmatic perspective by comparison to the semantically contrastive particles *ka'ch* and *kuúch* ('recently', 'a while ago').

kuúch has cognates in all Yukatekan languages, whereas *ka'ch* is only found in Yukatek and Northern Lakandon. *kuúch* and *ka'ch* are hypothesized to be two variants with one function in Lakandon; *kuúch* in the Southern dialect and *ka'ch* in the Northern one. According to McQuown (1967) the meaning of cognate forms in Colonial Yukatek turn on relative temporal proximity, i.e. *kachi*, refers to "a time earlier today" and *kuchi* refers to a time "before today" (McQuown 1967: 243).

In Lakandon, *kuúch/ka'ch* do not encode a temporal separation between the speech event and the narrated event in terms of proximity (see Jakobson 1990 [1957]), i.e. *kuúch/ka'ch* cannot be used to answer a when-question about a past event (Bergqvist 2008: 260–261). Instead, the speaker's assumption about the addressee's knowledge of a past event constitutes the encoded semantics of the forms. As an illustration, compare (7), to (8), both of which refer to past states/events that happened more than 20 years ago.

(7)	*aw-eer*	*mana'*	*ch'upraj*	*uúch*			
	2S.A-know	NEG.EXIST	woman	before.EXCL			
	'You know, there were no women before' (HB040917_1EChK_12)[1]						
(8)	*in-yuhm*	*cheen*	*b'in u-ka'*	*ich*	*este*	*chiwahwa*	*kuúch*
	1S.A-FB	only	go 3S.A-do	LOC	this(Sp.)	TN	before.INCL
	'Only my uncle was going to go to Chihuahua (as you already know)' (HB050328_1KYYM_1)						

Example (7) was uttered in the context of telling a story about the history of the Lakandones. In this story there are many instances of *uúch*, one of these marking a commentary on the shortage of potential wives for Lakandon males in the first half of the 20th Century, as seen in (7). The events it recounts were not experienced first-hand by the speaker although this piece of community history is told as the speaker's personal knowledge (although not his personal history).

1 The opening phrase *aweer* ('you know') does not mean that the speaker thinks the addressee knows about the contents of the ensuing proposition, but is used as an informative opener, which is what I have tried to convey in the English translation of the example. An analogous construction in English would be: *You know, most of the Vikings came from Norway and not from Sweden, as you might think.*

Example (8), on the other hand, was uttered when the speaker re-told the story of his uncle's going to Chihuahua to the researcher, who had failed to get the recorder to capture the story the first time. *kuúch/ka'ch* is not restricted to appear in repeated utterances, but is often found with them. *uúch* was used during the first telling of the story for the same reasons that are stated above for example (7).

In Lakandon, the meaning encoded in *kuúch/ka'ch*, a "past event known to the addressee" (shared knowledge) is in paradigmatic contrast with the meaning encoded in *uúch*, which is to signal a 'past event unknown to the addressee'. As stated above, a change from temporal operator to a marker that specifies the speech participant's respective access to knowledge aligns with the notion of intersubjectification in which the subjective stance of the speaker is extended to include assumptions about the addressee's perspective. Comparable changes have taken place in English time adverbs (e.g. *now*, *then*; see Schiffrin 1987), but in contrast to such discourse markers, the change in *uúch* stems from its relationship to a contrastive 'past time' deictic, namely *ka'ch/kuúch*, which originally was contrasted to *uúch* in terms of temporal distance. A temporal contrast between 'long ago' (*uúch*) and 'recently' (*ka'ch/kuúch*) has developed into a differentiation between what is assumed to be unknown to the addressee and known to the addressee, respectively. This development is outlined in Figure 15.2.

Interestingly, the proposed analaysis for *uúch* and *kuúch/ka'ch* in Lakandon has no synchronic correspondence in Yukatek. According to Vapnarsky (1999), using the terminal deictic suffix *-o'* together with *uúch* denotes a distance away from the interlocutors as well as 'shared information' (Fr. *savoir partagé*; Vapnarsky 1999: 202). This semantic analysis is however dependent on the presence of the terminal deictic *–o'* which allows (past) events to be referred to using *uúch*, but where reference to the speech participants' knowledge states is made by attaching one of the available terminal deictics, *-a'*, *-o'*, *-e'*, or *–i'*. The semantics attributed to these terminal deictics in non-temporal acts of reference, as reported by Hanks (1990), is also appropriate in the analysis of time words in Yukatek (p.c., Vapnarsky 1999: 200). In Lakandon, there is no semantic contrast in terms of knowledge (a)symmetry between attaching *–a'* or *–o'* to *uúch*. The function of these terminal deictics is to serve as devices for event tracking (see Bergqvist 2008: 226) and does not indicate the speaker's expectation with regard to the addressee's knowledge of an event.

kuúch/ka'ch:	temporal proximity → knowledge symmetry
uúch:	temporal distance → knowledge symmetry

Figure 15.2: Semantic changes in *uúch* and *kuúch/ka'ch* (after Bergqvist forthcoming).

Also according to Vapnarsky, the semantic value of *ka'ch* in Yukatek refers to a state which is no longer true, or which could have been true but did not occur (see Vapnarsky 1999: 206–209). While a hypothetical function of *ka'ch* is also attested for Lakandon, the contrastive function of *ka'ch* in Yukatek to signal a past event/state that no longer holds may also be found in the use of *uúch* in the case of Lakandon. These semanto-pragmatic differences in cognate forms from two closely related languages serve to illustrate the nebulous nature of shifters more generally.

The synchronic variation found with *uúch* in Yukatek must be understood in terms of contextualized token-usage, whereas these conveyed meanings have crystallized in Lakandon to become encoded in forms. While it is beyond the scope of this paper to determine the exact functional motivation behind these changes, the semantic path is clear from a comparison between *uúch* and *ka'ch/kuúch* in Lakandon to the synchronic (and diachronic) status of cognate forms in Yukatek.[2]

5 Sentence-type and person in Ika and Kogi

Ika and Kogi are two closely related Arwako-Chibchan languages spoken in the Sierra Nevada de Santa Marta region of northern Colombia. Ika has a variant of the egophoric marking pattern (see Section 5.1; Bergqvist 2012; Bergqvist in press), whereas in Kogi there is a form of epistemic marking that encodes knowledge (a)symmetries between the speech participants, tentatively named "complex epistemic perspective" (Section 5.2; see Bergqvist 2016; cf. "engagement", Evans et al. 2017a). The function of these (purportedly) unusual, grammatical sub-systems in two closely related languages begs comparison and a first stab at this is in Bergqvist (2011). Since then, a more nuanced analysis of both systems has been formulated and the following account (Section 5.3) thus differs in some respects from the one proposed in Bergqvist (2011).

5.1 Egophoric marking in Ika

Egophoric marking (a.k.a. conjunct/disjunct) is a form of epistemic marking that draws on both 'person' and 'evidentiality' for its definition. Broadly speaking, the egophoric marker targets the involvement of the speech participants in some event,

2 The process of grammaticalization can clearly be seen with other pre-clitic aspect-modal markers in both Yukatek and Lakandon, which tend to be subject to phonological reduction and a possible future status as prefixes.

and is as such restricted to occur in contexts where the speaker or the addressee are salient participants.[3] The prototypical egophoric pattern is as follows: the egophoric marker occurs with first person subjects in declaratives and second person subjects in interrogatives. The non-egophoric marker is reserved for all other combinations of subject person and the declarative/interrogative sentence-types. Egophoric marking must therefore be accounted for in both declarative and interrogative contexts. This pattern is demonstrated by data from the first description of such a system, namely the Tibeto-Burman language Kathmandu Newar (Hale 1980):

(9) a. *Ji ana wanā*
1S there go.EGO
'I went there.'

b. *Cha ana wanā lā*
2S there go.EGO INTERR
'Did you go there?'

c. *Cha ana wana*
2S there go.NON.EGO
'You went there.'

d. *Wa ana wana*
3S there go.NON.EGO
'He went there.'(Hale 1980: 95)

In (9), the egophoric *ā* is restricted to occur with first and second person subjects in accordance with the stated alternation of sentence-type. However, this prototypical pattern is not without attested exceptions, which stem from the relationship between sentence-type and subject person (see Bergqvist in press). Firstly, it is possible for interrogative sentences with first person subjects to feature the egophoric marker, despite the fact that such combinations of subject person and sentence-type should be marked as non-egophoric. This atypical combination often results in a rhetorical reading as in (10):

(10) *Ji ana wanā lā*
1S there go.EGO INTERR
'Did I go there? (I most certainly did not!' (Hale 1980: 100)

---

3 The Western philosophical tradition has focused on the (solitary) speaking subject to the exclusion of his/her interlocutor(s) something that is clearly reflected by the term egophoric marking. However, as should be clear from the discussion, the ego also houses the *tu*, in Benveniste's terms (from the point of view of the ego), allowing for a dialogical exchange of epistemic authority.

Aside from this exception to the prototypical pattern, it is also possible to signal a difference in terms of 'volition' by alternating the egophoric and non-egophoric marker in a context where a first or a second subject person would require the egophoric marker:

(11) a. *Ji* *danā*
1S go.EGO
'I got up (voluntarily)' (conjunct)
b. *Ji* *dana*
1S go.NON.EGO
'I got up (involuntarily)' (disjunct) (Hale 1980: 99)

In Kathmandu Newar, as in other languages with egophoric marking (e.g. Akhvakh, Creissels 2008) there is a restriction on the distribution of egophoric markers that depend on predicate type, where only predicates that signal the volition/control of the speaker can take egophoric marking (see Creissels 2009 for a discussion). While non-prototypical uses of egophoric forms, such as the ones described above, may produce pragmatic changes in meaning, these are not attested in all languages that feature egophoric marking (e.g. Bergqvist 2012; Curnow 2002).

In Ika, there are specific distributional restrictions with the egophoric marker and second person subjects that depend on the relationship between subject person and sentence-type, and which have consequences for the analysis of the system. In Bergqvist (in press), it is argued that these exceptions are consistent with the functional motivations underlying egophoric marking more generally, although they may in detail be specific to the system found in Ika. Prima facie, the distribution of the egophoric *-w* and the non-egophoric *-Ø/-y* in Ika appears to conform to the prototypical pattern:

(12) a. *(ən=)bunsi-w-in*
spin.yarn-EGO-DECL
'I am spinning yarn'
b. *nə=bunsi-k-w-e*
2S=spin.yarn-DIST-EGO-SUSP
'You are spinning yarn?'
c. *nə=bunsə-y-in*
2S=spin.yarn-NON.EGO-DECL
'You are spinning yarn./You spin yarn.'
d. *bunsə-y-in*
spin.yarn-NON.EGO-DECL
'He is spinning yarn.' (Landaburu 1992: 9–10 [my translation and glossing])

In (12) the egophoric *-w* is reserved for the same combinations of subject person and sentence-type that we saw for Kathmandu Newar in (10). However, a closer look reveals that there are exceptions to the egophoric pattern in Ika that involve the role of sentence-type and predicate type in the system. Most importantly, the declarative-interrogative alternation is not binary, given that there are two markers (*-e* and *-o*) used to produce questions (in a speech-act sense) of which only one (*-e*) is ever available for egophoric marking. It turns out that *-e* fails to meet the requirements for an interrogative marker given that the speaker's ignorance is only implied and may disappear with a change of subject person. Compare (12b) to (13) below:

(13) *bunsí-k-w-e*
spin.yarn-DIST-EGO-SUSP
'(When) I spun yarn/(that) I spun yarn.' (ELI_090823)

The translation of (13) suggests a subordinate clause, but egophoric marking only occurs in finite, main clauses. This form of "insubordination" has been attested for a number of languages where finite "modal" constructions have an origin in subordinate clauses (e.g. German *ob*-constructions; see Evans 2007 for a detailed discussion of 'insubordination'). Support for an analysis of clauses such as (13) with the egophoric marker and *-e* as finite is seen in example (14) where a rhetorical interpretation is also possible:

(14) *eya* *nuku-w-e*
this hear-EGO-SUSP
'(Do) I understand this? (Of course!) (ELI_120507)

By contrast, the interrogative marker *-o* is not available for egophoric marking. Compare example (14) with (15) below:

(15) *bunsə-k-Ø-o*
spin.yarn-DIST-NON.EGO-INTERR
'Do I (know how to) spin yarn?' (i.e. in your opinion; Bergqvist 2012:174)

A rhetorical reading is not available for the sentence in (15), where the ignorance of the speaker is implied by asking for the addressee's opinion/knowledge. A solution to the problem of accounting for *-e* in the framework of a traditional division into sentence-types is proposed in Bergqvist (2012), who draws on Landaburu (1992, 2000) and analyses *-in*, *-o*, and *-e* as markers of 'epistemic authority'. Instead of signalling a separation between declarative and interrogative sentence-types, it is argued that these markers encode three distinct (a)symmetries in terms of epistemic authority, namely "speaker asymmetric" (*-in*); "addressee asymmetric" (*-o*); and "speaker-addressee symmetric" (*-e*). This tripartite division of epistemic authority has direct bearing on the analysis of egophoric marking since only utterances that encode the speaker's authority, either as exclusive (*-in*, 'speaker asymmetric') or shared (*-e*, 'speaker-addressee symmetric') take egophoric marking. Instances where epistemic authority is in effect "handed over to the addressee" (*-o*) are non-egophoric regardless of subject person. This distribution is schematized in Table 15.1.

Table 15.1: Combinations of egophoric (EGO) and markers of epistemic authority

	–in, 'speaker authority'	*–e*, 'shared authority'	*–o*, 'addressee authority'
1Sg	EGO	EGO	–
2Sg	–	EGO	–
3Sg	–	–	–

The translation of (15) is also suggestive of another restriction found with egophoric marking in Ika, namely which predicates are available for egophoric marking. The already mentioned restriction in terms of 'volition' and/or 'control' is not applicable to Ika. Both *re'kich* ('jump') and *wa'na* ('fall') take egophoric marking as in (16), below:

(16) a. *re'kich-ən* *nuk-w-in*
jump-IMPF be.loc-EGO-DECL
'I am jumping.'

b. *ka'-se* *wa'na* *u-k-w-in*
floor-LOC fall.PERF do-DIST-EGO-DECL
'I fell to the floor.' (ELI_120508)

In Ika, only predicates that target socially and perceptually "observable" events and states can take egophoric marking, meaning that mental state predicates that concern the feelings, opinions, and wishes of the speaker (or the addressee) are not available for egophoric marking. This notion of observational access plays an important role in the Ika system, but is also underspecified with regard to how access to an event is acquired. 'Access', in this use distinguishes between events that are available to be experienced, and/or known, and those that are not. Inaccessible events (non-egophoric) include "public" events that do not directly involve the speaker or the addressee and the "private" inner states of the speaker and others (including the addressee). The notion of 'involvement' appears key, as any other form of perceptual access remains under-specified.

Egophoric marking in Ika is, because of the specific distributional constraints sketched above in terms of observability and access, hypothesized to encode the speaker's epistemic authority of an event that involves (at least) one of the speech participants. With second person subjects, egophoric marking is only possible by including the perspective of the addressee in the epistemic assessment of the speaker, not by means of epistemic "flip" or reversal, as suggested in other accounts of egophoric marking (see Creissels 2008; Curnow 2002).

A final argument to support this hypothesis comes from restrictions on egophoric marking with second person subjects in certain temporal contexts. Although tense marking in the strict sense has yet to be demonstrated for Ika, sentences with egophoric marking and second person subjects are always interpreted as "present". A past context rules out egophoric marking with second person subjects, but not with first person subjects, which may combine with egophoric marking in both past and present contexts. This restriction is analysed as a component of the egophoric system to only mark accessible events.

The development of egophoric marking in Ika is clearly an instance of the same process that gave rise to *uúch/kuúch/ka'ch* in Lakandon, namely the grammaticalization of one categorical expression into another. In the case of Ika, the egophoric –*w* is cognate to the first person marker –*ku* in the other two Arwako languages, Kogi and Damana. The meaning of the form has thus gone from indexing a participant (in a syntactic and speech-act sense) to signaling the involvement of a speech participant, subject to different configurations of epistemic authority. The role of the epistemic suffixes, -*in*, -*e*, and -*o* in Ika egophoric marking bridges this system to the Kogi "complex epistemic perspective" prefixes (below), which draw on some of the same semantic contrasts and involve cognates of these forms, but in the end results in a quite different system.

A summary of the features of egophoric marking in Ika, is as follows: (1) egophoric marking only occurs with declaratives featuring first or second person subjects; either ones that charge the speaker with exclusive epistemic authority (-*in*), or ones that share epistemic authority with the addressee (-*e*). Interrogatives that encode the speaker's ignorance and where the epistemic authority resides with the addressee (-*o*) are not available for egophoric marking, (2) the defining feature of (1) has the consequence of projecting a "present" interpretation on instances of egophoric marking with second person subjects. Actions/events that explicitly involve the addressee but which are inaccessible to the speaker's immediate experience/ observation, are marked non-egophoric and receive a default "past" reading, (3) 'volition' or 'control' does not determine the availability of egophoric marking with certain predicates in Ika. Instead, epistemic/observational access imposes a division between actions/ events and personal attributes that may take egophoric marking, and psychological/ cognitive and bodily states that may not combine with egophoric marking.

5.2 Complex epistemic perspective in Kogi

In Kogi, there is a paradigmatic set of epistemic markers whose primary function is to signal knowledge (a)symmetries between the speech participants with respect to an event (see Section 1, above). This (a)symmetry relation can be further divided into "speaker-perspective" and "addressee-perspective" forms. The set of epistemic markers consists of five prefixes: *na-/ni-/sha-/shi-/ska(n)-*, and are listed in Table 15.2.

The speaker-perspective forms, *na-/ni-*, target the epistemic perspective of the speaker. *na-* signals the speaker's exclusive knowledge of an event (speaker-asymmetry), whereas *ni-*, by contrast, signals shared knowledge between the speaker and the addressee (speaker-symmetry). The examples in (17) demonstrate this meaning contrast:

(17) a. *kwisa-té*[4] *na-nuk-kû*
dance-IMPF SPKR.ASY3M-be.loc-1S
'I am/was dancing.' {informing}(JM_130613)

b. *kwisa-té* *ni-nuk-kû*
dance-IMPF SPKR.SYM-BE.L3oc-1S
'I am/was dancing.' {confirming}(BUN_090824)

Example (17a) by default conveys a "past" action if no context specific circumstances are provided, even though the sentence does not feature any temporal operators. A "present" reading entails a situation where the speaker and the addressee e.g. are in separate rooms, given that the act of dancing is directly observable and thus does not permit being stated from the exclusive perspective of the speaker (see below).

Table 15.2: Epistemic marking prefixes in Kogi (after Bergqvist 2016)

	Speaker-perspective	Addressee-perspective
Asymmetric	*na-*	*sha-*
Symmetric	*ni-*	*shi-*
Non-Speech Participant	*ska(n)-*	

4 Acute accent (´) signals prosodic accentuation (see Bergqvist 2016).

Example (17b) is, by contrast, usually free from temporally tinged interpretations in that a statement regarding the speaker's act of dancing is expressed as symmetrically accessible to the both speech-act participants.

The addressee-perspective forms, *sha-/shi-*, focus on the epistemic perspective of the addressee. *sha-* signals the addressee's exclusive knowledge, while *shi-* signals shared knowledge between the addressee and the speaker. Consider the examples in (18):

(18) a. *nas* *hanchibé* *sha-kwísa=tuk-(k)u*
1s.IND good ADR.ASYM-dance=be.loc-1S
'I am dancing well?' {in your opinion} (BUN_090824)
b. *kwisa-té* *shi-ba-lox*
dance-IMPF ADR.SYM-2S-be.loc
'You are/were dancing?' {confirming} (BUN_090824)

Example (18a) targets the opinion of the addressee, which by social convention (not resticted to Kogi society) cannot be addressed without explicitly signalling the addressee's authority with regard to his/her own opinions. Example (18b) exemplifies a common use of *shi-*, which is to mark utterances concerning observable actions performed by the addressee. Statements featuring *shi-* may function as questions, but with an explicitly expressed expectation from the perspective of the speaker that the talked about event/action holds.

Despite this functional overlap with interrogatives, there are reasons to consider *sha-* and *shi-* as declarative by form. This analysis is supported both grammatically and pragmatically. Firstly, interrogatives can be formed without *sha-/shi-*:

(19) a. *sakí* *mi-k-zéi-shi*[5]
what 2O-DAT-feel-PTCP
'How are you?' (DAM_090819)
b. *néi* *ma-gu-ngu-é*
go 2S-do-PST-INT
'Did you go?' (DAM_090820)

Indeed, there is a complementary distribution between the polar interrogative marker *-e* (cognate to the 'suspensive' *-e* in Ika) and *sha-*, as illustrated in (20). It is not possible to combine the *sha-/shi-* prefixes with the interrogative *-e*. The

5 The participial suffix *-shi* has not been demonstrated to be cognate to the prefix (*shi-*) under discussion.

semantic difference between *-e* and *sha-* is suggested by the translation in (20) where 'thinking about something' differs from 'having an opinion about something' (cf. example 18a, above). Given an otherwise identical construction, this difference in meaning must be attributed to the semantics of these forms.

(20) a. *sakí* *hangwa-ba-lóx-e*
what think-2S-PROG-INT
'What are you thinking about?' (BUN_090826)
b. *sakí* *sha-hangwa-ba-lóx*
what ADR.ASYM-think-2S-PROG
'What do you think (about something)?' (BUN_090826)

The presence of the speaker's assertion in the addressee-perspective forms *shi-/sha-* is also apparent from the use of these forms in narratives. Depending on the specific setting for a narrative telling, an addressee-oriented stance may be adopted by marking monologic stretches of speech with *shi-/sha-* (see Bergqvist 2016, for details).

Pragmatic interpretation effects that cannot be attributed to the encoded meaning of the forms, but which may result from this in combination with certain contextual cues, include temporal displacement and attitudinal shades of meaning, such as 'familiarity' and 'affection' (see Bergqvist 2016, for details). Changes to the temporal interpretation of utterances that contain one of the prefixes are, as in the case of Ika, argued to be the result of the asymmetry notion. While *ni-/na-* do not specify a point in time, the combination of *na-* with a predicate denoting an observable act that is assumed to be available to both speech participants, may result in a 'past' interpretation if no other contextual cues are provided. This is why example (21a), repeated here, usually is translated 'I was dancing' instead of 'I am dancing'.

(21) a. *kwisa-té* *na-nuk-kú*
dance-IMPF SPKR.ASYM-be.loc-1S
'I am/was dancing.' {informing}(JM_130613)

Alternatives to this translation are possible if access to the event is reduced, e.g. if the act of dancing takes place in a dark room where the addressee cannot see the speaker. In that case, a present reading of the phrase is accepted. This means that temporality parameters are implied and not entailed. A sentence that does encode 'past' time must feature *-gu(a)*, as in (22):

(22) *kwisa-té* *ni-nu(k)-gu-kú*
dance-IMPF SPKR.SYM-be.loc-PST-1S
'I was dancing.' (BUN_090822)

The pragmatic restrictions sketched above arise from the primary function of complex epistemic marking in Kogi to signal knowledge access as either exclusive, or shared between the speaker and the addressee. This (assumed) (a)symmetric access can further be viewed from the speaker's (*ni-/na-*) or the addressee's (*shi-/sha-*) perspective.

5.3 Comparing Ika egophoric marking and Kogi epistemic marking

From the above descriptions of Ika egophoric marking and Kogi complex epistemic marking, we may conclude that cognates of the sentence marker *-in/ni* and the first person markers *-ku* (subject) and *na-* (object) play a role in comparing the two systems. In Ika, a cognate of the first person subject marker *-ku*, has developed into a marker of 'speaker involvement' (*-w*), which may be accounted for by comparison to available accounts of egophoric marking. The distribution of the egophoric *-w* is conditioned by a set of markers e.g. *-in/ni*, that turn on the notion of "epistemic authority", encoding an exclusive vs. shared contrast regarding who is charged with authority of an event in an epistemic sense.

In Kogi, a cognate of *-in/ni* encodes 'knowledge symmetry' as part of a system that also features a cognate of the first person object marker *na-*, which has grammaticalized to encode 'knowledge asymmetry'. The system in Kogi harbours additional complexity in the markers *shi-/sha-* which encode a corresponding (a) symmetry contrast from the perspective of the addressee. A plausible development of these forms consists of a combination of the *ni-/na-* contrast with the indefinite/interrogative *s-/sh-*.

The grammaticalization of sentence-type and person marking in Ika and Kogi is illustrated in Figure 15.3:

Ika:	'declarative' (*–in/ni*) → 'speaker authority'
	'1S.NOM' (*-ku*) → 'egophoric' (*-w*)
Kogi:	'declarative' (*–in/ni*) → 'speaker authority'
	'1S.ACC' (*na-*) → 'speaker asymmetric perspective'

Figure 15.3: Grammaticalization of sentence-type and person markers in Ika and Kogi.

The present comparison between the two systems focuses on *-in/ni*, which encodes 'the speaker's claim to epistemic authority' in Ika, and 'shared knowledge/attention' from the perspective of the speaker in Kogi. While these constitute opposed semantic contrasts in terms of authority and knowledge, such developments are not contradictory given their common origin as a marker of the declarative sentence-type. The marking of epistemic authority in Ika, retains some characteristics of sentence-type marking, and the once declarative *-in/ni* still features aspects of the speaker's prototypical role as provider of (novel) referential content (Givón 1990: 288–291). In Kogi, *ni-* also encodes the speaker's privileged perspective, but as shared with the addressee in terms of knowledge/attention. The form in Kogi that most obviously corresponds to the shared epistemic authority, *-e*, in Ika, is the addressee-perspective *shi-*. Both forms possess a "quasi-interrogative" function in the separate systems, clearly signalling attention to the perspective of the addressee.

The egophoric *-w* developed from a cognate of the first person subject marker *-ku* in the other two Arwako languages Kogi and Damana (see Trillos Amaya 1999). A separate development occurred in Kogi where the first person object marker *na-* became part of a distinct system for marking knowledge (a)symmetry. While the distribution of the egophoric *-w* in Ika co-varies with markers of epistemic authority and with properties of the predicate of the clause in terms of socially acceptable observability (i.e. public vs. private events), the distribution of *na-* in Kogi is not restricted by any comparable grammatical parameters in terms of subject person and/or a notion such as 'involvement'. Restrictions in the use of *na-* are only found on the level of the speech-event, where grounds for making assumptions about the knowledge and attention of the addressee are assessed by the speaker. The only grammatical restriction relevant to the Kogi system is found with sentence-type, since it is argued that complex epistemic marking only occurs in declarative contexts. In Ika, on the other hand, the markers of epistemic authority (*-in*, *-e*, and *-o*) arguably have retained a function as signalling sentence-type.

Although the notions of 'epistemic authority' and 'knowledge (a)symmetry' are distinct in targeting slightly different aspects of epistemic perspective-taking, they are very much comparable given the shared function of the markers that are analysed using these terms. These differences are reflected by grammatical features and distributional restrictions associated with the discussed markers. While epistemic marking in Ika consists of two inter-related systems, i.e. egophoric marking and the marking of epistemic authority, the Kogi system is formally less complicated, but conceptually richer in allowing the speaker to adopt a speaker-centred, or an addressee-centred epistemic perspective. It appears likely that similar functional pressures have given rise to distinct grammatical expressions that developed from cognate forms that index ‘person’ and ‘sentence-type’.

6 Your view in mine: implications for research on epistemicity

The very reason that prompts a speaker to signal his/her subjective point of view with regard to some event also underlies the development of intersubjectively grounded forms of epistemic marking, such as the ones detailed above. The speaker’s need to situate events with respect to other comparable and contrasting events includes a requirement to situate these in relation to the speech participants and to related aspects of the speech situation. While the traditional conception of epistemicity in language focuses on notions such as ‘necessity’, ‘possibility’, and ‘commitment’, these are intimately tied to other aspects of the speaker’s evaluation of events in terms of affect, attitude, and expectations. It is obvious that these notions must be kept separate, but it is also important to acknowledge their role in accounting for cross-linguistic variation in systems for epistemic marking. It is, in fact, reasonable to assume that most cross-linguistic research on epistemic marking systems is heavily biased in focusing on notions associated with modality and to a lesser degree on evidentiality, largely due to the frequent presence of these expressions in the languages of Europe. Even though there has been an awareness of intersubjectivity as a prerequisite for language ever since Benveniste’s formulation of subjectivity (see Section 2, above), it is only recently that this awareness has started to shape descriptive and comparative work on epistemic marking in lesser described languages. Viewing language as a tool for representing (potentially) objective knowledge about the world has been a fruitful perspective for linguistic research in many areas, but it has become increasingly clear that there are some severe limitations in this approach once descriptive linguists’ interest in language-use came on the agenda. When taking into account how language is used in order to analyse linguistic structures and demarcate language from competing and complementary forms of communication, an increasing emphasis on the embodied, intersubjective nature of language appears crucial. Understanding how pragmatics becomes grammar is key in accounting for forms of epistemic marking such as the ones outlined in Sections 4 and 5, where “objective knowledge” is a less relevant parameter than intersubjectively positioned knowledge from the inherently subjective perspective of the speaker.

An important issue that was discussed in Section 3 is how implied meaning becomes encoded in forms. This semantic development is at the heart of the grammaticalization process and the reason why it is regarded as semantically driven (see Traugott & Dasher 2002). This analytical aspect of intersubjectivized expressions of epistemicity is also important for understanding their place in grammar vis-à-vis other forms of epistemic marking such as modality and evidentiality. Functional pressures, shared by all languages, to provide the speaker with the means to position him/herself epistemically with regard to events may produce very different resources for doing so. Cross-linguistic observations concerning the correspondence between syntagmatic positioning, scope properties, and meaning content allows us to postulate a potential placement of intersubjective forms near the edge of the clause, corresponding to the gradual shift from subjective to intersubjective meaning as accounted for by the process of intersubjectification. Pragmatically conditioned meaning is likely more often found with forms such as second position enclitics and particles than with inflectional forms that occur close to the verb stem. The development of temporal adverbial clitics/particles in Lakandon and sentence-type markers in Ika and Kogi into resources for specifying the intersubjective distribution of knowledge and commitment between the speech participants aligns with such expectations. While intersubjective aspects of meaning are implied in some subjective forms expressing temporality and epistemology as part of the verbal template, this implied meaning may become encoded along with an increased displacement of forms towards the periphery of the clause.

Semantically, the (a)symmetry notion appears central in accounting for the distinct sub-systems outlined in the present paper. Originally adopted from Hanks (1990), the wide applicability of this notion connects to the basic concept of "intersubjective alignment" (and non-alignment) in stance-taking, as detailed by Du Bois (2007). While the notion of 'knowledge (a)symmetry' as discussed in this paper represents a specialized, technical use of the notion of (a)symmetry, the fundamental recognition that what the speaker knows may either overlap with someone else's knowledge, or be distinct from it, must be considered as the basis for this notion. The use of '(a)symmetry' in the languages discussed in Sections 3 and 4 matches perfectly Benveniste's formulation of subjectivity in language (see Section 2, above): the speaker's perspective holds sway over the addressee's even in forms that are defined as symmetric, i.e. encoding shared epistemic access/authority. In this sense, shared knowledge, or epistemic authority, is not the same as "equal" access/authority. The addressee can always disagree, or question the speaker's evaluation of information as shared, i.e. the speaker's assumption does not equal "fact" in this regard. This seemingly trivial observation has consequences for the analysis of forms where the secondary perspective of the addressee must be regarded as subordinate to the speaker's primary point of view. Forms that harbour two simultaneous perspectives in an epistemic sense arguably have one of these perspectives embedded in the other, making the embedded perspective a "second order" commitment (cf. Kockelman 2004) that stands in relation to the speaker's first order commitment to the event in question.[6] This mode of analysis also resonates with Schutz's observation that the proprioception of 'self' and the external perception of 'other' differ (see Section 2, above). The only commitment that the speaker has direct access to is his/her own. All other commitments must be assumed.

7 Conclusion

As this paper has shown, intersubjectification is not restricted to involve the development of modal adverbs into discourse markers, nor person forms that develop politeness distinctions (see Traugott & Dasher 2000, Ch 4, 6). The development of person markers and sentence-type markers in Ika and Kogi, and time deictics in Lakandon Maya, to express (a)symmetric access to events in an epistemic sense, may also be accounted for by the process of intersubjectification. Given this observed diversity, we may ask if any grammatical form may acquire intersubjective aspects of meaning. The answer is both yes and no. An observation that follows from the semantic changes accounted for in this paper as well as those reported by Traugott & Dasher points to the requirement that a grammatical expression must have the properties of a shifter (per Jakobson 1990 [1957]), such as tense, epistemic modality, evidentiality, sentence-type, and person. Aspectual forms, such as the 'progressive', are unlikely to be available for this kind of development unless they first acquire the meaning-function of a shifter, like the 'perfect' has in some European languages (see Lindstedt 2000 for a discussion of the 'perfect' in a number of European languages). Although suggested by the data discussed in this paper, this proposal remains a hypothesis until confirmed by more research on processes of intersubjectification in language.

The applicability of the (a)symmetry notion to define epistemic-intersubjective forms stands out, but is also expected from cross-linguistic research on modality such as Narrog (2012) and comparable research by Hengeveld & Dall'Aglio Hatthner (2015) on evidentials where a shift in the grammatical status of a

6 Kockelman's analysis builds in equal parts on Jakobson's notion of event types (speech event/narrated event [Es/En]; cf. Jakobson 1990 [1957]) and Goffman's notion of participant-roles (Goffman 1981), resulting in a proposal that allows for a separation between different forms of epistemic marking, as well as the embedding of these to produce stances about stances, either reflexively or with respect to someone else's viewpoint (see Kockelman 2004).

form towards the periphery of the clause corresponds to a shift in the semantics of that form to target the level of the speech-act and an increasing attention to the perspective of the addressee. If we wish to know more about markers of the kind discussed in this paper, this is an area of grammar where we should start looking.

Acknowledgements: The author gratefully acknowledges the financial support of the Swedish Research Council (dnr. 2011–2274) and Åke Wibergs Stiftelse. The formulation of the ideas and analyses proposed in this paper have greatly benefitted from collaboration and discussion with Nick Evans and Lila San Roque, although said ideas may not be shared by either of them, in detail. Many thanks to Zlatka Guentcheva for generous and patient guidance thoughout the process of submitting and revising the manuscript. I'm also thankful for suggestions and critisisms provided by two anonymous reviewers. Any remaining errors are my own. A final thanks to my host institution, the Department of General Linguistics at Stockholm University.

Abbreviations: 1 – first person; 2 – second person; 3 – third person; A – ergative agreement marker; ADR – addressee perspective; ADV – adverbial; ALL – allative; ANA – anaphoric; ASYM – asymmetric; B – absolutive agreement marker; CP – completive; DAT – dative; DEP – dependent; DEM – demonstrative; DET – determiner; DIM – diminutive; DIST – distal; DUB – dubitative; DUR – durative; EXCL – exclusive; EXIST – existential; FB – father's brother; FOC – focus; FUT – future; HAB – habitual; HYP – hypothetical; IM – imperative; IMPF – imperfect; INC – incompletive aspect; INCL – inclusive; IND –independent; IV – intransitive verb; LOC – locative; O – object; NEG – negative; NSP – non-speech participant; PERF – perfect; PL – (generic) plural; PLN –plain status; PN – person/place name; POS – possessive; POT – potential; PROG – progressive; PRTC – participal; PST – past; PURP – purposive, REM – remote; REV –reverential; S – subject; SG – singular; SOC – socialis; SPKR – speaker-perspective; SYM – symmetric; TD – terminal deictic; TOP – topic; TR – transitivizer

References

Aksu-Koç, Ayhan A. & Dan I. Slobin. 1986. *A Psychological Account of the Development and Use of Evidentials in Turkish*, In Wallace L. Chafe & Johanna Nichols (eds.), *Evidentiality: the Linguistic Coding of Epistemology*, 159–167. Norwood, New Jersey: Ablex.

Benveniste, Émile. 1971 [1958]. De la subjectivité dans le langage. In *Problèmes de linguistique générale*, Vol. 1: 258–266. Paris: Gallimard.

Bergqvist, Henrik. 2008. *Temporal reference in Lakandon Maya: Speaker and Event perspectives*. PhD dissertation, School of Oriental and African Studies, Endangered Languages Academic Programme: University of London.

Bergqvist, Henrik. 2011. *Complex perspectives in Arwako languages: comparing epistemic marking in Kogi and Ika*. In Peter K. Austin, Oliver Bond, David Nathan & Lutz Marten (eds.), *Proceedings of Conference on Language Documentation & Linguistic Theory* 3, 49–57. London: SOAS.

Bergqvist, Henrik. 2012. Epistemic marking in Ika (Arwako). *Studies in Language (News from the field)* 36:1. 154–181.

Bergqvist, Henrik. 2016. Complex epistemic perspective in Kogi (Arwako-Chibchan). *International Journal of American Linguistics* 82:1. 1–34.

Bergqvist, Henrik. 2017. The role of 'perspective' in epistemic marking. *Lingua* 186–187. 5–20.

Bergqvist, Henrik.in press. The role of sentence type in Ika (Arwako) egophoric marking. In Simeon Floyd, Elisabeth Norcliffe & Lila San Roque (eds.), *Egophoricity*. Amsterdam: John Benjamins Publishing Company.

Bergqvist, Henrik. forthcoming. Time and commitment: the grammaticalization of uúch in Lakandon Maya. Proceedings of the symposium *"Mesures et textures du temps chez les Mayas: le dit, l'écrit, le vécu"*, Paris, 7–10th October, 2014, *Journal de la Société des Américanistes*.

Bickel, Balthasar & Johanna Nichols. 2007. Inflectional Morphology. In Timothy Shopen (ed.), *Language Typology and Syntactic Description: vol 3 Grammatical Categories and the Lexicon*, 169–240. Cambridge: Cambridge University Press.

Bohnemeyer, Jürgen. 1998. *Time Relations in Discourse: Evidence from a comparative Approach to Yucatec Maya*. Katholieke Universiteit: Ph.D. diss.

Bybee, Joan L. 1985. Morphology: a study of the relation between meaning and form (Typological Studies in Language 9). Amsterdam: John Benjamins.

Cinque, Guglielmo. 1999. *Adverbs and Functional Heads: A Cross-Linguistic Perspective*. Oxford University Press.

Creissels, Denis. 2008. Person variation in Akhvakh verb morphology: functional motivation and origin of an uncommon pattern. *Sprachtypologie und Universalienforschung* 61: 4. 309–325.

Creissels, Denis. 2009. Language documentation and verb inflection typology: the case of Northern Akhvakh (Nakh-Daghestanian). Handout at Chronos 9, Paris, 2–4 October.

Crossley, Nick. 1996. *Philosophy and Social Criticism, Volume 4: Intersubjectivity: The Fabric of Social Becoming*. London: Sage Publications.

Curnow, J. Timothy. 2002. Conjunct/disjunct marking in Awa Pit. *Linguistics* 40 (3). 611–627.

Du Bois, John W. 2007. *The stance triangle*. In Robert Englebretson (ed.), *Stancetaking in discourse*, 139–182. Amsterdam: Benjamins.

Evans, Nicholas R. 2005. View with a view: towards a typology of multiple perspective. *Berkeley Linguistics Society*. 93–120.

Evans, Nicholas R. 2007. *Insubordination and its uses*. In Irina Nikolaeva (ed.), *Finiteness: Theoretical and Empirical Foundations*, 366–431. New York: Oxford University Press.

Evans, Nicholas R., Henrik Bergqvist, and Lila San Roque. 2017a. The grammar of engagement I: framework and initial exemplification. *Language and Cognition*, 1–31.

Givón, Talmy. 1990. *Syntax: A Functional-Typological Introduction, Vol. 2*. Amsterdam: John Benjamins.

Goffman, Erving. 1981. *Forms of Talk*. Philadelphia: University of Pennsylvania Press.

Hale, Austin. 1980. Person markers: finite conjunct and disjunct forms in Newari. In Ronald L. Trail (ed.), *Papers in Southeast Asian Linguistics 7*, 95–106. Canberra: Department of Linguistics & Australian National University.

Hanks, William H. 1990. *Referential practice: Language and lived space among the Maya.* Chicago: University of Chicago Press.

Hengeveld, Kees & Marize Mattos Dall'Aglio Hattnher. 2015. Four types of evidentiality in the native languages of Brazil. *Linguistics* 53:3. 479–524.

Hopper, Paul J. & Elisabeth Closs Traugott. 2003 (2nd edn). *Grammaticalization* (Cambridge textbooks in linguistics). Cambridge: Cambridge University Press.

Husserl, Edmund. 1931. *Ideas: General Introduction to Pure Phenomenology.* Trans. W. R. Boyce Gibson. New York: The MacMillan Company.

Jakobson, Roman. 1990 [1957]. *Shifters and verbal categories.* In Linda R. Waugh & Monique Monville- Burston (eds.), *On language*, 386–392, Cambridge, MA: Harvard University Press.

Jespersen, Otto. 1922. *Language; its nature, development and origin.* London: G. Allen & Unwin, ltd.

Kockelman, Paul. 2004. Stance and Subjectivity. *Journal of Linguistic Anthropology* 14. 127–150.

Landaburu, Jon. 1992. La langue ika ou Arhuaco: morphosyntaxe du verbe. *Amerindia* 17. 1–30.

Landaburu, Jon. 2000. La lengua ika. In *Lenguas indígenas de Colombia: una visión descriptiva.* Bogota: Instituto Caro y Cuervo.

Landaburu, Jon. 2007. *La modalisation du savoir en langue Andoke (Amazonie Colombienne).* In Zlatka Guentchéva & Jon Landaburu (eds.), *L'énonciation médiatisée II – Le traitement épistémologique de l'information: illustrations amérindiennes et caucasiennes*, 23–47. Paris: Éditions Peeters.

Levinson, Stephen C. 2000. *Presumptive meanings: The theory of generalized conversational implicature.* Cambridge: MIT press.

Lindstedt, Jouko. 2000. The perfect – aspectual, temporal and evidential. In Östen Dahl (ed.), *Tense and aspect in the languages of Europe*, 365–383. Berlin: Mouton de Gruyter.

McQuown, Norman A. 1967. Classical Yucatec (Maya). In Norman A. McQuown (ed.), *Handbook of Middle American Indians. Volume 5*, 201–247. Austin (Tex.): University of Texas Press.

Narrog, Heiko. 2012. *Modality, subjectivity and semantic change: A cross-linguistic perspective.* Oxford: Oxford University Press.

Schiffrin, Deborah. 1987. *Discourse markers.* Cambridge: Cambridge University Press.

Traugott, Elisabeth Closs & Richard B. Dasher. 2002. *Regularity in Semantic Change.* Cambridge: Cambridge University Press.

Trillos Amaya, Maria. 1999. *Damana* (Languages of the world. Materials 207). Munchen: Lincom Europa.

Vapnarsky, Valentina. 1999. *Expressions et Conceptions de la Temporalité Chez les Mayas Yucateques (Mexique).* Université de Paris-X Nanterre: PhD Dissertation.

Valentina Vapnarsky

Inference crisscross: Disentangling evidence, stance and (inter)subjectivity in Yucatec Maya

Abstract: This article aims to disentangle values related to evidence, epistemic judgement, and (inter)subjectivity as conflated in two epistemic markers of Yucatec Maya. The particles *míin* and *ma'ak* are partial support inferential markers that contrast on the (inter)subjectivity parameter. The analysis, based on a wide and varied corpus approached through token-level usage, provides support for considering (inter)subjectivity as a separate dimension of epistemicity, and proposes that it should be organized among three poles (subjective/intersubjective/collective-general knowledge).

Keywords: inferential, epistemic, subjectivity, intersubjectivity, stance, Maya, Yucatec

1 Introduction

Over the past decade, there has been an increasing number of studies exploring the relation between evidentiality and other epistemic notions, particularly epistemic modality and stance (De Haan 1999; Aikhenvald 2004; Boye 2012; Cornillie 2009; Guentchéva and Landaburu 2007; Hanks 2012, among others). Recent texts on (inter)subjectivity (Nuyts 2001; Narrog 2012) and multiple perspective (Evans 2005; Bergqvist 2015), taken as orthogonal parameters to epistemicity, have introduced new complexities. Analyses such as these have resulted specifically from the fact that values relating to these different notions are often combined in actual forms (a point addressed by most of the first references; see also Tournadre and LaPolla 2014). However, the precise relation between these values is often not easy to grasp and tends to be left unspecified, especially in under-described languages, few of which benefit from a wide and varied corpus. It is also difficult to disentangle those aspects of meaning which are encoded from those that result from different types of pragmatic inference. Although this is a basic requisite, cross-linguistic studies are too vague in this respect, or they resolve this issue too hastily.

Valentina Vapnarsky, National Centre for Scientific Research (CNRS, France)

https://doi.org/10.1515/9783110572261-016

This chapter aims to contribute to this field by disentangling values relating to evidence, epistemic judgement, and (inter)subjectivity as conflated in two epistemic inferential markers of Yucatec Maya, a language spoken by nearly 800,000 people in Mexico.[1] In keeping with a discourse-centred approach, the categories are apprehended "through token level usage, [by considering] the actual deployment of the forms under interactive circumstances" (Hanks 2012: 169). The two particles – *míin* and *ma'ak* – express the epistemic modality of uncertainty or possibility (or "partial support", Boye 2012), as do other Yucatec epistemic markers, in particular *wale'* "maybe" (Hanks 2007; Vapnarsky 2012, 2013a, in prep). But they differ from the latter because they are also inferentials, conveying that the predication results from a reasoning process based on perceptual evidence or knowledge. They are thus partial support inferentials. *Míin* and *ma'ak* contrast in terms of the type of access to, and epistemic judgement of, the referent they index. Broadly speaking, *míin* is subjective and *ma'ak* non-subjective, or to use different terminology, they instantiate a direct/non-direct or first-hand/second-hand opposition (De Haan 2001), or to put it in Aikhenvald's (2004) terms, the former would be an "inferred" evidential and the latter more of an "assumed" evidential (Aikhenvald 2004).[2] However, given the variety of their uses, the precise characterization of their encoded values is less straightforward than it might first appear. Even though *míin* might seem to encode subjective access to information, in some cases the access is mediated, and *míin* only conveys a subjective epistemic judgement. However, the hypothesis that views subjective judgement as the primary encoded value is weakened by other facts. As for *ma'ak*, even though it seems to primarily encode non-subjective access to evidence, one might be tempted to characterize it as an intersubjective form that also marks the speaker's expectation of shared knowledge. However, intersubjectivity might be more a matter of implicature, and

1 The study presented here is part of a more general investigation I have carried out in the last years on uncertainty markers in Yucatec Maya. Parts of the analysis of the inferential uncertainty markers dealt with in this chapter were presented in earlier versions in different meetings: *Talking through uncertainty: Linguistic and multimodal analyses of uncertain speech situations*, EASA Workshop, University Paris Ouest Nanterre, July 2012; *First International Meeting on Yucatec Maya*, El Colegio de México, D-F, 4-5 October 2012; ELIA III, *Encuentro de Lenguas Indígenas Americanas*, Universidad de Rio Negro, Bariloche, May 2013 and FAMLI IV, *Form and Analysis in Mayan Linguistics*, Universidad del Oriente, Valladolid, November 2016. I thank all the participants of these meetings for their precious questions and comments, in particular Michel de Fornel and Scott Anderbois, as well as the editor of this volume, Zlatka Guentchéva. All misunderstandings are mine.

2 Aikhenvald (2004) proposes the following terminology: "inferred evidential", defined as "information source based on what one can see, or the result of something happening" (Aikhenvald 2004: 393) vs. "assumed evidential", defined as "information source based on conclusions drawn on the basis of on logical conclusion and general knowledge and experience" (ibid: 391).

the encoded value might strictly reference collective or general knowledge. *Míin* and *ma'ak* are thus good examples of the challenge of understanding the semantic and pragmatic intricacies of epistemic and evidential markers.

In section 2, I will start by defining the concepts and corpus of our study. Section 3 offers an overview of the syntactic properties of the inferentials *míin* and *ma'ak*. Section 4 will present an analysis of the subjective *míin*: its use for the estimation of measurements (including a comparison with the other estimative *kex*), its use for indexing direct-access to evidence, or for indirect access but subjective epistemic judgement, and lastly, its use in questions and play speech. Section 5 will analyse the non-subjective collective *ma'ak*: its use for inferences based on collective shared knowledge, in the context of situation experienced – but involving some type of mediation, its lack of strict encoding of knowledge symmetry, and its relation with perceptual access. In each section, my aim is to provide the reader with a thorough presentation and illustrations of the different kinds of more or less typical contexts in which each marker is used, in order to clearly show the values they encode and the inference they commonly trigger. This will involve a number of long examples. These illustrations are important because the markers studied here have been described either little or not at all. The examples also show the importance of taking into account local cultural principles of communicative practice and interpretation when elucidating epistemic and evidential values. Section 6 offers conclusive remarks.

2 Concepts and corpus

I define *evidential* as the linguistic marking of the source and type of perceptual or cognitive access to knowledge. *Epistemic modality* is the expression of the speaker's evaluation of his/her own degree of commitment to the knowledge or belief upon which the statement is based. This includes *epistemic judgement*, which in the context of inferentials is the speaker's assessment of the degree of validity of the inference (cf. also commitment; or epistemic qualification in Nuyts 2001: 386). I understand *subjectivity* as applying to both areas: evidentiality and epistemic modality (here instantiated as epistemic judgement). The access may be subjective (personal perception and experience, individual practice, autobiographical memory ...) and the judgement may be subjective ("in my opinion"...), and the two are not always correlated.[3] Like Nuyts (2001), I assume that subjectivity enters

3 For example, a subjective epistemic judgement may apply to evidence to which the speaker has no subjective access. Obviously there are asymmetries, for instance, cases of non-subjective

into a parameter of (INTER)SUBJECTIVITY, but in my view this parameter is made up of (at least) three poles that account for the values potentially encoded by epistemic and evidential markers: subjectivity, intersubjectivity and the collective-general. For the purpose of my analysis, these terms will be restricted to the following definitions:

- *Subjective*: knowledge sourced/accessed from the field of the speaker's direct experience and/or personal epistemic judgement.
- *Intersubjective*: knowledge sourced/accessed from the field of the other speech participant(s); it is either shared (you and me) or unshared (you but not me); it reflects the speaker's expectations with regard to the speech participant's epistemic judgement in the here-and-now of the speech event.
- *Collective-general knowledge*: knowledge sourced/accessed from widely shared collective or general knowledge; the speaker is making reference to general opinion (beyond the speech event).

Intersubjective is understood here in a more restricted sense than "intersubjective" as employed by Nuyts (2001), who used it to encompass what I designate as *collective-general*. My view is closer to more discourse-oriented views such as Traugott (1995) or Traugott and Dasher (2002), although I restrict intersubjective here to values inherent to, or prototypically associated with, linguistic forms. In particular, differentiating intersubjective from collective-general knowledge allows us to distinguish among markers expressing that the speaker shares his knowledge with others, those markers which specifically make reference to the addressee's knowledge (they index shared knowledge as construed in earlier discourse and are often used discursively in agreement or disagreement strategies) from those markers signalling that the information or stance is more widely shared as collective-general knowledge (and often shared with the addressee as well, but not necessarily). While the latter can be found designated by the term "general knowledge" in the literature on evidential markers, I add "collective" to the label to refer to the fact that speakers are often aware that their epistemic world is made up of different types of collective knowledge, which is shared to varying degrees, and to which they relate discursively (and in some languages grammatically, as in the Mayan language under study here). In different pragmatic and cognitive theoretical currents (Lyons 1977; Langacker 1990, 2002, Verhagen 2005; Portner 2009), *subjective* has often been opposed to *objective*, with diverging views in how the two concepts should be understood (for an overview, see Narrog 2012: 15–24).

judgement applying to subjective evidence, which are rarer (see Heritage 2012; Gipper 2015, and the present chapter, section 3.4).

We take *objective* to apply to utterances in which the speaker is not indexing any reference to her/his knowledge or anyone else's (thus placing it outside the (INTER)SUBJECTIVE parameter defined here, although we do not rule out the possibility that "objective" could represent a point further away on the *subjective* ←→ *collective-general* ←→ *objective* axis). The question of whether such "objective" utterances exist at all in real life, and what type of communicative components should be included in the matter, lies beyond the scope of this paper. In line with Benveniste's pioneering proposals on subjectivity, by using the (inter)subjectivity parameter, our aim is to account for values attached as conventional meaning to specific linguistic forms (Benveniste 1958).

Intersubjective and *collective-general* can enter into "multiple perspectives" indexation (Evans 2005; Bergqvist 2015) – the property that causes some markers or grammatical constructions "to encode potentially distinct values, on a single semantic dimension, that reflect two or more distinct perspectives" (Evans 2005) – but they involve different types of shared perspective and knowledge dynamics in the interaction. For instance, *intersubjective* markers are much involved in agreement or disagreement strategies during the speech event, and tend to be interchanged by speakers during conversational interactions (Heritage 2012; Gipper 2015; Stievers et al. 2011), in contrast to *collective-general* knowledge markers, which may be triggered more by particular discourse genres. Distribution or a/symmetry of knowledge (Hanks 1990; Heritage 2012) is understood in relation to the speech interaction. Therefore, *subjectivity* always involves some asymmetry of knowledge. By contrast, *intersubjectivity* involves symmetric knowledge, unless the marker explicitly encodes a differential access or judgement. *Collective-general* tends to involve knowledge symmetry (the speaker assumes that the addressee and the other participants share the same collective knowledge), although the speaker may be aware that the collective knowledge of the addressee or the other participants is not the same as that which she/he shares with her/his own epistemic group of inclusion. In this sense, it seems relevant to distinguish shared knowledge (shared with others, including or not including the addressee) from symmetric knowledge (shared with the addressee).

I use *stance* to refer to "the semiotic means by which we indicate our orientation to states of affairs, usually framed in terms of evaluation (e.g. moral obligation and epistemic possibility) or intentionality (e.g. desire and memory, fear and doubt)" (Kockelman 2004). In my view, stance also includes the speaker's evaluation of evidential aspects.

The analysis is based on data recorded in villages of the municipio of Felipe Carrillo Puerto, Quintana Roo, Mexico between 1994 and 2015. In these villages,

Maya is the dominant language in all types of daily interaction (except in school, and recently, in an increasing number of young parent to young children interactions). The corpus used for the study is based on approximately fifty hours of recorded audio and video, as well as transcribed verbal interactions, representative of different conversational and narrative genres. The data was supplemented by examples noted on the spot in day-to-day interactions, as well as by metalinguistic and elicitation sessions on the epistemic markers under study, held in Maya with four native speakers from the village of x Kopchen (*x K'oopch'e'en* in Maya). The aim of these sessions was to gain a more thorough understanding of the linguistic forms and recorded examples. However, with the exception of one small paradigm of examples, all of the illustrative utterances I present in the chapter come from natural interactions.[4]

3 Syntactic properties of the inferentials mîin and ma'ak

Amerindian languages are famous for grammaticalizing epistemic modality and evidentiality (Aikhenvald 2004; Guentchéva and Landaburu 2007). In these languages, markers of evidentiality usually seem to be inflectional affixes or clitics, contrasting with other languages such as those of Europe, where these notions tend to be expressed by lexical roots or verbal inflexion linked to tense. Yucatec Maya presents what could be seen as an intermediate case, since most epistemic markers are particles that, in this mildly polysynthetic language, have a status midway between grammatical and lexical elements.[5] They are not affixes, but cannot serve as the base of any affixation or derivation in the way that lexical roots do. They have linear constraints. They are not syntactically obligatory, but pragmatically they often are. The range of epistemic particles of Yucatec Maya present diverse syntactic properties (in particular in relation to linearity and predication). Among this range, however, *mîin* and *ma'ak* share the same morpho-syntactic

4 At this stage, we do not have access to diachronic data on the inferential markers to complete the analysis and better evaluate some hypotheses presented below concerning semantic and pragmatic changes. In any case, given the limited range of written genres which make diachronic data available in Yucatec Maya, and the discursive nature of the markers analysed, it is most probable that a diachronic analysis would provide a very partial image of their use in earlier times.

5 Aikhenvald (2004: 69) presents a few other Amerindian languages that mark evidentiality with particles (Hopi, Arizona Tewa, and Kamaiurá).

properties (for *míin*, examples of most of these properties can be found in Hanks 1984 and Anderbois 2013; the examples given in the next sections of the present chapter complete the illustration for *míin* and provide them for *ma'ak*). As shown by the properties below, *míin* and *ma'ak* precede the constituent over which they have scope. This implies that with these markers, the speaker first communicates her/his epistemic commitment to the proposition, framing the utterance from the outset as a conjecture or supposition (contrary to other Yucatec Maya particles which are clause final, and hence modalize the information only after its statement, such as the uncertainty marker *wale'*, the mirative *bakâan* (Anderbois 2016) or the confirmative *lo'obal*).

a. they precede the predicate (and the focalized constituent, but appear after topic), Yucatec Maya being a predicate-initial language, with the topic usually preceding the predicate, as shown in table 16.1.

Table 16.1: Position of inferential particles *míin/ma'ak* in the clause structure

(Topic)	*míin/ma'ak*	(Focus)	Predicate	Arguments

b. they apply to independent clauses (except in the case of the estimative use of *míin*, see 3.1);
c. they cannot function as the main predicate, nor can they be negated;
d. they cannot function as the base of morpho-phonological processes.

4 The subjective inferential *míin*

The epistemic particle *míin* is used to modalize a statement as a conjecture, as a hypothesis that the speaker cannot fully substantiate. It conveys possibility and inference. But *míin* also encodes a relation to the subjective field: in most cases the speaker uses *míin* when the inference is rooted in direct, perceptual evidence from the situation. We will show that *míin* can also be used in situations of indirect evidence, in this case, it conveys a subjective stance about what is inferred, similarly to "in my opinion" or "in my view". The subjectivity entailed by *míin* is also revealed by the translations provided by Yucatec bilingual dictionaries: Bricker et al. (1998: 185) give "I suppose", and the Maya Popular dictionary (2003: 164) proposes "creo que, quizá, a lo mejor" ("I think that, maybe, perhaps"). In addition to these brief mentions, *míin* is analysed as conjectural in Hanks 1984 and Anderbois 2013 (see 4.6).

4.1 Estimation of measurements

A very common function of *mı́in* is to indicate the estimative nature of a measurement, which can be of any type, such as size in examples (1) and (2), quantity in (3) and (5), or temporal location in (4). This function represents about a third of the examples of our corpus. The measure is generally expressed as a nominal clause or an adverbial complement. In (1), a woman explains that when she was hunting for an agouti, a big stone fell on her as she tried to enter a cave. To estimate the size of the stone in her story, she compares it to the hearthstone she is looking at while speaking. This perceptual act of approximate comparative measurement is expressed by *mı́in*.

(1) 1. *Noxi woolis tunich nojoch buka'aj!* ***Mı́in*** *buk le k'ooben-o'.*
Big round stone big MEASURE INF.S MEASURE DET hearth-TD$_2$
A big round stone, as big as this! **About** the size of the hearth stone.

2. *Buka'aj le tunich lúub t inwóo'lo'!*
The stone that fell on me was this big! [xisa-vva0154-1996]

In (2), the speaker estimates how old he was when he lived through the period of poverty that followed the war. His words *mı́in buka'ajena'* "maybe about this size" are accompanied by a gesture pointing at a child of an equivalent age.

(2) 1. *Teene' 'oora'ako' inwilmaj pero teene' ma' nojochen 'oora'ako'*
Me, at that time, I saw it (= experienced it), but I wasn't big at that time,

2. ***mı́in*** *buka'aj-en-a'!*
INF.S MEASURE-B1-TD$_1$
I was **about** that size!

In (3), an old man remembers the farm where he lived as a child, and the many domestic animals they had; he estimates their number by recalling personal memories of his life.

(3) 1. *Pos tene', ka j lúuk'en ten Xek Pich, tu'ux kajakbalo'ono',*
Well, when I left Xek Pich, where we used to live,

2. *yaan-Ø ten* ***mı́in*** *kwareenta jun-túul u-kaax,*
EXIST-B3 PR1 INF.S fourty one-NC A3-chicken
I had **about** forty chickens,

3. *kaax-óo' bey tak e x-nuk kaax-o' je'el-a',*
chicken-3PL MOD until DET FEM-old chicken-3PL OST-TD$_1$
chickens, the hens were as big as this,

4. *yaan-Ø to'on* **míin** *kex dyes wa kiinse jun-túul u-k'éek'en,....*
EXIST-B3 PR2PL INF.S CONC ten or fifteen one-NC A3-pig
we had **about** ten or fifteen pigs... [mak-vva0091-1996]

In (4), the speaker is describing the onset of a cyclone that he experienced years ago. He remembers that it started around the same time of day as when he was talking.

(4) 1. *pero le ka a'la'* **míin** *walaaji-ak tuka'aten-o' ...*
but DET CONJ say INF.S TP.ADV-PAST again-TD$_2$
But when it was **about** this time of day again,

2. *tuka'aten u-líik'-i muunyal-óo'*
again A3-rise-VL cloud-3PL
again the clouds rose [mak-vva0085-1997]

Finally, in (5), the speaker estimates the size of the field in which he is currently planting beans.

(5) 1. *ten ba'ax kinpak'ik be'ooráa' estee bu'ul,*
Me, what I'm planting now it's ... beans,

2. **míin** *t-in-pak'-ik* **míin** *seys mekates bu'ul, tsama'-bu'ul,*
INF.S PROG-A1-plant-IPF.TR INF.S six mecate bean *tsama'*-bean
let's say I'm planting **about** six *mecates* of beans, *tsama'* beans

All these examples are very representative of *míin* uses. In all instances, the estimation involves direct personal access to the referent, which is evaluated through perception, practice and/or personal memory.

4.2 The subjective estimative (*míin*) vs. the neutral estimative (*kex*)

When the estimation is not based on direct subjective access to the referent, another particle, *kex*, is favoured. *Kex* is a concessive marker that serves to introduce "even if" clauses, as in (6).

(6) ***kex*** *tâant* *u-sîij-l-e'* *bey-a',* *túun-chu'uch-(i)k* *u-chan k'a'*
CONC RETROS.IM A3 -born-VL-TD_4 MOD-TD_1, PROG.A3-sucke-IPF.TR A3-small hand
Even though she's just born, she's (already) sucking her little hand

But *kex* also signals approximation when estimating measurements. The facts presented below confirm that *mîin* indexes subjectivity of access in the estimation of measurements, and also that contrary to *mîin*, in its estimative function *kex* is neutral in terms of the type of evidential access.

It is not unusual for *kex* to co-occur with *mîin*, as in (3) above, line 4. However, *kex* is used on its own, without *mîin*, when the estimation is based on indirect access to the referent. This is typically the case in traditional narratives. A survey of the distribution of *kex* vs. *mîin* in this genre shows that *kex* is considerably more frequent, and that the few instances of *mîin* are framed as quoted speech, in which *mîin* indexes the perspective of the quoted character.[6] For this analysis, it is important to clarify that Yucatec Maya has both a generic hearsay marker (*bin*, hearsay most often from an indefinite source, translated in the examples as "they say") and a quotative marker (*k*-ABS). Only the latter presents the reported statement as a verbatim quotation and maintains the indexical frame of the reported speech event (see also Lucy 1993). All three examples below come from the same story about the origin of the sacred crosses in the region. The story takes place during the "war", in the early days of what is regarded as present-day humanity, a time the speaker has heard much about but did not see.[7] In (7), the estimation, which concerns the size of the tree on which the very first of these crosses is said to have been found, is explicitly presented as part of reported speech, signalled by the hearsay clitic *bin*.

(7) 1. *Si le* *che'-o'* *yaan-Ø* ***kex*** *bin* *de* *seeys* *meetros*
Si DET tree-TD_2 EXIST-B3 CONC REP CONJ six meters
but this tree, it's **about**, they say, six meters ...

2. *wa* *de* *syeete* *meetros* *ka'anl-i(l)!*
DISJ CONJ seven meters high-NOM
or seven meters high! [mak-vva0098-1996]

6 There are a very few exceptions to this. One possible way to explain them is to consider that they occur when the narrator adopts the perceptive of a protagonist, as an instance of discursive polyphony. We leave this topic for further investigation.

7 The "war" the Mayas refer to is the indigenous rebellion historically known as the Caste War, which took place on the Yucatan Peninsula, 1847–1901 according to Mexican history, although the Mayas consider that it lasted much longer.

In (8), the sizes of some parts of the tree are now described, a branch fork and a little hole in the trunk. Note that for the latter, the speaker adds a gesture to his description to show the approximate size of the hole. Despite this gesture – reinforced by the terminal deictic *a'*, which signals immediacy of access, and typically accompanies ostensive gestures – no *míin* is used, only *kex*. This choice reveals that in selecting an estimative marker, indirect access to the primary referent (the speaker never saw the tree) predominates over the speech event context. This indirectness/non-subjectiveness is also overtly signalled by the recurrent use of the reportative *bin*.

(8) 1. *koomo le seedro*
as DET cedar
as the cedar,

2. *yaan-Ø* ***kex*** *buk u-nak' uy-óox toop'-i le seedro*
EXISB3 CONC MEASURE A3-belly A3-three bud-NOM DET cedar
tun bin-a',
thus REP-TD$_1$
it was **about** that size, the three-forked branch of the cedar tree, they say

3. *te' tun bin uchan kweeba yan* ***kex*** *buk ujoboni bina',*
there, in its little cave, the hole was **about** that size they say
[mak-vva0098-1996]

By contrast, (9) illustrates one of the very few instances of *míin* (co-occurring with *kex*) in the same narrative. *Míin* occurs here in the context of direct quoted speech, signalled by the verbatim quotative *k-*. The narrator speaks as the "animator" (below, "animator" and "author" are used in Goffman's sense) of the main character's words: with *míin*, the main character – or "author" – estimates the time the candle must have been burning on the tree, given the large drops of wax that cover the trunk. *Míin* is allowed and expected here because now, given the quoted-speech framing, it is the narrated event (and the author's perspective) rather than the speech event (and the animator perspective) that determinates the indexical marking, and this triggers a subjective estimation.

(9) 1. *Le ba'ala' ma' táantike' senyoora!* ***Ki' bin.***
This thing, it's not new madam! **He said they say.**

2. *Le ba'al-a'* ***míin*** *yaan-Ø* ***kex*** *siinko wa seeys aanyos*
DET thing-TD$_1$ INF.S EXIST-B3 CONC five DISJ six years
this thing, **I suppose it must** have been burning for **about** five or six years

3. *ts'óok uyeele' le saanto kib te'la',* ***ki' bin.***
The candle there, **he said they say.** [mak-vva0098-1996]

The distribution of *kex* (with no *mı́in*) vs. *mı́in* (in quoted speech) in narrative genres confirms that *mı́in* conveys subjective access (and most often direct perceptual access) when used in measurement contexts. The next section will show that *mı́in* also indexes subjectivity in non-measurement-estimation uses, but that in these other cases, subjectivity of epistemic judgement can surpass subjectivity of access.

4.3 Other inferential uses based on direct access to evidence

In non-measurement uses, *mı́in* most often occurs in situations where, similarly to the measurement-estimation use, the inference is based on premises connected with the perceptual field of the speaker, or direct cognitive knowledge, such as in (10) and (11) below. *Mı́in* also helps signal that the statement is a personal supposition. This subjective stance is very often reinforced by the combination of *mı́in* with the idiomatic subjective attenuators *(in)wake* (< *kinwa'alike'* "I say it") "according to me" "to my opinion", as in (10) to (13), or *bey inwoojle'* "to my knowledge".

In (10) a man (S1) visits a ritual specialist, *j meen*, (S2) for a purification sweeping. Shortly after he arrives, he explains his pains by pointing at different parts of his body, and then suggests a hypothetical cause. His aetiological guess (a bad wind) comes from the feelings in his body, as well as from his personal knowledge of occasions when the wind might have caught him. And this is just a supposition. All of this is conveyed by the use of *mı́in*.

(10) 1. S1: *(...) Ma' chen junp'e diya ka tyala tunk'ı́inam te'ela', tunk'ı́inam,*
And is it not that one day, it was hurting here, it was hurting,

2. *ka j lı́ik' te'la', ka p'u bin te'la'*
and it went up here, and then it started to go here
(shows how the pain rose from his arm to his shoulder and neck),

3. *myeentras tak inkaal ubin, chachmil umenmile';*
and at that time, it was even going to my neck, it grabbed me

4. *Junp'el ink'ab je'la', maadre lelo' jach utopmaj! Chiingas uk'ı́inama tun!*
This one hand, my gosh it really ruined it! Damn, what pain!

5. S2: *bey, jach jaaj xı́ib*
That's how it is, that's very true man

5. S1:

Puuta	*k-inw-a'a-(i)k*	*le*	*ba'al-a'*	***mı́in***	*iik'-Ø*
damn	ICP-A1-say-TR.IPF	DET	thing-TD$_1$	INF.S	wind-B3

k-inw-a'a-(i)k-e'.
ICP-A1-say-TR.IPF-TD$_4$

Damn, I say, this, this **may be** wind, I say.

6. S2: (to other visitors) *P'aat injan atender le 'aamigoe'.* (to S1): *Mâaneni'.*
Wait, I'm quickly attending to the friend. (to S1): Come in.
[tor-D3-GA-P2-2007]

The following example (11) is taken from the same conversation as (3) above. The man had moved to a new home, where his poultry and pigs had quickly begun deteriorating and dying. Before going to see the ritual specialist, the man had had a conversation with his brother, which he re-enacts in his long story. In this extract, he is suggesting to his brother that the field is cursed. The personal, autobiographical experience on which the events are based and the subjective nature of the supposition are reflected in, and asserted with, the use of *míin*. The discourse is framed as quoted speech by the quotative *k* in first person (*ken*) at the end, line 3.

(11) 1. – *'Pos le ba'ala' 'ermaano', de por sile',*
'Well, this, my brother, in fact,

2. *inw-a'-k-e'* **míin** *waay-bi* *meent-ab-Ø* *le* *teereno'*
A1-say-TR.IPF-TD$_4$ INF.S curse-PART do-PAS.CP-B3 DET field
tu'ux *yaan-ak-en,*
where EXIST-INTR.SBJ-B1
I'd say that the field where I was **might** have been cursed,

3. *yóosa munyaanta to'on mix junp'e klaase 'áalak' waye', ken ti'.*
so that we couldn't have any sort of domestic animal there, I said to him.
[mak-vva0091-1996]

4.4 *Míin* use with non-direct evidence, but subjective epistemic judgement

Rarer, but nevertheless possible, are uses where the conjecture presented by *míin* is not based on direct subjective evidence. This is found especially in comments about old non-biographical times, or prophesied times-to-come such as in (12) and (13), or in speculations about matters to which one has no experiential access, such as in (14). As we will see in the section 5, in these contexts, the expected inferential marker is *ma'ak*. But the use of *míin* in such cases signals that, despite indirect access to the referent, the conjecture is a personal opinion of the speaker. Thus here, *míin* does not index subjective access to the evidence, but rather a subjective judgement on the facts.

(12) was uttered after the speaker had narrated the story of a fantastic animal, said to have killed and eaten people a few generations ago. In this extract, the speaker supposes that what was known as the *boob* might in fact be the "lion", which he has heard about and once saw in a picture (this was recorded before the introduction of electricity and television in the village). All the speaker's references to the *boob* are indirect (hearsay and mediated visual access).

(12) 1. *as.kweenta boob tumen (.) pero* ***míin*** *let e leon inw-ay-ik*
CONJ boob because but INF.S PI3 DET lion A1-say-IPF.TR
we can think it's the boob because... but **I suppose** this is the lion I'd say

2. *faasil beyo' tumen úuchben nukuch máakob-o'*
it's probably that because the ancestors

3. *boob ya'ako' jaaa bey uts'a'amilob uk'aabao'*
they said Boob, haa, that's the name they gave to it. [pascbob-1994]

In (13), an old woman talks about the different doomsday prophesies, a topic often discussed in the region. Her knowledge of the prophecies is hearsay; but here she suggests the doomsday that she personally thinks would be the least painful.

(13) 1. *pero t-inw-a'a-(i)k ke* ***míin*** *mas uts geera ka*
but PROG-A1-say-IPF.TR CONJ INF.S more good war CONJ
líik'-ik-Ø
raise-SBJ.INTR-3B
but I say that it would **probably** be better if war arises

2. *ke yete le eele ka meeto'*
than that fire occurs [xisa-vva0153-1995]

Finally, in (14), another woman is answering a question I had asked about the location of the sun, during an interview about cosmology. She can see the sun of course. But this does not provide her with the clues necessary for understanding precisely where the sun is located in the different sky layers that make up the Maya cosmos. With *míin*, she hypothesises that even those who travel in planes cannot know. This thought has just occurred to her, and she has never expressed it before. It is based on indirect knowledge but she experiences and conveys it as a very personal opinion on that topic.

(14) 1. V: *tu'ux yan le k'iino'?*
Where is the sun?

2. J: *lelo' ken sa' tu'ux?! tu'ux t at'aan le je'elo'?*
   That who knows where?! Where is it according to you?

3. *lelo' mix máak ojeelmil inwa'ik. Lelo' mix máak ojeelmi!*
   That, nobody knows I'd say. That, nobody knows!

4. ***Míin*** *mix* *le* *k-u-bin-o'* *ka'an-o'* *muny-il-ik-óo',*
   INF.S NEG.EMPH DET ICP-A3-go-3PL sky-TD$_2$ NEG.PROG.A3-see-IPF.TR-3PL
   I suppose not even those who travel to the sky, they don't see it

5. *munk'uchlo'bi', ay wa k'uchke' yeelo'be'!*
   they don't get there, uy if they got there, they would burn!
   [xjua-III-5-1994]

These examples show that even if direct access to the evidence is an important feature of *míin*, it is not a necessary value (see also sections 4.1.1 and 4.1.2).

The subjectivity encoded by *míin* is further confirmed by the fact that *míin* is most often combined with first-person predicates, as in (10) and (11). Naturally, the third person appears more often in the indirect access cases presented in this section. As for second-person subject predicates involving *míin*, these mostly concern polar questions, to which we now turn.

4.5 Questions and play speech

4.5.1 Polar questions (about facts concerning the addressee)

As a corollary of the cases analysed above, *míin* is also frequently used in questions that offer a personal supposition calling for a confirmation from the addressee. In the situation, the supposition is generally based on some immediate aspect that is perceived by the speaker, but concerns the addressee. In (15), after I step on a dog's tail and shout in surprise and fear, the worried owner of the house promptly approaches me and asks if her dog has bitten me. She did not see the incident but heard my shout (sensory-auditory access), and is guessing what happened.

(15) 1. V: – *Ay!*
   – Ow!

2. R: – *Bik* *u-chi'-ech!* ***Míin*** *t-u-chi'-ech* *Balentiina ?*
   ADM A3-bite-B2 INF.S CP.TR-A3-bite-B2 PN
   – Careful it doesn't bite you! **Might** it have bitten you Valentina (**as it seems to me**)? [xros-D3G2-06-2006]

In (16), a woman reports her conversation with a woman who has come to attend the village festival with her daughter. The conversation is rendered in quoted speech, framed by the verbatim quotative *k*. When she saw the woman waiting for a van, she asked her if she was planning to take her daughter back to their village. Again, the supposition is based on some perceptual-visual evidence (the visitor waiting for the van) and presented as a personal guess.

(16) 1. *tinw-a'al* *t* *e* *nojoch* *máako',*
PROG.A1-say PREP DET big person-TD_2
I said to the lady,

2. ***míin*** *yan* *a-bi-s-(i)k* *a-'iija-o'* *ken* *ti,*
INF.S OBL A2-go-CAUS-IPF.TR A2-daughter-TD_2 QUOT.B1 PR3
maybe you're taking your daughter away (as it seems to me)? I say to her.

Notice that in both (15) and (16), *míin* modalises a predicate concerning an addressee's circumstances to which the speaker has some perceptual access, though less than the addressee her/himself. These examples could therefore be considered cases of (relative) symmetric knowledge (the speaker shows that s/he is aware of some circumstances concerning the addressee). However, basic Mayan principles of communicative interaction rather tend to favour the interpretation that the speaker uses the subjective *míin* to avoid making an assumption about the viewpoint and experience of the addressee/other without previous confirmation. This is part of a more general cultural and linguistic stance to avoid asserting something that one is not entirely sure of and has no direct access to. Consequently, here *míin* also indexes an asymmetric relation to evidence.

4.5.2 Play speech

Finally, *míin* is characteristic of the genre *báaxal-t'aan* (play speech), in its gentle form.[8] In this dialogic genre, speakers make clearly false statements to their addressee. The humorous statement connects a detail of the situational context to a fact about the addressee, one that the speaker might want to indirectly criticise, compliment, or just make fun of. In (17), one woman teases another who arrives very late for group work during the village festival.

8 Other languages have been reported to use inferred inferentials for irony and sarcasm (see Aikhenvald 2004: 322).

(17) ***Mı́in*** *jóok'-ech* *cha'an* *'óonyak!*
INF.S go.out-B2 watch last.night
Maybe you were out watching [the festival] last night?! [maakan-2007]

(18) was said to me during the first minutes of a visit with some friends. When I arrive without my son, the man makes fun of me, referring to the fact that I often left my young son in the care of other women in the village. Notice that both jokes are based on perceptual evidence, as is common in the genre and correlates with the subjectivity of *mı́in*.

(18) *Tu'ux* *yaan-Ø* *e* *Mateo* *x* *Balen?* ***Mı́in*** *t-a-si-aj?*
Where EXIST-B3 DET PN FEM PN INF.S CP.TR-offer-TR.PF
Where is Mateo Balen? Or **maybe** you gave him away? [rosi8:17.40-2008]

Besides being triggered by the direct-access evidence condition, *mı́in* in *báax-al-t'aan* forms seems to help attenuate the provocation by marking the idea implied by the question as only assumed by the speaker (and potentially not shared by others).

4.6 Summary and discussion of *mı́in*

The analysis of the different uses of *mı́in* shows that this particle is often linked to the expression of subjective perceptual access to information, indicating an asymmetry of knowledge distribution among the speech participants. This is typically the case in the measurement-estimation function of *mı́in*, which represents a large proportion of its uses. It is also predominant in non-measurement cases, but among these it is possible to find contexts in which *mı́in* is used in situations of indirect non-subjective access to evidence, in order to signal more that the inference is a personal judgement.

One question is whether or not the marker should be analysed as basically a marker of subjectivity of epistemic judgement (a value that always appears to be present when *mı́in* is used) on which the value of direct access, or asymmetric knowledge, would be dependent. At first sight, this analysis would seem more economical, and could explain the fact that (i) *mı́in* is used even in cases of indirect access if there is subjectivity of epistemic judgement and that (ii) we have found no clear case of direct access and non-subjective (or intersubjective) judgement expressed by *mı́in*. Recent analyses of epistemic markers have offered similar interpretations, in which access to evidence or the indexation of knowledge distribution is seen as dependent on (inter)subjective epistemic judgement (e.g. Gipper 2015: 216). However, as Gipper (2015) mentions in her study of the Amazonian language Yurakaré and two of its epistemic forms that seem semantically very similar to *míin/ma'ak*, subjective judgement is rather neutral in terms of expectations regarding access to knowledge. In fact, for the Yurakaré subjective marker that Gipper analyses (*-laba*), subjective stance occurs just as frequently in cases of both symmetric and asymmetric (access to) knowledge. This contrasts with Yucatec uses of *míin*. In my view, the fact that *míin* occurs predominantly with direct access and asymmetric knowledge (including when it functions as a measurement-estimative) argues in favour of considering these values an essential part of its meaning. Furthermore, *míin* is not commonly used in responses marking the kind of disagreement or misalignment that would be expected with a marker primarily expressing epistemic judgement. Consequently, I would hypothesize that subjective access is the primary (diachronic) encoded meaning of *míin*, the subjective epistemic judgement being pragmatically conveyed. Through the conventionalization of pragmatic implicatures, the subjective stance becomes tightly attached to the form, to the point that in some uses, a shift occurs from subjective access to subjective epistemic judgement.[9] This explains why *míin* can be used in cases of indirect access to evidence or more symmetric knowledge, though these are less common. Moreover, the fact that sentences with *míin* are very often modalized by additional subjective attenuators like "in my opinion" or "according to me" confirms that *míin* tends to occur with an overall subjective stance, but it also reveals that the speakers need these expressions to explicitly express a personal judgement that is, or was, only inferable when using *míin*.

Anderbois (2013) analyses *míin* as a conjectural evidential, following Hanks (1984) and Faller (2002)'s subcategorization of inferentials. Anderbois argues that *míin* can be used for the two sub-types of inference that, according to Faller, characterize "conjectural": (i) inference with direct evidence and (ii) "reasoning" based on general knowledge and personal experience. We have shown several contexts in which *míin* can be used with direct evidence. This is its typical subjective frame of reference. As for "reasoning" as defined above, according to our data, *míin* can only be used (a) if the reasoning is also grounded in aspects of the predication to which the speaker has direct perceptual, practical or memory access or, (b) in cases where there is no such direct access, if the speaker wishes to express the subjectivity of her/his epistemic judgement. We will now see that in

9 Our conclusion contrasts with Anderbois (2013 submitted)'s analysis which considers that *míin* is primarily an epistemic modal and that the restriction to indirect evidence is an epiphenomenon of the semantics of uncertainty (Anderbois 2013: 9).

Yucatec Maya, a different marker is used when the inference is based exclusively or primarily on general knowledge.

5 *Ma'ak*: Inference and uncertainty in the field of collective knowledge

The particle *míin* contrasts paradigmatically with a second inferential epistemic marker: *ma'ak*. The particle *ma'ak* shares the same syntactic properties as *míin*, and the two never co-occur. Furthermore, *ma'ak* also expresses inference and conveys the same epistemic form of possibility or partial support as *míin*: the statement is presented as inferentially obtained (through presumption, deduction or abduction) and subject to a degree of scepticism. But in contrast to *míin*, *ma'ak* signals that the statement is a supposition whose clues are not centred on the speaker's subjective field, are not the immediate evidence of perception or personal memory, but are rather indirect and mediated. However, the distribution of the domain of *ma'ak* does not neatly complement that which is covered by *míin*. Whereas *míin* rather widely indexes directness of access and subjectivity, *ma'ak* is more specifically used for non-subjective evidence falling into the category of collective-general knowledge, based mostly on hearsay (but distinct from the hearsay markers).[10] This also means that it is not intersubjective in the strict sense of the definition in the introduction. Intersubjectivity (the expectation of symmetric knowledge) is nevertheless often conveyed by implicature.

The combination of *ma'ak* values of inference and non-subjectivity of access can lead to two apparently opposite epistemic interpretations, depending on the context: it can be considered (i) dubious, because the evidence does not come from the personal field, or (ii) probable, because it is linked to (widely) shared knowledge and presumably, for the speaker, a shared stance.

The particle *ma'ak*, often contracted to *mak*, is not reported in published dictionaries of contemporary Maya, most probably due to dialectal variation. My own data suggests that it is rarely or never used in Campeche and Yucatán, where most of the lexicographic work has been done.[11] However, it is frequently used in the eastern dialects spoken around Valladolid and Felipe Carrillo Puerto.

10 Hearsay is expressed by other particles: the reportative *bin* and the quotative *k-*, previously illustrated with *míin* and appearing in an example with *ma('a)k* in (21) below; see also Lucy 1993.
11 Also pers. com. by Briceida Cuevas Cob for Campeche and Fidencio Briceño Chel for Yucatán.

An arguably related form, *ma'k* or *ma'ki'* (Diccionario de Motul), *(ix) ma'kil* (Vocabulario de Viena) "por ventura no, quizá no" ("by chance no, maybe not"), is reported in the earliest colonial dictionaries of the 16th and 17th centuries (Barrera-Vásquez 1981: 480, 482). The form of the dictionaries' quotations and their proposed translations could indicate that the particle is etymologically related to the negative marker *ma'*.[12] In any case, these early reports suggest that the dialectal variation observed nowadays results from the decreasing use in some regions of a particle that was once more common.

5.1 *Ma'ak* for inferences based on shared collective knowledge

Given the meaning of *ma'ak*, it is not surprising that it is most frequently used in talk about old times, prophesied future times, folktales and matters to which the average person has only indirect and mediated access, such as the details and intricacies of the non-visible supernatural world. The following examples illustrate these contexts.

The first example, (19), is taken from a long conversation between two men, Don Juan (J) and Don Eu (E) (see Vapnarsky 1999, vol. II text 6). In this extract, the men are talking about former times and how people used to live. Don Juan, the oldest man in the village, is very confident about facts (which is typical of him, but is reinforced by my presence and the recording situation), whereas Don Eu, in his forties, adopts a much less affirmative stance, inquiring and supposing rather than asserting. This is seen clearly in the following extract, in which Don Eu introduces the topic of the clothes worn by the elders. At that moment, Don Juan had just talked about his father, and Don Eu is making reference to that generation of people, whom he did not know, or only knew when he was very young, and does not remember clearly.

(19) 1. J: *(...), pos inpapa leti' koomo ya'ab ubeetik koole', pos ma' t seen'ilaj o'tsilili'.*
My dad, as he worked a lot of fields, we didn't experience much poverty.

2. E: ***Mak*** *le úuchij,* ***mak*** *bey tak le nook'-o'* ***mak*** *mina'an-Ø?*
INF.C DET long.ago INF.C MOD even DET cloth-TD$_2$ INF.C NEG.EXIST-B3

12 Pérez (1866-77) suggests another possible etymology *maaki* "puede ser que no, parece subjuntivo de maakhal [no ser, no llegar a ser o tener resultado]" ("maybe not, it seems a subjunctive form of maakhal [not to be, to not manage to be or have results]") (Barrera-Vásquez 1981: 483). Pio Perez seems to have based his mention of *maaki* on the use of the particle as found in the *Arte* of Beltran de Santa Rosa (Beltran de Santa Rosa 1859 [1746]).

Maybe in old times, **maybe** clothes like those, **maybe** thereweren't any (as we can suppose from what we know)?

3. J: *Ba'ax nook'e' tun kunyaanta tech! Ba'ax 'óosa tun kak'uuch?*
What clothes could one have had! And what did one spin for, then?

4. E: *Chen bey uweenelo'bo', chen j wi'it'!*
They slept just like this, they were just people with loincloths!
[jua-eul-vva0028-1995]

The use of *ma'ak* in line 2 by Don Eu signals that the statement "there were no clothes (like today's)" is a supposition based not on personal experience, nor on anything the speaker has previously heard about in these precise terms, but rather on his general knowledge of those times, about which he has good reason to think his interlocutor knows more. In Don Eu's words, the intonation and the use of *ma'ak* also have a questioning effect. They call for a confirmation from Don Juan, his elder addressee. Don Juan's answer emphatically confirms Don Eu's supposition. And Don Eu's subsequent comments in line 4 show that he is falling into line with the elder's words.

In example (20), a man comments on the success of a ritual for rain, and on the powerful action of the guardian spirits that are invoked during this type of ceremony. Not being a ritual specialist himself, he has no legitimate reason to assert any direct personal knowledge on the matter. In Mayan terms, what he knows or can infer has to be presented as second-hand information. Furthermore, the inference expressed by *ma'ak* is itself part of a statement expressing a commonly shared conjecture.

(20) 1. *(...) máan le 'áaka'bo', graasya tunmeyaj,*
the night passed, and the offerings were working

2. *beendisyon jajal dyoos, ubendisyoon le nukuch máak,*
this was the blessing of True God, the blessing of the guardian-spirits,

3. ***ma'ak*** *e* *nukuch.máak-o'ob-o'*
INF.I DET big.PL.man-3PL-TD_2
probably the guardian-spirits,

4. *leti'-o'o'* *manejar-t-ik* *tulaaka* *le* *meyaj* *bey-a'.*
PR3-3PL govern-TRZER-TR.IPF all DET work MOD-TD_1
they govern this type of work [mak-vid1:29 :52-30 :02-2005]

The next example (21) shows a similar type of inference, but it does this by combining different epistemic-evidential markers. After relating a well-known episode from a mythical story about how in ancient times, people used to carry their firewood just by whistling, the speaker speculates on how this might have worked. He suggests that the whistle probably had special powers.

(21) 1. *(...) tujun kutaal! Teeche' tâanxûu'xu'!*
It came on its own! You, you were whistling!

2. ***Mak*** *espesyal-Ø* *u-xûu'xu'* *bin* *wal-e'.*
INF.C special-B3 A3-whistle RS POSS-TD$_4$
Their whistling **may** have been special maybe they say.

3. *Bey u'istoorya bey utsikbatik 'aanima inmaadrinai.*
That's the story as my godmother used to tell me. [mak-vid145:20-2005]

Notice that the statement is framed by three evidential-epistemic particles: *ma'ak*, the reportative *bin* and the epistemic *wale'* conveying possibility (Hanks 2007; Vapnarsky 2012). *Ma'ak* introduces the hypothetical statement as an inference that is based on collective knowledge. The use of the reportative *bin* (hearsay without a definite source) in the same predicate makes it explicit that the supposition (and not only the evidence) is shared by hearsay. Therefore, the final comment of the speaker in line 3 ("That's the story as my godmother used to tell me") is easily understood as referring not only to the narrative events but also to the speaker's tentative explanation of the special powers of men in old times. However, despite the supposition on the nature of the whistle also being hearsay, it is not part of the narrative itself, or at least it is not on the same epistemic level (otherwise it would not be introduced by the inferential *ma'ak*). The co-occurrence of *ma'ak* and *bin* in the same clause confirms that their values are distinct though not incompatible, and are clearly connected to the same domain of reference to cultural knowledge. The use of *wale'* in final position of the *ma'ak* clause reinforces the hypothetical character of the inference.

Whereas the use of the reportative *bin* is rampant in traditional narratives, *ma'ak* is used much less systematically and does not constitute an index of this genre. The following example clearly shows how *ma'ak* introduces the speaker's inferences and epistemic judgements on events repeated in canonical stories. This example is also very revealing of the specific values that *ma'ak* does or does not convey in terms of evidential access and epistemic symmetry.

After a conversation on various subjects, mostly surrounding the guardian spirits of different forest places, I had asked Don Torib, a man in his 70s, if the cenotes (the natural wells formed in sinkholes characteristic of the Yucatan peninsula) also have guardians. He answers affirmatively, but frames his assertion with two hearsay markers, the reportative *bin* and the reduced form *ya'ala* (> *kuya'alal* "it is said"), and in so doing, he explicitly roots his assertion in shared traditional knowledge. Don Torib then tells a well-known story about a "waterer" who got caught by a snake in a cenote, and whose rifle exploded so powerfully, it made the cenote collapse. With this story, Don Torib is suggesting that the "guardians of the water" or "of the cenote", about whom I had just asked, are in fact the *aj jóo'ya'o'ob* "waterer" guardian-spirits. Mayas commonly believe that these beings inhabit the lower layer of the sky and come down to earth to fill their gourds from the cenotes; with this water, the "waterers" create rain.

Notice first that the speaker introduces the *aj jóo'ya'* "waterer" character with *ma'ak*, a quite unusual incipit for a Maya folk story (line 3). This reveals that the speaker is still preparing his arguments at that point, using *ma'ak* to make explicit the inferential nature of the equivalence he is establishing between "the master of the water" (*uyuumil ja'*) and the "waterer" from the sky (*aj jóo'ya'*). The speaker then continues the story, constantly punctuating his words with the reportative *bin* and other hearsay markers, as is usually the case for traditional narratives (lines 4–36). It is only after the end of the story that *ma'ak* shows up again. Don Torib uses it twice, this time to equate the explosion produced by the rifle (on earth, at the cenote) with celestial thunder and lightning. This is done with a two-step/two-*ma'ak* inference: firstly, by suggesting that the sound of the rifle was just like the sound of thunder, and secondly, by suggesting that the small rifle found near the cenote must have been the same weapon that thunders in the sky. In both *ma'ak* sentences, Don Torib explicitly appeals to my personal knowledge: to my experiential knowledge in the first sentence (lines 37–40): "like **when you hear** the thunder of the lightning"; and to my knowledge of things "that are said" in the second (lines 41–46): "**don't you hear** its shake, its explosion; and **you hear it is said** the guardian spirits are shooting, it is said. that's it, that thing thunders".[13] Therefore, in this example, the speaker appeals to both traditional cultural knowledge and the addressee's experience. *Ma'ak* is used to draw on shared collective knowledge of the matters in which the inference is rooted, while explicit references to the addressee's experience are made to include this knowledge as part of the shared knowledge. As for the supposition (inference) itself, it is not symmetric, but is what Don Torib wants me to understand.

(22) 1. *Ka' bin úuch bin unp'ée beesak bin úuch bine'*
They say it happened once, they say, a long time ago, they say
(+ 1 they say)

13 Notice also that in these sentences, the reportative *bin* is not used in the same way as it was in the previous part, and this creates a clear contrast with the storytelling section.

2. *kya'ik bin e máak bino'*
   the guy says, they say,

3. | *pero* | ***mak*** *(.) aj jo'yab* | *e* | *le* | *éem-Ø* | *bey* | *ch'u_ chup* |
   |---|---|---|---|---|---|---|
   | pero | INF.C (.) AG to.water | DET | DET | go.down-B3 | MOD | fill_fill in |

u-chuuj-o'
A3-calabash-TD_2

   but **maybe** it was the waterer who went down to fill his gourd

4. *ti' yáana tun bin e 'áaktun beya'*
   below the cave, they say, like this,

5. *ti' yaan u yook yáan e 'áaktuno' beey tuchupk uchan chuuj beya'*
   his feet were under the cave's stone while he was filling his little gourd like this...

6. *kya'ik bin ti'e'*
   he says they say

7. *túuchupk uchuuj bine'*
   he was filling his gourd, they say

8. *e kutíip'l ula' juntúu máak beey kóomo ja' de uk'bile'_*
   when another man appears, since it was drinking water...

9. *ka' taal uch'a ja' bini'*
   and he came to fetch water they say,

10. *kya'ala bin ti', kya'ik bin e máako'*
    it is said to him, they say, the guy says, they say

11. *ichil uchupk uchuuj e aj jóo'ya'óo' máa ka' chu'uki'*
    As the waterer was filling in his gourd, suddenly he got caught

12. *ka' j k'a'ax men junp'e (no)xi kaan*
    and he got tied up by a big snake

13. *t ujool le ja' beyo', kya'ik bine'_*
    at the entrance of the water source like this, he says they say
    (...) (...) (here a section of the narrative is omitted for reasons of space)

36. *Tuntronáart e' ba'alo' ka j k'aschaj e (.) ts'ono'ot bino'*
    The thing thundered and the cenote got ruined.

37. | ***Ma'k*** *lee* ***ma'k*** *(.)* | *je'ex* | *je'ex* | *u-tronar* | *raayo* | *k-aw-uy-ik* |
    |---|---|---|---|---|---|
    | INF.C DET INF.C | as | as | A3-thunder | lightening | ICP-A2-hear-IPF.TR |

    It must have been like when you hear the thunder of the lightning

38. *[bey uwa'ak'a] uwíinkili máak bey úuchk utronark le ts'ono'oto'!*
    just like a body explodes, that's how the cenote thundered!

39. *ka j ts'o'okej nojochajij*
    and after that, it got bigger

40. *bey bin*
    that's how it is they say
    (... .... 30 s. not reproduced)

41. ***Ma'ak*** *le* *ba'a* *taa-s-a'ab-e'*
    INF.C DET thing come-CAUS-PAS.PF-TD$_4$
    It must have been the thing that he brought (lit. was brought)

42. *lete'* *le* *k-u-tronar-o'* *te'* *ka'an-l-o',*
    PR3 DET ICP-A3-thuunder-TD$_2$ LOC sky-NOM-TD$_2$
    that thundered in the sky,

43. *máa' [k]awuyik u ukíilba uwa'ak'a,*
    don't you hear its shake, its explosion;

44. *kawuyik ya'alalo' tunts'oonóo' le yúuntsilo'obo' kya'alale'*
    and you hear it is said the guardian spirits are shooting, it is said

45. *aja lete' je'elo' kutronartik le' ba'a je'lo'.*
    that's what it is, the thing that thunders things.

46. *Bey bin.*
    That's how it is they say. [tor-D3G4P2-2007]

The examples above are typical of the majority of the instances of *ma'ak* found in our corpus, in that they involve non-subjective indirect access to the evidence on which the inference is based, and concern different kinds of traditional collective knowledge. Since they concern traditional collective knowledge, they also tend to imply symmetry of knowledge. Indeed in these cases, we have seen that most instances also imply the speaker's supposition or expectation that both the evidence and the inference are shared by others, usually – but not always – the other speech participants. This is seen in example (19) because the speaker is convinced that his addressee knows more than he does about what he is supposing, in example (20) because the inference reflects a shared conjecture, and in example (21) because the inference is grammatically marked as hearsay. However, notice that in (21) the inference is marked as shared with others (hearsay), but is not expected to be shared by the addressee (myself). The last example (22) shows a similar but more complex situation in which *ma'ak* is used because the speaker thinks the knowledge behind the inference is shared (either as common experience or as common traditional lore) but the epistemic judgement is not (although the speaker's aim is to change this).

5.2 *Ma'ak* in the context of situations experienced

The next examples are especially instructive because they present cases in which *ma'ak* modalizes statements related to autobiographical events. In this context, the subjective *mı́ın* rather than *ma'ak* would be expected in terms of knowledge access and asymmetry. But we will see that in fact, despite being rooted in a personal experience, the inference introduced by *ma'ak* always concerns an aspect of the situation to which the speaker has only non-subjective or mediated access, following the general pattern of *ma'ak* uses.

This is clear in example (23). The situation mentioned is a very concrete event that the speaker, an elderly woman, experienced and is remembering: while hunting, she got trapped in a cave after a stone fell and blocked the entrance. The speaker then speculates about why the cave closed, and *ma'ak* introduces the hypothetical cause. Notice however, that the cause is not related to anything the speaker has directly seen or experienced. It is instead related to a supernatural power, the guardian-spirit of the cave, knowledge of which is, as we saw in (20), indirect, based on comments and stories of all kinds (see also Vapnarsky 2013b). This reference to common and mediated knowledge can explain the use of *ma'ak*.

(23) 1. *Pos leti',* ***mak*** *u-yuum-il le 'áaktun*
CONJ PR3 INF.I A3-master-NOM DET cave
well it's him, **it must be** the guardian of the cave

2. *leti' leen-ch'in-t-ej le ba'a t-inw-óok'ol-o', leti'!*
PR3 flash-throw.at-TRZER-B3.SBJ DET thing PREP-A1-on-REL-TD_2 PR3
he's the one who threw the thing on me, it's him!

3. *Yaan uyuumil (...) (...) la'tene' tunmeetiko' teen beyo'.*
It [the cave] has its guardians, that's why they did that to me.
[xisa-vva0154-1996]

The following example involves another type of mediation. It is taken from the account of a boy abducted by guardian-spirits and taken to live with them for some time. In quoted speech, the extract presents the dialogue between the parents and the son, now back home. At first sight, *ma'ak* seems clearly unexpected here because it introduces a statement relating to an action of which the boy was the direct patient, and which is reported as verbatim quotation. However, notice that this action took place when the boy was living with the guardian-spirits, in a somewhat different world, and in an abnormal state of consciousness. *Ma'ak* appears to index the indirect perception of this extraordinary experience. Here it might also be used as a way of creating a sense of distance while relating events that, according to cultural values, should be left unmentioned, or be only very vaguely referenced.

(24) 1. – *Ay pero núux, kuya'alaj bin ti', yaan tak x nóok'ol tech!*
Oh but son, it was said to him they say, you even have worms!

2. – *Xíib yaan wale', (...) pos teene', teene' tin-máan,*
Man, I have maybe (...) well me, me, I was going,

3. *chen ween-(e)k-en, **ma'ak** tun-ts'a'ab-a ten xnóok'ol*
just sleep-SBJ-1B INF.C PROG.A3-give-PAS-IPF PR1 worm
wal-e' kij bin...
POSS – TD_4 QUOT RS
and when I went to sleep, **maybe** they put worms on me (lit. I was put worms) maybe,
he said they say... [mak-vva0087-1996]

The last example in this section is probably the most atypical of our corpus. It is nevertheless perfectly explainable from what we saw before. The sentence was spoken by a young mother while she was bathing her little girl in an elevated washing tub. The girl laughs with joy. The mother then tells of another child she once saw, a boy who cried and resisted while being bathed in the same way. Using *ma'ak*, she then hypothesizes that the boy might have been suffering because he was not used to that way of bathing. The speech event takes place in the kitchen of her mother-in-law (where the girl's mother lives) with various family members around. None of them knows the boy she is talking about.

(25) ***Mak** ma' súujk uy-ich-kúun-s-a'a(l) bey-o'*
INF.C NEG HAB A3-bathe-FACT-CAUS-PAS.IPF MOD-TD_2
Maybe he wasn't used to being bathed like that?! [fieldnote-2012]

The speaker is reporting a situation she observed, and is drawing an inference about this situation. There is clearly asymmetric knowledge, since the inference is addressed to speech participants who were not present when the reported event occurred. Despite the fact that this asymmetry and the speaker's perceptual access to the evidence (the boy crying) would make *míin* the expected inferential, *ma'ak* is used instead. We can identify a number of relations – of the speaker to the reported facts, as well as to the speech participants' assumed knowledge – that lead the speaker to use *ma('a)k*: (i) perceptual and corporal mediation (the mother observed the situation but she was not bathing the child herself; the child was bathed by a third person who is absent from the speech situation);[14] (ii) inference addressed to a third party (the mother is addressing not the person who was bathing the boy, nor the boy himself, but rather people who did not observe the situation; this context can be contrasted with the uses of *míin* in questions, seen in section 2.4.1); (iii) the inference has to be confirmed by drawing on second-hand cultural knowledge (given that the speech event participants have no access to aspects or participants of the reported bathing situation).[15] All of these elements converge to exclude the use of *míin* in this experienced situation and, by contrast, to justify the use *ma'ak*.

5.3 *Ma'ak*: The lack of coding of knowledge symmetry

We have seen that all of the instances of *ma'ak* found in our corpus reflect various types of knowledge-access indirectness, but mainly relating to references to shared collective knowledge. The recurrent use of *ma'ak* to draw inferences from this type of knowledge may lead to the analysis that *ma'ak* is a marker of symmetric knowledge. However, some of the previous examples did not fit this analysis ((21), (22), (25)). Other examples, some of them from elicitation sessions, confirm that symmetry of knowledge is not a necessity. For instance, *ma'ak* was chosen in an imaginary context in which a speaker, seeing seeds he did not know about as a child (*tumen teene' ma' inwili'* "because I didn't see them (the seeds)") assumes they did not exist back then. He comments on this to a co-worker, asking for confirmation:

(26) ***Ma'ak*** *mina'an* *áa úuchij ?*
INF.C EXIST.NEG INTER in.the.old.times
Doesn't it seem that there weren't any before? [elicitation-epist-2012]

The interviewee improvised an answer for the addressee, who contradicts the inference, replying that the seeds must have existed because his grandfather told him so. The fact that *ma'ak* was used in a polar question, and that the answer is incongruous with the proposition introduced by *ma'ak*, reveals that symmetry of knowledge was not expected by the speaker.

---

14 See also Kwoon (2012: 963) on the use of an indirect inferential marker in Korean with third-person subject experiential predicates.

15 In a way, this is similar to example (19) with the speaker asking for help to confirm a hypothesis based on cultural knowledge.

5.4 Prevalence of collective-general knowledge over visual access

Interestingly, the elicited data also reveals a preference for *ma'ak* when the inference concerns matters of the past and of collective history, even if the evidence also comes from personal memory or perceptual access. This was already present in the earlier example where the speaker, imagining the scene associated with the *ma'ak* sentence, said that he was drawing his inference from old memories. This is even more striking in the contrast between the next two examples. In (27), the imagined situation involves a person discovering traces of an old wall in the forest, and inferring that there once must have been a village at that location. She expressed this with *ma'ak.*

(27) 1. ***Ma'ak*** *yan-Ø* *máak* *kaaj-l-a'an-Ø* *way* *úuch-ej*
INF.C EXIST-B3 person village-posit-PART-B3 here long.ago-TD_4
It seems there were people living here before.

2. *pos tumen umeyajo' way p'aatla', wa kex nukuch máakóo' meetej.*
Well because, their work has stayed here, it could have been done by old generations. [elicitation-epist-2012]

In (28), the speaker was asked to imagine someone discovering that a stool had changed place in her house while she and the other inhabitants were absent, and inferring from this that someone must have entered the house. In this case, the speaker clearly preferred to express the inference with *míin:*[16]

(28) 1. ***míin*** *yaan-Ø* *máak* *óok-Ø* *t* *in-na(j)-i,*
INF.S EXIST-B3 person enter-B3 PREP A1-house-NOM
Apparently someone entered my house,

2. *ba'an.ten le ba'al-a' bey yaan-ik-a'? (..)* ***míin*** *yaan-Ø máak*
WHY DET thing-TD_1 MOD EXIST-MAF-TD_1 INF.S EXIST-B3 person
óok way-e'.
enter-B3 here- TD_3
why is this thing like this? (.) **Apparently** someone entered here.

3. *Beey, inwa'ake' yan máak óok waye'. Aaja ooko máak waye'! kech xan*
That's it, I'd say someone entered here. Aha, someone has entered here! You (should) say also. [elicitation-epist-2012]

16 Similar answers to both contexts were given by three other speakers.

Both situations imply that the inference is drawn from visible evidence. However, in the first case, the epistemic judgement is also informed by common local historical knowledge about the existence of abandoned dwellings in the forest, and this led to the use of *ma'ak*. By contrast, the second case corresponds to an individual fact linked to present-day life and the immediacy and singularity of a situation that has just occurred and that no one knows about, which triggered the use of *míin*.

Similarly to the ancient dwelling example, but taken from a natural context, our final example confirms the prevalent relation of *ma'ak* to matters of traditional knowledge. When I asked a friend if Maya had been their language since old times, my addressee, a woman in her forties, exclaimed:

(29) – ***Ma'ak*** *bey-o!*
INF.C MOD-TD$_2$
Probably yes, it has!

She immediately supported her assertion by mentioning that her grandfather used to speak Maya. She had known her grandfather well, and clearly remembered interacting with him in Maya until his death when she was about 20. The evidence she invokes is thus based on personal memory access (which is more of the field of *míin*). However, as also shown by the above example (26), and as supported by other facts, here the reference to the grandfather mainly serves as a typified source of collective knowledge, which triggers the use of *ma'ak*.

Examples (27) and (29) show interesting cases in which the evidence comes from both subjective and collective-general knowledge. Remarkably, the fact that the latter is favoured in the marking choice does not follow the common salience hierarchy generally observed for evidential (visual > non-visual > inferred) (Aikhenvald: 2004) or for deictic markers in Yucatec (asymmetric/perceptual > symmetric/perceptually more distant) (Hanks 1990, 2005) (where > means that the value to the left of the sign outweighs the one on the right, and the marker encoding the "heavier" value is given preference when both compete in a given speech context).

5.5 Summary of *ma'ak* and its contrast with *míin*

The particle *ma'ak* signals that the statement under consideration is a partial-support inference based on non-subjective knowledge. This characterization makes it the exact complement of *míin*. However, I have shown that the evidential anchoring of *ma'ak* does not apply to any kind of mediated non-subjective access, and that *ma'ak* is mostly connected to collective-general knowledge. In particular, I have not found cases of *ma'ak* being used for knowledge that is accessible to the other speech participants, especially the addressee, but is inaccessible to the speaker. Since *ma'ak* appeals to collective-general knowledge, it generally presupposes that the knowledge is shared with the addressee, although this is not always the case. Instances of a speaker using *ma'ak* based on a presumption of knowledge asymmetry with the speech participants can occur. The speaker might conceive the knowledge as being shared not with the speech participants, but rather with others not present in the speech event. Thus in the strict sense of the definition in the introduction, symmetry of knowledge and intersubjectivity is not codified by this marker.

The fact that *ma'ak* and *míin* are not used in intradiscursive, dialogic strategies of agreement and disagreement confirms that they do not primarily encode intersubjectivity (even though *ma'ak* often anticipates alignment from the other speech participants, because the inference is drawn from collective knowledge, and often resonates with common presumptions or explanations). The same is true concerning the fact that in dialogic exchanges, I did not observe changes from *míin* to *ma'ak* that indexed a shift from asymmetric to symmetric knowledge. This dimension is instead expressed by other markers in Yucatec, particularly the pervasively used terminal deictics *a'* (asymmetric) /*o'* (a/symmetric) which do evolve intradiscursively (Hanks 1990). Nevertheless, it is worth noting that in my corpus, the instances of *ma'ak* that appear in sentences with terminal deictics all involve the clitic *o'*. This is not surprising given that *o'* indexes shared access to the referent, typically associated with collective-general knowledge. In contrast, *míin* occurs in utterances with *a'* or *o'*, and this correlates with its broader usages, and with the fact that it applies to more varied and indexically complex speech events.

Other correlations would appear to be relevant for understanding the contrast between *ma'ak* and *míin*. The particle *ma'ak* is used with third-person predicates, whereas *míin* is found with a variety of persons (since the subjective stance it encodes may apply to statements about other people or things, even though first-person predicates are most commonly used because of the subjective access value). The particle *ma'ak* tends to be used in or next to predicates with the indefinite reportative (*bin*), whereas *míin* appears more frequently in quoted speech marked with the quotative (*k*-ABS) (and this is required in traditional narratives for the measurement-estimation use). Finally, *ma'ak* does not co-occur with subjective modal attenuators, contrary to *míin*, which is very commonly found with them. Instead, *ma'ak* occurs with expressions such as *keensa*, which signals shared lack of knowledge (Vapnarsky 2012). All of this confirms the link of *ma'ak* with collective-general knowledge and traditional lore. Table 16.2 below presents the main properties of *míin* and *ma'ak*.

Table 16.2: Synthesis of *mîin and ma'ak* properties

	mîin	*ma'ak*
Access to information	Subjective ++	Non-subjective = Collective-General knowledge
Epistemic judgement	Personal	Shared
Knowledge symmetry (with respect to speech event)	Asymmetric	(Symmetric +)
Typical uses	estimation of measurements; inference based on premises connected with the perceptual field of the speaker or direct cognitive knowledge	talk about old times, prophesied future times, folktales and matters to which speakers only have mediated access (e.g. the non-visible supernatural world)
Combination with person	any	3rd person
Combination with reportative markers	quotative	indefinite reportative
Combination with subjective modal attenuators	very common	none

6 Conclusion

As a general characterization, the particles *mîin* and *ma'ak* can be defined as partial support inferential markers that contrast on the (inter)subjectivity parameter. However, we have seen that, as commonly understood, this characterization is insufficient for understanding the specific uses and speaker choices connected with this form. Firstly, one needs to determine whether the subjectivity applies to access or to epistemic judgement. Secondly, the pole contrasting with "subjective" needs to be specified. Besides "intersubjective", which I restrict to knowledge as constructed in the speech event, I have proposed to introduce "collective-general" knowledge as a third pole of the (inter)subjective dimension. Thirdly, although (inter)subjectivity often correlates with symmetric/asymmetric knowledge distribution among speech participants, the particles analysed here confirm the need to keep both dimensions very separate. As we have seen with the contrast between Yucatec Maya and Yurakaré, languages with markers conveying apparently very similar values may differ in terms of which dimension is encoded and which is inferred.

Lastly, the analysis shows that even though *mîin* and *ma'ak* form a paradigmatic contrast in a two-member syntactic category of inferentials, their use does not cover all possible semantic and pragmatic possibilities relating to inference reasoning (for example inference based on something the speaker has previously heard said about the addressee). This is the case particularly because *ma'ak* is connected with collective-general knowledge and rarely used for other types of mediated access to knowledge. It is also linked to the scattered distribution of evidentiality in the Yucatec Maya grammatical and lexical system, which is expressed by different sub-groups of particles with limited contrasts. Last but not least, it probably also results from constraints dependent on local linguistic ideologies regarding what can be said and what should remain implicit, as well as on more universal communicative principles of knowledge sharing. To better understand these crucial issues, further investigation will be needed in Yucatec Maya, as well as in many other languages.

Abbreviations: 1 – first person; 2 – second person; 3 – third person; A – SET A (ergative); ADM – admonestative; ADV – adverb; AG – agent; B – SET B (absolutive); CAUS – causative; CONC – concessive; CONJ – conjunction; CP – completive; DEM – demonstrative; DET – determinant; DIS – disjunctive; EMPH – emphatic; EXIST – existential; FACT – factitive; FEM – feminine; HAB – habitual; ICP – incompletive; IPF – imperfective; INF – inferential; INF.C – collective-general knowledge inferential; INF.S – subjective inferential; INTER – interrogative; INTR – intransitive; IPF – imperfective; LOC – locative; MOD – modal deictic base; like; MAF – manner adverb focus; NC – numeral classifier; NEG – negation; NOM – nominal suffix; OBLIG – obligative; proyective; OST – ostensive; PART – participial; PAS – passive; PF – perfective; PL – plural; PN – proper noun; POSS – possibility; epistemic deictic; PR – independent pronoun; PREP – preposition; PROG – progressive; QUOT – quotative; REP – repetitive; RS – reported speech; RETROS – retrospective; SBJ – subjunctive; TD_1 – terminal deictic (immediacy, asymmetry); TD_2 – terminal deictic (less immediate, symmetric) TD_3 – terminal deictic (neutral); TD_4 – terminal deictic (topic); TP – temporal; TR – transitive; -VL – suffix attached to nominal and imperfective stems realized as – *Vl* (vowel harmony).

References

Aikhenvald, Alexandra. 2004. *Evidentiality.* Oxford/New York: Oxford University Press.
Anderbois, Scott. 2013. Míin en maya yucateco: evidencial o modal? Paper presented at CILLA VI, Austin, Texas, October 2013.
Anderbois, Scott. 2016. Illocutionary mirativity: the case of Yucatec Maya *bakáan*. Paper presented at SULA 9.
Anderbois, Scott. Submitted. Conjecturals seem like evidentials, but they might not be.
Barrera-Vásquez, Alfredo (ed.). 1981. *Diccionario Cordemex Maya-Español, Español-Maya.* México: Editorial Porrúa.
Beltrán de Santa Rosa María, Pedro. 1859 [1746]. *Arte del Idioma Maya reducido a sucintas reglas y Semilexicón yucateco.* Mérida : Imprenta de J.D. Espinosa.
Benveniste, Emile. 1958. De la subjectivité dans le langage. *Journal de Psychologie.* Paris: PUF.
Bergqvist, Henrik. 2015. Epistemic marking and multiple perspective. An introduction. *STUF. Language Typology and Universals.* Special Issue. Epistemic marking in typological perspective 68 (2). 123–122.
Boye, Kasper. 2012. Epistemic Meaning. A cross-linguistic and functional-cognitive study. Berlin/Boston: De Gruyer.
Bricker, Victoria, Eleuterio Po'ot Yah & Ofelia Dzul de Po'ot. 1998. *A Dictionary of The Maya Language as Spoken in Hocaba, Yucatán.* Salt Lake City: University of Utah Press.
Cornillie, Bert. 2009. Evidentiality and epistemic modality. On the close relationship between two different categories. *Functions of Language* 16 (1). 44–62.
De Haan, Ferdinand. 1999. Evidentiality and epistemic modality: setting boundaries. *Southwest Journal of Linguistics* 18. 83–101.
De Haan, Ferdinand. 2001. The place of inferential within the evidential system. *International Journal of American Linguistics* 67 (2). 193–210.
Evans, Nicholas. 2005. View with a view: Towards a typology of multiple perspective. *Berkeley Linguistics Society*, 31 (5). 93–120.
Faller, Martina. 2002. *Semantics and pragmatics of evidentials in Cuzco Quechua.* Stanford: Ph.D. thesis.
Gipper, Sonja. 2015. (Inter)subjectivity in interaction: Investigating (inter)subjective meanings in Yurakaré conversational data. *STUF. Language Typology and Universals.* Special Issue. Epistemic marking in typological perspective, 68 (2). 211–232.
Guentchéva, Zlatka & Jon Landaburu (eds.). 2007. *L'énonciation médiatisée II. Le traitement épistémologique de l'information : illustrations amérindiennes et caucasiennes.* Louvain: Éditions Peeters.
Hanks, William F. 1984. The Evidential Core of Deixis in Yucatec Maya. In *Proceedings of the Chicago Linguistic Society*, 154–172.
Hanks, William F. 1990. *Referential practice. Language and lived space among the Maya.* Chicago/London: The University of Chicago Press.
Hanks, William F. 2005. Explorations in the Deictic Field. *Current Anthropology*, 46 (2). 191–220.
Hanks, William F. 2007. The evidential core of deixis in Yucatec Maya. In Guentchéva, Zlatka & Jon Landaburu: *L'énonciation médiatisée II. Le traitement épistémologique de l'information : illustrations amérindiennes et caucasiennes*, 311–331. Louvain: Éditions Peeters.
Hanks, William F. 2012. Evidentiality in social interaction. *Pragmatics and Society*, 3 (2). 169–180.

Heritage, John. 2012. The Epistemic Engine: Sequence Organization and Territories of Knowledge. *Research on Language and Social Interaction* 45(1). 30–52.
Kockelman, Paul. 2004. Stance and subjectivity. *Journal of Linguistic Anthropology* 14. 127–150.
Kwoon, Iksoo. 2012. Please confirm what I inferred: On the Korean inferential-evidential marker -napo-. *Journal of Pragmatics* 44. 958–969.
Langacker, Ronald. 1990. Subjectification. *Cognitive Linguistics* 1. 5–38.
Langacker, Ronald. 2002. Deixis and subjectivity. In Frank Brisard (ed.), *Grounding: The Epistemic Footing of Deixis and Reference.* 1–28. Berlin/New York: Mouton de Gruyter.
Lucy, John. 1993. Metapragmatic presentationals: reporting speech with quotatives in Yucatec Maya. In John Lucy (ed.), *Reflexive language: reported Speech and Metapragmatics*, 91–126. Cambridge: Cambridge University Press.
Lyons, John. 1997. *Semantics* vol. 2. Cambridge: Cambridge University Press.
Narrog, Heiko. 2012. *Modality, Subjectivity, and Semantic Change.* Oxford/New York: Oxford University Press.
Nuyts, Jan. 2001, Subjectivity as an evidential dimension in epistemic modal expressions. *Journal of Pragmatics* 33. 383–400.
Pérez, Juan Pio. 1866–77. *Diccionario de la Lengua Maya.* Mérida: Imprenta Literaria de Juan Molina Solis.
Portner, Paul. 2009. *Modality.* Oxford: Oxford University Press.
Stievers, Tanya, Lorenza Mondada & Jakob Steensig. 2011. *The Morality of Knowledge in Conversation.* Series Studies in Interactional Sociolinguistics. Cambridge: Cambridge University Press.
Tournadre, Nicolas & Randy J. LaPolla. 2014. Towards a new approach to evidentiality: issues and directions for research. *Linguistics of the Tibeto-Burman Area* 37(2). 240–263. Amsterdam: John Benjamins Publishing Company.
Traugott, Elizabeth C. 1995. The Role of the Development of Discourse Markers in a Theory of Grammaticalization. Paper presented at ICHL XII, Manchester 1995; Version of 11/97. http://web.stanford.edu/~traugott/papers/discourse.pdf (accessed 7 June 2017).
Traugott, Elizabeth C. 2003. From subjectification to intersubjectification. In Raymond Hickey (ed.), *Motives for Language Change*, 124–139. Cambridge: Cambridge University Press.
Traugott, Elizabeth C. & Richard Dasher. 2002. *Regularity in Semantic Change.* Cambridge: Cambridge University Press.
Verhagen, Arie. 2005. *Construction of Intersubjectivity: Discourse, Syntax, Cognition.* Oxford: Oxford University Press.
Vapnarsky, Valentina. 1999. Conceptions et expressions de la temporalité chez les Mayas Yucatèques. PhD Université de Paris X, Nanterre. vol. 2.
Vapnarsky, Valentina. 2012. The grammar of uncertainty in Yucatec Maya. Paper presented at *Primer Coloquio Internacional de Estudios de Maya Yucateco*, El Colegio de México, D-F, October 2012.
Vapnarsky, Valentina. 2013a. Mandatos y solicitudes: el arte cotidiano del pedir en maya yucateco. In Alain Breton & Philippe Nondédéo (eds.), *Maya Daily Lives*, 169–183. Mark Schwaben, Germany: Verlag Anton Saurwein.
Vapnarsky, Valentina. 2013b. Le passif peut-il éclairer les esprits ? Agentivités, interactions et esprits-maîtres chez les Mayas. *Ateliers d'Anthropologie. LESC, Nanterre.* http://ateliers.revues.org/9449
Vapnarsky, Valentina. 2017. *The indexical field of uncertainty. In* Valentina Vapnarsky, *Senses of time: Exploring temporality in Mayan discourses, experiences and remembrances,* chap. 7, p. 273–291. Manuscript presented for the Habilitation à Diriger des Recherches. Paris: EHESS.

Part V: Theoretical perspectives

Jean-Pierre Desclés

Epistemic modality and evidentiality from an enunciative perspective

Abstract: The aim of this article is to briefly compare and distinguish epistemic modalities and mediative enunciation in a network of concepts and to propose a semantic map construed within the framework of enunciation theory. Using the concept of enunciative stancetaking (Fr. 'prise en charge énonciative'), we will show that it must not be confused with the notions of commitment and engagement (e.g. in assertions) which are more specific than general stancetaking. We will show that the notion of evidentiality, does not constitute a homogeneous area because it is grounded in semantic categorizations reflecting cognitive mechanisms which it is important to highlight and describe in precise detail.

Keywords: enunciative stancetaking, enunciative and modal operators, semantic map, mediative enunciation, epistemic modality

1 Introduction

The aim of this article is to briefly compare and distinguish epistemic modalities and mediative enunciation in a network of concepts and to propose a semantic map construed within the framework of enunciation theory. Using the concept of enunciative stancetaking (Fr. 'prise en charge énonciative'), we will show that it must not be confused with the notions of commitment and engagement (e.g. in assertions), which are more specific than general stancetaking. The concept of enunciative stancetaking is close to that given in Kockelman (2004: 128): "[...] commitment events are particular instances of stancetaking, when the idea of stance has been semiotically operationalized and cross-linguistically theorized." Despite intensive research since the publication of the volume by Chafe and Nichols (1986) and the reference work by Aikhenvald (2004), we will show that the notion of evidentiality does not constitute a homogeneous area because it

Note: I would like to thank Bernard Pottier and Zlatka Guentchéva for their constructive discussions, suggestions and exchanges of ideas on the complex field of modalities. I am grateful to Margaret Dunham for her dedicated and accurate translation of this article.

Jean-Pierre Descles, University Paris-Sorbonne & STIH

https://doi.org/10.1515/9783110572261-017

is grounded in semantic categorizations reflecting cognitive mechanisms which it is important to highlight and describe in precise detail. Our position partially overlaps with that of Nuyts (2017: 80):

> In sum, there appear to be strong reasons to assume that – just like modality – evidentiality is not a coherent category. Among the classical and less classical 'evidential' categories there are a few substantially different subtypes.

2 Enunciative stancetaking

As in many cases, the term evidentiality is not used with a generally consistent meaning and it is often applied to a heterogeneous area of linguistic phenomena. It appears useful to attempt to draw a semantic map where modalities, especially epistemic modality, and evidentiality can be located and distinguished from other types of enunciative stancetaking.[1] Our approach is developed in the framework of enunciative theory, grounded in the modern works of the Prague School (with Pauliny (1948)) and those of Bally (1932 [1965], Benveniste (1966, 1974), Culioli (1968, 1990), Desclés (1976) . . . to name but a few). In this approach, utterances are the result of stancetaking operations by an enunciator (Fr. énonciateur) regarding contents organized in the form of a clause constituted through predicative operations (the application of predicative operators to actants) and other operations (determination, diathesis, topicalization, etc.).[2] Taking Bally's decomposition of an utterance into modus and dictum, stancetaking operations become the constituents of a modus analyzed as a complex operator, the operand of which is a propositional form (or dictum) and the result of which is an utterance. These operations contribute to making public a propositional form while also expressing the various perspectives[3] and viewpoints of the enunciator who takes a stance with regards to the propositional contents; they describe what is often called "the attitude of the speaker towards the propositional content" in the literature. The enunciative operations are obtained by the combination of various operators, namely enunciative operators, aspect-tense operators and modal operators.

1 A semantic map linked to enunciative operations has already been presented in Desclés (2009). The map proposed below builds on the latter.

2 For a presentation of the various aspects of enunciation, see the collective work edited by Colas-Blaise et al. (2016) and on the author's enunciative approach, see Desclés (2016a), where many bibliographical references are cited; see also Desclés & Guibert (2011: 15–121) and Desclés & Guentchéva (2015).

3 The term perspective is used with a meaning close to that in Evans (2005).

2.1 Minimal enunciative stancetaking

The minimal enunciative operator in the production of an utterance is that which expresses the necessary stancetaking by an enunciator 'EGO' in the form of an incomplete process, which can be glossed as 'EGO-AM-SAYING (…)'. Without this stancetaking an utterance cannot be enunciated. The enunciator EGO indicates a role distinct from that of the co-enunciator YOU who may either accept to constitute a shared enunciative reference frame and engender a dialog, or not; the enunciator EGO is also able to indicate the role of an absent person in the initial dialogic dipole between EGO and YOU. The enunciator, like the co-enunciator, must not be assimilated to speakers and hearers denoting directly external persons and implying pragmatic knowledge beyond the utterances.

2.2 Various types of enunciative stancetaking

Some stancetaking operators combine with the minimal enunciative operator. Thus aspectual operators, where the operand is a predicative relation, specify aspectual actualizations in the form of state, event, processe, resultant state, etc.,[4] with temporal relations (with regards to the enunciation process), and they generate various aspect-tense operators which can be traced in the various more or less grammaticalized aspect-tense morphemes found in languages. The linguistic units languages used to express modality are also traces of modal operators which are necessarily combined with the minimal enunciation operator and with aspectual operators and temporal relations. These modal operators also express various forms of (modal) stancetaking, which is to say various enunciator attitudes.

Other stancetaking operators which cannot be analyzed as modal operators also combine with the minimal enunciative operator. The enunciator can express an observation drawn from direct perception; some languages grammaticalize the cognitive source of the observation stated, using distinct markers to express the various sensory sources: vision (*Regarde, un sanglier passe* 'Look, there's a boar coming'), hearing (*J'entends le son de l'orgue de la chapelle* 'I hear the sound of the church organ'), smell (*Je sens l'air frais du printemps* 'I smell the fresh scent of spring'), touch (*C'est du velours* 'It's velvet') or even in reference to a known event (*La grande Guerre a opposé l'Allemagne à la France et ses alliés anglais*

4 On these aspectual distinctions, see Comrie (1976) and Lyons (1977) as well as the semantic map of aspectuality in Desclés (2016b).

et américains 'The Great War pitted Germany against France and its British and American allies').

Simple declarations by an enunciator (*Il fait très chaud aujourd'hui* 'It is very hot today') must be distinguished from assertions (*Aujourd'hui, je t'assure, il fait très chaud* 'I'm telling you, it sure is hot today'). Assertion is a language act which fully engages the speaker's responsibility, it is a commitment, whereas simple declarations are less binding. Moreover, simple declarations can be the beginning of dialogic adjustments (the co-enunciator could reply: *Pour moi, ce n'est pas encore ce que je caractériserais comme 'très chaud'* 'For me, this isn't yet what I would call 'very hot''), which is not the case for assertions since the co-enunciator must either accept the assertion within the single shared dialogic reference frame, or refuse it by being entirely opposed and thus institute a reference frame distinct (at least on some points) from that of the enunciator. The enunciator can also institute an entirely personal reference frame, to create his or her own "universe of belief" (*ce que je crois* 'what I believe' / *ce que je pense* 'what I think'. . .),[5] regardless of the co-enunciator he or she is addressing. Enunciator assessment (*luckily* / *unfortunately* / *unimportantly* . . .) constitutes the modalities which combine with purely declarative or assertive enunciative acts. Deontic modalities directly concern obligations which enunciators impose on others (*You must / It is indispensable to*) or on themselves (*I must...*).

With performatives (*I baptize you / I declare the session open / I forgive you*) the speech act is effective and performs actions in the world. The speech acts theory of Searle and Vanderveken (1985) is grounded in this type of enunciative acts. It would be highly interesting to systematically compare enunciative theory with that of speech acts to explore differences and similarities.

Human languages have a remarkable feature which is not found in animal communication systems. Indeed, all languages have specific semiotic means to report (directly or indirectly) speech previously uttered by a speaker.[6] The enunciative stancetaking for the propositional forms listed above is obtained by combinations with the minimal enunciation of more specific operators, for example "it is true in the outside world that (. . .)", "what others say is (. . .)", "the personal belief or thought system is (. . .)", etc.

5 On the universe of belief, see Martin (1983, 1987) and the article by Gosselin (this volume).
6 See among others Benveniste (1966) who notes this characteristic on the subject of the communication system of bees analyzed by Von Frisch. Recent studies on communication among the great apes come to similar conclusions.

2.3 On possibility

There are several sorts of specifically modal stancetaking operators, of which modality markers are the trace, in more or less grammaticalized form depending on the language. Since Aristotle and on through the Middle Ages and in modern logic,[7] it has become usual to distinguish alethic modalities from epistemic modalities,[8] even though the same markers are sometimes used to express both: *it's necessarily true, it's possible, it's impossible, it isn't necessary (or it's possible to not . . .)*. Epistemic modalities express uncertainty as to the enunciator's stancetaking on a proposition. The modality expressed by *it's possible* (or its variants such as *can, possibly, perhaps...*) is particularly complex as it denotes, in a language like French, not only capacity (*Luc peut nager, il en est maintenant capable* 'Luke can swim, he is now able') but also permission (*Luc peut nager, il en a reçu la permission de son éducateur* 'Luke may swim, he has permission from the teacher') and judgment expressing uncertainty as to the actualization of a situation (*A cette heure de la journée, Luc peut nager dans la piscine, c'est dans ses habitudes* 'At this time of day Luke can be swimming in the pool, it is usual for him').[9] The epistemic uncertainty expressed by possibly (Fr. *c'est possible*) is often indeterminate because it can denote (i) the modal extension of a certainty (*Luc vient demain, du moins c'est possible* 'Luke is coming tomorrow, at least possibly') since what is certain is of course possible but not the reverse; (ii) variable uncertainty positioned between certainty and impossibility (*Attention, c'est possible que Luc vienne demain car, selon moi, c'est loin d'être certain et, en même temps, l'impossibilité de sa venue ne doit pas être totalement exclue* 'Warning, Luke may possibly come tomorrow because, according to me, it is far from certain but, at the same time, the impossibility of his coming must not be entirely excluded'); (iii) uncertainty which is better specified because geared towards what is only possible, distinct both from what is deemed probable and what is deemed improbable (*Il est peu probable que Luc vienne demain, mais c'est cependant possible et pas improbable* 'Luke's coming tomorrow is unlikely, but it is however possible and not improbable'). This semantic indeterminacy is often reduced by the context.

---

7 The reader can refers to the historical overview of Van der Auwera and Zamorano Aguilar (2016) and the references cited therein.

8 On alethics in linguistics, see Kronning (1996) and Pottier (2000: 195). For a presentation of modalities in logic and the epistemic / alethic distinction, see Blanché and Dubucs (1970/1996), Kneale & Kneale (1962), Grize (1973).

9 See Herslund (this volume) for similar phenomena in Danish, and Kiefer (this volume) in Hungarian. On the semantic distinction between *pouvoir*, *vouloir*, and *devoir* in French, see Desclés (2003).

As shown in the preceding examples, alongside the traditional modal operators expressed by *il est possible* 'it is possible', *il est impossible* 'it is impossible', *il est nécessaire* 'it is necessary', *il n'est pas nécessaire* 'it is unnecessary' (i.e., in the latter case, contingency modality) studied in modal logic, languages also make use of other expressions of uncertainty such as:

> *c'est hautement probable / c'est presque certain / il n'est pas tout à fait impossible / il est fort possible et même probable / il n'est guère possible et même improbable / c'est à la limite possible mais peu probable / Il est possible bien qu'improbable…*
> *it is highly probable / it's a near certainty / it's not completely impossible / it is entirely possible and even probable / it's hardly possible and even improbable / it's almost possible but unlikely / it's possible but improbable, etc.*

A large number of examples extracted from the French database Frantext confirm the variations with regards to uncertainty in the area of possibility[10]:

(1) *César, c'est probable, mais ce n'est pas sûr.* (M. Pagnol, *Fanny*, 1932, p. 118)
'Cesar, it's probable but it isn't sure'

(2) *C'était probable, mais non certain, car avant même qu'elle ne le présente à Sarah, Nil se rendait souvent à Bruxelles* […] (G. Matzneff, *Ivre du vin perdu*, 1981, p. 354)
'It was probable, but not certain, because before she even introduced him to Sarah, Nil often went to Brussels'

(3) *Il est possible et probable même que 150 millions d'années ne représentent qu'une fraction très faible de ce temps.* (H. Poincaré, *Leçons sur les hypothèses cosmogoniques*, 1911, p. 65).
'It is possible and even probable that 150 million years only represent a small fraction of this time span.'

(4) *Cette attaque vous semblait-elle probable, ou seulement possible?* (P. Bourget, *Un drame dans le monde*, 1921, p. 71).
'Did this attack seem probable to you, or only possible?'

(5) *Bref, il n'est pas médicalement impossible, mais il est tout à fait improbable que* […] *vous ayez contracté le bacille* […] (H. Montherlant, *Les lépreuses*, 1939, p. 1453).

---

10 A systematic analysis of these markers may be found in Vinzerich (2007); see also Desclés and Vinzerich (2008).

'In short it is not medically impossible but highly improbable that [...] you have contracted the bacillus [...]'

(6) *Mais on voit l'aléa de ces pronostics, qui ne font aucune part aux accidents, une collision, quoique improbable, n'est pas absolument impossible* [. . .] (*Histoire générale des sciences*, dir. by R. Taton: t. 3: *La Science contemporaine*, vol. 2: *Le XXe siècle*, 1964, p. 587).
[But one sees the randomness of these prognostics, which leave no room for accidents, a collision, although improbable, is absolutely not impossible]

The analysis of the notion of "possibility" can be structured with quasi-topological concepts. Indeed, the domain of modal places is structured as follows:

- Certain is the modal place where the actualization of the proposition 'not(p)' is completely excluded;
- No Certain contains the modal places:
  - Possible , the place where the actualization of the proposition 'p' is possible but that of 'not(p)' is also possible;
  - Probable, the place where the actualization of the proposition 'p' is more probable than that of 'not(p)' (the actualization of 'not(p)' is still possible);
  - Only Possible, the place where the actualization of the proposition 'p' is possible but not probable and not improbable;
  - Improbable, the place where the actualization of the proposition 'not(p)' is more probable than that of 'p' (the actualization of 'p' is still possible);
  Impossible is the modal place where the actualization of the proposition 'p' is completely excluded.

The notion of possible is linked with impossible, certain, probable, improbable (Figure 17.1). We deduce a structuration where the topological parts are abstract places of actualization of modal predicative relations. In fact, it is a quasi-topological structuration (an extension of the classical topological of abstract places) where Possible is an cognitive and abstract place which is located between on one hand, the 'strict interior' Certain (the open place of actualizarion of certain predicative relations, necessarly true) and on the other hand, the open exterior Impossible (the place of actualization of impossible predicative relations). In a quasi-topological stucturation, there are two boudaries between Certain and Impossible: the internal boundary (the Probable or the Only Possible) and the external boundary (the Improbable or the Only Possible) (Figure 17.1).

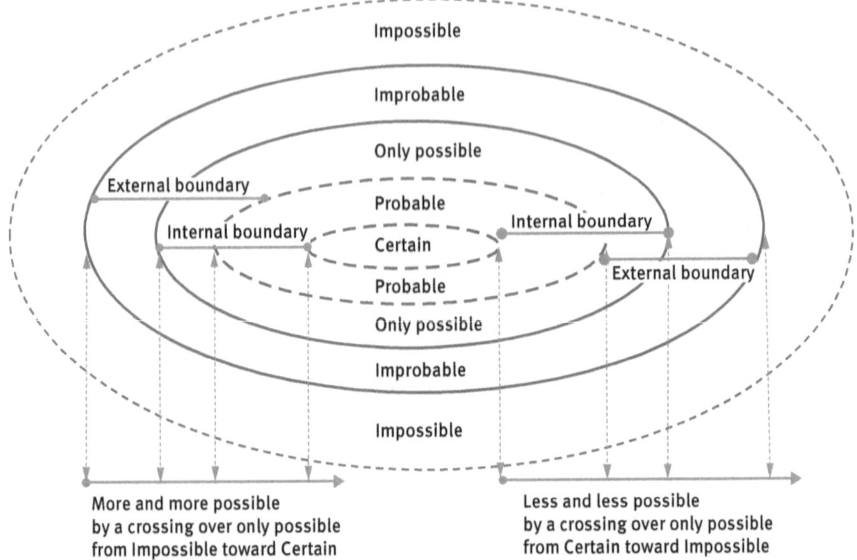

The quasi-topologiacal space of modal places with an internal boundary and an external boundary between the strict interior (the place of actualization of certain situations) and the exterior (the place of actualization of impossible situations).

Figure 17.1: Quasi-topological structuring of the notion of possibility.

Different modalities around the possibility constitute cognitive and abstract places organized by a quasi-topological structuring[11] which makes it possible to grasp, using specific operators, the clearly topological[12] notions of *presque* 'almost', *pas tout à fait* 'not quite', *à la limite* 'at the border', *à peu près* 'nearly', *proche de* 'close to', *dans le voisinage de* 'in the neighborhood of'. Unfortunately there is no place here for examining this structuring because this would entail major theoretical developments and arguments which go beyond the scope of this book.

---

11 Topological and quasi-topological structurings are highlighted in various language domains: lexical semantic analysis (prepositions and movement and changing verbs represented by semantic-cognitive patterns), grammatical analysis (aspectual actualizations such as uncompleted / complete / completion / resultant states, etc.; various phases in an event – see Desclés and Guentchéva (2010); typical and less typical categorizations – see Desclés and Pascu (2011). It is useful to study the field of modalities using logical-topological tools to underline that the quasi-topological patterns transcend several language domains with clearly cognitive relevance; this helps shed light on the relations between cognitive representations, language acts and language diversity.

12 See the *Leçons d'à peu près* by Guilbaud (1985), a mathematician interested in the mathematical study of the human and social sciences. The topological and quasi-topological structurings are similar on many points to the figural structurings put forth by Pottier (2000, 2012).

Epistemic modalities indicate judgments which are linked to enunciators' uncertain knowledge, and denote the wish to not fully commit to the information relayed in their utterance. These epistemic modalities are distinct from the more consensual alethic modalities (necessity, impossibility, possibility, contingency) and from inter-enunciator modalities (give an order, make a promise, ask a question, etc.).

In section 3, we will examine the specificities of mediative enunciation and how it is conceptually distinct from various epistemic judgments obtained through inference based on direct sensory perception (*I see* / *I hear*, etc.), from the indirect speech of more or less determined other speakers (with markers such as *according to the press* / *following the declaration of the Minister of Employment*). Such stancetaking belongs to the field of evidentiality, the boundaries of which are sometimes fuzzy. We believe it would be useful in this field to clearly distinguish categories differentiated by specific properties, even though these categories are often expressed by the same linguistic units within a given language. This is a question of grammatical polysemy which must be expressly studied for each language.

2.4 Semantic map of enunciative stancetaking

The various enunciative and modal stances are analyzed by combinations between more specific and more or less complex operators and the enunciator's minimal enunciation operator. They are all specifications of the minimal enunciation. In the semantic map (Figure 17.2), each stance positioned at a graph node is linked by an arrow which establishes a relation from a more general concept to a more specific concept. By reversing the direction of the arrow (interpreted as a subsuming relation or conceptual subordination), the map takes on the form of an ontology (to borrow a term from Artificial Intelligence), not an ontology of objects, but a linguistic ontology. The compounds of each stance positioned at each node are formulated within a system of formal applicative metalinguistic representations (because they are essentially composed of various operator types which apply to operands to form applicative expressions which become, depending on the context, either operators or operands). We will not provide here the metalinguistic formulas of the operator combinations, this would entail a degree of technicality[13] which is beyond the scope of this volume.

13 See Desclés, Guibert and Sauzay (2016).

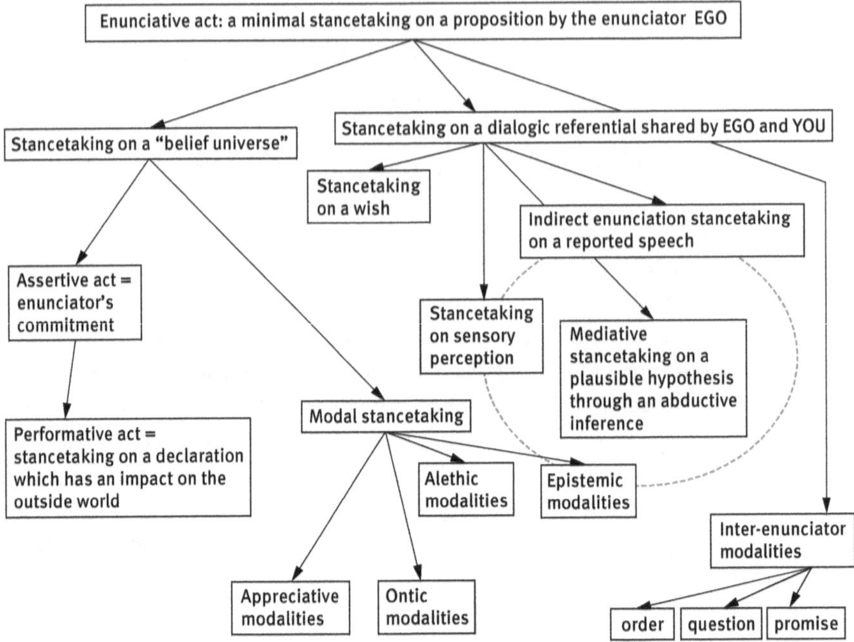

Figure 17.2: Simplified semantic map of stancetaking on proposition.
Note: The arrows express specifications from a general concept towards more specific concepts.

The general and heterogeneous domain of that is often called evidentiality intersects with the category of epistemic modalities, the category of stance directly taken on sensory perception, the category of stance taken on a reported speech. The mediative stancetaking through an abductive inference constitutes the core of evidentiality categorized in some languages.

3 Mediative enunciation

It is important to avoid confusing epistemic modalities structured around possibility with inference modes which, as we shall see below, result either in a probable consequence or a plausible hypothesis. Mediative enunciation is the utterance of a plausible hypothesis where it is (implicitly) indicated that the hypothesis was reached based on observed clues (representing forms of mediativity,[14] sometimes

14 The term *médiatif* 'mediative', coined by Lazard (1956) for the verbal paradigm in Tadjik, is restricted to cover the so-called indirect evidentials; the term *énonciation médiatisée/médiative*,

also called sources of information) through abductive inference (in the sense of Peirce),[15] which is not a logical inference, contrary to deductive inference (which, grounded in a true proposition, leads to a true consequence based on an implication also recognized as true). Let us examine these various inference modes in more detail.

3.1 Inferences by deduction versus inferences by abduction

Let us take two series of examples in context:

(7) a. [Context: Karen has the flu.]
Il est donc fort probable que Karine ait de la fièvre
'It is thus highly probable that Karen has a fever'
Karine doit avoir de la fièvre.
'Karen must have a fever'.
b. [Context: Karen's face is flushed and she has a fever.]
Karine aurait ainsi attrapé la grippe
'So Karen will have caught the flu'
Karine serait donc grippée.
'Karen must have the flu'.

These examples contain modal markers of uncertainty, but the semantic values of the markers are determined by inferences grounded in shared knowledge. In the interpretation of (a), the shared knowledge is grounded in frequent observation:

> (7a') When one has the flu (p) one very often has a fever (q), which can also be formulated as the implication 'p => probability(q)' ('if p is true then q is probably true') where the consequent 'probability(q)' has only a probability of being actualized. The probability can be further specified by contextual information.
>
> In the interpretation of (b), the shared knowledge is:

used by Guentchéva (1996) is associated with the concept of stancetaking (Fr. prise de charge) and abductive inference.

15 Abduction is an inference mode described by Peirce (1965, vol. 2, ch. 5), who distinguishes it from reasoning by deduction and induction; see also Pottier (2000: 196). Polya (1958, ch. 12 and 13), using the label hypothetical syllogism, also defines such formulations of a plausible hypothesis, common in mathematics and in ordinary reasoning.

(7b’) When one has the flu (p), one has a fever (q1) and one is flushed (q2), this is a statement of the implication ‘p => [q1 & q2]’ (‘if p is true then q1 and q2 are always also true’).

In (7a), it is a case of inference by deduction: based on the observation (p) ‘Karen has the flu’ and on the general knowledge (7a′), grounded in a significant sample of highly frequent statistical correlations between p and q, one deduces the probable consequence ‘Probability(q)’. In 7(b), it is a case of inference by abduction which, based on the two observed clues (q1) ‘Karen has a fever’ and (q2) ‘Karen’s face is flushed’ and general knowledge (7b′), points towards the plausible hypothesis (p) ‘Karen has the flu’ and states this by indicating, more or less directly through linguistic traces, that it is the result of reasoning.

To systematize the two inferences:[16]

Deduction of a probable consequence	**Abduction of a plausible hypothesis**
1°) Observation: p	1°) Observation of clues: q1 & q2 . . .
2°) Shared knowledge:	2°) Shared knowledge:
p => probability (q)	p => [q1 & q2]
3°) probability (q) [by deduction]	3°) plausibility (p) [by abduction]
4°) enunciation of probability (q)	4°) enunciation of plausibility (p)

In the case of deductive inference, shared knowledge is construed by induction based on highly frequent correlations, whence the implication relation p => probability(q)’, meaning that if ‘p’ is observed then there is also a strong possibility of ‘q’. In abductive reasoning, the shared knowledge is often a general law: when there is ‘p’ there is always ‘q’, whence the implication relation ‘p => q’.

3.2 Probable consequence versus plausible hypothesis

In the two preceding inference modes, the result obtained is uncertain since, in deduction, the consequence is simply probable, and, in abduction, it is based on observed clues, and is presented as only plausible. The absence of certainty as to the results of the inference in the two cases must not however lead to confusion between the two inferences, they are clearly different cognitive mechanisms.

16 See Desclés and Guentchéva (2013) and (2015).

It is well documented that some languages directly grammaticalize the enunciation of a plausible hypothesis based on observed clues and knowledge shared with the co-enunciators. These clues may be sensory, i.e. obtained through sight, smell, sounds, etc. Thus tracks left by an animal can constitute clues as to its recent presence and proximity (*Attention, un sanglier est passé par là* ! 'Careful, there's been a boar around here!'); a smell perceived becomes a clue as to food to be served (*Toi, tu as préparé du poisson* ! *Je l'ai senti. 'You've prepared fish! I smell it.'); a characteristic piano performance heard on th*e radio is a clue for recognizing the pianist Glen Gould (*C'est évidemment Glen Gould qui joue ces variations de Goldberg* !... 'That's obviously Glen Gould playing Bach's Goldberg Variations!). Such indications are grammaticalized in these languages through so-called 'evidential' markers. Other clues may be involved in grammaticalized abductive inference, e.g. hearsay ('a large number of people agreeing on something is a clue in favor of the plausibility of what they agree on'), the words of an indeterminate third party who may have been the direct witness to an event which thereby becomes plausible and is presented as such by the enunciator, despite not having been a witness to the event in question. The enunciation of a plausibility sanctioned by intermediate witnesses bears the technical label "mediative enunciation" and contrasts with the direct statement of sensory or cognitive observations which directly commit the enunciator ('I'm saying this because I saw / heard / observed it for myself...'). In having recourse to mediative enunciation, the enunciator avoids taking full responsibility for the contents of what is being presented as plausible, thus allowing for the possibility of other (or better) hypotheses in lieu of the one expressed, all while explaining the observed clues. Consider the following examples:

(8) a. *Il y a eu un naufrage cette nuit : j'en suis l'un des rescapés.*
'There was a shipwreck last night: I am one of the survivors.'

b. [Context: There was a shipwreck last night]
On va trouver probablement ce matin des cadavres échoués sur la plage.
'There will probably be bodies washed up on the beach this morning.

c. [Context: We found bodies washed up on the beach this morning.]
Il y a eu très probablement un naufrage cette nuit.
'There was very probably a shipwreck last night

Sentence (8a) states a fact directly observed by the speaker. Sentence (8b) states a probable fact based on the following reasoning: everyone knows that very often when there has been a shipwreck, one finds bodies washed up on the beach. Sentence (8c) denotes the plausibility of a shipwreck, the hypothesis being grounded in general knowledge ("every time there is a shipwreck, the bodies of the victims always wash up on the beach"), and in the discovery of bodies on the beach; that observation was the clue which led the speaker to the plausible hypothesis, without excluding other possible hypotheses to explain the bodies on the beach. In sentences (8b) and (8c) the results of the inferences are uncertain, and are based on deductive inference in (8b) and abductive inference in (8c). In languages where mediative enunciation is grammaticalized, distinct morphological markers are used: an epistemic modality marker for judgments based on the probability of an event in the case of (8b) and a marker signaling abductive inference in the case of (8c), with the speaker taking no responsibility for the hypothesis. In languages such as French and English which have not grammaticalized mediative inference hypotheses, additional information is necessary if the speaker wishes to distinguish between inference modes to avoid possible confusion.

Several types of clues (or sources of plausible knowledge) are susceptible of triggering abductive inference: (i) clues from sensory perception or cognitive observations; (ii) clues linked to rumor or hearsay; (iii) information not obtained directly but through intermediaries; (iv) observed states concomitant with states interpreted as states resulting from (plausible) occurrences of prior events. Such clues only lead to abductive inference if there is shared knowledge (or knowledge construed and demonstrated within a theoretical framework) of a stable relation explicitly linking the formulation of the hypothesis in question to the observed clues. We reproduce here the map of evidentiality (Figure 17.3) so as to highlight within it the map of mediative enunciation (construed and uttered following abduction) and to show how evidentiality can denote different types of inference as well as directly observed clues, but which do not come under the domain of what we label mediative enunciation.

This type of semantic map corresponds to the epistemological remarks of Blanché (1969: 11) on the subject of conceptualization:

> A concept is never alone. Without speaking of the infinitely complex network which links it, step by step, to the set of all other concepts and which makes this set, as well as the words which express it, a global system where elements can only be exactly determined through their relation to the whole, each concept is linked, by much closer relations, to a restricted group of other concepts with which it forms a family.

It is clearly highly instructive to compare this mediativity semantic map with the underlying concepts which justify its structure, to those of Van der Auwera and Plungian (1998), Boye (2012, chap. 3) and Wiemer (forthcoming) on the relation between evidentiality and epistemic modality.

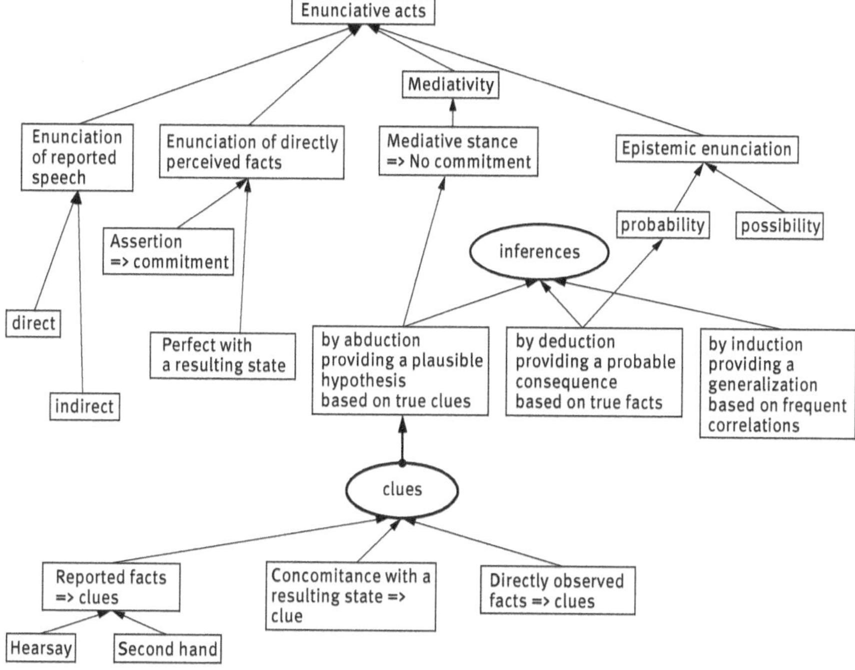

Figure 17.3: Semantic map of mediativity (Desclés & Guentchéva, Summer School of typology, Leipzig, 2010).

Note: The arrows express generalization relations from a specific concept toward a more general concept.

4 Concluding remarks

The semantic analysis of modal expressions is complex because one must take into account several types of modalities which in some cases are expressed using the same markers. For example, a marker such as *must* indicates, depending on the context, possibility (*At this hour on a Monday Luke must be swimming at the pool*), but also self-obligation (*He must swim at least an hour every day to stay in shape*), obligation (*Luke must swim to join the Navy*) and even an order to be executed (*I am telling you and I won't repeat it: You must swim!*).

Some modalities indicate a form of uncertainty; this is naturally the case for epistemic modalities but also for mediative enunciation since this expresses situations that are only plausible, and therefore uncertain. It is important to avoid confusion between on one hand the notions of possibility, probability, improbability, with their various modal intensifiers mentioned above, and the notion of plausibility on the other hand. Both notions express a form of uncertainty, but notions pertaining to possibility are directly linked to a lack of knowledge whereas plausibility is tightly linked to inference through abduction based on observed clues. Some utterances of probable facts are obtained, as explained above, through deductive reasoning which calls upon observed – and therefore true – facts, which are not clues in favor of a hypothesis but premises in an implication which makes it possible to deduce simply probable facts, given that the implication is the result of induction, i.e. a frequent statistical correlation (which is not necessarily always actualized) between what is posited as premise 'p' and what is probably expected 'q'.

> **Remark:** In the implicative proposition 'p => probability(q)', the expression 'probability(q)' is indeed a proposition which is true when the proposition 'q' is effectively probable (with a probability greater than 1/2) and false otherwise.

Obviously the construals and semantic differences laid out in this article should be further developed technically. This is still a work in progress. For linguistics considered as a science, we believe it useful to combine, on one hand, the formulation of sometimes abstract semantic theorizations aiming to highlight conceptual networks which can lead at times to the formulation of general operational invariants with, on the other hand, a more empirical typological approach covering a diversity of languages. In our view, such issues must be broached from both angles to confirm, or disconfirm, plausible hypotheses on the cognitive aspect of language activity, to refine the hypotheses formulated, to shed light on little known categorization processes which are grammaticalized in various languages, because these must be recognized and accounted for theoretically, even if it means reviewing certain fundamentals hitherto considered solidly established. We adhere to the wish expressed by several authors[17] calling for heightened cooperation between typology and formal semantics. Even though the field of epistemic modalities and other forms of enunciative stancetaking such as mediative enunciation is complex, and often referred to as "the cross of logicians" (and therefore also of linguists), it is an area where cognitive semantics, formal semantics and language typology devoted to the search for invariants should collaborate to better improve our understanding of the relations between cognition, language activity and the semiotic organization of languages.

---

17 For instance, see Evans (2005).

References

Aikhenvald, Alexandra Y. 2004. *Evidentiality*, Oxford University Press.

Bally, Charles. 1965 [1934]. *Linguistique générale et linguistique française*, 4th edn. Berne: Francke.

Benveniste, Emile. 1966. *Problèmes de linguistique générale*, Tome 1. Paris: Gallimard.

Benveniste, Emile. 1974. *Problèmes de linguistique générale*, Tome 2. Paris: Gallimard.

Blanché, Robert. 1966. *Structures intellectuelles. Essai sur l'organisation systématique des concepts*. Paris: Vrin.

Blanché, Robert & Jacques Dubucs. 1996 [1970]. *La logique et son histoire*. Paris: Armand Colin.

Boye, Kasper. 2012. *Epistemic Meaning. A crosslinguistic and Functional-cognitive Study, Empirical Approaches to Language Typology*, 43. Berlin/Boston: De Gruyer.

Chafe, Wallace & Johanna Nichols (eds.). 1986. *Evidentiality: The Linguistic Coding of Epistemology*. Norwood, NJ: Ablex.

Colas-Blaise, Marion, Laurent Perrin & Gian Maria Tore (eds.). 2016. *L'énonciation aujourd'hui, un concept clé des sciences du langage*. Limoges: Lambert-Lucas.

Comrie, Bernard. 1976. *Aspect*. Cambridge: Cambridge University Press.

Culioli, Antoine. 1968. La formalisation en linguistique. *Cahiers pour l'analyse* 9 : 106–117. Paris: Seuil.

Culioli, Antoine. 1999. *Pour une linguistique de l'énonciation. Formalisation et opérations de repérage*, Tome 2. Paris: Ophrys.

Desclés, Jean-Pierre. 1976. Description de quelques opérations énonciatives. In Jean David & Robert Martin (eds), *Modèles logiques et niveaux d'analyse linguistique*, 213–243. Paris: Klincksieck.

Desclés, Jean-Pierre. 2003. Interactions entre les valeurs de pouvoir, vouloir, devoir. In Merete Birkelund, Gerhard Boysen & Poul Soren Kjaersgaard (eds), *Aspects de la modalité*, Linguistische Arbeiten, 469, 49–66. Tübingen: Max Niemeyer Verlag.

Desclés, Jean-Pierre. 2009. Prise en charge, engagement, désengagement. *Langue française*, 162: 29–53.

Desclés, Jean-Pierre. 2016a. Opérations et opérateurs énonciatifs. In Marion Colas-Blaise, Laurent Perrin & Gian Maria Tore (eds.). *L'énonciation aujourd'hui, un concept clé des sciences du langage*, 69–88. Limoges: Lambert-Lucas.

Desclés, Jean-Pierre. 2016b. A cognitive and conceptual approach to tense and aspect markers. In Zlatka Guentchéva, *Aspectuality and Temporality, Descriptive and theoretical issues*, 27–60. John Benjamins Publishing Company.

Desclés, Jean-Pierre & Zlatka Guentchéva. 2010. Quasi Topological Representation (QTR) of spatial places and spatio-temporal movements in natural Languages. In Giovanna Marotta, Alessandro Lenci, Linda Meini & Francesco Rovai (eds). *Space in Language* [Proceedings of the Pisa International Conference, 213–233. Edizioni ETS.

Desclés, Jean-Pierre & Zlatka Guentchéva, 2015. Metalinguistic enunciative systems. An example: temporality in natural languages. In Viviane Arigne & Christiane Migette, *Metalinguistic Discourses*, 85–92. Cambridge: Cambridge Scholars Publishing.

Desclés, Jean-Pierre & Zlatka Guentchéva (forthcoming). Inference processes expressed by languages: deduction of a probable consequent vs. abduction. In Viviane Arigne & Christiane Roque-Migette (eds.), *Theorization and Representations in Linguistics*. Cambridge: Cambridge Scholars Publishing.

Desclés, Jean-Pierre & Gaëll Guibert. 2011. *Le dialogue, fonction première du langage*. Paris: Honoré Champion Editeur.

Desclés, Jean-Pierre, Gaëll Guibert & Benoît Sauzay. 2016. *Calculs de significations par une logique d'opérateurs*, Vol. 2. Toulouse: Cépaduès.

Desclés, Jean-Pierre & Anca Pascu. 2011. Logic of determination of objects (LDO): how to articulate "extension" with "intension" and objects with concepts, *Logica Universalis* 5 (1): 75–89.

Desclés, Jean-Pierre & Aude Vinzerich. 2008. Epistemic Modalities and Temporal Reference Frames, International Congress of Linguistics, CIL XVIII, Korea University, Séoul, July 24, 2008.

Evans, Nicholas R. 2005. View with a view: towards a typology of multiple perspective, Berkeley Linguistics Society, 93–120.

Gosselin, Laurent (this volume). French expressions of personal opinion: je crois / pense / trouve / estime / considère que P.

Grize, Jean-Blaise. 1973. *Logique moderne*, Fascicule III. Paris: Gauthier-Villars.

Guentchéva, Zlatka (ed.). 1996. *L'énonciation médiatisée*. Paris: Édition Peeters.

Guentchéva, Zlatka & Jon Landaburu (eds.). 2007. *L'énonciation médiatisée II. Le traitement épistémologique de l'information: illustrations amérindiennes et caucasiennes*. Louvain: Éditions Peeters.

Guilbaud, Georges Théodore. 1985. *Leçons d'à peu près*. Paris: Christian Bourgeois éditeur.

Herslund, Michael (this volume). Epistemic modality and the tripartition of the sentence illustrated by the Danish modal verbs.

Kiefer, Ferenc (this volume). Two kinds of epistemic modality in Hungarian.

Kneale, William K. & Marta Kneale. 1962. *The development of Logic*. Oxford: Clarendon Press.

Kronning, Hans. 1996. *Modalité, cognition et polysémie: sémantique du verbe modal devoir*. Uppsala: Acta Universitatis Uppsaliensis.

Kronning, Hans. 2003. Modalité et évidentialité. In Merete Birkelund, Gerhard Boysen & Poul Soren Kjaersgaard (eds.), *Aspects de la modalité*, Linguistische Arbeiten, 469, 131–151. Tübingen: Max Niemeyer Verlag.

Larreya, Paul. 2003. Types de modalité et types de modalisation. In Merete Birkelund, Gerhard Boysen & Poul Soren Kjaersgaard (eds.), *Aspects de la modalité*, Linguistische Arbeiten, 469, 167–180. Tübingen: Max Niemeyer Verlag.

Lazard, Gilbert. 1956. Caractères distinctifs de la langue tadjik. *Bulletin de la Société de Linguistique de Paris* 52, 117–186.

Martin, Robert. 1983. *Pour une logique du sens*. Paris: Presses Universitaires de France.

Martin, Robert. 1987. *Langage et croyance*. Bruxelles: Mardaga.

Nuyts, Jan. 2017. Evidentiality Revisited. In Juana Isabel Marín Arrese, Gerda Haßler & Marta Carretero (eds.), *Evidentiality Revisited. Cognitive grammar, functional and discourse-pragmatic perspectives*, 57–83. Amsterdam: John Benjamins.

Pauliny, Eugène. 1967 [1948]. La phrase et l'énonciation. In *Recueil Linguistique de Bratislava*, 59–66. Reprinted in Josef Jachek, *A Prague School Reader in Linguistics*, 1967: 391–397. Bloomington & Lonndon: Indiana University Press.

Peirce, Charles S. 1965. *Collected Papers of Charles Sanders Peirce*, edited by Charles Hartshorne & Paul Weiss. Cambridge, Massachusetts: The Belknap Press of Harvard University Press.

Polya, George. 1958. *Les Mathématiques et le raisonnement "plausible"*. Paris: Gauthier-Villars.

Pottier, Bernard. 2000. *Représentations mentales et catégorisations linguistiques*. Louvain-Paris: Editions Peeters.

Pottier, Bernard. 2012. *Images et modèles en Sémantique*. Paris: Honoré Champion.

Searle, John R. & Daniel Vanderveken. 1985. *Foundations of Illocutionary logic.* Cambridge: Cambridge University Press.

Van der Auwera, Johan & Vladimir Plungian. 1998. Modality's semantic map. *Linguistic Typology* 2: 79–124.

Van der Auwera, Johan & Alfonso Zamorano Aguilar. 2016. The History of Modality and Mood. In Jan Nuyts and Johan Van der Auwera (eds.), *The Oxford Handbook of Modality and Mood*, 9–27. Oxford: Oxford University Press.

Vinzerich, Aude. 2007. *Étude linguistique sur les modalités aléthiques et épistémiques*. PhD, Université Paris-Sorbonne.

Wiemer, Björn. 2018. Evidential and Epistemic Modality. In Alexandra Y. Aikhenvald (eds.), *The Oxford Handbook of Evidentiality*, 85–108. Oxford: Oxford University Press.

About Contributors

Henrik Bergqvist is Associate Professor in the Department of Linguistics at Stockholm University. He has a PhD (2008) in Field linguistics from the School of Oriental and African Studies, University of London. For his thesis, he documented aspects of Lakandon Maya grammar and he has continued to focus on field work-based research at Stockholm University where he has worked since 2008. Areas of grammar that are central to his research are categories and constructions that relate to epistemicity and intersubjectivity. In joint work with Nicholas Evans (Australian National University) and Lila San Roque (Radboud University), Henrik Bergqvist has explored the notion of 'engagement' as a potential category in languages that have grammaticalized means to signal who has the right to knowledge and whether knowledge of and attention to an event is shared between the speech participants or not.

Anna Paola Bonola graduated in 1986 from the Università Cattolica del Sacro Cuore (Milan – Italy) and in 1991 she was awarded a PhD in Slavic Studies at the Ludwig-Maximilians-Universität in Munich (Germany). Since 2011 she has been Full Professor of Slavic Studies at the Faculty of Foreign Languages of the Università Cattolica del Sacro Cuore. Her research activity focuses on different aspects of Russian-Italian contrastive linguistics: diathesis, particles and lexicology (changes in contemporary Russian, word-formation and the role of culture and ideology in the evolution of word semantics). In the last years she has focused on linguistic analysis of Russian literary texts and their translation into Italian. She is now working on the Italian-Russian bidirectional parallel corpus.

Agnès Celle received her PhD from the University of Paris Diderot in 1995. She is Professor of Linguistics in the Department of English at Paris Diderot. In 2018 she is a Prestige fellow and a Marie Curie fellow visiting the University of Colorado at Boulder. She has worked extensively in the areas of Tense, Aspect, Modality and Evidentiality in English and French. She was responsible for the linguistic part of an interdisciplinary project on surprise funded by the National Agency for Research, the Emphiline project (ANR-11-EMCO-0005; La surprise au sein de la spontanéité des émotions: un vecteur de cognition élargie) from 2012 to 2015. Her current research interests include modality and evidentiality in interrogatives.

Adrián Cabedo is Lecturer in Spanish Linguistics at the University of Valencia (Spain). He has published on phonetics and pragmatics in several international journals and books, such as *Journal of Politeness Research*, *Onomazéin* and with John Benjamins. His main interests are forensic linguistics, discourse markers, evidentiality, prosody and pragmatics. He maintains the Val.Es.Co 2.0 Spanish Conversation Corpus, in collaboration with Salvador Pons. He is also editor-in-chief of the Spanish Journal *Normas* and webmaster of the Spanish Linguistics Society (SEL).

https://doi.org/10.1515/9783110572261-018

Bert Cornillie is Associate Professor of Spanish Linguistics at the University of Leuven (Belgium). He has published on modality and evidentiality in international journals and thematic volumes. He has also edited books and special issues of journals on discourse-grammatical phenomena such as (inter)subjectivity, modal auxiliaries, diachronic morpho-syntactic variation and discourse traditions, modal particles and discourse markers. Bert Cornillie has supervised doctoral dissertation on English tag questions, the Spanish copula expressing change, Spanish clitic doubling and Spanish insubordination. He served as the conference manager of Societas Linguistica Europaea (SLE) from 2008 to 2013. Between 2010 and 2015 he was the coordinator of the Leuven Research Group FunC (Functional and Cognitive Linguistics: Grammar and Typology).

Jean-Pierre Desclés is Professor Emeritus in Computer Science and Linguistics at University Paris-Sorbonne. He was the head of the research team LaLIC (Languages, Logics, Informatics, and Cognition). He received his PhD in 1970 and his Doctorat d'Etat in 1980. He collaborated with linguists such as A. Culioli (University of Paris Diderot) and B. Pottier (University Paris-Sorbonne), and S. K. Shaumyan (Yale University). He uses topology and combinatory logic to formalize basic aspectual concepts (state, event, process, bounds...), temporal relations, and the place of inference (deduction and abductive reasoning) in an enunciative and cognitive framework. Jean-Pierre Desclés is member of the International Academy of Philosophy of Sciences (Brussels).

Lionel Dufaye is Full Professor of Linguistics at the University of Paris Est Marne-La-Vallée, member and director of the LISAA research team, EA 4120. His research interests focus mainly on the semantics and semiotics of English (although he has also been working on French markers over the past few years). In the continuation of his PhD thesis, he wrote a number of articles on the paradigm of modal auxiliaries within a cognitive and enunciative framework. He then worked on adverbial and prepositional particles in English, and published some ten articles dealing notably with *by, over, away* and *on*. Lionel Dufaye is the author of two textbooks, *Pour en finir avec les auxiliaires de modalité* (Ophrys, 2006) and *L'épreuve de grammaire à l'agrégation d'anglais* (Ellipses, 2006), as well as two monographs, one of them on modal auxiliaries: *Les Modaux et la négation* (Ophrys, 2001) and *Théorie des opérations énonciatives et modélisation* (Ophrys, 2009).

Laurent Gosselin is Professor of French linguistics at the University of Rouen (France). His research focuses on time, aspect and modality. He is the author of numerous articles and four books on these issues: *Sémantique de la temporalité en français* (Semantics of Temporality in French) (1996), *Temporalité et modalité* (Temporality and Modality) (2005), *Les modalités en français* (Modalities in French) (2010), and, in collaboration with computer scientists, *Aspects de l'itération* (Aspects of iteration) (2013). He developed a time and aspect model that has been applied to a wide variety of languages, and has been computer-implemented. His current research focuses on the verbal system of French, appreciative and axiological modalities and causality.

Michael Herslund is Professor Emeritus at Copenhagen Business School. He has taught Old and Modern French language and medieval culture and literature in the universities of Copenhagen and Trondheim, Norway. In 1987 he was appointed Professor of French Linguistics at Copenhagen Business School. He obtained his doctoral degree (dr. phil.) from the University of Copenhagen in 1989 with the dissertation *Le datif en français* (Leuven – Paris 1988). He has been in charge of the research group TYPOlex (studies on the lexical typological of the Romance languages compared to other languages) from its start in 1997. From 2004 to 2017 he has been head of the Centre for the Study of Europe at CBS. He has published widely on general, Romance and Danish linguistics, and on European history and politics. Michael Herslund has received the University of Copenhagen's gold medal (1970). He was a member of the Royal Danish Academy of Sciences and letters and in July 2003 he was made Knight of the Order of Dannebrog.

Axel Holvoet, formerly Professor of Baltic linguistics at Warsaw University, is now Professor of General Linguistics at Vilnius University. His research focuses on the Baltic and Slavic languages, with special emphasis on morphosyntax – argument realization and grammatical categories (voice and argument structure, case, definiteness, mood, modality and evidentiality). His books include *Transitivity and Clause Structure in Polish* (1991) and *Mood and Modality in Baltic* (2007). He is managing editor of the journal *Baltic Linguistics* (2010–) and editor of the series *Valency, Argument Realization and Grammatical Relations in Baltic* (Amsterdam-Philadelphia: John Benjamins), reflecting the results of a similarly named research project.

Ferenc Kiefer is Research Professor at the Research Institute for Linguistics of the Hungarian Academy of Sciences and Professor Emeritus of Budapest University (ELTE). His main interest is morphology and the semantics-pragmatics interface. He has published an important number of research articles on these topics. He is also a specialist in Hungarian linguistics. Professor Kiefer has been guest professor at several universities (Stockholm, Paris, Uppsala, Aarhus, Stuttgart, Antwerp, Vienna) where he taught mainly semantics and Hungarian linguistics. He has received honorary doctorates from the universities of Stockholm, Paris and Szeged.

Hans Kronning is Full Professor and holder of the Chair of Romance Languages at Uppsala University. His research is mainly devoted to modality, evidentiality and conditionality in French, but also in other Romance languages (Italian, Spanish, Catalan, Portuguese) and in Swedish, from a semantic, pragmatic, variational and predominantly comparative perspective. It is also dedicated to developing a modal theory of linguistic polyphony, to tense and aspect, auxiliarihood, coordination and subordination, reported speech, theme-rheme structure and focalization, pragmatic connectives and argumentation, as well as to translation studies. He was elected a Fellow of the *Royal Swedish Academy of Letters, History and Antiquities* in 2008.

Brenda Laca obtained her PhD at the University of Tubingen and is currently Full Professor at the University Paris 8. She is interested in the semantics of grammatical categories and in cross-linguistic variation. Her main research interests in the past decades comprise aspectual categories and temporal-modal interactions. She has published a number of papers and co-edited three volumes on these topics. Besides, she has contributed to several reference grammars of the Romance languages.

Jean Léo Léonard is Full Professor of General Linguistics and Linguistic Typology at Paris-Sorbonne University, France. He was initially trained as a dialectologist and a Finno-Ugrist (1980–86), and he has extensively published on Finnish, Estonian, Vepsian and Mordvin dialects (1988–). He later became involved in Romance dialectology and sociolinguistics (PhD dissertation on Noirmoutier island's linguistic anthropology, 1991), and he has explored several non Indo-European empirical fields of research, such as Basque/Euskara (1998–), Mayan (1999–), Otomanguean languages, especially Mazatec (2010–), but also Huave (2012), Totonacan (2015) and, more recently, Caucasian languages (IDEX EMERGENCE project *Language Dynamics in the Caucasus*, 2017–18) and South American languages of Colombia and Southern Central America (2017–). He claims a strong commitment to fieldwork, to applied linguistics and to endangered language documentation, and to revisiting descriptive categories and models applied to "lesser described" languages and dialects – as in his contribution in this volume. Since 2013, he has been strongly involved in projects integrating Complexity Theory and Complex Systems as fundamental methodology, from a multidisciplinary standpoint, and as a framework to foster new prospects for general dialectology.

Daniel Petit received his PhD at the Sorbonne University of Paris (1996) on the Greek reflexive pronoun, and his Habilitation at the Sorbonne University of Paris (2002) on ablaut and grammatical categories in Baltic. He has been Professor of Greek and Indo-European Linguistics at the Ecole Normale Supérieure (Paris) since 2003, Director of Studies for Baltic and Indo-European Studies at the Ecole Pratique des Hautes Etudes (Paris) since 2011, Vice-President of the Indogermanische Gesellschaft since 2016.

Mario Squartini (PhD, Scuola Normale Superiore, Pisa, 1995) is Professor of Linguistics at the University of Turin. His research interests concentrate on grammatical marking of tense, aspect, and modality, especially focusing on complex semantic boundaries (aspect and *Aktionsart*, epistemic modality and evidentiality). He has written a book on aspectual matters, *Verbal Periphrases in Romance: Aspect, Actionality and Grammaticalization* (Mouton de Gruyter, 1998). As to epistemic modality and evidentiality, he has published articles in *Studies in Language*, *Lingua*, *Linguistics*, *Journal of Pragmatics*, edited a special issue of the *Italian Journal of Linguistics* (*Evidentiality between Lexicon and Grammar*, 2007) and written survey chapters for the Oxford Handbooks of Modality and Mood (2016) and Evidentiality (2018).

Valentina Vapnarsky is a linguist anthropologist, specialized in Mayan languages. She is Researcher at the CNRS (National Centre for Scientific Research, France) and the director of the *Centre Enseignement et Recherche en Ethnologie Amérindienne* of the LESC Lab (CNRS & Université Paris Nanterre). Based on seven years' fieldwork in Guatemala and Mexico since 1991, and the analyses of situated verbal interactions in a great variety of discursive genres, her main topics of research and publication are temporality, agency and epistemicity, categorization, as well as the dynamics of Mayan oral and written traditions. She has directed international projects in linguistics and anthropology, such as POLYCAT and FABRIQ'AM on the new processes of cultural heritagization in Amerindian societies. She teaches at the University of Paris Nanterre and at INALCO.

Zuzana Vokurková studied Sinology and English and American Philology at Charles University, Prague (Czech Republic), and Tibetan Studies at INALCO, Paris (France). In 2001 she continued her studies for the doctoral degree of General Linguistics at Charles University and Université Paris 8 – Saint-Denis (France). In 2008 she defended her thesis on epistemic modality in Standard spoken Tibetan. She currently works as a Researcher and Senior Lecturer in the Seminar of Mongolian and Tibetan Studies of the Institute of South and Central Asia, Faculty of Arts, Charles University, teaching the grammar of modern spoken Tibetan. The field of her research is the grammar of spoken Tibetan (Standard Tibetan) and Tibetan dialectology.

Author Index

https://doi.org/10.1515/9783110572261-019

Subject Index

https://doi.org/10.1515/9783110572261-020

Language Index

https://doi.org/10.1515/9783110572261-021

www.ingramcontent.com/pod-product-compliance
Lightning Source LLC
Chambersburg PA
CBHW031721230426
43669CB00007B/199

* 9 7 8 3 1 1 1 0 8 6 1 8 7 *